Torture Porn in the Wake of 9/11

War Culture

Edited by Daniel Leonard Bernardi

Books in this new series address the myriad ways in which warfare informs diverse cultural practices, as well as the way cultural practices—from cinema to social media—inform the practice of warfare. They illuminate the insights and limitations of critical theories that describe, explain and politicize the phenomena of war culture. Traversing both national and intellectual borders, authors from a wide range of fields and disciplines collectively examine the articulation of war, its everyday practices, and its impact on individuals and societies throughout modern history.

Kerner, Aaron Michael. *Torture Porn in the Wake of 9/11: Horror, Exploitation, and the Cinema of Sensation*

Levinson, Nan. *War Is Not a Game: The New Antiwar Soldiers and the Movement They Built*

Torture Porn in the Wake of 9/11

Horror, Exploitation, and the Cinema of Sensation

AARON MICHAEL KERNER

Rutgers University Press

New Brunswick, New Jersey, and London

Library of Congress Cataloging-in-Publication Data

Kerner, Aaron, 1972-
Torture porn in the wake of 9/11 : horror, exploitation, and the cinema of sensation / Aaron Michael Kerner.
pages cm.—(War culture)
Includes bibliographical references and index.
ISBN 978–0-8135–6403–6 (hardcover : alk. paper)—ISBN 978–0-8135–6402–9 (pbk. : alk. paper)—ISBN 978–0-8135–
6404–3 (e-book (web pdf))
1. Horror films—United States—History and criticism. 2. Torture in motion pictures. 3. Sadism in motion pictures. I. Title
PN1995.9.H6K44 2015
791.43'617—dc23 2014030637

A British Cataloging-in-Publication record for this book is available from the British Library.

Visit our website: http://rutgerspress.rutgers.edu

Manufactured in the United States of America

Perhaps too much value is assigned to memory, not enough to thinking.
—Susan Sontag, *Regarding the Pain of Others*

This book is dedicated to President George W. Bush, Vice President Dick Cheney, and John Yoo, sadists par excellence—they are the true authors of torture porn.

Contents

Preface

The genre of torture porn—a brand of horror film that emerged in the wake of 9/11 and the War on Terror—attempts to negotiate the angst-filled years colored by the devastating terrorist attack. The subsequent wars lasting more than a decade in Iraq and Afghanistan will certainly be recorded in history as one of our darker moments. In the same way that the slasher films of the 1970s and 1980s demonstrated a deep-seated fear of female sexuality (as explored by Carol Clover, Barbara Creed, and others), revealing a veiled truth within patriarchal culture, in certain instances torture porn films expose our own abject nature and our violent disposition. Decades before 9/11, critics and scholars drew correlations between the Vietnam War and the horror genre—specifically with such films as *Night of the Living Dead* and *The Texas Chain Saw Massacre*. In a somewhat ironic twist, some of those very same critics and scholars now cannot fathom what torture porn films, which supposedly host such nihilistic violence, are about. This is not to suggest that torture porn is to be hailed as progressive once you just cut through the gore; rather, no film is made in a cultural vacuum, and these films are highly reflective of the culture that made them. And if we treat torture porn as an archeologist does an excavation site, then, these films begin to disclose something about us. Torture porn in certain instances effectively pulls back the curtain to reveal the naked truth of what we both fear and desire. While the fear of terrorism in part fuels these narratives, what is also at stake is the startling realization of who we are—ignominiously exposed in the post-9/11 world. Torture porn narratives might express a desire for security at any expense, while also negotiating the dreadful realization that the American regime enlists brutal tactics (namely torture) to maintain this security. Something similar might be said of popular film criticism and scholarship that reflects our culture's disavowal of the violence that is perpetrated on our behalf. And to this end, some popular film reviews are subject to analysis—not simply for what they say about the respective film being reviewed but also for how the criticism reflects cultural attitudes.

Many of the films discussed here are quite accessible, others less so. I would like to thank my local video store, Le Video, the single most important resource for locating films—mainstream, obscure, cult, foreign. This book would not be possible without it. Sadly, "Netflix killed the video store," and it was scheduled to shutter its doors spring 2014.

I would also like to acknowledge my colleague Julian Hoxter—my regular source of all things popular culture. We would frequently discuss progress on the book, and he was always a great sounding board. Likewise, Daniel Bernardi, the chair of the Cinema Department at San Francisco State University, has been tremendously supportive.

I would also like to thank Steve Jones at Northumbria University for generously sharing his work with me.

I am *deeply* indebted to Jonathan Knapp, who read an early version of the book and helped to shape it.

My fall 2012 Film Aesthetics graduate seminar functioned as a research workshop for the present volume—I owe a great deal to all my students. Throughout the volume, individual contributions are acknowledged.

Torture Porn in the Wake of 9/11

1

Torture Porn

From 9/11 to the Multiplex

> Somewhere the secret impulse of the revolutionary mass had to be laid bare. For this impulse had not been laid bare in its political manifestation, since even when the revolutionary mass beat to death, drowned, hanged, pilloried, burned, and raped, it always did so in the name of the sovereign people.
> —Pierre Klossowski, *Sade My Neighbour*

> It seems that the appetite for pictures showing bodies in pain is as keen, almost, as the desire for ones that show bodies naked.
> —Susan Sontag,
> *Regarding the Pain of Others*

Torture Porn Is the Theory, Torture Is the Practice

Imagine this scene: a bound and hooded man, his leg severely wounded—shot when he was captured. His wound is allowed to fester for days on end; it oozes and produces a pungent odor. His bindings are so tight they cut off circulation to his extremities, causing excruciating pain. He is held in a bare and dark room for an undetermined time. His only contact is with his captors, who take turns berating him and peppering him with threats.

Imagine another scene: a man imprisoned in a cell six feet long, three feet wide, a low ceiling, and closed off by a heavy metal door; virtually no light penetrates this space save a small crack in the ceiling that lets a faint beam of light through. Imprisoned in this space for weeks, during the first two weeks of his captivity he is routinely beaten and whipped. In a "waiting room," the man listens to others being beaten, their screams echoing through the facility—all the while waiting for his turn.

There is no need to imagine these scenes; they are not from the latest installment of the *Saw* franchise but are real-life accounts of torture conducted by Americans or their surrogates. The first scene is an account of the treatment of John Walker Lindh, the so-called American Taliban fighter captured in Afghanistan, at the hands of his American captors. The second scene details a case of extraordinary rendition, a program in which the United States effectively, for the lack of any better term, kidnaps suspected terrorists and takes them to CIA "black sites" (most of which are thought to be in eastern Europe) or hands the suspect over to another country.

The latter scene just described is an account of the Syrian-born Maher Arar. En route to Canada—Arar is a Canadian citizen—U.S. officials detained him at Kennedy International Airport after he tried to change planes following a trip to Tunis. Denied an opportunity to speak to a lawyer or to his family for several days, Arar was finally "deported" to Syria and held captive for ten months.[1] Speaking to *Washington Post* reporters Dana Priest and Barton Gellman regarding the extraordinary rendition program, an American intelligence official stated, "We don't kick the shit out of them. We send them to other countries so they can kick the shit out of them."[2] The rendition program offers thinly veiled legal coverage to American military and security agencies by outsourcing torture.

Whereas the Jordanians, Egyptians, and Syrians torture, Americans utilize "enhanced interrogation techniques." This specious coding, for Cullen Murphy, "brings to mind the euphemism for torture that the Roman Inquisition employed—*rigoroso esamine*, or 'rigorous examination.'"[3] What is now popularly known as the "Torture Memos," authored by John Yoo, provided legal cover for American agents to use a wide array of techniques in the interrogation of a presumed terrorist or associated subjects. The legal opinion effectively made allowances for torture techniques, such as waterboarding, that stop short of killing or causing permanent physical or psychological damage. One of the questions that surfaced in the wake of the "Torture Memos" is whether we have ceded the moral high ground and have now stooped down to the terrorist's level.

Torture porn potentially posits that we have become the very thing that we are fighting. Revelations about abuses at Abu Ghraib and Guantánamo Bay Prison, disclosures regarding the "Torture Memos," and the rendition program fuel torture porn narratives. Torture and violence are certainly not new phenomena; rather, what is different here is that our violent disposition has been publicly exposed. New technology—digital photography, Internet distribution—makes keeping secrets a far more difficult task.[4] When CIA operatives trained their Central American counterparts in the art of torture during the Cold War, it was kept largely from public view. Following the events of 9/11, however, these tactics—though now thinly cloaked behind euphemisms—materialized in public discourse. During the Cold War, in places such as Guatemala, Americans could displace violence onto others—violence is "expected" from the exotic other or from those less "civilized" corners of the world. And in this displacement of violence, it was possible to uphold the Manichean worldview, in which Americans might consider themselves a force for "good." More to the point, though, while torture porn might have been prompted by specific historical incidents, what it finally reveals is that violence lurks within the sinews of American culture. Torture porn negotiates the violence we can no longer disavow.

Horror has played host to other uncanny themes. For instance, whereas *The Texas Chain Saw Massacre* "thematizes the horrific 'un-repression' of a mode of commodity production," namely, the production of meat, something that most Americans would prefer not to think about, Jason Middleton observes that "*Hostel* adapts this structure of reversal for the context of the contemporary American 'war on terror' and the positions of torturer and tortured. Where the working-class labor of meat production represents the repressed in *Texas Chainsaw Massacre*, the analogous object in the thematics of *Hostel* is the United States' dirty business in the 'war on terror'—the abuses that are intended to stay hidden from view."[5] This fetishistic logic implicitly proclaims, "I know, but . . ."—for example, "I know how hot dogs are made, but . . . ," "I realize that cheap clothes are possible because of sweatshops in South East Asia, but . . ." Torture porn potentially undoes this fetishistic logic and confronts the spectator with his or her complicity in the American institutionalized campaign of violence.

Torture porn does not coddle its spectators. It does not offer, as Elizabeth Swanson Goldberg terms it, "counterhistorical" narratives that locate violence in the other or in other places but rather presents violence as intimate to the American disposition.[6] True, we find examples of films set outside the United States—*Hostel* and *Turistas* to name a couple, with the latter featuring a Brazilian torturer—but Americans or their "civilized" Westernized partners (Dutch, German, Japanese) are more often than not the perpetrators of violence.

Likewise, on the flipside of this equation, in these examples (*Hostel* and *Turistas*), it is the "civilized" body that is subject to torture.

In torture porn, victims are typically confined or otherwise imprisoned in some fashion. Victims are not just impaled or cut; they are frequently dismembered or mutilated. They are not merely subjected to savage physical brutality but are also tormented emotionally and psychologically, for instance, in films such as *Captivity*, *The Strangers*, and *Chained*. In some instances, victims are compelled to perpetrate acts of violence against others (in a bid to save their own lives), faced with some sort of grievous choice usually involving bodily mutilation, as in *The Final*, the *Saw* franchise, *The Experiment*, and *Chòose*. Jeremy Morris distills the genre to a handful of basic elements: (1) torture is noninterrogational, (2) torture is "the source of horror," (3) "the transformation of torturers and victims" prompts role reversals, (4) the reversal of victim-turned-torturer justifies the exhibition of violence, and (5) most importantly, there is a "realist element; . . . torture-horror is never supernatural, magical, or religious—at least not primarily."[7] Morris offers a brief summation of the genre, but there is obviously more to it (see the following chapter).

Whether we are speaking of real-world violence or the fictional worlds that reflect it, one does not have to look far to see that there is nothing new here. And this is all the stranger when some film critics and scholars wonder, if only implicitly, "Where did all this nihilistic violence come from?" Cullen Murphy's book *God's Jury: The Inquisition and the Making of the Modern World* demonstrates that many of the current enhanced interrogation techniques date to the Spanish Inquisition or earlier. The Spanish, for instance, called waterboarding by another name, "toca, meaning cloth," referring "to the fabric that plugged a victim's upturned mouth, and upon which water was poured. The effect was to induce the sensation of asphyxiation by drowning."[8] Water torture has been used in many forms and in many cultures throughout human history. And yet many senior policy makers during the prosecution of the War on Terror deny that waterboarding is torture. Vice President Dick Cheney, for instance, "called waterboarding 'a dunk in the water.' Defenders of the practice insist that waterboarding is not torture, on the grounds that the procedure does not cause lasting impairment," which was precisely the Inquisition's position. Whereas many conservative pundits and officials in the Bush administration refused to recognize that waterboarding is torture, the Inquisition understood that it was.[9] For nearly every one of the "enhanced interrogation techniques" used in the prosecution of the "War on Terror," a corresponding torture technique can be found in the Inquisition.

Real-world violence informs the visual culture of torture porn. In Errol Morris's 2008 documentary *Standard Operating Procedure* (*SOP*), which shares certain affinities with torture porn, we witness the intersection of nonfiction and fiction. This is not simply because Morris employs reenactments (which he is so well known for) but also because of the aesthetic tropes he utilizes to represent real torture. The parade of naked prisoners, bound by handcuffs to their bunks or to prison bars, hooded—both in the photographs taken at Abu Ghraib and in Morris's reenactments—at first glance, this calls to mind the victims in the *Hostel* films. This is all self-evident; one need not look any further than the surface of the image to recognize the semblance between the real world as depicted in *SOP* and torture porn. What is particularly striking, though, are the highly stylized cinematic and audio elements in *SOP* that, taken on their own, could quite easily be mistaken for shots in one of the installments in the *Saw* franchise.

Morris clearly sympathizes with the low-ranking men and women that took the fall for higher-ranking officers and other government agencies conducting interrogations at the prison. The "torturers" that Morris features in the film contextualize and justify their actions, and we come to sympathize with them as characters. Even if we find their actions reprehensible, and without question they are, we begin to view the "torturers" as something different: victims. They are not the antagonists of the *SOP* narrative, but they are not exactly the heroes of the narrative either. And like Jigsaw in the *Saw* franchise, they appear to occupy a space somewhere in between—pro(an)tagonists.

Morris uses diegetic and nondiegetic sound for dramatic effect (this is what cinema does, even documentaries—no revelation here). Take, for instance, the moment that features "Gus," as he is dubbed by the American MPs at Abu Ghraib, the Iraqi detainee seen on all fours at the end of a leash held by Lynndie England. Partitioning one sequence from the next, Morris cuts from a black frame to what we are led to believe is archival material of a handwritten prison log from October 24, 2003; the nondiegetic sound, like the abstracted sound of a whirring saw blade (12:40 [DVD time code]), underscores the horror of what we see—the clear abuse of Iraqi detainees. This whirring sound is nearly identical to the soundscape that composer Charlie Clouser sculpts in the *Saw* films, particularly at moments of revelation and typically accompanied by a flashback. It is quite striking that Morris uses this particular sound element over a piece of archival material, which in the diegesis of a documentary shares a kinship with the flashback in torture porn, which likewise intends to facilitate a revelation.

Photography is not necessarily a featured trope of torture porn, but it does materialize in some of the films in the genre. For instance, one of the victims in the first installment of the *Saw* franchise, Adam, is a photographer, and he uses his photographic flash to navigate through his unlit apartment. Photography is, of course, a significant element in *SOP*; this is how the world came to know of the abuses committed at Abu Ghraib, and subsequently Morris emphasizes the medium of digital photography in his stylized reenactments. In the single most reproduced and sadly iconic image from the Abu

Ghraib scandal, we see "Gilligan," as the American MPs named him, arms outstretched in the form of the crucifixion, standing on a box, hooded, and with a blanket covering his body. Electrical wire is wrapped around his index and middle fingers. Although the wires were completely harmless, he was told that he would be electrocuted if he stepped off his box. In Morris's reenactments, we see a consumer-grade Sony digital camera in extreme close-up—the camera more than fills the frame, while the unseen photographer, save his or her hands, wearing protective green latex gloves, snaps a picture. The camera's flash floods the frame with a blinding hot white light that is immediately followed by a cut to Gilligan standing on his box, with only his feet and the fringe of his blanket being visible. The manner in which Morris uses the flooded screen—washed out in white—as an editing device is characteristic of the *Saw* films and of the torture porn genre in general. And more than this, accompanying the brilliant white light of the flash is the click of the camera shutter and the whir of the discharging flash. These diegetic audio elements that we associate with the camera (an audio-designed conceit to be certain) are precisely what we find in the *Saw* films—which in turn might find their antecedents elsewhere, namely, police procedurals including the *CSI* series and films such as *Se7en* and even the opening of *The Texas Chain Saw Massacre.*

One of the distinct traits of torture porn is the containment of violence in hermetic spaces, and the interviews in *SOP* strangely replicate this. In addition to highly stylized reenactments, Morris is well known for his interview

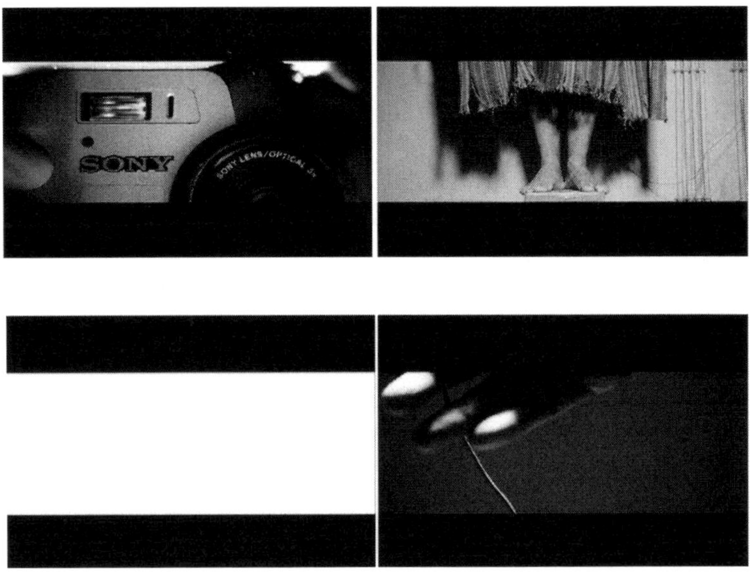

1.1 Errol Morris uses an editing device characteristic of the *Saw* films in *Standard Operating Procedure* (Errol Morris, 2008).

tactics. He uses what he calls the Interrotron, effectively a video-mediated "face-to-face" interview. While Morris sits in one room, his interviewee sits in another. Both Morris and the interviewee can see each other via a reflective glass mounted over the camera lens, and what results is something like a face-to-face conversation, though one mediated through the video image. The violence that is discussed—what each of the MPs did and what they observed—stays within a confined hermetic space, which Morris consciously dresses with a drab concrete-like background that gives the feeling of "imprisonment," or a torture chamber. In one instance, Military Intelligence Interrogator Roman Krol walks right up to the camera, or in reality the Interrotron, to inspect an image that Morris is apparently holding up for his interviewee to see. Krol's head, in extreme close-up, nearly fills the frame, as just his eyes and nose are visible, though in deep shadow. The effect here illuminates the divide between the space that the interviewee occupies and Morris; in a strange sense, it is almost as if Krol is looking through a small opening in a jailhouse door, apparently groping to identify people in a photograph that Morris is holding up for him to see. The power differential is in this case fairly evident, but it is also evident in the ways in which Krol is presented—in a position to-be-seen, isolated, a subject of interrogation. In the *Saw* films, as one character puts it, Jigsaw liked to "book himself a front-row seat." Jigsaw is a voyeur par excellence. In many of the *Saw* films, a video monitor—though it does not open a line of two-way communication, as does the Interrotron—mediates spaces in which victims play their violent games (the use of video to mediate events is actually a trait common to a number of torture porn films). At the end, though, what the Interrotron does is locate discrete spaces, an inside and an

1.2 Roman Krol appears to look through the window of a prison door in *Standard Operating Procedure* (Errol Morris, 2008).

outside, the site where the interviewee recounts violence and the space outside where the viewer's surrogate, Morris, interrogates his subject. It is interesting, then, how Morris and the spectator come to occupy something akin to Jigsaw's viewing position—a front-row seat to our own little sadistic theater.

I do not expect that Morris ever intended to replicate the aesthetics of the torture porn genre. However, the subject of torture—whether fiction or nonfiction—virtually screams for certain elements: a heterotopic non-site removed from proper society; isolated victims who are confined within a highly controlled space, bound, placed in stress positions; the administration of violence eliciting pain and suffering; and accompanying diegetic and nondiegetic audio elements that convey the gravity of the situation. While these basic aesthetic tropes cross multiple genres—just as likely to be found in nonfiction as they are in police procedurals, thrillers, or torture porn—what sets these scenarios apart is their (narrative) contextualization (or lack of it), and this begins to approach the reasoning for the critical ire heaped on torture porn.

What Is David Edelstein's Problem—Really?

In the *Scream* series, characters within the narrative diegesis are aware of film history, specifically the horror genre, and in the opening moments of Wes Craven's 2011 film *Scream 4*, a pair of female characters talk about what film they are going to watch. Sherrie says, "We're gonna go scary—*Saw IV*." Her interlocutor, Trudie, protests, "I saw that in theaters. It sucks. It's not scary—it's gross. I hate all that torture porn shit." And indeed one of the frequent criticisms horror fans have leveled against torture porn is that it is less about making spectators jump from their seats and more about turning their stomachs. Defending the virtues of torture porn, the other young woman returns, "Well, I like Jigsaw. I think he kills people very creatively." Echoing the criticism that torture porn lacks narrative, Trudie complains, "But you don't give a shit who dies, because there's no character development. There's just body parts ripping and blood spewing. Blahh!" For Trudie, because torture porn tends to emphasize spectacle over narrative, the genre is somehow "less worthy," not up to the standards of the "good old days" when horror films had substance. Popular film critic David Edelstein seems to share a lot in common with Trudie's assessment.

Edelstein coined the term "torture porn" in his *New York* magazine article "Now Playing at Your Local Multiplex: Torture Porn."[10] Edelstein reflects on the trend within mainstream horror of exhibiting graphic images of torture and mutilation; for him, this is the province of 1970s exploitation films, relegated to grindhouse theaters. What Edelstein finds shocking is not the images themselves but rather their context (the multiplex), their proliferation, popularity, and production values. "As a horror maven who long ago made peace, for better and worse, with the genre's inherent sadism," nevertheless, Edelstein puzzles, "I'm baffled by how far this new stuff goes—and by why America seems so nuts these days about torture."[11] Profits bear this out: during torture porn's reign, it was enormously successful at the box office—the *Saw* series (2004–2010) is the single largest grossing horror franchise of all time.

Edelstein establishes a common critical refrain: that torture porn lacks character development and that the graphic spectacles of violence are unmotivated, being without any narrative pretense. The self-professed "horror maven" argues that earlier films, especially the slasher films from the 1970s or even their ironic metacinematic remakes, such as *Scream*, offer a modicum of character development and violence couched within narrative motivations. Whereas slasher films feature "masked maniacs" that punish "nubile teens for promiscuity (the spurt of blood was equivalent to the money shot in porn)," in torture porn, victims are interchangeable and expendable.[12] Moreover, for Edelstein, torture porn films go nowhere, offering no resolution, no reaffirmation of order, and presenting violence that is often inexplicable and goes unanswered. In slasher films, the final girl set the world right again, at least for the time being, but Edelstein laments, "the 'final girls' in *Wolf Creek* and *The Devil's Rejects* [two films that he equates with torture porn] die ghastly deaths, and while *Hostel* ends with bloody retribution, it's set in a world in which people pay big money for the opportunity to torture and murder—a world of latent serial killers."[13] While Paxton, the surviving male character in the first *Hostel* film, raised the hopes among some critics (and horror fans) that we might witness a new era of horror featuring the "final boy," no such trend materialized; in fact, Paxton is the first victim of *Hostel: Part II*.[14] In addition, though Paxton dispatches the individual responsible for torturing his friend, the syndicate that caters to the sadistic tastes of those who can afford it is completely untouched, save for losing a (paying) client and a couple of employees along the way.

Edelstein also resents being made complicit in the acts of brutal violence. He cites Will Self's commentary on Quentin Tarantino's 1992 film *Reservoir Dogs*, "The American Vice," in which Self expresses frustration over Tarantino's cinematic syntax. Self maintains that, during the infamous torture sequence of the bound policeman, the subjective shots are impossible to place: does the victim, the accomplice, or the sadist conducting the torture own the gaze? "For in such a situation," Tarantino, in Self's view, "is either abdicating—or more likely *foisting*—the moral responsibility for what is being depicted onscreen from himself to the viewer."[15] Following this line of reasoning, Edelstein suggests not only that torture porn "rubs our noses" in the explicit, graphic, and prolonged exhibitions of violence but also that these films flout moral culpability and through cinematic syntax apparently leave the veteran film critic wondering, "What's next?" Torture porn does destabilize viewers' identification, or even aligns our identification with the perpetrators of violence, and on top of that allows violence to go unchecked by any moral agent and in some instances features an affable serial killer.[16] Not surprisingly, Edelstein, like so many other critics, takes issue with torture porn, but what is his problem—really?

One of the issues, I would posit, is that of critical paradigms—where conventional modes of cinematic assessment (e.g., character development/motivation, plot, narrative arc) confront a genre that privileges cinematic embellishments. And this calls to mind the very prejudice that Tom Gunning exposes in his seminal essay "The Cinema of Attractions." Gunning is largely concerned with the historical context that gave rise to "the narrativization of the cinema," which he places between 1907 and 1913,[17] but prior to this, the cinematic elicited a different sort of pleasure from the spectator—one closer to the amusement-park ride or attraction. The cinema of attractions offered visual spectacles (relatively) unencumbered by the obligations of narrative, as Gunning states, "emphasizing the direct stimulation of shock or surprise at the expense of unfolding a story or creating a diegetic universe. The cinema of attractions expends little energy creating characters with psychological motivations or individual personality." Rather than directing attention toward the interior world of the diegetic text (whether fictional or nonfictional), the cinema of attractions "moves outward towards an acknowledged spectator."[18] Torture porn, to one degree or another—in an effort to viscerally address its audience and to negotiate a painful history in a tactile manner—mobilizes the cinematic attraction. Adam Lowenstein argues this precise point in his assessment of Eli Roth's 2005 film *Hostel*, noting that the film, "like its early cinema cousins . . . channels . . . spectacle horror through spectator desires to feel history."[19]

Employing the criterion of narrative assessment is perhaps not always the most effective or appropriate measure. Should all films be expected to adhere to the conventions of narrative? Though Edelstein never says as much, he objects to torture porn due to his unstated prejudice against the cinema of attractions and a privileging of (literary) narrative conventions. "I've described all this freak-show sensationalism with relish," Edelstein admits with guilty pleasure, "enjoying—like these filmmakers—the prospect of titillating and shocking."[20] The freak show, the sideshow, the amusement park—these are all the analogies that have been applied to the cinema of attractions. The convergence of torture porn and the amusement park seems quite fitting, then—take, for instance, Thorpe Park's Saw: The Ride (a *Saw*-themed roller coaster) in Lincolnshire, United Kingdom, or the *Hostel*-themed attraction (a haunted maze) at Hollywood's Universal Studios. Whether it is cinematic torture porn or a torture-porn-themed amusement-park attraction, they both aim for the gut.

In addition, torture porn adopts the pornographic regime to play to the sensorial experience and does not necessarily appeal to a spectator's emotions. (The pornographic regime is discussed at length in the following chapter.) Whereas conventional narratives invite the spectator to make an emotional investment into a character's arc—Will Prince Eric come to realize that it is Ariel that he truly loves in Disney's *The Little Mermaid*? Will Ariel's dream of being human and finding love be fulfilled?—our investment in torture porn characters is less of an issue, as critics and scholars are so keen to point out. This, however, is not to say that torture porn is "meaningless" but rather that it mobilizes a narrative structure (episodic) and aesthetic regime (highly embellished audio/visuals) that constitute an alternative storytelling paradigm. And this appears to be one of the issues that is persistently overlooked; it is not that torture porn films are inherently "bad" but rather that they do not subscribe to conventional modes of storytelling that appeal to our emotions per se. Furthermore, critics and scholars alike either conflate or fail to substantially differentiate between emotions and sensations, making it all that more difficult to offer a judicious reading of the torture porn text. Appealing to our senses, torture porn, as Adam Lowenstein also observes, finds affinities with the cinema of attractions and opens "the possibility of *feeling* the past as an embodied experience." Lowenstein continues, "This 'return of history through the gut' points toward a largely unacknowledged historical underside to the cinema of attractions, one where spectacle does not necessarily halt at sensation alone but opens out toward history."[21] Torture porn, then, negotiates the conflicted, and frequently contradictory, sentiments regarding the War on Terror, through narratives that play to not only a sentient spectator but a sensorial one as well.

Linda Williams makes something of a similar argument in her "Discipline and Fun: *Psycho* and Postmodern Cinema," taking David Bordwell, among others, to task for their assessment of Alfred Hitchcock's 1960 classic thriller *Psycho*. What Bordwell is missing, Williams argues, is the funhouse element of the film, which Hitchcock himself comments on: "You have to remember that *Psycho* is a film made with quite a sense of amusement on my part. To me it's a *fun* picture. The processes through which we take the audience, you see, it's rather like taking them through the haunted house at the fairground."[22] Bordwell and others view the conventions of cinema as "stable and permanent" and so pervasive that they accommodate all manner of cinema, expecting that cinema will conform to "strong narrative logic, coherence of cause and effect, space and time, psychological motivation, and character-driven events."[23] Williams views *Psycho* through a different lens "to account for some of its more sensational and 'fun' appeals."[24] *Psycho* marks an important step in mainstream Hollywood production—those films that are destined for the multiplex, including horror films—and in viewers' expectations, as they "began going to the movies to be thrilled and moved in quite visceral ways, and without much concern for coherent characters or motivations."[25] It is precisely in these terms that I treat torture porn.

The vignettes of violence in horror films (and not just torture porn) have been compared to the song-and-dance numbers in the musical genre; Cynthia Freeland, in her discussion of the *Hellraiser* films, does exactly that. "Some people would say," Freeland summarizes, "that the numbers in graphic spectacular horror are sheer pyrotechnical displays of monstrousness that serve only the end of meaningless violence." She insists on greater nuance, noting that the numbers should not be dismissed as simply gratuitous accessories to the otherwise legitimate narrative. Rather, the numbers in horror films frequently "convey information about the monster, its nature and its desires, and who it will attack and why."[26] Similarly, while song-and-dance numbers generally bring the narrative to a snail's pace, we nevertheless learn something of the nature of our characters and their desires—Dorothy in *The Wizard of Oz*, for example, wants to escape, to go "somewhere over the rainbow."

Linda Williams, in her discussion of pornography, refers to the episodes of sex in hardcore films as "numbers" and explicitly compares pornography to the musical. Much in the same manner in which torture porn is dismissed, Williams observes, "it is commonplace for critics and viewers to ridicule narrative genres that seem to be only flimsy excuses for something else—musicals and pornography in particular are often singled out as being *really* about song and dance or sex."[27] This is not to say, however, that the episodic spectacles—song-and-dance routines in musicals, sex in pornography, or exhibitions of violence in torture porn—are completely devoid of narrative. "Narrative informs number," Williams insists, "and number, in turn, informs narrative."[28] Williams adds later that "as in the movie musical, the episodic structure of the hard-core narrative is something more than a flimsy excuse for sexual numbers: it is part and parcel of the way the genre goes about resolving the often contradictory desires of its characters."[29] Musicals frequently work out these contradictory desires—usually between male and female characters—through the song-and-dance numbers ending in a heterosexual union. In torture porn, (satisfactory) resolutions are few and far between, whether it is within the discrete torture number, which usually ends with the rending of a body, or the narrative as a whole.

While different in certain respects, these genres—musicals, pornography, torture porn—rely on the exhibition of bodies. In musical numbers, the channels of sensation are loaded up with aural and visual stimulus; on display are bodies that gyrate, writhe in pain, contort, and are thrown into ecstatic motion—bodies that wail, howl, and scream. Frequently bodies are reduced to props or materialize as (subjectless) elements of the scene—think of the large

Busby Berkeley set pieces or the famous "Diamonds Are a Girl's Best Friend" number in Howard Hawks's 1953 film *Gentlemen Prefer Blondes*, where in the background women are literally made into chandeliers—that is to say objects. In these moments, narrative progression slows down, and much of this holds true for torture porn; however, the visceral numbers in torture porn are not devoid of meaning but rather potentially connect the viewing body into the complex and even contradictory narratives regarding the American sadistic disposition.

Moreover, Edelstein's very term "torture porn" is suggestive of the attraction as well. Pornography is designed with an explicit and, to be frank, a singular objective in mind: sexual arousal. If a pornographic film exhibits any narrative pretense, this is secondary at best and, at its worst, frustrating, as it interferes with the express intent of the pornographic genre.[30] Films in the torture porn genre, then, are little more than a series of violent vignettes loosely tied together with a narrative that is secondary to the exhibition of brutality. At least, this is how Edelstein apparently views it. While by no means as dismissive as Edelstein, Jason Middleton observes that there are clear affinities between pornography and the exhibition of violence in Eli Roth's 2005 film *Hostel*. Roth draws visual parallels between the Amsterdam brothel that the two male protagonists, Josh and Paxton (along with Oli, their Icelandic buddy), patronize and the Slovakian torture facility in the latter part of the narrative.[31] In both cases, patrons pay for the privilege of doing something to another—in the former case, people pay to have sex; in the latter, people pay to torture. In *Hostel*, the sexual episodes are set in contrast with the torture numbers in the latter half of the film, but it is not a simple analogy (sex scene = torture scene); rather, the composition and choreography of the torture numbers replicate the pornographic regime. In both cases, there is the ratcheting up of tension that eventually ends in the discharge of bodily fluids.

Consider, for a moment, Darren Lynn Bousman's 2005 film *Saw II*, in which several characters are compelled to play a series of "games" typically ending with a gruesome death.[32] In a structure resembling pornography, each game is like the sexual episode in porn, culminating in the rending of a body, sharing affinities with the climactic cum shot.[33] Each of the violent spectacles is bookended with scraps of narrative to offer the semblance of motivation and progression. While torture porn outlines the choreography of the pornographic genre, it is nowhere near as graphic as most critics and detracting scholars have suggested.[34] This point aside, when held to the unspoken criteria by which most people assess films—where the narrative is held as paramount—the entire *Saw* franchise might be considered a fantastic failure. But is this the only criterion on which to assess film? Is it then possible to critically approach cinema from a different paradigm?

What I am suggesting here is that Edelstein finds the films grouped under the heading of torture porn to be lacking narrative, or "narratively challenged," and as a consequence, he can dismiss them as pornography. And if we accept that the (literary) narrative is the critical paradigm on which to assess a film such as *Hostel*, then Edelstein is absolutely correct in his assessment. If, however, we make allowances for other critical paradigms, then we might consider these films in a new light. I actually find the term "porn" fitting, but not for the reasons that Edelstein does; it is abundantly clear that the term "porn" is mobilized as a pejorative.[35] "Porn" is perfectly acceptable precisely because the genre emphasizes the body. Torture porn does not rely on narrative per se, as it is about spectacle, about excessive violence and the body. And there is no need to be coy here; many of the films in the genre are crass kitsch, but this does not make them somehow illegitimate. (Linda Williams's analysis of the pornographic genre in her influential book *Hard Core: Power, Pleasure, and the "Frenzy of the Visible"* substantiates this latter point quite clearly.) In addition, it is not that the films in the genre are morally bankrupt but rather that they trade in obscene currency—namely, the American foreign policy that sanctions torture and our sadistic disposition that subsequently fuels the visual culture of torture.

Adam Lowenstein also challenges Edelstein's conception of torture porn, arguing "that 'torture porn' does not exist, that a far more useful concept to work with is 'spectacle horror': the staging of spectacularly explicit horror for purposes of audience admiration, provocation, and sensory adventure as much as shock or terror, but without necessarily breaking ties with narrative development or historical allegory."[36] Lowenstein continues to distinguish these spectacle-driven horror films from those more psychological narratives in what he calls "ambient horror."[37] I most certainly concur with the tenor of Lowenstein's position, but as I have already suggested, the term "torture porn" enjoys popular currency. Lowenstein is absolutely correct in his characterization of torture porn as a genre driven by spectacle, but "spectacle horror" appears to be an effort to legitimize the genre. I, on the other hand, feel no compulsion to apologize for it.

In Dean Lockwood's assessment of the genre, he meets Edelstein and Gunning somewhere in the middle (without mentioning the latter). "The *affect* is the affect of the fairground ride; a contained, familiar sort of threat which is easily assuaged."[38] The "contained"—and thus safe—thrill of the cinematic attraction is precisely what torture porn offers its audience. This claim parrots Gunning's argument relating cinema to the tamed attractions of the amusement park, such as the roller coaster or the haunted house, which are intended to thrill or scare. Horror cinema, perhaps even from its very inception, offers its audience a visceral experience, as Gabrielle Murray suggests: "What the cinema mostly does, and one of the main reasons we continue to engage with its content, is that it *affects* us—it makes us feel."[39] Commenting on this point, Lockwood says, "Seen from the frequently limiting perspective of effect, new horror looks like moral pollution, but seen in terms of affect theory, it may have a transformative and liberating potential."[40]

But most of these torture porn films need "to experiment more drastically with 'style' in the Deleuzian sense and come up with truly unknown pleasures."[41] Lockwood's assessment concludes not that torture porn films are too excessive but that they are "not extreme enough." This is an argument that to my mind has traction. It seems to me that elements of the *Saw* franchise, for instance—especially in the application of cinematic embellishments, in the mobilization of cinematography, editing, and audio design—begin to approach something quite interesting; where they (potentially) fail is in narrative. And as a consequence, film critics who review torture porn films through the lens of narrative find them deficient. Lockwood continues, "Controversies around images such as those in torture porn are typically framed in terms of a naturalized moral interpretation and logic which deters consideration of the ways extreme images can move us and experimentally switch us into different connections with the world. Foregoing moral stances, we might also engage affirmatively with the capacity of horror cinema to elicit an authentic encounter, the eruption of something new."[42] Knee-jerk moralizing potentially plugs the sensory nodes, thus precluding or attenuating the opportunities for "the eruption of something new." Critics predisposed to the conventional narrative paradigm might in fact be untouched by the sensorial attributes of these films or unwilling to view films through another lens. But it is not simply extreme images that are at issue, because of course (even "good") cinema is littered with the carcasses of dismembered living creatures—think, for instance, of the horse's head in *The Godfather* (Francis Ford Coppola, 1972).

Jeremy Morris reminds us too that torture in cinema is not limited to the horror genre. "For example, the fact that a central character is tortured in *Syriana* (2005) does not mean that it is a torture-horror film," Morris notes. "Rather, the apparent intent of *Syriana* is to lead its audience through situations that include torture for the sake of a story about international politics." Contextualized torture within a narrative—in other words, there is a clear cause-and-effect relation between the character and his or her situation within the diegesis—offers sufficient narrative motivation for its occurrence. "Horror is very different," Morris reasons; "generally speaking, the intent is to lead the audience through horrifying experiences for the sake of those experiences."[43] Narrative motivations are not at stake in torture porn; rather, what is at stake is the "horrifying experience" for the spectator. The difference, of course, between torture porn and narrative films such as Gavin Hood's 2007 film *Rendition*, Pierre Morel's 2008 film *Taken*, *Syriana*, or even television programs such as *24* and nonnarrative films for that matter—think of Errol Morris's

Standard Operating Procedure—is that the depictions of torture are contextualized within complex (read: sophisticated) narratives. In *Hostel*, as Kevin Wetmore observes, little is made of Paxton's killing of the Dutch businessman: "The audience does not perceive this action as evil, as he deserves to die—he tortured and killed *first*, and thus is not innocent and therefore morally culpable and deserving of death. If someone deserves to be tortured and killed, then we do not object when they are."[44] I find this logic deeply troubling and morally dubious (to be clear, Wetmore is not arguing for this but rather relating the general expectation of viewers): dispatching characters sometimes in the most gruesome manner—whether it is the Dutch businessman in *Hostel* or the rapists in *I Spit on Your Grave*—when set in the context of narrative motivation is somehow more acceptable, while the depictions of rent bodies outside the conventions of narrative (cinema) are somehow more prurient? This is in fact Wes Craven's point in his 1972 film *The Last House on the Left*—that the violence in the first half of the film is little more than a narrative conceit that sanctions the violence in the latter half—is it not?

"The appeal of retributivist torture-horror consists in a comprehension and evaluation of the torturer's motives and methods."[45] The assumption here is that these films (1) are guided by narrative conventions and (2) rest on plots governed by retribution. Like Edelstein, Morris uses "sadism" as a dismissive pejorative, admitting that retribution cannot account for all films in the torture porn genre and explaining that the appeal of many of these films is "purely sadistic."[46] The suggestion here is that there is no (narrative) motivation. Describing Rob Zombie's 2005 film *The Devil's Rejects*, Morris observes that while "part of the story is driven by Sheriff Wydell's quest for revenge for his brother's murder, the most prominent torture scenes of the film have no such retribution purpose."[47] The trope of retribution for Morris amounts to narrative motivation and finally propels a narrative toward a resolution, perhaps (without ever making the connection) aligned with the conventions of the final girl. In his calculus, the retributive character in torture porn occupies the position formerly held by the final girl in the slasher genre. Morris, in his effort to evacuate *The Devil's Rejects* of any redeeming qualities, hollows out any pretense of retribution (read: narrative)—"part of the story is driven by Sheriff Wydell's quest for revenge for his brother's murder"—and instead situates Zombie's film as "purely sadistic" (read: narrativeless)—"the most prominent torture scenes of the film have no such retribution purpose."[48]

"They sure don't make them like they used to" seems to be the shared (though unspoken) mantra of film critics and scholars who years earlier had praised the horror genre for its intervention in a culture torn apart by the upheavals of the Vietnam War. George A. Romero "seem[s] lost on the current generation of filmmakers and audiences," Christopher Sharrett says, bemoaning the state of the horror genre. He continues, calling torture porn "a form alarming in its diminishing of the genre, and its disregard of the psychological content and social criticism of the horror film at its height (although *Saw* and its sequels try mightily to mask their intellectual bankruptcy and retrograde politics)."[49] This comment echoes the initial response to Romero's 1968 film, which Sharrett, coincidently, calls our attention to, saying, "By far the most vilified form of violent representation is the horror genre, and in particular its 'gorefest' subgenre." Specifically, Sharrett cites *The Texas Chain Saw Massacre* and *Night of the Living Dead*, which were "vilified by the mainstream press" but then later recouped by figures such as Sharrett himself and Robin Wood and even canonized by the Museum of Modern Art.[50]

Sharrett's and Edelstein's views seem to line up insofar as their focus is on narrative failure. Sharrett observes that torture porn films and their fans relish the spectacle of bodies destructed "to the near-total exclusion of context, aside from outright absurd ruminations about the villain's motivations. The consequences of violence for the individual and society, for all the bogus moralizing of these films, is nowhere in evidence."[51] Like Edelstein, Sharrett too appears to view cinema through the singular lens of narrative and as a consequence only "sees" the "exclusion of [narrative] context," "absurd [read: lack of or thin] . . . motivations [for the villain]," and "bogus moralizing." Sharrett cannot see the "meaning" of these films because they are narrativeless (to his mind), and he presumes, then, that they are regurgitating the neoconservative agenda, apologizing for and/or legitimizing the use of torture. And this certainly might be true of some films (the television program *24* can certainly be read in these terms). Sharrett laments that, in torture porn, "the subversive component nearly vanished, as the genre was relegated to a lowbrow vehicle for shouting 'boo!' that its snobbish attackers accused it of being since its inception."[52] Films that have "meaning"—that is to say, that are "subversive" in Sharrett's terms—are films that are set within a narrative properly speaking. The problem here is that Sharrett cannot "see" the potentially subversive (or, at least, critical) elements in torture porn, because they lurk in the form of torture porn films, not necessarily in the narrative as such.

Film critic Kim Newman, certainly no stranger to the horror genre, shares Sharrett's opinions. He too lauds the great horror films of old (as does Edelstein, of course). "Audiences coming out of *Night of the Living Dead* or *The Texas Chain Saw Massacre* were horrified but exhilarated, encouraged to make connections between what they'd just seen and what was happening in the world," the critic nostalgically dotes. "There was a sense that these films were really 'about' Vietnam or social class in America." When contemporary audiences, Newman posits, leave the theater, they "are upset and depressed, not like veterans of a rollercoaster but survivors of some Jackass-like self-imposed ordeal." He finally concludes, "The 'message' of horror in the 1970s tended to be that there was something seriously wrong with society; the 'message' of

2000s horror is that Other People Are Shit."[53] The message is "people are shit" because there is nothing else in the narrative? Newman does not explain. But what appears self-evident is that the narratives are too thin for him to see anything else—and so they are, for Newman, effectively "meaningless."[54]

What such a vociferous lambasting of spectacle-driven horror reveals, though, is that it is in fact highly psychological and affecting. One of the most frightful things that we might experience is violence without context. Torture porn is, of course, littered with context when one is open to it; however, when film critics and scholars are so beholden to the canonized figures of horror and the conventions of narrative, they fail to recognize the paradigmatic shift that has occurred in the genre.

From Edelstein, Newman, and popular critic Roger Ebert[55] to film scholar Christopher Sharrett[56] and a whole host of pundits that wag the finger of discontent, their criticism regarding the lack of any apparent redeeming moral qualities in torture porn is, in my view, largely a veiled prejudice against films that emphasize spectacle or fail to adhere to conventional narrative structures (e.g., narrative resolutions that result in the reaffirmation of "proper order"). *Saw*, for instance, is actually quite narrative heavy. There is in fact little gore in the first film; director James Wan, after watching a fine cut of the film, lamented that he had made a PG-13 drama and went back to shoot close-ups (e.g., Amanda's hands sifting through guts) to give the film a bit of an edge. Films judged morally vacuous, then, are little more than code for "narrative failure"—either the film lacks narrative cohesion, drowned in spectacle, or does not conform to conventional narrative resolutions. Edelstein's real problem, then, is a matter of critical paradigms, as opposed to any inherent problem with the genre of torture porn.

Furthermore, those who vociferously hail that torture porn signifies the moral corruption of the United States or that the end-times are upon us are misdirecting their energy. Indeed, it might be true that the United States has lost its moral compass, but it is not because of torture porn but rather because we torture.[57] Critics that lambast torture porn on moral grounds marshal arguments that are intellectually dishonest, for at their core, they proclaim in effect, "That's not me. I could never do that." But as Susan Sontag acknowledges in her discussion of the Abu Ghraib photographs, "the photographs are us."[58] Edelstein, for instance, acknowledges that "fear supplants empathy and makes us all potential torturers, doesn't it? Post-9/11, we've engaged in a national debate about the morality of torture, fueled by horrifying pictures of manifestly decent men and women (some of them, anyway) enacting brutal scenarios of domination at Abu Ghraib."[59] In a few quick strokes, Edelstein at once acknowledges the source of torture porn but in the very same instance disavows any stake in it, effectively foreclosing any possibility that torture porn might have something legitimate to say about the culture of violence nurtured by the American disposition. Edelstein implies that he could never be a torturer and apparently resents having his identification aligned with characters that are. And more than this, what his assessment leaves in place is the "few bad apples" argument propagated by the Bush administration, to conceal a culture of torture. And this is precisely what torture porn draws from: not that there are a few misbehaved people out there or that other people are shit but that not only does our culture perpetrate acts of violence but this violence is institutionalized.[60] In a sense, to treat torture porn as legitimate is to recognize this latter fact and moreover that we are complicit in the culture of torture. So yes, indeed, Edelstein or anyone of us might be able to deny our capacity to personally participate in violence. What we cannot escape, though, is our complicity in it. Registering moral repugnance is intended to proclaim innocence, but in the end, it also confirms our impotence—the inability to consider where torture porn is really coming from: us.[61]

What Is to Come

The working assumption of the present book is that torture porn is a genre. More precisely, it might be categorized as a subgenre of horror. Upon close review, however, we will discover that torture porn also shares affinities with other genres—exploitation, thriller, police procedural, suspense, and, of course, pornography. The fact of the matter is that any one category is likely to trespass on another. Rather than getting hopelessly mired in the nature of genres (or subgenres), I work with the assumption that torture porn is a self-contained genre, understanding that this is something of an agreed-upon fiction.

At certain moments throughout the book, I discuss elements of audio design, but unlike the visual field, where I can describe gestures or identify specific visual elements (e.g., a color, an object) or even include a still, sound—and particularly nondiegetic sound—is harder to specify in the written form. Subsequently, I have in some cases offered the time when the specific audio element is heard on the American commercially released DVD. For example, I earlier discussed the use of nondiegetic sound in Errol Morris's *Standard Operating Procedure*, specifically identifying the abstracted sound of a whirring saw blade (12:40).

While we might be able to glean some information regarding the characteristics of the torture porn genre from the present chapter, I leave a detailed discussion of the general motifs and themes, characters, and aesthetic tropes for chapter 2, while chapter 3 contextualizes torture porn within cinematic traditions. From the trope of sadism as drawn from Pier Paolo Pasolini's infamous 1975 film *Salò, or the 120 Days of Sodom* through the influence of spectacle-driven exploitation cinema of the 1970s—that in some cases assimilated plot elements of Pasolini's film and other less-than-scrupulous meditations on the nexus of fascism and sadism—what is clear is that torture porn did not spontaneously emerge at the dawning of the twenty-first century. Certain evolutions in the slasher genre as well, particularly in the treatment of the monster and the final girl, might also be seen as contributing to the torture porn genre.

Chapter 4 focuses on James Wan's 2004 film *Saw*, which might be viewed as the inaugural film of what we now identify as torture porn. The subsequent six films in the *Saw* franchise utilize the tropes established in the first film while developing increasingly more elaborate numbers. Among the tropes that the *Saw* franchise adopts is that of the gaming motif, which is explored in some detail in this chapter, including the adaptation of the discourse of videogames in the series. The pro(an)tagonist Jigsaw is a sadist par excellence, and this is also given considerable attention as viewed through the post-9/11 lens.

Of all the films discussed in this book, the *Hostel* films exhibit the most overt references to the post-9/11 experience and the so-called War on Terror—and this is the subject of chapter 5. The Slovakian factory converted to a complete in-house torture facility finds affinities with CIA-operated detention and interrogation facilities known as black sites. The progenitor of the film series, Eli Roth, is a self-professed cinephile in the spirit of Quentin Tarantino (the producer of the first two *Hostel* films). The *Hostel* films are inflected with a multitude of cinematic influences—extreme cinema coming out of Asia, as well as *giallo* films, slashers, and exploitation cinema. Whereas the appropriation of the discourse of videogames sets the *Saw* franchise apart, the two *Hostel* films that are directed by Roth are haunted by the specter of the Holocaust.

Chapter 6 is more eclectic than chapters 4 and 5, focusing on the general horror trope of the "wrong turn." This trope is found in a wide range of films and owes a large debt to films such as *The Hills Have Eyes* and *The Texas Chain Saw Massacre*. In films such as *Captivity*, *The Final*, *Steel Trap*, and *Chained*, characters are led astray. In other films, we find the return of the colonial oppressed—the prime example being *Turistas*, in which Australian, Swedish, British, and American travelers in Brazil find themselves unwilling organ donors. In the domestic setting, the Appalachian hillbilly is figured as the American other—from the inbred mutants in the *Wrong Turn* films (there are five in the series) to the redneck Firefly family in Rob Zombie's film *House of 1000 Corpses* and its sequel, *The Devil's Rejects*.

Whereas many of the films discussed in this volume offer the tacit promise of delivering unadulterated gore and nihilistic violence to its niche market, television caters to a much wider audience and is more reserved in its exhibition of violence—offering audiences soft-core torture porn. The television series that are discussed in chapter 7 do not necessarily fit into the category of horror (this genre has rarely been featured in the television format) but rather adopt various torture porn elements. The Fox Network's thriller/suspense series *24* negotiates the post-9/11 experience and the efficacy of torture. *The Following*, also on the Fox Network, can potentially be read as a soft-core version of the *Saw* franchise. The Showtime series *Dexter*, being on premium cable, has a lot more latitude in the exhibition of violence. Dexter, like the ostensible hero of *24*, Jack Bauer, is a contemporary cowboy—living on the fringes of society and doing whatever it takes to keep the marauding hordes at bay.

Rather than a formal conclusion as such, chapter 7 looks outward, surveying the ways in which torture porn influences our contemporary visual culture. Police procedurals have become increasingly more violent with elements of torture. Popular programs such as *Game of Thrones*, particularly in the third season, have introduced torture into their narratives. New television series feature serial killers as their pro(an)tagonists. Torture porn no doubt has changed the landscape of the horror genre in general. I think I can safely conclude, though, that the torture porn cycle is dead—arbitrarily we might cite the 2010 film *Saw 3D: The Final Chapter* as the end of the cycle, if for no other reason than we witnessed the birth of the genre with the first film in the franchise. The political environment changed dramatically in 2008 with the end of the Bush-Cheney administration, and President Obama has made efforts to "reset" our foreign policy—changing rhetoric, for instance, by referring to Osama bin Laden and Al-Qaeda specifically, rather than to the more opaque "War on Terror"; terminating the use of torture; attempting to close Guantánamo Bay Prison (though thwarted by conservative factions); and adopting an overall tenor that is markedly different from the belligerence of the previous administration. Moreover, from 2010, we begin to see parodies and metacinematic elements, a sort of genre autopsy—for instance, Dick Chibbles's 2010 pornographic film *Saw: A Hardcore Parody*. Regardless of where we might locate the demise of torture porn, its impact is sure to be felt for a long time to come.

2

The Torture Porn Genre

Key Tropes

To date there has been no definitive or substantive effort to outline the genre of torture porn, and even with its tacit recognition, there is no real consensus on its defining tropes, let alone agreement on its name. Steve Jones laments, "it is remarkably difficult to pinpoint precisely what the characteristics of Torture Porn films are."[1] With reference to the explicit gore associated with torture porn, it has alternatively been called by critics and horror fans "splatter horror," "spectacle horror" (Adam Lowenstein), or "torture-horror" (Jeremy Morris), and the directors commonly associated with torture porn—Roth, Wan, Zombie—have also been dubbed "the splat pack." Interestingly, if you type "torture porn" into the *Wikipedia* search field, what comes up is "splatter film." Most critics, though, seem to agree with this basic principle: the genre of torture porn emerges in the wake of 9/11, and it is a distinctly American genre. While other genres, and films from outside the American market, bear some of the hallmarks of torture porn, they are not within the genre properly speaking; for the most part, these films are governed by a different set of anxieties (social inequities, the return of the colonial repressed). In order to clarify the bounds of the genre, I offer a taxonomical survey of the general motifs and themes (divided into secondary sections), aesthetics, and character tropes of torture porn.

General Motifs and Themes in Torture Porn: Post-9/11 Resonance

Torture porn as the post-9/11 horror genre draws from a deep well of anxiety spawned by the fear of terrorism, amplified by American media and government officials. Leveraging post-9/11 fears, neocons pushed their agenda and justified the invasion of Iraq and the so-called War on Terror. Condoleezza Rice and other Bush administration officials argued their case in the media with such refrains as "We don't want the smoking gun to be a mushroom cloud." The United States came to a halt on the morning of September 11, 2001, and not because of a massive military onslaught or monster robots from another world but rather because of a small band of determined men armed with nothing more than box cutters. The terrorists were not monsters; they did not possess special powers. Muhammad Atta, the supposed lead hijacker on September 11, was no boogieman; he was no Jason, no Michael, no Freddy Kruger. In the wake of 9/11, what scares us the most is not some supernatural boogieman lurking in the dark waiting to pounce but simply the potential of ordinary people undertaking terrible things. There is no need for the boogieman, because people are scary enough. As a consequence, one of the key features of torture porn is that its plots are based in "reality"—its characters are set in a mundane world where horrific things happen, perpetrated by flesh-and-blood mortals.

The history of horror cinema is littered with the remains of monstrous or supernatural entities—transmogrified cinematic hosts of real-world fear. The 1958 film *The Blob* and Don Siegel's 1956 film *Invasion of the Body Snatchers* are widely read as narratives that express American fears of communist infiltration. The figures that haunt the slasher genre—Freddy, Michael, Jason—have frequently been read as moral vigilantes, policing the bounds of normative heterosexuality. So why is there an emphasis on "reality" in torture porn? What sets torture porn apart is that these earlier transmogrified monsters stood in for more abstract ideological regimes—the Red Scare, conservative patriarchal "family values." In these "battles of ideas," the individual human agent is less apparent, not immediately tangible. And as more abstract ideas, these fears materialized in forms unchained from the bounds of any one mortal human being. One might argue that terrorism, as a tactic, achieves something similar—it is the idea of terrorism that is frightening, not necessarily the individual terrorists—but, nonetheless, the post-9/11 era elicits anxiety that is immediately tactile. In the wake of 9/11, terrorism was made tangible to Americans, the palpable realization of an abstract fear—our unassuming neighbor could be a terrorist; terrorism is random and does not take into consideration the guilt or innocence of a victim; and 9/11 brought the violence "home" in a very real, concrete, and spectacular way. In short, there is an immediate and direct recognition: "I, just as much as anyone else, could be a victim of terrorism." Victims in torture porn are effectively random, and torturers are in all other aspects ostensibly normal—take, for instance, the unassuming Dutch businessmen in *Hostel* and a whole host of other working professionals. And as for torturers who effectively lead two lives, this begins to approach the idea of a terrorist sleeper cell. Or, even more than this, the tidy "moral binary" that popular American culture proffers, if not always a fiction, is certainly shown to be one in our post-9/11 world. "With an unrelenting insistence," Dana Polan observes regarding the horror genre, "horror is not merely among us, but rather a part of us, caused by us."[2] Torture porn, perhaps more so than any incarnation of the horror genre before it, starkly vivifies this idea.

Jason Middleton similarly observes that "the ostensible alignment of *Hostel*'s diegesis (and that of other films grouped within the 'torture porn' category) with the 'real world' creates, for some viewers, the sense that these films are scarier than older horror films premised upon elements of the supernatural, because 'this could really happen to you.'" Middleton is prepared to accept that torture porn relies on "real world" fears but presses this point further. If the formula of a torture porn film is "this could really happen to you," Middleton asks, "who is the you" in this configuration?[3] Middleton argues that in the real world, it is ultimately those figures that have limited or no access to social/economic privilege—in a word, "non-Americans"—that are subject to torture. And he argues that this disjunction between the real world and its fictional representation "can be seen as *Hostel*'s progressive gesture."[4] I would add, though, that it is not simply that "you" might well be a victim but that "you" might well be a torturer (or at the very least complicit in torture). "Ordinary Americans" might be immune to torture, as Middleton argues, but the anxiety that torture porn negotiates is not simply the fear of being a victim but rather more frightening still that "I am a torturer."

It is not just the terrorists that frighten us, then, but ourselves, or at least those who are waging the War on Terror on our behalf. The existential realities of the War on Terror began to emerge in news reports about the abuse of detainees, public acknowledgment of the extraordinary rendition program, the Bush administration's brazen dismissal of the Geneva Conventions—which White House Counsel Alberto Gonzales casually brushed aside as a "quaint" relic of the past—and the drafting of the "Bybee Memo" (more commonly known as the "Torture Memos") giving the CIA and other American operatives effectively carte blanche in the interrogation of individuals in their custody, short of killing them. The rooting of horror in torture porn in "reality," then, draws from not only the terrorist attacks but also our loss of faith in the Manichean world order. The American public still has not really come to terms with the fact that, despite our self-image of being the purveyor of human rights and dignity, we are a violent people, and we have caused (and are causing) a great deal of suffering. I would posit that torture porn narratives, in part, serve as a device to work through this inherent contradiction. On the one hand, we imagine ourselves as agents of righteousness, the torchbearers of freedom and democracy, and on the other hand, we have to acknowledge our implicit or even explicit sanctioning of torture, even if it is designed ostensibly to keep us safe.

One of the most shocking revelations that came to light after 9/11 was the CIA's extraordinary rendition program. In this program, terrorist suspects are secreted away to another country (e.g., Egypt, Syria) to be detained and tortured. Thus, the narrative trope of abduction finds its real-world analog in rendition. It is the fear of (randomly) being picked up off the street, waking to find yourself in a small cell and subject to brutal treatment. The *Saw* franchise, the *Hostel* films, *Captivity*, *Dexter*, and others all incorporate abduction in their plots. *Dexter*, which ran on the Showtime network for eight seasons, might be considered soft-core torture porn and is the subject of chapter 7.

In torture porn, nowhere is safe. Even the safety and security of home can be turned against the victims (it is usually plural). Terrorism works precisely because it breeds fear: When and where will the next attack take place? What form will it take? In addition, and I suspect that this has largely left public consciousness now, shortly following the 9/11 attack, the American public was rocked by the threat of germ warfare. Envelopes of Anthrax mailed to public officials and media outlets fueled the anxiety of an already anxious public; experts on news programs encouraged Americans to be ready for a bioterrorist attack and to prepare a "safe room" that could be sealed with duct tape and plastic sheeting.[5] Predictably, shelves were soon cleared of emergency supplies to prepare for the bioterrorist Armageddon. This effectively meant turning one's own home into a prison, but at the end of the day, it also meant that nowhere, not even home, is truly safe.[6] Home-invasion films (*The Strangers*, *Funny Games*, *The Collector*) or the use of homes as torture facilities (*Saw II*, *The Final*) are indicative of another trope that we find in torture porn narratives.

What is considered safe turns into something cruel. These films are replete with narrative reversals or inversions. The *Hostel* films, in particular, place Americans as victims in foreign lands. One of the critical questions raised in the wake of the 9/11 attack but never addressed is, "Why do they hate us so much?" This question effectively gets parroted in torture porn films in various ways: "Why are you doing this?" or "What did I ever do to you?" The failure in American public discourse to address this question is motivated by the fact that any answer would probably be terribly unflattering. Moreover, the question itself is an inversion, because the dispossessed of the world might ask Americans the very same question: "Why do you hate us so much?" Slavoj Žižek observes, "Is this not the truth behind the fact that Bin Laden and the Taliban emerged as part of the CIA-supported anti-Soviet guerrilla movement in Afghanistan, and behind the fact that Noriega in Panama was an ex-CIA agent? Is not the USA fighting its own excess in all these cases?"[7] While we imagine that we are fighting an alien enemy, completely antithetical to Western culture, the fact is that the terrorist is our strange bedfellow.

There is an utter disavowal of the suffering that we have caused, and in its place, we view ourselves as the sole victim. "You weep over your own misfortune, and at the same time you are the best," Jean Baudrillard reflects on the 9/11 experience. "And what gives us the right to be the best is that from now on, we are victims. This is the perfect alibi; it is the whole mental hygiene of the victim, through which all guilt is resolved, and which allows one to use misfortune as though it were, so to speak, a credit card."[8] Indeed, viewing ourselves as the victim offers a limitless credit line, unburdened by guilt to rectify the wrong perpetrated against us. Torture porn flirts with this constantly and in its negotiation of the subject begins to reveal the moral bankruptcy of the position. Tortured Americans reaping vengeance against their captors; Americans perpetrating violence against one another; antagonists that take on the attributes of a protagonist—torture porn employs reversals, inversions, maybe even perversions, and what gets revealed is that, finally, the tidy "mental hygiene of the victim," which whitewashes our own violence in the real world, does not add up. Part of this victim's calculus is, of course, to sustain the lie that American prosperity comes at no expense to others around the world.[9]

Capitalizing on victimization gives license to retribution. It is little wonder, then, that retribution is a significant feature in torture porn, and it is commonly associated with an inversion—the tortured becomes torturer. Ripping a page from Wes Craven's playbook, many torture porn films load up the first two-thirds of their narrative with abusive violence to justify the retaliatory violence in the final third of the film—following the basic plot of *The Last House on the Left* (Wes Craven, 1972). This particular plot is evident in the *Hostel* films, *Captivity*, and the 2010 remake of *I Spit on Your Grave*. "It is difficult to find an instance of torture-horror that is completely devoid of retributivism," Jeremy Morris insists.[10] Without wholly dismissing Morris's position, it could be argued that not all torture porn films incorporate retribution—*The Strangers*, *Funny Games*, and *Vacancy* are examples, and it is debatable whether the *Saw* franchise is genuinely fueled by retribution. Violence in these films is random, or in the case of the *Saw* films, Jigsaw generally does not have a *personal* stake in the victim's supposed transgression. Furthermore, Jigsaw orchestrates traps as an opportunity for rehabilitation, rather than executing revenge. Nevertheless, Morris's general point remains: the trope of retribution is certainly a common feature of the genre, and it resonates with an American audience that feels that it is the victim.

Regardless of how the moral calculus works out, the American public finds satisfaction in retribution. "Violence is not to be denied," René Girard writes in his volume *Violence and the Sacred*.[11] An outlet always has to be found, Girard insists, and if not directed toward the "correct" object, a substitute might be taken (Saddam Hussein, as a convenient sacrificial substitute for Al-Qaeda, for instance). From this perspective, torture porn might be viewed as little more than a ritual that exorcizes violence. A ritual, as viewed through Girard's work, is always a reenactment of some original violent event. The violence in torture porn narratives, then, enters the ritualistic economy in a compulsive rehearsal of post-9/11 violence. The multiple sequels (seven, for instance, in the *Saw* franchise; five *Wrong Turn* films) and reappropriations of the *Saw* plot (*The Collector*, *Captivity*, *Steel Trap*, *Choose*) speak to this ritualism as well. Carol Clover also observes that the horror genre is "organized around the experience of fear" and that its compulsion to repeat is rooted in an effort to negotiate suffering.[12]

Narrative Tropes: Conflicts, Common Devices, and Structure

Some film critics and scholars routinely lambast torture porn for lacking narrative—offering little or no context for the exhibition of violence. David Edelstein certainly frames it this way (as discussed in the previous chapter). While it is true that some torture porn films do not subscribe to the conventions of (dramatic) narrative, tending to favor an episodic structure rather than cohesive linear narratives, this is not to say that they are as utterly devoid of narrative as some claim. So what are the central narrative tropes that are associated with the genre?

What is "wrong"—that is to say, the core narrative conflict—in torture porn films is not the lascivious behavior of women, as found in the slasher genre, but instead agents of paternal authority perverting the Law in the form of the sadistic disposition. Torture porn represents a paradigmatic shift in the governing anxiety of the horror genre. Whereas the "presence of the monstrous-feminine in the popular horror film" spoke to male anxieties in earlier incarnations of the horror genre, as Barbara Creed cites in her introduction to *The Monstrous-Feminine*,[13] it is abject fathers, not mothers, that spawn dread in torture porn. Dexter, in the Showtime series, lives by the Code of Harry as dictated by his father, Harry Morgan; similarly, the serial killer Bob in *Chain* instructs his adopted son, Rabbit, on how to take women apart; Jigsaw and the Elite Hunting syndicate (headed by the paternalistic Sasha) in *Hostel* subscribe to libertinage. In all these cases, we witness the perversions of "proper" Law by paternal figures.

With these twisted paternal figures, we find the outlines of a Frankenstein motif in torture porn. Madeleine Smith, along these lines, observes that the

Saw franchise is populated with the monstrous-masculine (set in contrast to Creed's monstrous-feminine).[14] The monstrous-masculine gives birth to abject agents. Dexter is the clearest example of this, and in the final season, Dexter explicitly recognizes the affinities between himself and Frankenstein's monster. (This is discussed at some length in chapter 7.) The torture chamber, like Frankenstein's laboratory, might be viewed as an artificial womb from which monsters are conceived. Paxton in *Hostel*, an ordinary college-aged young man, survives his ordeal in the Slovakian torture facility and emerges a vengeful murderer. Jennifer in *Captivity*, likewise, suffers the abuses of her male captors in their subterranean torture chamber and is reborn as a vigilante killer. In *Chain*, Rabbit, despite his most vigilant efforts to reject the sadistic teachings of his adoptive father, cannot escape fate and becomes a murderer. In the finale of the *Saw* franchise, Doctor Gordon surfaces as Jigsaw's heir, assuming, as Smith argues, "the role of abject, punishing father."[15] The torture-chamber-cum-womb witnesses the transformation of characters as (perverse) paternal agents—and they generally emerge, like a baby, from the monstrous site bloody, gasping, and crying. In many instances, revelations on how monsters are conceived are delivered through flashbacks.

The flashback—or even, in some cases, the flashforward—is a common narrative device. The flashback is a significant feature of the *Saw* franchise. Unique to the *Saw* films, the flashbacks allow for later sequels in the franchise to contextualize events in the serialized narrative. In fact, Jigsaw dies in the third installment, but his character reemerges in the diegesis of later films through the narrative device of the flashback. In addition, common to the *Saw* franchise and other films, a flashback might be used at a moment of revelation either (1) when characters find themselves in some torture chamber, and the flashback reveals how they arrived there (e.g., on moral grounds—punished for some transgression—or in a literal sense relating to their abduction), or (2) at the conclusion of a narrative, to elaborate how all the pieces fit together (as in *The Tortured*). This latter variant might have its cinematic roots in the expository conclusion of *Psycho*, where the psychiatrist explains Norman's motives.

Read through the post-9/11 lens, the flashback follows the contours of questions such as "Why do they hate us so much?" "Were the abuses at Abu Ghraib an aberration or symptomatic of a culture of torture?" While at a narrative level the flashback, or the flashforward for that matter, illustrates how a character arrives at a certain place, conceptually the device gestures toward the incomplete project of post-9/11 reflection. *Captivity*, for instance, opens with a flashforward—Jennifer, the victim-turned-torturer, dispatches her victim—the whole of the film effectively details Jennifer's transformation into a torturous killer. The structure and application of devices such as the flashback in torture porn narratives, then, in some oblique way approaches questions about our sadistic disposition and our culpability in violence.[16]

In certain instances, narratives do not employ conventional cues that allow viewers (at least initially) to read the images as a flashback/flashforward. For instance, in the unrated version of *Captivity*, as noted earlier, the film opens with a man, bound to a bed and tortured by an unseen perpetrator—save for their gloved hands.[17] The audience is led to believe that this opening prelude is the work of Jennifer's abusive captor. Only at the end is it revealed that the unseen perpetrator is Jennifer exacting vengeance, like Dexter Morgan, on those who have escaped justice. Apparently taking a lesson from her own captivity, she hunts down those who "deserve" to die slow, painful deaths. Leaving flashbacks/flashforwards uncoded as such tends to build tension into torture porn narratives, destabilizing the viewer's command of the narrative's overall coherence. However, when flashbacks/flashforwards are viewed in the context of the overall narrative, like a piece in a puzzle, this allows the spectator to see the whole picture.

The game motif derives in part from the *Scream* series, in which the perpetrator(s) plays little games with the victim(s). Games are found, not surprisingly, in *Funny Games* and are a significant feature of the *Saw* franchise. The gaming motif materializes in any number of forms, sometimes quite explicitly and on other occasions in more implicit ways—perpetrators might "toy" with victims, play hide-and-seek, hunt victims like big "game." The *Saw* franchise incorporates videogame discourse into its plots and parlance—with phrases such as "let the game begin" or "game over." Likewise, victims in the *Saw* franchise are frequently compelled to play games, to play against other "players," to solve a riddle. In films such as Marcus Graves's 2010 film *Choose*, characters are compelled to make choices with severe consequences, for one person or another, a plot device clearly inspired by the basic premise of the *Saw* films.

Puzzles, riddles, videogames—torture porn does not simply draw on these as plot elements but rather weaves them into the overall narrative. Drawing from the well of (video)gaming discourse, though, shifts storytelling modes, accounting for some of the negative reviews of torture porn that attempt to map more conventional narrative modes over the genre. Jeffrey Sconce finds a similar critical prejudice against the slasher genre, specifically discussing the last in the *Nightmare* series, *Freddy's Dead: The Final Nightmare* (Rachel Talalay, 1991). The film features a sequence in which a stoner is lured into a videogame landscape only to engage in mortal combat with Kruger.[18]

> The *Nightmare* films are not unlike another popular youth visual entertainment medium—video games. Both reward viewers for acute perception and nimble subjectivity in relation to constantly transforming perceptual data, usually based

> on a minimal narrative premise. Both are also often incomprehensible to the adult community. The reference here to Freddy and his stoned victim as video characters is thus both apt and perhaps even a bit calculated. The scene confirms that having the skills of [a] good Tetris player is probably more valuable in either watching or eluding Freddy than possessing a highly developed sense of narrative acumen.[19]

Torture porn, and specifically the *Saw* franchise, is less likely to "connect" with an audience that is not familiar with gaming discourse. As Sconce notes, films that draw from videogaming discourse "have little need or regard for qualities of narrative causality, probability, and complexity, textual features that" film critics and film scholars prize. And because these films do not adhere to conventional narrative paradigms, they serve as "ripe targets for abuse by a community committed to more 'sober' and 'realistic' filmmaking."[20]

Thus, torture porn narratives, and particularly the *Saw* narratives, being governed according to gaming discourse, do not subscribe to the imperatives of character-driven or plot-driven storylines per se but instead follow the internalized logic of specific narratives. In the *Saw* franchise, characters must strictly adhere to the rules of Jigsaw's games, in the *Hostel* films, characters must win/gain access to the Elite Hunting syndicate and abide by its code of conduct. Narrative closure in torture porn, then, has very little to do with reaffirming moral order or witnessing the transformation of a character and more to do with mastering the internal logic of the game being played.

As a consequence, there tends to be no satisfactory resolution in a torture porn film. The order of things does not change, and the villain might even walk away unscathed and unpunished. Kevin Wetmore makes a similar observation: "Characteristic of this nihilism is the impossibility of rescue." He continues, "There are no more 'final girls,' or heroes, or authority figures who know what is going on and can stop it. In post-9/11 horror cinema, there is no God, there is no authority figure that can fix the situation, nothing saves us and everybody or almost everybody dies."[21] What we find, then, is not a conventional catharsis arising from narrative form but rather a negotiation of a complex and violent world.

The lack of "proper" narrative closure arises from Bush-era rhetoric. Branding the fight against Al-Qaeda as the "War on Terror" effectively places us in a state of perpetual and hopeless war. By declaring war on "terror," the Bush administration mobilized the nation against an undefeatable hydra-headed tactic, as opposed to an identifiable and thus "defeatable" enemy. This unwinnable war against terror materializes as part of the radical paradigm shift in the horror genre following 9/11—specifically in the denial of restorative closures. Prior to 9/11, the conclusion of horror films generally brought about the (temporary) restoration of order. "In pre-9/11 horror, there is almost always a way to stop evil," Wetmore notes. "Jason, Michael and Freddy, though they return in the next sequel, can be defeated by the 'final girl.' . . . The horror film ends in hope up to September 10."[22] In the post-9/11 world, the restoration of proper order seems utterly trite, and torture porn responds with narratives that are deeply cynical and refuse conventional narrative closure.

Mediated Images: Moralizing Assaults, Surveillance, and the Consumption of Violence

One of the contemporary terrorist's most powerful weapons of choice is video: videos documenting terrorist attacks (used for recruiting purposes), videos ranting against the evils and excesses of Western culture, videos of beheadings, videos claiming responsibility for this or that attack. In all these examples, frequently broadcast on YouTube, the underlying message, whether implicit or explicit, is a moralizing one. Wetmore argues that Jigsaw, in the *Saw* films, "is on a moralistic crusade": "Like the Islamic extremists his work imitates, he sees Western society as decadent."[23] Individuals caught in a Jigsaw trap, then, are confronted with a video (or audio) recording dictating the sins for which they must atone. In torture porn, videos can also be used as an actual element of torture. In *Captivity*, for instance, a video showing the torture of another victim is shown to Jennifer, the primary victim of the narrative, to terrorize her by demonstrating what presumably awaits her. American agents interrogating terrorist suspects have also used video to manipulate detainees and to compel them to divulge information. This is fictionalized in the Fox Network television series *24*, in which Jack Bauer stages a mock execution of the son of a terrorist via a video feed.

In addition to these narrative conceits (which in large part are generated through editing—a subject discussed later), flashbacks are in a number of instances mediated through video. The second installment of the *Saw* films, for example, happens effectively on two stages: (1) the abandoned house filled with a nerve agent, where victims progress through rooms in an effort to retrieve hidden syringes filled with an antidote, and (2) Jigsaw's lair, where, while in police custody, Jigsaw and the investigating detective watch the games playing out on surveillance monitors. What we do not realize, until the climax of the film, is that the events on the surveillance monitors and the subsequent cuts into that narrative space took place long ago; what is coded as a live video feed turns out to be a recording. Video, and surveillance video particularly, is coded as "neutral," a static objective view of an event; what potentially emerges from this is a critique of commonly held assumptions about the medium. Though a surveillance image might typically be understood as a "straight-on shot" and relatively "objective" and "unmanipulated," what torture porn potentially reveals is how "truthful" images can manipulate our perception.

2.1 Use of surveillance monitors in *Saw II* (Darren Lynn Bousman, 2005).

Likewise, cameras, and the viewing window on (digital) cameras, or recorded video also function as a convenient device to introduce past events. *Vacancy* provides a good example. A road-weary couple is forced to stop at a grungy roadside motel after their car breaks down. Unable to find anything on television, David, the primary male character, inserts a nondescript VHS tape found in their room into the VCR, implicitly hoping that the tape contains pornographic material. He is instead disturbed to discover a scene of brutal violence. Playing another tape, which enacts a similar scene of violence, David soon realizes that both scenes are set in the very room in which they are staying. The VHS tape at once gives us direct access to violent acts and at the same time functions as a mediating device offering a degree of safety—it places the horrific violence at a distance, a film in a film and an event that by virtue of being recorded is past. There are a number of other films that use this or a similar device, including *Captivity*, *Rest Stop*, and the 2010 remake of *I Spit on Your Grave*. The use of video as a device to return to "the scene of the crime," so to speak, can be traced to its roots in films such as John McNaughton's 1986 film *Henry: Portrait of a Serial Killer* and Michael Powell's 1960 classic *Peeping Tom*.

One of the most common examples of a mediated image in torture porn is that of the surveillance video. Surveillance has a lot to do with power—the power associated with subjects that see as opposed to subjects that are seen. In the *Saw* franchise, traps are monitored through surveillance equipment, the torture chambers in the *Hostel* films are likewise monitored, and the same is true of *Captivity*. Michael Haneke's work, though generally outside the scope of torture porn, properly speaking, is especially attuned to this subject—his films are about the mediation of violence. While on the surface Haneke's

2.2 David realizes that the recorded scene is set in his motel room in *Vacancy* (Nimród Antal, 2007)

2.3 Entering the site of violence through the mediated image in *Captivity* (Roland Joffé, 2007), *Henry: Portrait of a Serial Killer* (John McNaughton, 1986), and *Peeping Tom* (Michael Powell, 1960).

films *Benny's Video* (1992), *Caché* (2005), and *Funny Games* (1997/2007) appear worlds apart from the *Saw* films, Catherine Zimmer views these in "a contiguous relationship," both addressing "the cinematic mediations on video surveillance."[24] To contextualize Haneke's work, I would tentatively assert that his American 2007 remake of his 1997 film *Funny Games* qualifies as torture porn—the setting, the historical context of the film, the consideration of mediated images, and the sadistic tropes offer evidence to support this position. Understandably, some people might contest this claim, noting that his work is highly self-conscious and coming from the European art film tradition. As Zimmer does, though, it seems productive to view *Funny Games* (2007), and Haneke's work in general, as sharing certain affinities with torture porn.

Zimmer also suggests that the mediated image potentially calls into question a spectator's culpability in the exhibition of violence. Exemplary of this is Gregory Hoblit's 2008 thriller *Untraceable*, which features Jennifer, an FBI agent on the cyber-crime unit, as she hunts down the individual responsible for the website killwithme.com. Visitors to the site effectively participate in an individual's torture and murder, which is streamed live over the Internet. Clear boundaries between the representatives of "good" and "bad" begin to blur, as does the spectator's position. As Steve Jones notes, the "narrative does not create a simplistic moral dichotomy where the police are faultless."[25] Far from it—agents of authority appear to be some of the most avid consumers of the live-streamed violence. FBI agents boisterously cheer for Jennifer as they watch her dispatch the antagonist through the live-streaming video. "Parallels are made between the site users and the FBI," Jones recounts, "debunking any implication that the police are self-evidently righteous simply because they are law enforcers."[26] The exhibition of violence mediated through streamed video, commoditizing the exhibition of violence, emphasizes the fraught tension built into *Untraceable*. The mediated images in torture porn narratives wield the potential to do the same.

Violence, Torture, and the Torture Chamber

Obviously, torture is a significant narrative element in torture porn. It is certainly fueled by reports of rendition, by the scandalous photographs and the facts that emerged from the Abu Ghraib incident, and by the frightening latitude given to American operatives under the aegis of "enhanced interrogation techniques." While torture is central to the torture porn narrative and is informed at least in part by reports of American agents utilizing torture to extract information, Jeremy Morris observes that torture-horror utilizes "non-interrogational torture."[27] Ostensibly, torture intends to solicit from the subject a confession of one type or another—despite the fact that the efficacy of torture is deeply in doubt.[28] Torture porn, to one degree or another, wrestles with the monster that we have conceived, and what generally materializes onscreen is torture for the sake of torture, rather than any attempt to extract information from a character.

The nature of the violence and suffering, which all but necessitates proximity between torturer and tortured, nearly precludes the use of weapons in the conventional sense. Guns are few and far between, though there certainly are exceptions. Guns, for instance, in the *Saw* films are more frequently mounted *within* a Jigsaw trap than brandished by perpetrator or victim. The relative absence of guns might well be a holdover from the slasher genre, as Carol Clover observes: "In the hands of the killer, at least, guns have no place in slasher films." Rather, as Clover argues, the instruments of death in a slasher film emphasize intimacy between the killer and the victim.[29] In certain instances, the intimacy between the perpetrator and the victim might be quite pronounced (the *Hostel* films, the remake of *I Spit on Your Grave*, *The Tortured*, *The Final*). It is worth noting, though, that while Jigsaw is typically not physically close in the *Saw* franchise, he is embodied in the games and the machinery that rips victims asunder. Finally, what is more important is the promise of protracted grievous bodily injury that might prove fatal in the end but in all cases "leaves a mark."

In *Hostel*, for instance, during Paxton's escape, he finds an American in the torture facility's locker room; the American, believing that Paxton has just finished up torturing his own victim, quizzes him in a frenzied and excited tone, "'Cause here's why I asked for the fucking gun, 'cause I just wanted to do it quick! You know what I mean—get it over with. But now I'm thinking, maybe . . . maybe . . . I want to feel it! I mean, I want to fucking feel that shit! So, I don't—what . . . what do you think I should do?" In the end, the manic character elects not to use the gun, preferring instead to savor the moment. Guns would be too compassionate, too quick, and would mitigate the suffering that is endemic to the genre of torture porn. When guns are employed in the *Saw* franchise, as I mentioned, they are typically mounted within a trap, detached from a human agent, and it is the threat that the gun will be triggered that produces the suffering, rather than the discharge of the weapon. As with real-world examples of torture, as recounted by Elaine Scarry, innocuous things (in another context—industrial work, construction) are transformed into instruments of pain.[30] Fire, ice, drugs or toxins, acid, chains, power tools, pruning shears, the threat of being smashed, drowned, or buried, industrial-aged versions of quartering, or other modern takes on medieval punishment—the litany of the instruments of torture knows no bounds. Whether in the *Hostel* films, the *Saw* franchise, or a host of other films, rarely are the instruments of torture new; on the contrary, they are frequently aged—tarnished or rusty.

It is evident that torture porn is drawing from the long history of torture, from medieval racks to CIA-trained paramilitary groups in Latin America. The cinematic torture chamber, like its real-world analog, is typically dark, where no natural light penetrates, in a number of cases subterranean, and is relatively sparse. In cinematic terms, the torture chamber, as seen in torture porn, is drawn from what Carol Clover calls "the terrible place"—usually houses or tunnels.[31] The torture chamber tends to be a hermetic space and, more than this, a nonplace, sequestered from the day-to-day civilized world—what Michel Foucault called a heterotopia. Set in contrast to utopias, heterotopias are "sites with no real place"; they exist contiguous with the inhabited world and yet are set apart, sequestered.[32]

In addition, heterotopias are "out of time"; they are places where time stands still, frozen in time, the place that time forgot. Like the archive, a sort of time capsule that insulates its holdings from the ravages of time, torture chambers are frequently windowless, completely shut out from the cycles of the day.[33] Access to the heterotopic site is limited and is usually monitored (hence the proliferation of surveillance monitors in the torture porn genre). Whether it is a victim that is imprisoned or the perpetrator, "the individual has to submit to rites and purifications. To get in one must have a certain permission and make certain gestures."[34] In the broadest sense, torture porn frequently ritualizes the stalking and abduction of a victim (*Captivity*, *Dexter*, *Hostel*, *Saw*), while the perpetrator is inducted as a member of an exclusive organization—Elite Hunting in the *Hostel* films, Jigsaw's inner circle of acolytes, or Dexter's partners in crime. And to be sure as well, the heterotopic sites in torture porn are "consecrated," sites that witness "activities of purification." Dexter "takes out the trash" and satiates his Dark Passenger (what he calls his compulsion to kill), members of Elite Hunting get to "blow off steam," Jigsaw and his disciples execute their pedagogical agenda, getting victims to reexamine their lives and to value the preciousness of it. In all cases, the heterotopic sites in torture porn host a cathartic potential—a procedure of purification that evokes to one degree or another an almost religious (*Saw*, *Dexter*) and/or hygienic system (*Dexter*).[35] This should not be confused with narrative catharsis, or closure, though.

Foucault cites brothels and colonies as "two extreme types of heterotopia," and it is fascinating how, in certain torture porn films, these two heterotopic sites intersect—Slovakia in the *Hostel* films and Brazil in *Turistas*. Prior to the prevalence of air travel, travelers—that is to say, those with the means of traversing spatial bounds and especially the colonizing subject venturing into the colonial frontier—traversed from home ports to colonial outposts on ships. "And if we think, after all," Foucault asserts, "the boat is a floating piece of space, a place without a place, that exists by itself, that is closed in on itself and at the same time is given over to the infinity of the sea, . . . the ship is the heterotopia par excellence."[36] Think, for instance, of *Zero Dark Thirty*, which depicts a CIA black site on a ship anchored in an eastern European port (a plot element probably based in fact). Casting off the moorings, a ship, like a torture chamber, becomes untethered from the land and the laws associated with it. The torture chamber, like the ship, is detached, in other words, "floating" within a spatial field, and is "a place without a place, that exists by itself."

In the spirit of earlier generic conventions, the torture chamber can also be read as an uncanny site, along the lines of the haunted house or "terrible place."[37] Evangelos Tziallas observes that whereas the horror genre is filled to the hilt with phallic weapons, torture porn witnesses "the overwhelming presence of 'vagina dentata' or 'vaginal weaponry.'"[38] The torture chamber threatens to (re)absorb the body, to consume it. The Slovakian factory in the *Hostel* films, formerly the site of *labor* and the fabrication of individuated products (finding analogies with the birthing process), works in reverse and destroys. In the *Saw* franchise, rooms become tombs, and Tziallas describes Jigsaw's traps as vaginal weapons that threaten to engulf and suffocate, rather than to penetrate, characters.[39] The governing anxiety that galvanizes torture porn is quite different from its slasher predecessor—which was largely fueled by patriarchal angst and fears of female sexuality. Tziallas notes that torture porn subverts the conventional demographics, so that victims who are made to suffer protracted ordeals are just as likely to be men as women and "there are a surprising number of female killers."[40] This is not to suggest that sexual politics are absent from torture porn or that the genre casts off the yoke of misogyny; rather, we might locate these same anxieties in the heterotopic site of the torture chamber, which "transforms the entire setting into a 'vaginal space' and weapon."[41] And from this perspective, the torture chamber as an uncanny site dovetails with the devouring mother, a figure, as Barbara Creed observes, that is "associated with the dread of the generative mother seen only as the abyss, the all-incorporating black hole which threatens to reabsorb what it once birthed."[42]

Aesthetic Tropes: The Look and Feel of Torture Porn

The antonym of "aesthetic" is "anesthetic," that which dulls the senses. The "aesthetic," then, stimulates the sensorial experience. This section, consequently, outlines not only the stylistic elements common to torture porn but the ways in which the genre addresses the viewing body and how it makes us feel. There is something almost nostalgic in the torture porn genre for "real" bodies—in the first *Hostel* film, for instance, the Dutch businessman, while on the train to Slovakia, explains that he prefers to eat his food with his hands, because it reaffirms the connection between the death of an animal and sustenance. He says all this as he is seated next to Josh, the Dutchman's soon-to-be-victim. Jigsaw, too, while "keeping his hands clean," never directly sullying his hands with torture properly speaking, relies on "old" industrial age technology—gears, springs, metal parts with a distinctly rusted patina—that has very real consequences for bodies. The obsession for countdowns, while frequently displayed in digital readouts, also heralds back to clockwork (with all the connotations of industrialized labor). In *Saw IV*, Jigsaw, for instance, marvels at a three-hundred-year-old clock that still works—its springs and gears inspiring his torture devices.[43]

This emphasis on analog technology at the same time turns our attention to bodies. The treatment of the body in torture porn is peculiar, because one might automatically assume that the genre eroticizes bodies, especially given the moniker "torture *porn*," and indeed some bodies are undoubtedly eroticized (see, for instance, the opening of *Saw 3D*). But surprisingly, on many occasions, the sexual economy is skirted in preference for a decidedly asexual biological approach to bodies of multiple types—old and young, fit and rotund, men and women, an array of classes and races. This is particularly true of the *Saw* franchise. Obviously, given the pretense of the genre, and the anticipated young male audience, many films are littered with the mutilated corpses of nubile female bodies (the *Hostel* films, *The Final*). What sets these films apart, particularly from the slasher genre, is that bodies are not engaged in sexual activity (slasher victims are frequently killed prior to, during, or immediately following the coital act). There is almost something stoic or scientific in the approach to the destruction of bodies in torture porn. The *Saw* franchise in particular might be viewed as a compendium of industrial accidents—limbs cut off, chemical burns, bodies torn asunder by mechanized devices.

In our postindustrial culture, there is, to one degree or another, a sense of alienation from the body. Technology that ostensibly is designed to bring us closer together in fact encourages just the opposite—mobile devices that allow us to connect with others but remove us from our immediate environment; social media, and the commodification of "friends" and "like-ing" something. And in this technologically rich environment, there is a poverty of real bodies. Slavoj Žižek argues that 9/11 functions as a pivotal moment in American (or Western) history. The terrorist attack, if only briefly, pulled the curtain back to reveal the body in what Žižek calls the "passion for the Real." We are inundated with products that at once satisfy basic (bodily) needs but in the same stroke deny (or deprive) the body: "coffee without caffeine, cream without fat, beer without alcohol." Žižek continues, "what about virtual sex as sex without sex, the Colin Powell doctrine of warfare with no casualties (on our side, of course) as warfare without warfare, the contemporary redefinition of politics as the art of expert administration, that is, as politics without politics, up to today's tolerant liberal multiculturalism as an experience of the Other deprived of its Otherness."[44] The "reality" of the 9/11 attack—the live broadcast, the recorded phone calls from the World Trade Center or hijacked flights, the bodies falling/jumping from the towers, the cloud and dust that settled on lower Manhattan following the collapse of the towers—certainly had all the hallmarks of a movie, but more potent or palpable. Žižek asks, "And was not the attack on the World Trade Center with regard to Hollywood catastrophe movies like snuff pornography versus ordinary sado-masochistic porno movies?"[45] Žižek is certainly not the first to refer to the spectacle of 9/11 as pornographic.[46] To posit a rhetorical question of my own, as Žižek's certainly is, Is not one of the critical elements of the pornographic genre the body—real bodies in genuine sex acts? And does this then also get to the very reason why the genre is dubbed "torture porn," precisely because of its emphasis on the body? True, the acts of torture onscreen—confinement, administration of pain, mutilation, dismemberment, rending of the body—are simulated. There is, nevertheless, in this historical moment a desire to reacquaint ourselves with the body, perhaps more importantly not the body onscreen but the one that we inhabit. Furthermore, this begins to approach Adam Lowenstein's account of torture porn and post-9/11 history—in which films such as *Hostel* in a tactile sense allow the spectator to "feel history" and confront "the audience with American responsibility for Abu Ghraib rather than dismissing it."[47] Torture porn confronts spectators with not only allegorical narratives but ones laden with affect.

We might consider, for a moment, the origin of the term "torture," which comes from the Latin *tortūra*, meaning "twisting, wreathing; torment, torture"; it also corresponds to *torquēre*, meaning "*tort*—to twist, torment."[48] Indeed, bodies onscreen are "twisted"; think, for instance, of the rack in *Saw III* that Tim is strapped into: his extremities—arms, legs, and head—are slowly twisted until bones crack, and his head is turned clear around. The scene is grisly, no doubt, but what we might consider here is not just the tortured body onscreen but also the tortured spectator. David Edelstein, for instance, commenting on loathsome violence in Gaspar Noe's 2002 film *Irreversible* [*Irréversible*] (which is not a torture porn film), notes, "For a while I stared at the EXIT sign, then closed my eyes, plugged my ears, and chanted an old mantra. I didn't understand why I had to be tortured, too."[49] Obviously, the spectator's body is never in peril,[50] but scenes of torture, graphic gore, the explicit rending of bodies—frequently enhanced with a highly embellished audio design—encourage spectators to cringe, to furrow their brow, to avert their eyes, to squirm, or returning to the Latin root of "torture," "to twist" or to writhe. The aesthetics of torture porn elicit sensations from the spectator, and the spectator effectively "replicates," if only in faint outlines, what is onscreen.

Finally, the "tortured spectator," then, is made to experience the body that he or she inhabits. This is precisely why Linda Williams refers to the horror genre (as well as pornography and melodrama) as a "body genre," and with a body genre, "the body of the spectator is caught up in an almost involuntary mimicry of the emotion or sensation of the body on the screen."[51] The visceral affects of body genres rely not only on what is seen but also on what is heard. The aural signifiers that slop/slurp generally signify, whether in pornography

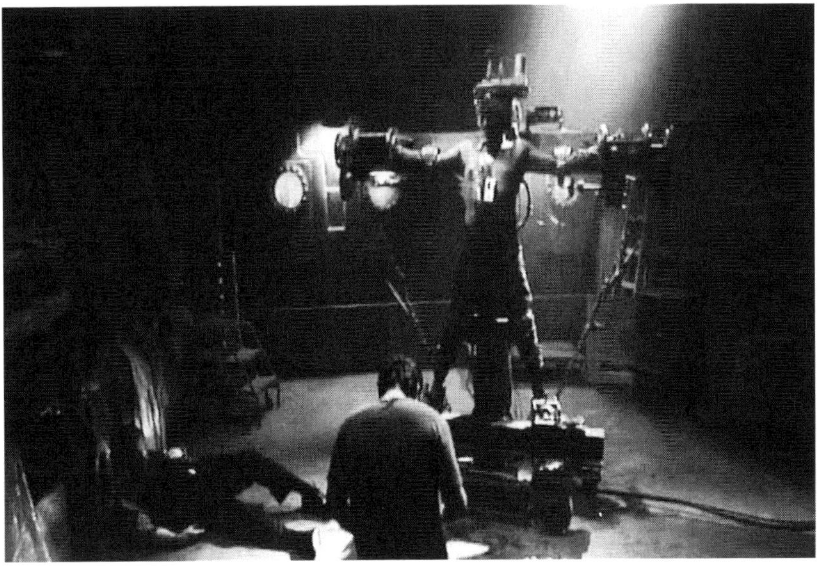

2.4 Tim twisted on his cross in *Saw III* (Darren Lynn Bousman, 2006).

or horror, the traversal of boundaries and the exchange/expulsion/loss of bodily fluids. In torture porn, then, we witness the highly embellished audio designs, including "sounds of blood," as Jeffrey Bullins observes, that strive "to deliver a greater amount of 'horror ecstasy' to the viewer."[52] Williams does observe, however, that conventionally the body that writhes onscreen—whether in agony or ravished frenzy—is typically a female body. This might be one of the clear differences of torture porn from earlier horror genre conventions, because in torture porn, the gender of the tortured body is almost negligible.

Regardless of the gender, the exhibition of the body is one of the central tropes of the genre. And there is a medicalization of horror that emphasizes the destruction of bodies. Many of Jigsaw's traps, for instance, are about testing the physical limits of the body—how much can the body endure before it breaks? how much blood loss can the body tolerate? David Edelstein opens his torture porn piece with, "Seen any good surgery on unanaesthetized people lately? Millions have, in *Hostel*, which spent a week as America's top moneymaker."[53] Indeed, Josh's torturer, the aforementioned Dutch businessman, in *Hostel* could never qualify as a surgeon (on account of his shaky hands), but he nevertheless fulfills his dream of practicing medicine on unwilling patients. Surgery is also an important feature of *Saw III*, *The Tortured*, and *Turistas*. And even Dexter in his methodical killing ritual in a room lined with plastic sheeting, taking a sample of blood for a trophy by lacerating a victim's cheek with a scalpel, also has medical characteristics. Dexter too is a blood-spatter expert

2.5 The trope of the dentist chair as found in *The Final* (Joey Stewart, 2010).

working as part of the Miami Police Department's forensics team, which of course is intimately associated with the medical profession. Unwanted dental procedures—drawn from films such as John Schlesinger's *Marathon Man* (1976), Wes Craven's *The Last House on the Left* (1972), and more recently, Chan-wook Park's *Oldboy* (2003)—can also be found in torture porn; the dental chair in particular is a significant visual trope and is found in *The Final* and *Captivity*, among others.

These medical tropes are not the sole province of the cinematic imagination, though; there are historical analogs to it. In Elaine Scarry's seminal book on torture, *The Body in Pain*, she observes, "Reports of torture from prisoners in the Philippines include references to 'unwanted dental work.' . . . In Brazil, there were forms of torture called 'the mad dentist' and 'the operating table.'"[54] This medicalization of horror in torture porn in part corresponds to the focus on the body and is drawn to a large extent from its cinematic inheritance—namely, the influence of exploitation films (especially from the 1970s). Exploitation cinema frequently showcased medical experiments designed to emphasize gore, with the objective of eliciting a visceral response in the viewer. (I discuss this genre in the following chapter.)

The banality of the space, the decor, and the instruments displayed before the victim/character in the context of torture are charged with a wholly different quality, rather nefarious in fact. (Here we have yet another example of inversion, which I addressed earlier.) The everydayness of torture objects—a drill, a dentist's pick, a chair—recontextualized in the framework of torture become weapons, which are designed to evoke dread in the character subjected to torture and in the spectator, for whom the stability of the order of things is undone. Scarry discusses this precise issue: "The room, both in its structure and its content, is converted into a weapon, deconverted, undone." And this inversion, turning things on their head, is designed to elicit fear in the victim (and the spectator). Scarry continues, "Made to participate in the annihilation of the prisoners, made to demonstrate that everything is a weapon, the objects themselves, and with them the fact of civilization, are annihilated: there is no wall, no window, no door, no bathtub, no refrigerator, no chair, no bed."[55] In a topsy-turvy world, all objects have the potential to execute pain. Torture porn, then, is littered with everyday objects employed in the administration of pain—chairs, for example.

Tied, duct taped, shackled victims in torture porn repeatedly find themselves bound to a chair. From the interrogation of terrorist suspects in *24* or for noninterrogational purposes as found in *Saw*, *Hostel*, and many other films, this is a motif that is endlessly recycled. (It is even found in horror films of the era outside the realm of torture porn, including Rob Zombie's 2007 neo-slasher film *Halloween*.) This trope has clear antecedents in the real world and in cinema—Roberto Rossellini's 1945 film *Rome, Open City*, for instance.

Exploitation films of the 1970s loosely and shamelessly adapted for the screen historical accounts of torture, though without regard for historical fidelity or context—accounts of torture in concentration camps, Nazi medical experiments, and reports of disappearances and torture at the hands of Latin America paramilitary. Torture porn assimilates many of the tropes found in exploitation films and, at the same time, draws from the well of contemporary stories and images of torture, largely at the hands of Americans. Images of detainees in Afghanistan in jumpsuits, hooded, and shackled, in transit to Guantánamo Bay Prison (re-created in uncanny detail in Mat Whitecross and Michael Winterbottom's 2006 film *The Road to Guantánamo*) finds its corresponding image in films such as *Hostel*—Josh, for instance, shackled and hooded before his tormentor enters the torture chamber. The "cat in a bag" game in *Funny Games* is also an example of a hooded victim. Likewise, the leaked images from Abu Ghraib inspired many of the images found in torture porn.[56]

As much as these contemporary images inform the aesthetic tropes of torture porn, there is, at the same time, a visual deficit veiled behind American secrecy. (For instance, we saw only a small portion of the Abu Ghraib catalogue; there were apparently over twelve hundred photographs.) First introduced during the Clinton administration, the existence of the CIA's extraordinary rendition program was acknowledged in the wake of 9/11. The CIA operates a clandestine fleet of aircraft to transport detainees to a network of CIA prisons known as black sites or to third-party countries (e.g., Egypt, Jordan).[57] Coupled with these revelations, the George W. Bush administration brazenly mobilized legal opinions that sanctioned torture. In the concluding remarks of what is now popularly known as the "Torture Memos," John Yoo, who wrote the opinion (for Jay S. Bybee, the assistant attorney general), concludes that torture "covers only extreme acts." Torture in Yoo's estimation results in "serious physical injury such as death or organ failure" or causes "lasting psychological harm. . . . Because the acts inflicting torture are extreme, there is significant range of acts that though they might constitute cruel, inhuman, or degrading treatment or punishment fail to rise to the level of torture."[58] Giving American operatives wide latitude in their treatment of detainees, under the aegis of enhanced interrogation techniques, stokes the imagination: what exactly are they doing in these CIA black sites? Torture porn, to one degree or another, fills this deficit in the economy of our visual culture.

Perpetrators in torture porn are frequently quite banal in their demeanor and dress. No trademark striped pullover such as we find with Freddy, no masks as we find with Jason or Michael—there are, however, quite a number of perpetrators in hooded cloaks. The antecedents of this attire are clearly drawn from the tradition of the hooded (and sometimes cloaked) executioner. In her commentary on the Abu Ghraib photographs, Catherine Soussloff associates hoods and cloaks with the Ku Klux Klan; specifically, she discusses the ways the poignantly iconic man on the box (Gilligan, as the MPs dubbed him), the hooded figure covered with a poncho and arms outstretched in a cruciform, echoes the profile of KKK regalia and that "putting prisoners in Klan regalia reverses the victim/abuser roles that we expect from the symbols themselves."[59] This once again returns us to the idea of an inversion, where the victim is dressed in the guise of the reprehensible perpetrator. There is more to consider here, though, because the Klansman's regalia too has antecedents: the capirote is a conical-shaped head piece, usually covering the face, worn by the Christian flagellants that ritualistically whip themselves in a penitential procession[60] or is in other cases worn by condemned individuals while they atone for their transgression (the likely source of the "dunce cap"), or alternatively by those who administered punishment (torture or an execution) in Spain. In particular, it is associated with the Spanish Inquisition. In visual culture, then, the hood is a slippery signifier, vacillating between the poles of torturer and tortured. It is little wonder that the hood, rooted in the tradition of torture and capital punishment, is found in torture porn worn by perpetrators and victims alike. For the latter, a victim, such as Josh in *Hostel,* is seen with a hood immediately prior to his torture. As for the former, Jigsaw wears a black, satin hooded cloak with a deep red lining. The "Countess Bathory" character in *Hostel: Part II* dons a full-length crimson velvet cloak. Ben Dexter, the portly, "brainy" brother in *Captivity*, lounges in a terrycloth bathrobe with a hood.

An admirer following the journalistic accounts of a vigilante killer illustrates Dexter as "The Dark Defender," a gothic comic-book vigilante superhero, with a long sweeping overcoat topped with a hood that keeps most of his face in shadow. This is a fantastic vision, though; typically when Dexter makes a kill, he wears practical clothing, dull and dark earthen hues and a heavy apron. The perpetrators in the *Hostel* films wear something quite similar. In these cases, the heavy apron, made of vinyl or leather, has the qualities of abattoir gear, which points us back once again to *The Texas Chain Saw Massacre*. There is poetry in their attire—perpetrators tend to treat their victims as nothing more than animals for the slaughter; consequently, the abattoir's apron is very appropriate.

Similarly, victims are, on a number of occasions, placed in situations or traps that are designed to deliver some sort of "poetic justice" or, if not "justice," then a torture befitting the character. In the first *Saw*, Paul, apparently facing a bout of depression, cuts himself; he is subsequently compelled to tunnel his way through razor wire. Whitney in *Hostel: Part II* is a stereotypical vivacious sorority girl, and she is made to play the part to the hilt. Danica in *Saw III* is the eyewitness to a fatal hit-and-run accident, but she refuses to testify to what she witnessed; for her moral paralysis, she is encased in ice. Torture is not always customized to the victim, though. In many instances, scenes of torture are intended to elicit a "sick" thrill from the audience that laughs, screams, squirms, or averts their eyes at the sight of an "ingenious" number or the crass spectacle of gore, but nevertheless with a degree of purpose. While torture porn films might be structured around a series of violent vignettes, they should not be confused with films that are made in the spirit of the Grand Guignol—the *Final Destination* series, for instance, showcases a string of grim accidents exhibiting the various ways in which a body might be destroyed.[61] Torture porn is generally different insofar as it encourages the spectator to read the embellished violent numbers through the post-9/11 matrix.

The exhibition of violence and suffering in torture porn is protracted—indeed torturous. In the slasher genre, male characters are typically dispatched quickly; female characters, on the other hand, are stalked, and once confronted with the monster, they tend to plead for their lives before they are finally cut down after a struggle or chase. And this is certainly one of the defining elements that set torture porn apart from its predecessor, the slasher, in which gender politics arguably is the prevailing anxiety. Carol Clover observes that in slashers, "crying, cowering, screaming, fainting, trembling, begging for mercy belong to the female [character]. Abject terror, in short, is gendered feminine, and the more concerned a given film is with that condition—and it is the essence of modern horror—the more likely the femaleness of the victim." Clover continues by noting, "It is no accident that male victims in slasher films are killed swiftly or offscreen, and that prolonged struggles, in which the victim has time to contemplate her imminent destruction, inevitably figure females. Only when one encounters the rare expression of abject terror on the part of a male (as in *I Spit on Your Grave*) does one apprehend the full extent of the cinematic double standard in such matters."[62] Whereas slasher victims are dealt merciful blows, victims in torture porn are not let off so easily. Furthermore, the demographics of victims in torture porn are far more "egalitarian"; men are just as likely to be subjected to protracted suffering and made to utter "expressions of abject terror." Regardless of the gender, victims in torture porn typically endure extended torment and in fact might even live through their ordeal, but they usually remain mentally and physically scarred for life.

The color of age, or of wear, is characteristic of the overall color palate of torture porn. The *Hostel* films—and in particular the torture sequences—are dominated by earthen hues. The color palette is muted: dark browns, blacks, or fecal in nature. Films that include medicalized horror, on the other hand, tend to be bathed in a sickly bluish-greenish light, and this is particularly true of the first *Saw* film and *Saw III*. But this bluish-greenish tint, like *Hostel*'s muted palette, also suggests age or wear. The bluish-greenish light is attributed in part to the industrialized fluorescent lighting—the light of an aging Cold War–era institution. The color scheme of the second installment of the *Saw* franchise, which is largely set in an abandoned house, shares more in common with the *Hostel* films, with its sickly sepias and dingy yellows. Whether the pale bluish green of medicalized horror or the more organic palette—ranging from black/brown to begrimed yellows—torture porn lacks natural light. And this is especially true of the spaces where violence occurs. The hermetic torture chamber (a characteristic intimately associated with the sadistic disposition—discussed in the following chapter) is typically lit with functional bare lights; rarely if ever does the sun penetrate these spaces.

The color and lighting scheme of these films relies heavily on cinematography to convey isolation, doom, and dread. Torture porn, and here I am specifically addressing torture scenes, relies on a steady diet of medium shots and two-shots (in the instance when the perpetrator is present with the victim). While medium-long and long shots establish the immediate surroundings—the torture chamber, the tools of torture, the character's (or characters') predicament—close-ups, on the other hand, offer the signifiers of suffering—tense muscles, clinched fists, a face furrowed, sweaty, tearful, filled with anguish. The close-ups also provide forensic details—for instance, the power drill penetrating Josh's thigh in *Hostel*, the scalpel cutting open Amy's abdomen in *Turistas* to harvest her organs, the self-extraction of teeth in *Saw 3D: The Final Chapter*, or the extraction of teeth in the remake of *I Spit on Your Grave*. Aside from the forensic close-ups, much of the violence in torture porn is set in medium shots.

In short, torture sequences in torture porn are shot in the same way that contemporary hardcore pornography is. The sexual episode in (mainstream heterosexual) pornography typically begins with a long or medium-long shot that introduces the spectator to a space—a bedroom, a living room, a hotel room, a doctor's office—and usually to the featured female performer. This is quickly followed with the entrance of the male character who prompts the sexual number; shots become increasingly tight—medium long, medium, medium close-up shots. Intercut into these shots are close-ups that reveal, like torture porn, muscles tensing, hands clinching body parts or clinging to bedsheets or furniture, and ecstatic faces in contorted gestures. As for these latter shots, taken on their own, without the auditory cues and the context of other shots, one could easily confuse the expression of ecstasy for agony. In addition to these close-ups that detail facial expressions and tense musculature, pornographic films also include an abundance of forensic close-ups, commonly referred to as "meat shots." As Linda Williams observes, no pornographic feature film would be "complete without a great many meat shots in any given sexual sequence," which offer to the spectator "visual evidence of penetration." Indeed, the forensic shots in torture porn typically offer something analogous—proof of penetration of a different kind. In torture porn, as with conventional pornography, the meat shot is not in itself enough, though, because there is "a 'higher' narrative goal: to prove that not only penetration but *also* satisfaction has taken place."[63] In pornography, the money shot, frequently choreographed as the male character ejaculating on the ecstatic female character's face, serves this function—proving that orgasm has occurred and signaling the end of the number. Likewise, in torture porn, the culmination of shots typically leads to the rending of a body or the discharge of blood, which like the facial cum shot (the discharge of a bodily fluid) also serves as the climactic event within the torture sequence. Eli Roth refers to the severing of Kana's eye in his film *Hostel* (2005), which when cut emits a milky pus, as an "eyegasm," and Tom Shankland refers to the climax of his torture numbers in his 2007 film *WΔZ* (also known as *The Killing Gene*) as the money shot.[64]

Camera movement and editing can vary quite dramatically from film to film, and even within individual films. The *Hostel* films, for instance, might be divided into three parts: the first part of the film introduces a cadre of characters, which is subsequently followed by the torture numbers, and finally the films conclude with an escape. The composition and editing for each discrete section is quite different. While the introductory segment generally follows the conventions of dramatic narrative (or, more specifically, the bromance), the torture sequence follows the conventions of the pornographic regime, and finally the escape draws on the conventions of the action thriller.

Frenetic cinematography is generally reserved for moments of terror—for instance, those moments when characters find themselves in a Jigsaw trap. Tracking or crane shots might even fully circle a character to reveal the gravity of the situation: such shots might be repeated but reframed as a canted shot and/or sped up or slowed down. These highly stylized shots are frequently accompanied with an equally frenetic editing regime. Editing, like the cinematography, is generally restrained (at least by contemporary cinematic standards) throughout most of the narrative diegesis, however. Adhering to the conventions of continuity editing, a moment of dread might be amplified with the abrupt use of fever-pitch editing—for instance, when a victim realizes he or she is in trouble or moments of revelation, such as the end of a *Saw* film, when it is shown how all the pieces fit together.

Whereas slasher films usually rely on the monster lurking in the shadows, jumping out from behind a corner, from behind a tree, or whatever it might be, torture porn instead relies on the editing to generate fear. Adam's abduction in the first installment of the *Saw* films seems to straddle both conventions. The assailant, wearing a pig's-head mask, jumps out of a dark closet. This certainly corresponds to the conventions associated with the slasher genre, but it is also the editing that greatly enhances the tension. Whereas slashers use the sudden emergence of the monster onscreen (or perhaps just the monster's weapon—recall how Kevin Bacon's character is dispatched in Sean Cunningham's 1980 film *Friday the 13th*), torture porn might suddenly insert a close-up, or extreme close-up, commonly accompanied with a jarring (non)diegetic audio element. And when the editing is mobilized to scare, it is usually done with a rapid succession of shots, each individual shot onscreen for no more than a split second. The inserted (extreme) close-ups in some fashion capture the expression of pain, suffering, or terrified anticipation—a face wracked with fear, a hand thrown up in a defensive gesture. Jeffrey Bullins's excellent assessment of the audio design in the *Saw* franchise makes the same argument, noting that the "shock cut combines a quick visual cut with a sudden aural event in the attempt to cause the viewer to actually 'jump out of their seat.'"[65]

Adam's abduction in *Saw* is notable too for its use of the photographic camera flash, the instantaneous lighting up of a space quickly washed out in hot white before returning to dark. Camera flashes are a fairly common trope in the torture porn genre.[66] The flash is used as an editing device, as cuts are made with the rhythm of the blown-out light; this editing technique is probably traceable back to the opening of *The Texas Chain Saw Massacre*. Blown-out or hot white shots, even independent of any diegetic motivation (e.g., a camera flash), coupled with rapid editing, are also a fairly common device for transitions—moving from one spatial and/or temporal field to another, bracketing, for instance, a flashback from the primary narrative diegesis. This device is used quite extensively in the *Saw* franchise but is also found in other films and television programs. Lumen in season 5 of *Dexter*, for instance, is besieged by flashbacks, returning in lightning-fast takes, when she and Dexter return to her torture chamber.

Whether to elicit a scare from the spectator, to illustrate some revelation, to serve as a vehicle to enter a flashback, or to act as a cinematic transition, these editing devices are frequently accompanied by a highly embellished audio design. In some cases, a diegetic audio element—a scream or the wail of a power tool—might be engineered in such a way that it slips into the nondiegetic soundscape. Sound is paramount in torture porn, because as realistic as torture porn is, the graphic images are never fully convincing (despite what detracting critics and scholars claim). In the pornographic genre, the meat shot is intended to deliver proof of penetration; the meat shot in torture porn, however, the forensic close-up, does not command the same evidentiary weight. The drill bit boring into Josh's leg, for instance, clearly is a cinematic prosthetic, and the potency of the shot relies heavily on the sound. The "meat sound," then, might be torture porn's true meat shot, its means of delivering what the forensic shots alone cannot. The surgery sequence in *Saw III* might cause spectators to avert their eyes, but what ultimately transcends the ruse of cinematic trickery (the fake blood, the prosthetic head) is the diegetic audio design that emphasizes what we see—the drill bit coming to rest on the skull with a "tap," the sound of blood oozing from the incisions, the roar of the cutoff saw cutting through the skull, the "gooey" sound of the skull fragment being pulled back to relieve the pressure on Jigsaw's brain. Audio design, perhaps even more so than the visual image, wields the most potential to elicit an affective response in the viewer. Sound can easily be unhinged from its signified, slipping into the realm of the nonobject, the abject. Sounds that are in between, composites, signifying the instability or the violation of borders—these instances are pregnant with affective potential.

In addition to emphasizing gore, the diegetic sound design of torture porn helps to define the spatial environment. Torture chambers are most commonly little more than concrete rooms or situated within an industrialized setting, and as a consequence (at least when we are speaking of torture sequences), the sound tends to be fairly live. Voices or the racket of torture reverberate (if only slightly), bouncing off the live surfaces. Think for instance of the first *Saw* film, which takes place almost entirely in a bathroom—sound reverberating off glass and ceramic tiles. In these live spaces, the audio accouterments of horror echo: footsteps on concrete floors, doors creaking open or slamming closed, chains rattling, metal pipes and metal instruments of all sorts scraping, the whir of a power tool that trails off, the dripping of water or blood. These sounds tend to reverberate; they hang in the air, haunting the spaces of violence.

Although torture porn includes no supernatural elements, the nondiegetic sound design has a ghostly character. It is as if the nondiegetic elements—an abstraction of power tools, scraping metal, screams—stand as aural vestiges of violence. The score and a lot of the sculpted audioscapes in the *Saw* franchise are the work of Charlie Clouser. Having played with the industrial band Nine Inch Nails, among others, Clouser is intimately familiar with the sampling of audio elements, manipulating them through processors and weaving them together in a richly textured design. (I discuss Clouser and his role in the *Saw* franchise at some length in chapter 4.) Though Clouser's work is quite distinctive, similar nondiegetic sound designs are evident in other torture porn films. The low dissonant rumble—not exactly music and not attributable to a diegetic source either—is quite typical of torture porn; these ambient low drones, particularly at scary moments, might be abruptly shattered with a high-pitch squeal. And these audio elements that shatter the drone, or pierce relative silence, are difficult to categorize—not exactly a scream, not exactly the scratching of metal, and not exactly a growl or howling of a fierce animal but somewhere in between these things. And it is the in between, the uncategorized element, that elicits affect. Disproportionate (negative) critical attention has been given to the graphic images found in torture porn; the affective charge associated with these images, however, relies heavily on embellished audio elements.

Character Tropes: Victims, Perpetrators, and Those In Between

Victims in the slasher genre have some sense that they are misbehaving (even if it is only normal high school high jinx); in torture porn, on the other hand, victims are often completely oblivious to their transgressive behavior. Torture porn victims typically perceive themselves to be innocent and may in fact be so. Victims are generally ill equipped and/or confounded by the situation in which they find themselves and are incapable of processing what they did to deserve such a fate. Ignorance might be transgression enough for a perpetrator to select a victim and to execute a punishment, prompting that frequently asked question in torture porn: "Why are you doing this?"

As with most things in the genre, though, torture porn stubbornly refuses to uphold clear moral categories—victims are not always innocent, and perpetrators are not always nefarious. Good or bad misses the point. "Ultimately," Catherine Zimmer concludes regarding the *Saw* films, "it would be reasonable to suggest that the films posit every character as both guilty and innocent."[67] Rob Zombie's 2005 film *The Devil's Rejects* also features brutal killers that are subject to gruesome torture at the hands of Sheriff Wydell. In fact, in many instances, the boundary between good and malevolence is difficult to ascertain in these narratives—Dexter is a serial killer (of serial killers), but he works for the Miami Police Department as a blood-spatter expert; many of the torturers in the *Hostel* series are respectable in every other way—they are captains of industry, doctors, professionals; Jigsaw in the *Saw* series is an altruistic engineer, and he counts among his disciples a police officer.

Be that as it may, and understanding that a character might vacillate between victim and perpetrator, efforts to save victims are either thwarted or useless. This is due in part to the representatives of authority—doctors, police, agents of the state apparatus—who are either ineffectual, hamstrung, or even at times complicit in the deadly game being played, creating an environment permeated by fear and hopelessness. At the conclusion of a torture porn film, malevolence still exists in the world, and there is no overarching authority poised to set things right. Actually, it is quite the opposite; spectators leave a torture porn film knowing that malevolence lurks "out there" and could pounce at any moment. While earlier film such as *Halloween* and *The Texas Chain Saw Massacre* conclude without (wholly) vanquishing the representatives of malevolence, they nonetheless locate a degree of solace in the final girl's triumph; torture porn, on the other hand, emphasizes bleaker outlooks. This captures the American zeitgeist in the post-9/11 era, when the nation waited—and indeed is still waiting—for the next shoe to drop.

Characters in torture porn films, while hardly fixed, in the broadest of brushstrokes might be placed in one of two camps—victims and perpetrators. In the slasher genre, victims are typically punished for some moral transgression, indulging in the vice of sex, alcohol, or drugs. In torture porn, on the other hand, victims might be perfectly modest. True, some victims are not saints. Amanda, for instance, in the *Saw* franchise, is tested by Jigsaw because she is a drug addict. However, victims frequently are quite naïve. The first installment of the *Hostel* series features two American characters, Josh and Paxton, who are emblematic, buying into a wide-eyed and unsophisticated understanding of "exceptionalist" rhetoric. The pair carry themselves confidently, secure in the knowledge that they are Americans. They are both "book smart"; both are presumably off to graduate school in the near future. Paxton encourages his friend to be more adventurous because soon Josh will be "writing his thesis," and he will be studying for the bar exam. On their European trip, sowing their wild oats before they embark on their imminent success, Josh and Paxton are the epitome of the American sense of entitlement. They carry themselves with an abundance of confidence and presume that they are entitled to the world's bounty—namely, European women. But precisely because of their sense of license, and its concomitant gift of self-assurance, they are also incredibly ignorant of the world that they inhabit. What the *Hostel* films exhibit, as do other films that feature Americans abroad (or in foreign-like environments—such as rural spaces), is that Americans are targets. Victims are not selected because of their behavior but rather for the simple fact that they are Americans, and they happen upon the perpetrator at an opportune moment.[68]

On some occasions, a victim is selected effectively at random. Bryan Bertino's 2008 film *The Strangers*, for example, features a young couple returning to the male protagonist's—James Hoyt's—family home. Late at night, the couple is disturbed by a knock at the door, and a petite woman, one of the strangers, asks, "Is Tamara home?" (No one has ever heard of a "Tamara.") The filmmaker describes the film as a "terror" film, and indeed the stranger, along with her two colleagues, terrorizes the couple over the course of the night. When Kristen McKay, Hoyt's girlfriend, asks for a third time, "Why are you doing this to us?" the masked stranger simply responds, "Because you were home."

Victims suffer at the hands of sadistic characters, and they are usually sadistic in the clinical sense of the term. (I discuss the nature of sadism in the following chapter.) The perpetrators are usually very intelligent, cool, calm, and collected. While malice might be a motivating factor, the perpetrator in torture porn usually remains composed. Perpetrators do not act capriciously but rather meticulously execute their plans; everything is premeditated. And just as with Sade's libertines, perpetrators establish and are governed by a set of rules, sometimes manifesting as some sort of game.

While a torture porn perpetrator might abduct a victim outside, in the world, he or she does so cautiously and reserves the most vicious acts for a space that is typically designed for the explicit purpose of executing torture. If a victim is not abducted, a perpetrator might set a trap to lure a victim or cast of victims to the torture chamber. In both Luis Cámara's 2007 film *Steel Trap* and Joey Stewart's 2010 film *The Final*, victims are lured into the torture space with an invitation to a party. The use of the hermetic torture chamber is drawn directly from the sadistic disposition, in which the sadist acts only within prescribed spaces and within a closed network of friends. This ensures that the perpetrator's highly scripted episode of violence can take place beyond prying eyes and ensures the perpetrator's security. Indeed, frequently the violent vignettes in torture porn are highly scripted—the perpetrator knows precisely how the scene is supposed to unfold.

The perpetrator then begins to resemble a film director. The perpetrator manipulates victims like puppets on a string and in some cases, rather than actually participating in the violence, watches from a distance—Jigsaw watches from a peephole in a wall, and the perpetrator in *Captivity* watches events on a bank of video monitors.[69] This also corresponds to our new reality: the terrorist as auteur, as Michael Ignatieff has phrased it. "We now have the terrorist as film director," Ignatieff writes. "One man taken hostage recently in Iraq described, once released, how carefully his own appearance on video was staged, with the terrorists animatedly framing the shot: where the guns would point, what the backdrop should be, where he should kneel, what he should be scripted to say."[70] The terrorist video and the torture vignettes in torture porn are, then, impossible to view completely independent of the imagery of terrorism. Furthermore, as this real-world example indicates, perpetrators intend that violence should be premeditated, scripted, highly controlled.

Finally, perpetrators are, at their core, corrupt. On the one hand, Jigsaw desperately wants to bring order to the world, and yet he lives in a chaotic space, littered with the wreckage of twentieth-century hardware. The perpetrators in the *Hostel* films live two lives. While on the one hand they are working professionals, on the other they are bloodthirsty killers. Dexter works for the Miami Police Department but satiates the cravings of his Dark Passenger, what he calls his compulsion to kill, with his ritualistic killing of other murderers and justifies it as a public service. "The traitor, the liar, the criminal with a good conscience, the shameless rapist, the killer who claims he is a savior," this is the very face of the abject as Julia Kristeva deems it.[71]

While the perpetrators very well might be abject, they are not evil as such. Evil generally does not exist in torture porn; evil is inescapably bound to religious connotations, and torture porn narratives—while evoking the specter of Islamic terrorists, if obliquely—are by and large secular in nature. Perpetrators might be disgruntled in some fashion (Jigsaw in the *Saw* franchise, Dexter) or simply bored (the "Johns" in the *Hostel* films), but they are not evil; a maleficent spirit does not beckon them to commit acts of violence. They are not possessed. True, a perpetrator may be "soulless" (Dexter) and commit acts of violence for no apparent reason whatsoever (*Funny Games*, *The Strangers*). The perpetrators might be well endowed with great intelligence, but they are not supernatural entities (or Satan's spawn). In fact, they might even be social "insiders." Take, for instance, the saintly looking pair in *Funny Games*, who are "themselves white, educated, 'proper' young men," as Catherine Zimmer observes. She marvels at Haneke's positioning of these characters, who "even in a home-invasion narrative . . . seem more like insiders than outsiders," emphasizing the fact that the roots of violence are closer to home than we might care to admit.[72]

On the other hand, the intentions of the perpetrator very well might be "altruistic." The nerdy crowd in *The Final* wants to teach the popular kids a thing or two about compassion. Jigsaw's purported mission is to rehabilitate individuals so that they might cherish the gift of life. Malevolence and sometimes even (a perpetrator's) agency is taken out of the equation altogether, because in many instances, the perpetrator places a victim within a system—a game, a riddle, a trap. A perpetrator, without contradicting the idea of highly scripted episodes, might relinquish immediate control of a situation, allowing the chips to fall where they will, permitting the rules of the game, or the laws of nature, to dictate the final outcome. In torture porn, it is frequently a system that is lent agency, rather than the perpetrator's personal vendetta. Human compassion, human emotion, is dispensed with altogether, another trait highly characteristic of the sadistic disposition.

Usually, a perpetrator, or perpetrators, confines violence to a hermetic space—a torture chamber/facility, a home, a basement. Outside the confines of this hermetic space, perpetrators in torture porn conforms to conventional social mores. They have all the mannerisms and characteristics of social insiders, a far cry from the social outcasts of the slasher genre. And this is what is so frightening in these films: the perpetrators are out there among us, and perhaps even more frightening still, they are no different from us. Torture porn films do not paint a neat Manichean worldview. Victims are not always likable characters, and when given the chance, the victims prove to be just as brutal as the perpetrators. And this is probably torture porn's most distinct characteristic, and presumably it registers a crisis of faith in the Manichean worldview. While the Bush administration attempted to construct a narrative of good versus evil (e.g., the conception of the Axis of Evil, which also points to the division of powers in the Second World War, or even the efforts to make Al-Qaeda play Indian to our Cowboy, e.g., George W. Bush's rhetoric of "dead or alive" and "we're going to smoke them out"), the effort to cast the post-9/11 experience in such clear-cut black-and-white narratives rings false, and torture porn (if only by coincidence) speaks truth to power. It could be argued that the crass narratives that torture porn proffers reveal the more complex moral truths about the nature of violence, innocence, retribution, and the inversion of moral order that are hidden behind the official narrative that the Bush administration and conservative pundits peddle. This is analogous to the high/low distinction that Carol Clover identifies in rape-revenge narratives: "What disturbs [us] about *I Spit on Your Grave* is the way it exposes the inner workings of *The Accused* and films like it. . . . *I Spit on Your Grave*, in short, is the repressed of *The Accused*, and I suspect that it is for this reason as much as any other it has met with the punitive response it has."[73] The scathing critical reception of torture porn might be read in these terms as well—these are the repressed narratives of a violent culture.

Earlier I positioned torture porn characters in one of two camps—victims or perpetrators. There is, however, a third category. In a number of cases, the perpetrator straddles boundaries in a morally ambiguous world, and I would posit that a number of the perpetrators that populate torture porn are pro(an)tagonists—sympathetic in their intentions, seductive in their cunning and capacity to immediately effect change, but ultimately dubious in their methodology. The nerdy crowd that reaps revenge on the popular kids in *The Final* might be an example of this category. Dexter, Jigsaw, and Jack Bauer are most certainly the pro(an)tagonists of their respective narratives. Configured in the rape-revenge narrative, Jean Lerner, in *WΔZ*, deals "righteous vengeance" to those who abused her. And because the pro(an)tagonists are generally affable, our identification is commonly aligned with them; the cinematic syntax tends to reinforce this alignment. We want Jack Bauer to break fingers, we want Dexter to dispatch scum, and we are eager to see poetic justice delivered in the form of a Jigsaw trap. This is not necessarily unique to torture porn; it is also evident in the slasher genre. "Within the *Nightmare* formula," Jeffrey Sconce observes, "it is easy to see why Freddy is the star protagonist and chief point of identification rather than the menaced teens." While the stalked teenagers are stock characters and readily interchangeable, it is "Freddy [who] continues from film to film. The teenagers do not."[74]

This idea of the pro(an)tagonist finds certain affinities with Robin Wood's fifth principle, "ambivalence," under the general heading of "the return of the repressed." It is not simply that the monster (in whatever form it takes) in the horror film is sympathetic but rather, as Wood posits, that the monster fulfills "our nightmare wish to smash the norms that oppress us and which our moral conditioning teaches us to revere."[75] The difference here is that the pro(an)tagonist does not necessarily smash norms but frequently reaffirms them. The acts that the torture porn pro(an)tagonist performs no doubt counter "our moral conditioning," but there is a tacit understanding—especially in the case of Dexter and Bauer—that this is in the service of the supposed "greater good."

Part of the intention here in my mobilization of the pro(an)tagonist is to complicate the loci of identification. Frequently what we find in both scholarship and popular criticism is the unquestioned assumption that identification lies with the tortured victim (there is a moral assumption that the victim deserves our sympathy and, thus, our identification). Implicit, then, in some of the critical reviews of torture porn is an expression of frustration over the genre's tendency to align our identification with the perpetrators. Lurking within the haranguing dismissal of torture porn is the defensive gesture, "That's not me." But this vehement denial probably has more to do with the critic's inability to negotiate the violence perpetrated on our behalf in the real world. Catherine Zimmer posits that "despite the critical marking of these films as a disturbing symptom of the bloodlust of our times, they are also oddly trying to work through some of the complexity of the experience of violence (and the anger with current formulations of and responses to these violences) in a less pedantic way than more explicitly political films addressing topics such as torture."[76] Zimmer adds that Darren Lynn Bousman's 2007 film *Saw IV* made more in box-office returns than did Gavin Hood's 2007 film *Rendition* and Robert Redford's 2007 film *Lions for Lambs* combined. Zimmer is addressing the *Saw* franchise in particular, but her interpretation generally applies across the genre; there is a critique of power in many of these films. What these films potentially ask of the audience is to consider whether there is such a thing as "righteous torture"?[77] Aligning our identification with the pro(an)tagonist invites us to reflect on our complicity in the American sadistic disposition.

While these character, aesthetic, and general tropes are in many instances informed by our post-9/11 experience, they are not completely new. Edelstein even notes this in his 2006 *New York* magazine article. It is not simply that Edelstein is disturbed by the graphic exhibition of violence but rather that it is found in mainstream fare. The veteran film critic has seen it all before, but what used to be confined to crass exploitation films (particularly those coming out of Italy in the 1970s) is simply another choice among many in the bastions of consumer capital (the multiplex), no longer relegated to inner-city second-run movie theaters or the "naughty" back end of a video store in the cult section nestled right next to the pornography. A good share of the tropes identified here originate elsewhere. I address the cinematic antecedents of the torture porn genre in the following chapter.

3

Some Antecedents

Sadism, Exploitation, and (Neo-)Slashers

Sadism 101

Torture porn did not spontaneously arise from the ashes of the World Trade Center; it locates its heredity in a multiplicity of sources. And we might be too hasty in locating the source of torture porn exclusively in the post-9/11 experience. "If anything," Steve Jones observes, "the obscenity of the 'porn' aspect of Torture Porn is the cruelty one human being is willing to inflict on another, and this is a more universal theme than the majority of War on Terror readings of Torture Porn account for."[1] Indeed, torture porn negotiates complex, sometimes even contradictory matrixes of cinematic narrative, sociopolitical, cultural, and economic forces. What I intend to do here is to survey some of the generic tropes in the torture porn genre that find their antecedents elsewhere—from the conceptual framing of sadism and its cinematic representations to the cinematic conventions of exploitation and slasher films that inform visual and narrative motifs in torture porn. Perhaps one of the most misunderstood concepts in torture porn is that of sadism.

Because everything is accounted for, nothing is abject in the Sadean universe, Julia Kristeva proclaims.[2] The libertine's code of conduct accommodates all manner of sexual excess and violence, but—and this is absolutely paramount—within a highly circumscribed space and regimented procedure. Contrary to our colloquial understanding of sadism, the libertine is not capricious. Jeremy Morris, in his assessment of torture porn, for instance, uses this more colloquial conception of sadism, associating it with sexual pleasure and the "delights in controlling others and making them suffer."[3] The libertine—the clinical sadist—does not act on erotic feelings or bestial passion; rather, the sadist is scrupulously calculated. While by no means a shrinking violet, the sadist nevertheless revels more in intellectual mastery than in sexual excess. The patently ritualized encounters between a sadist and his or her subject share more in common with games or sports than with unbridled lust.[4] Only viewing sadism through the colloquial lens, Morris fails to see that the pleasure of sadism resides in the execution of rules, not in sensual pleasures as such. And because he views sadism through this narrow lens, Morris concludes that the spectator locates pleasure in the sadistic spectacle as a matter of "sickness," "enjoyment, even that which is sadistic, is infectious."[5]

The strict code of libertinage is not only a prerequisite for (sexual) gratification, but it also ensures the sadist's security. The sadist, then, rarely exercises his or her desires in a public arena but rather does so within hermetic spaces and within a closed-circuit economy among friends. Inspect Sade's novels, and one discovers that they are populated with a close-knit network of libertines and countless episodes that unfold in secluded chateaus, private residences (frequently shuddered up), cloistered monasteries, exclusive brothels, and so on. Jane Gallop's discussion of Sade arrives at the conclusion that so many have failed to recognize, and I would like to emphasize this point: "Sade: the name screams sex and violence—but community?" Georges Bataille, Maurice Blanchot, Pierre Klossowski, Jacques Lacan, Simone de Beauvoir, Roland Barthes—many have turned to Sade but overlook the significance of a close network of associates. For instance, "Bataille's dream of Sade is too pure," Gallop insists, "because it leaves out the friends."[6] The reliance on a network resonates with torture porn; Elite Hunting, the crime syndicate in the *Hostel* films, for instance, is an exclusive club that caters to the taste of rich patrons and operates a facility—an abandoned Slovakian factory—that is fully self-contained and where torture takes place. In other words, it is a close network of friends.

Jean Baudrillard, in his response to the 9/11 terrorist attack, "The Spirit of Terrorism," observes that Western philosophy operates according to a complete misunderstanding "on the part of the Enlightenment, or the relation between Good and Evil." He continues by noting, "We believe naively that the progress of Good, its advance in all fields (the sciences, technology, democracy, human rights), corresponds to a defeat of Evil. No one seems to have understood that Good and Evil advance together, as part of the same movement. The triumph of the one does not eclipse the other—far from it."[7] Indeed, and despite Baudrillard's strong assertion otherwise, someone did understand this all too well: the Marquis de Sade. His novels can be read as cautionary tales. As the streets ran red with blood, which Sade witnessed with his own eyes, barbarity shadowed the progress of liberal human values that in the same stroke cast off the yoke of aristocracy.

Read through the lens of allegory, Sade's work is a critique of the Enlightenment and specifically the autonomy of reason—human agency unbound from the governing sovereign or theocracy. In short, Sade's literature envisions the logical end of reason unbound by ethics. This line of thinking corresponds to Theodor Adorno and Max Horkheimer's assessment of Sade and Kantian ethics in their coauthored volume *Dialectic of Enlightenment*, which features a chapter titled "Juliette, or Enlightenment and Morality." The sadist eroticizes the execution of law (or duty, in the Kantian paradigm). And subsequently, the sadist's stringent adherence to the laws of libertinage decouples him or her from any ethical obligations. Sadism, then, at its core is the practice of reason divorced from ethics. For instance, understood from this perspective, the eugenics project might be a sadistic enterprise insofar as it is the application of Darwinian science without regard to ethics, to humanitarian compassion.

The sadistic disposition might also explain the paradigmatic shift in the governing anxiety fueling torture porn. Whereas pre-9/11 horror films—the slasher genre in particular—were largely preoccupied with the abject monstrous-feminine, to use Barbara Creed's term, torture porn features abject fathers. The *Saw* franchise, for instance, "takes place not in the realm of the Spectral Mother," as Brian Collins observes, "but the Law-giving Father."[8] The figures of authority—Harry Morgan in *Dexter*, Jigsaw in the *Saw* franchise, the Elite Hunting syndicate in the *Hostel* films—dictate a corrupted form of the Law. The awe-inspiring generative powers of the female body—its transformations (pubescence, pregnancy) and emissions (menstruation, lactation), its contextualization as the male other—are the currency with which many horror films trade. Torture porn, on the other hand, elides proper Law and preaches the Gospel of Libertinage in its place. What is "wrong" in torture porn films is not women behaving badly but rather the corrupted agents of "proper" paternal order. "Any crime" is abject, Julia Kristeva posits, "because it draws attention to the fragility of the law, . . . but premeditated crime, cunning murder, hypocritical revenge are even more . . . [abject] because they heighten the display of such fragility."[9]

American foreign policy in the post-9/11 era, and the execution of the so-called War on Terror, bears the hallmarks of the sadistic disposition. John Yoo, deputy assistant attorney general during the George W. Bush administration, wrote what has come to be known as the "Torture Memos," providing legal cover for American operatives to conduct enhanced interrogation techniques.[10] Bush himself, in a dubious assertion during an October 5, 2007, news conference, stated, "This government does not torture people. We—we—we stick to US law and our international obligations." He continued by adding,

"There are highly trained professionals questioning these extremists and terrorists. In other words, we got professionals who are trained in this kind of work—to get information that will protect the American people." (Is Bush describing CIA agents? Or is he describing Jack Bauer in *24*?) The sadistic disposition is on exhibit here, in the calloused mobilization of legal reasoning to justify torture, alleviating government officials, American operatives, and even the American people of any ethical concerns because the acts perpetrated on our behalf fall within legal bounds. There is no excess in the libertine's universe precisely because everything is accounted for under strict principles. Analogously, American officials can categorically hail, "we do not torture people," because the laws account for a wide range of activities, short of causing grave bodily injury or death. Moreover, the sadistic disposition allows for a more complex assessment of torture—whether real or its fictional cinematic depiction; it is freed from the shackles of tawdry good/bad binaries. The act of torture takes place within a regime, and a torturer very well might not even "like" what he or she is doing but is acting in accordance with the Law or duty.[11] The calculated perpetrator in *WΔZ*, for instance, reaping revenge against her rapists, declares to one of her victims, "I don't enjoy any of this!" She even becomes physically ill; nonetheless, governed by scientific principles, she is compelled to act. Similarly, Jack Bauer foists responsibility on his torture subject: "Damn you for making me do this!" Satisfaction is located in the execution of the law.

The sadistic disposition materializes in the post-9/11 American genre of torture porn. The single most astute cinematic representation of sadism is Pier Paolo Pasolini's 1975 film *Salò, or the 120 Days of Sodom*, which is adapted from Sade's novel *The 120 Days of Sodom*. Pasolini's film has subsequently been (poorly) emulated by exploitation films through the 1970s and '80s and in turn has influenced the contemporary genre of torture porn.

Exploitation: Cannibalized Cinema and the Ecstatic Body

In the latter part of the 1970s, a glut of exploitation films cannibalized basic plot elements and themes from European prestige films released earlier in the decade. From Pier Paolo Pasolini's 1975 film *Salò* to Liliana Cavani's 1974 film *The Night Porter* and Lina Wertmüller's 1975 *Seven Beauties* and even dating back to 1969 with Luchino Visconti's *The Damned* and perhaps to a lesser extent Bernardo Bertolucci's 1970 film *The Conformist*—all these films in some fashion approach the subject of fascism through the lens of aberrant sexuality or sadomasochism. The exploitation films that appropriated the theme of fascism and exhibited it in its naked form (i.e., films about evil Nazis doing horrific things) are commonly referred to as Naziploitation, while other films—women-in-prison films, for instance—drew from sadomasochistic elements, without the explicit hallmarks of Nazism (e.g., Nazi regalia, swastikas, concentration camps). These films in particular—Naziploitation films and women-in-prison films—along with other exploitation films that reveled in the exhibition of gore, such as Herschell Gordon Lewis's 1963 film *Blood Feast*, inform the narrative themes and visual motifs found in torture porn.

It is no accident that the vast majority of the Naziploitation films were released between 1975 and 1977, quick on the heels of *The Night Porter* and *Salò*. Mikel J. Koven situates Naziploitation films in almost the same terms: "What emerges from a study of these films' influences and precursors is a genetic/generic code that moves downward from 'art' films like Visconti's through [Tinto] Brass's glossy but salacious re-working, into the Nazi sexploitation period proper."[12] Koven explores how Naziploitation films brazenly replicate serious films about sadism and the Holocaust. In one case, he notes how closely the plot of Cesare Canevari's 1976 film *The Gestapo's Last Orgy* follows that of Cavani's *The Night Porter*. But true to the conception of kitsch, Koven concludes that the comparisons between these "cultured" films and their less esteemed counterparts "end at . . . [the] surface level," because while a film such as Cavani's is "*about* sexual exploitation," Canevari's film *is* "sexual exploitation."[13]

Whereas the tradition of horror and melodrama is to render phallic power in authority figures, or other symbolic ways, representations of phallic punishment are made more explicit in exploitation films—subtlety is not exploitation's forte. For instance, in Don Edmonds's 1975 film *Ilsa: She-Wolf of the SS*, the title character, Ilsa, administers electrical shocks to female victims with an electrified dildo. Abused characters are also whipped, strapped, and literally beaten into submission. When the tide turns at the end of the film, and Ilsa is made to pay for her crimes—namely, exercising phallic power—the American detainee, who is endowed with an unyielding member, ties her up and leaves her for dead. A German compatriot, finding Ilsa bound to her bed, instead of saving her shoots her in the head, which explodes in a gruesome spectacle. Whereas melodrama tends to exercise phallic punishment in subtler forms (horror perhaps offers slightly more explicit forms of phallic punishment—knives, machetes), in exploitation, it materializes in fairly explicit if not quite literal forms, as in *Ilsa*—an electrified dildo, whips, the American's erect penis, the German's gun.

Viewing positions tend to be very different in exploitation films, compared to their more culturally esteemed counterparts. In *The Night Porter* and most especially in *Salò*, the viewing body is consciously aligned with subjective perspectives, and in the latter film, the audience is made painfully aware of its complicity in the spectacle of suffering. No such critical perspective is fostered in exploitation cinema. Rather, exploitation promises to deliver guilt-free spectacles of violence that treat the female form both as fetish object and as a prop on which sadistic punishments are exercised. Comparing *The Night Porter* and

The Gestapo's Last Orgy, Koven observes that in the latter film, "the spectator is positioned more or less objectively to the horrendous events on screen. The horrors are presented as if on some kind of Grand Guignol stage."[14] Mobilizing the "objective" viewing position does not invite spectators to question their own visual pleasure; *Cannibal Holocaust* (Ruggero Deodato, 1980), read from a particular perspective, for instance, even adopts the documentary mode to exhibit horror and gore unfettered by critical consideration, unlike *The Night Porter* or *Salò*.[15]

Ilsa: She-Wolf of the SS is exemplary of the Naziploitation genre. Made on a shoestring budget and shot in only nine days, the film was put into development following the box-office success of Lee Frost's *Love Camp 7* in 1969. The self-professed "Sultan of Sleaze," David F. Friedman, produced both films and secured the use of the former set of *Hogan's Heroes*, the popular comedy television series about Allied soldiers in a German POW camp. The set in fact was scheduled to be razed to make way for a condominium development, allowing the film crew free rein over its use and destruction.

The success of *Ilsa: She-Wolf of the SS*, and its subsequent cult status, led to a number of other films that used the Nazi concentration camp as a plot device for salacious and sadistic spectacles. Despite the fact that the title character is killed in the first film—such a trivial detail hardly matters in the exploitation genre—in quick succession, three sequels to the first *Ilsa* film were released: Don Edmonds's 1976 film *Ilsa: Harem Keeper of the Oil Sheiks* and, one year later, *Ilsa: The Tigress of Siberia*, directed by Jean LaFleur, and finally the 1977 unauthorized film *Ilsa: The Wicked Warden*, directed by Spanish director Jesus Franco.[16]

The title character, Ilsa, is a composite drawing on historical figures such as the notorious doctor Josef Mengele, the Angel of Death, and others who conducted medical experiments on concentration-camp internees. (This much the filmmakers openly admit.) Her namesake, though, is assuredly premised on Ilse Koch, popularly known by various titles including "the Bitch of Buchenwald," "the Witch of Buchenwald," and "the Beast of Buchenwald." As the wife of SS *Standartenführer* (Colonel) Karl Otto Koch, the commandant of Buchenwald, she exercised her privileged position with the utmost brutality. Ilse Koch was put on trial three times: first, by the Nazi regime for corruption (Karl Koch was convicted and executed, while Ilse Koch was acquitted); second, by the war crimes tribunal, which found her guilty and sentenced her to prison; and, finally, by the postwar German government, ensuring that she would spend the rest of her life in prison.[17] (She eventually committed suicide in her prison cell, but not before bearing a child while incarcerated—the paternity of the child is unclear, but a prison guard probably fathered it.) Among her acts of naked cruelty, for which she was tried as a war criminal, "she allegedly had more than forty inmates killed for their tattooed skins.

The report commissioned by the US Army immediately after the liberation of Buchenwald also documented the reign of terror of the 'homosexual' commandant Karl Koch and his 'nymphomaniac' wife Ilse."[18] With the case of Ilse and Karl Koch—proving that life can be stranger than fiction—one might see how historical events and figures can be used as narrative fodder.

The iconography of Ilsa's character in Edmonds's cult film points back to the historical record. In her regalia, Ilsa is typically seen wearing a white shirt—unbuttoned to emphasize her buxom cleavage, of course—black riding boots, riding pants, and riding crop in hand. Such attire is not entirely unusual to exploitation films, nor is it completely alien to the world of sadomasochistic fetishism (closely associated with the exploitation genre). Reportedly, Koch's abuses took place in an indoor horse-riding ring, which was built on the grounds of Buchenwald by concentration-camp inmates at Ilse Koch's behest. In addition to the fetishistic accouterment of horse riding (i.e., riding boots, pants, and crop), it was popularly reported that Koch was inclined to wear revealing clothing, further evidence of her sexual deviance. The salacious court proceedings, along with testimonial accounts of Ilse Koch's brutal character, prone to exact punishment with her riding crop, and her predilection for provocative clothing, were the catalyst for the fictional character of Ilsa. These details about Koch and her cruel sensibility were widely reported in the press. Throughout Edmonds's film, Ilsa is shown in a white blouse with cleavage exposed, and she has an insatiable sexual appetite. She also conducts gruesome medical experiments and collects body parts (e.g., penises) for her colleague in Berlin, characteristics clearly derived from the historical figures Ilsa Koch and Mengele. While Koch serves as a model for many of the sadistic female characters in exploitation cinema, the historical figure of Mengele also informs exploitation character traits. Filtered, then, through the genre's historical and cinematic heritage, these character types can also be found in torture porn films.

As much as characters and themes are drawn from history, *Ilsa: She-Wolf of the SS* is more accurately a picture of male anxiety in the 1970s in the wake of the women's liberation movement than it is a depiction of the historical horrors of the concentration camp. Whereas fear of terrorism and the conflicted attitudes regarding the execution of the so-called War on Terror play a significant role in torture porn, gender wars fuel the narratives of many exploitation features from the 1970s. Ilsa is what patriarchal culture fears the most: a woman "on top," authoritative, an independent woman with sexual agency. It is fitting that the film opens with Ilsa having sex with one of the male internees, on top, astride him. Gendered tropes such as pink ballet slippers and beauty products lining an ornate vanity quickly give way to a decidedly masculine and merciless character. As the commandant of Medical Camp 9, Ilsa is the lord of her domain and exercises her privilege over it by conducting cruel medical experiments and using internees to satisfy her sexual desires.

In the first scene, there is nothing that contextualizes the sex act with conventional representations of feminine sexuality. Rather, we find the couple in the midst of the coital act with Ilsa on top—in control and enthralled with pleasure. Immediately, it is clear that the order of things is not in line with the traditional patriarchal paradigm. Pleasure in this opening scene quickly gives way to disappointment when Ilsa's male partner climaxes, despite her pleas to hold on, leaving the insatiable Ilsa unfulfilled. Sullenly, she slumps down and rests on her spent sexual partner, saying under her breath, "You should have waited." Unsatisfied by her male partner, Ilsa retreats to the shower, where she pleasures herself. Returning to the bedside, she orders two female associates to take the hapless man away; soon we find him in Ilsa's lab, nude and strapped to an examination table. Like the female praying mantis—which devours its mate after copulating—Ilsa and her two female accomplices castrate the internee and presumably allow him to bleed to death. The scene ends with blood pouring down a trough that captures and dispenses with bodily fluids coming from the examination table.

The misogyny of patriarchal culture is projected in reverse, with highly embellished scenes of women perpetrating violence against and sexually exploiting men (and other women), rendering them as objects of satisfaction and, when through, casting them away like rubbish. Ilsa is less a vision of a real Nazi (or the real Ilse Koch) than she is a signifier of the monstrous and what in the 1970s was perceived by patriarchal culture to be the quintessence of evil: a woman with agency. Ilsa is the literal embodiment of the "femi-Nazi." The Holocaust, in this case, is merely a narrative device—or an excuse—on which contemporary social anxieties are projected; the grotesque horror of the spectacle that we see onscreen amounts to an articulation of male hysteria.

As with many of the Naziploitation films, in women-in-prison films, characters are introduced into the prison and confront a sadistic warden or prison guard. Much of the iconography here is drawn from the civil rights movement and the searing imagery from the Watts Riots (1965)—racist police violently rounding up people of color, and firefighters turning hoses on protestors. Exploitation sensation Pam Grier plays Alabama, the sadistic master in Gerardo de Leon's 1971 film *Women in Cages*, and those characters that run afoul of her authority are sent to the "playpen." Hardened by racism, Alabama is incapable of feeling pity—we learn that a white man raped her, and she resorts to hustling the streets of Harlem by the age of twelve. There are clear affinities between Alabama and Ilsa: they occupy positions of authority, wear revealing uniforms to emphasize their buxom figures, have voracious sexual appetites, and are prone to violence—torturing their captive parties and using them to satisfy their own sexual desires. Women subject to punishment are stripped bare, or nearly bare, bound to one torture device or another, and made to endure excruciating pain. Like Naziploitation, it is quite typical for women-in-prison films to exhibit the female body in excess—electrocuted, whipped, beaten, maimed, burned, raped; the body is made to convulse, writhe in agony, scream, bleed, and tearfully beg for mercy.[19]

Sex slavery is also a common element in Naziploitation and women-in-prison films. In *Women in Cages*, for instance, a narrative parallel is established between the prison that Alabama oversees and a ship, the *Zulu Queen*, anchored off the coast (a scary prophetic vision of CIA black sites, some likely based on ships and thus "nowhere"—a heterotopic site). The film is set in an undisclosed foreign country, but it is quite clearly the Philippines. Whereas the land-based prison is governed by the general principles of legitimate law and order (though the execution of law and order is less than scrupulous), a crime syndicate governs the *Zulu Queen*. Aboard the *Zulu Queen*, vice pervades—a subjective shot carries us across the threshold from the sanctioned world of law and order into Sodom and Gomorrah. An Orientalist fantasy greets the spectator: a male character wearing a turban welcomes us, opening the door and inviting us into the bar of the *Zulu Queen*. Inside, debauchery awaits—hostesses flirt with male customers, prostitutes seductively wait to be propositioned, a stripper entertains patrons (and fellow sex workers). Cubicles on a lower deck of the ship offer a modicum of privacy where sexual services are rendered. A theater screens pornographic films entertaining male customers and their female companions. Some of the women, perhaps all of them, are bound to the ship—the syndicate keeps the "working women," who are addicted to heroin, in line by supplying them with their fix. There are affinities with the *Hostel* films in the Orientalist fantasy as well. The correlation between the torture trade and the sex trade is made fairly explicit in both the *Hostel* films but is particularly evident in the first installment. (Jason Middleton, in his article "The Subject of Torture: Regarding the Pain of Americans in *Hostel*," addresses this subject at some length.)[20] The primary male characters in Roth's film are lured away from the pedestrian state-sanctioned sex trade in Amsterdam to the wild frontier of eastern Europe.

Whether we are discussing Naziploitation or exploitation films generally, these films are designed to elicit sensations from the viewing body by combining elements of horror and pornography and thus mixing sexual stimuli (pleasurable feelings, sexual arousal) with violence and gore (feelings of displeasure, repulsion, or disgust). In the Naziploitation and women-in-prison genres, women are most often the targets of abuse. More often than not, female victims are in a state of undress; they are paraded about and made into a spectacle. The gender-targeted violence found in exploitation films is not necessarily perpetuated in torture porn films; rather, male suffering can be quite protracted and excruciating. In addition, and more to the point, torture porn carries on the tradition of eliciting a visceral response from its spectators in its unabashed exhibition of tormented bodies—both male and female.

Gender is still very much an issue in torture porn films—how can one, for instance, view the castrating of Stuart by Beth in Eli Roth's 2007 film *Hostel: Part II* in any other way but through a gendered lens? It is true, nevertheless, that sexuality is not or is certainly less of an issue than it has been in earlier iterations of the horror genre.[21] Interestingly, male characters in torture porn are more than twice as likely to meet some grisly fate as their female counterparts are. "In the 42 films referred to as torture porn by three or more major international English language publications," Steve Jones observes, "228 men and 108 women are killed and 275 men and 136 women injured."[22] It would be a mistake, nonetheless, to cite these statistics and conclude that torture porn is somehow more progressive than its progenitors. And just as Carol Clover argued with respect to earlier rape-revenge narratives, it is not simply that "women are [just] as capable as men of acts of humiliating violence" and thus that "men are off the guilt hook that modern feminism has put them on."[23] Bound bodies subjected to sadistic abuse are undeniably charged with sexual politics. There is, though, something qualitatively different. The governing anxiety driving torture porn narratives is situated elsewhere; at the same time, we cannot ignore the fact that (torture) porn concerns the body, and gender politics is never that far removed.

As previously theorized, the spectator is invited to viscerally share in the experience of ecstatic screen bodies. Melodrama might elicit tears, pornography intends to arouse, and horror might startle us, making us jump from our seats, gasp, cringe, or avert our eyes at the sight of gore. With torture porn, bodies are torn asunder, wrenched, and contorted. Spectators obviously are not subjected to grievous bodily injury, but they are nevertheless compelled to mimic onscreen violence—flinching, tensing up, wrenching the body away from the depiction of pain. There is in that sense a degree of violence inflicted on the viewer. We are, if you will, manipulated, and we have established colloquialisms that express the implicit violence inflicted on us, the viewing body: we refer to the weepie as a "tear jerker"; in cruder terms, we might say that a horror film "scared the shit out of me," and as Linda Williams adds, with pornography, "some people might be inclined to 'jerk off.'"[24]

In the opening moments of *Ilsa: She-Wolf of the SS*, the audience is treated to doses of highly embellished eroticism and violence—Ilsa's pursuit of erotic pleasures and the subsequent castration of her male partner. As for the latter experience, the male internee is lost in uncontrollable convulsions as he pleads with Ilsa not to dismember him, finally giving way to screams of pain, writhing, and blood. The female body here is out of control too, not only in Ilsa's penchant for violence but also in her insatiable sex drive. In addition, by castrating the male character, she effectively makes him a woman—an idea furthered by the body being strapped to an examination table and thrashing wildly, an image more commonly associated with female characters. The spectacle of violence and eroticism elicits from the viewing body, then, a conflicting array of sensations oscillating between pleasure and repulsion. Arriving at a similar conclusion, Rikke Schubart argues that the "function of the *Ilsa* series is the display of a perversion—male masochism—that is taboo and therefore fascinating."[25] Indeed, there is a conflicting set of feelings/sensations that occurs when watching *Ilsa* (or other exploitation films): a mix of fascination, revulsion, and perhaps even erotic arousal, leaving the viewing body to wrangle with a range of conflicting sensations and negotiate the (visual) pleasure derived from the representation of suffering. The exhibition of and the violence directed toward the male and female bodies in torture porn finds its heredity here. Clearly, torture porn owes a debt to exploitation cinema, but it also evolved from earlier conventions in the horror genre—specifically, the slasher.

The Evolution of Slashers

Many of the tropes that we find in torture porn are drawn from the waning moments of the slasher genre. It is possible also to identify instances of cross-pollination in the slasher's anemic resurrection in the form of the neo-slasher—Rob Zombie's 2007 remake of *Halloween* or Marcus Nispel's 2009 remake of *Friday the 13th*—which is contemporaneous with the torture porn cycle. The exact date of the slasher genre's demise is contested. Adam Rockoff, for instance, situates the slasher genre between 1978 and 1986 in his study of the genre, *Going to Pieces: The Rise and Fall of the Slasher Film, 1978–1986*, but this historical framing then places Wes Craven's 1996 *Scream* outside the slasher cycle (something Rockoff is certainly aware of). And there is no doubt that *Scream* is different from the canonical films in the slasher genre. I have no intention of arguing about the historical placement of the slasher genre; suffice it to say that *Scream* bears the hallmarks of the genre. Indeed, I consider *Scream* an important transitional film, leaving bare the characteristics of the slasher in its metacinematic irony and evolving toward something new. In these mutations of the genre, the film exhibits some of the nascent characteristics of torture porn.

Like torture porn, *Scream* is certainly a product of its time. Set in the midst of the Clinton administration and its relative prosperity and stability, *Scream* has the luxury, if I might call it that, of focusing on interpersonal relations. While torture porn, by comparison, is shackled to the post-9/11 Bush era and the anxiety spawned by terrorism and war, *Scream* instead focuses inward. Kevin Williamson, who wrote the screenplay for *Scream*, explicitly strove to appeal to the "concerns particularly relevant to teenage girls."[26] He explains in a *USA Today* article, "I try to write very smart women," and he wrestles "with issues of betrayal and trust." In the same article, Craven too suggests that *Scream* "has the emotional appeal of a soap opera, which he thinks plays better to women than men. There are secret loves, haunting pasts, snobs, nerds and badly behaved boyfriends, twists that normally drive soaps."[27] Couched in gender stereotypes to be sure, the film focuses—as the filmmakers contend—on matters of trust among its female characters. (This is even more evident in the sequel, Wes Craven's 1997 film *Scream 2*, which is more romantic comedy than horror film.) In the first film, the central character, Sidney Prescott, a high school student, pieces her life back together following the rape and murder of her mother a year prior. And just as life appears to be returning to normal, a rash of murders suddenly engulfs the community of Woodsboro, California, and Sidney and her friends find themselves in grave danger.

There are three critical elements in *Scream* that set it apart from the slasher genre and set the stage for torture porn: (1) the evolution of the final girl, (2) the characteristics of the monster (or monsters—as it so happens in *Scream*), and (3) the game motif. Craven and his screenwriter are extremely self-aware, and the film even includes the now famous "rules sequence" that explicitly details the tropes of the slasher genre. Not only are the filmmakers (Craven and Williamson) aware of the genre tropes, but so too are the characters within the diegetic narrative. This self-awareness invites the filmmakers, the characters, and even the audience all to revel in the comfort of genre conventions, while at the same time authorizing—because once you know the rules, you can break them—the deconstruction or violation of those rules to spawn surprise and innovation.

Sidney conforms to the conventions of the final girl: she is fairly modest in her behavior, speech, and dress; she is intelligent, self-reliant, and resourceful; she is quite capable in physical confrontations; she borders on being a tomboy (her name, sometimes shortened to Sid, clothing, and hair are not particularly "feminine" in the conventional sense, and this is particularly true compared to her peer group); and where figures of authority fail, Sidney succeeds in protecting herself, finally vanquishing the killers. It is clear that Sidney conforms to the characteristics that we commonly assign to the final girl, but her character also diverges from some of these tropes. To begin with, she is not puritanical like some of her predecessors. We learn that Sidney and her boyfriend, Billy, have been dating for two years, and the relationship, as Billy nostalgically recalls, "started off hot and heavy. Nice solid R-rating on our way to an NC-17." Sneaking into Sidney's room, Billy vows not to break Sidney's "underwear rule" but hopes they might have a little "bump and grind"—"a little on-top-of-the-clothes stuff." Sidney cheerfully obliges but stops Billy when he gets a bit too randy. Though she routinely rebuffs the sexual advances of her boyfriend, a common final-girl trope, it is Sidney that eventually initiates sex with the long-denied Billy.

Sidney is not as wholesome as the conventional final girl and not simply because she engages in, as she refers to it in the film, "PG-13" sexual activity but also because she is traumatized. Sidney's mother, Maureen Prescott, was raped and murdered a year prior; her body was discovered a short distance from the Woodsboro town square. On the basis of Sidney's testimony, Cotton Weary was convicted of the crime and is appealing his death sentence. Cotton and Maureen, in fact, had an illicit sexual affair, and word on the street is that, as two gossiping girls rant in bathroom banter, Sidney's "mother was a tramp." Sidney is forced to come to terms with her mother's promiscuity, leading her to question her own mores—as she confesses to Billy, "I'm scared that I'm gonna turn out just like her, you know? Like the 'Bad Seed' or something. And I know it doesn't make sense." The dialogue between the pair has more resonance than Sidney realizes, because Billy reassures her that he does in fact understand—and he understands all too well, given that he is the killer, in other words, a bad seed. The intimacy between the final girl and the monster points toward one of the critical traits of the torture porn genre: the effacement of a clear distinction between good and bad characters and the trope of the pro(an)tagonist (e.g., Jigsaw, Dexter, Jack Bauer).

And this point brings us to one of the most important evolutionary elements of the final girl as embodied in Sidney: she exhibits certain affinities with the monster and even effectively assumes the role of the monster. True, the kinship between the monster and the final girl has been an important feature of the slasher genre—notably, in Rick Rosenthal's 1981 *Halloween II*, we learn that Laurie Strode and the boogieman, Michael Myers, are brother and sister. John Carpenter also admits, "The one girl who is the most sexually uptight just keeps stabbing this guy with a long knife. She's the most sexually frustrated. She's the one that killed him. Not because she's a virgin, but because all that repressed energy starts coming out. She uses all those phallic symbols on the guy." Carpenter adds, "She and the killer have a certain link: sexual repression."[28] The final girl in *Friday the 13th Part Two* sees Jason's enshrined head of Mrs. Voorhees and, because she is a psychology major, understands what she must do to survive and intones, "I am your mother, Jason. Put down the knife."[29] Mrs. Voorhees, of course, was the monster in the first film, and the final girl emasculates Jason by donning the guise of the monstrous-feminine. What makes *Scream* different is the degree to which Sidney embraces her position as monster, stalking the killers, appropriating their tools of terror—phone, voice modulator, mask, outfit, and weapon. This trope of brother and sister, and the relationship between the monster and the final girl, comes full circle in Wes Craven's 2000 film *Scream 3*, in which Sidney's brother, Roman Bridger, born by Sidney's mother out of wedlock, turns out to be the killer. Furthermore, like Freddy, Michael, and Jason, Sidney too bears the weight of (sexual) trauma. Freddy was accused of being a pedophile, and the neighborhood takes justice into its own hands and burns him alive; Michael witnesses the "original sin" when his elder adolescent sister has sex with her boyfriend, in a household left unsupervised by negligent parents—Michael viciously stabs his sister to death as a result; and Jason drowns because the camp counselors were having sex, rather than supervising the youngsters at Camp Crystal Lake.

Like the monsters from these canonical slasher films, Sidney too bears the traumatic weight that couples sex and violent death. It is effectively impossible to decouple sex from violence as embodied in the monsters (Freddy and pedophilia; Michael and "original sin"; and Jason and premarital/teen sex), and this too is evident in Sidney's character. Unlike the final girl, who is virginal in character (if not in actual fact), Sidney is sexually frigid because of the trauma of sexual violence. And while there are debates about whether monsters in the slasher genre are born that way or shaped by some other means, Sidney, in this case, is made into a monster. Many of the perpetrators in the torture porn genre are made—the nerdy group in *The Final*, Dexter, and Jigsaw in the *Saw* franchise.

And this point brings us to the second critical element in *Scream* that signifies a significant shift in the genre—the characteristics of the monster. In *Scream*, the monster is actually plural—Billy, Sidney's boyfriend, and Stu alternately don the ghost mask and wreak havoc on their peers. Once again, like *Halloween II*, the intimacy between the final girl and the monster is made explicit in the intimate relation between Billy and Sidney. Unlike monsters from the conventional slasher tradition, Billy and Stu come from the very peer group that is stalked. The two young men are, if not attractive, then perfectly normal by all outward appearances, unlike the monstrosity that is the standard slasher antagonist—Michael is exceptionally tall and wears a mask, Freddy bears the scars of being burned alive, Jason is ghostly and in later films dons a hockey mask. The monster in a slasher exhibits a degree of supernatural abilities; in Carpenter's original installment of *Halloween*, Michael disappears in the closing moments of the film despite being shot a handful of times at close range; Freddy appears in nightmares; and Jason haunts the landscape—like a specter, seemingly appearing and disappearing without so much as a trace. Billy and Stu, on the other hand, are bound to the earthly laws of physics; any miraculous characteristics attributed to the presumed singular monster are explained in the multiplicity of monsters. With *Scream*, the monsters are flesh-and-blood mortals and are not social outsiders but intimately related to the peer group subjected to violence. Torture porn assimilates this move toward mundane monsters.

Brian Collins notes that the ghost mask and the modulated voice allow for other flesh-and-blood mortals to step into the role as killer in the *Scream* series. And this idea might correspond, as Collins argues, to the *Saw* franchise, in which "the idea of Jigsaw" constitutes a role, rather than a specific individual. Collins points out as well that the advertisement for *Saw V* features an anonymous male figure wearing "what appears to be the death mask of John Kramer strapped to his face."[30] This idea—that the character of the killer is an empty variable, filled by anyone—comes full circle in Kevin Williamson's television series *The Following*, which airs on the Fox Network. The serial killer, Joe Carroll, like Jigsaw, enjoys the company of faithful acolytes that execute Carroll's murderous schemes. Carroll presumably dies in the finale of the first season, but followers (or copycats) continue to carry out his mission in the second season, wearing Carroll masks, and to terrorize the public. (*The Following* is discussed at some length in chapter 7.)

In the opening moments of *Scream*, littered with references to canonical slasher films, Casey (played by the well-known star Drew Barrymore) is home alone when the phone rings. Dismissing the call as a wrong number, Casey thinks little of it and hangs up. This happens a couple of times before the unidentified male caller strikes up a conversation with her. The slightly malevolent sounding crank caller begins to quiz Casey about scary movies when the conversation turns frightening: "You never told me your name." Casey asks, "Why do you want to know my name?" "'Cause I wanna know who I'm looking at," the caller insists. Presuming (correctly) that she is being surveilled, Casey is visibly alarmed. Following additional tense exchanges, Casey again answers the phone, "Listen, asshole!" before the crank caller angrily demands, "No, you listen, you little bitch! You hang up on me again I'll cut you like a fish, understand?" In a timid voice, Casey asks, "Is this some kind of joke?" The caller responds, "More of a game, really. Can you handle that, blondie?"

Casey runs to lock all the entrances into the house, but her efforts are quite futile. Eventually, Casey is coaxed to turn on the back patio lights to discover her football-star boyfriend, Steve, gagged and bound to a patio chair. (This same motif appears in Craven's 2011 film *Scream 4*.) Casey pleads for the caller not to hurt him. "That all depends on you," the caller returns. "Why are you doing this?" Casey asks tearfully. Notably, this latter question is also something that is repeated in torture porn films ad nauseam. "I wanna play a game," the caller reminds Casey—a game based on movie trivia. If Casey answers the questions correctly, Steve will be allowed to live. The game motif that is woven through *Scream*, and through the whole series, finds its way into the fabric of torture porn—particularly the *Saw* franchise.

The neo-slashers assimilate many of the evolutionary traits identified in *Scream*—specifically the close affinities between the monster and the final girl and "humanizing" the monster. Furthermore, these films are made well within the torture porn cycle and are either (1) drawing from the tropes of torture porn, (2) responding to contemporaneous cultural anxieties in which human beings are more terrifying than any fantasy-world boogieman, or (3) some combination of these two.[31] For instance, Marcus Nispel's 2009 remake of *Friday the 13th* dispenses with Mrs. Voorhees in the prologue of the film, opening with her beheading, and transforms Jason into a flesh-and-blood human being—albeit quite a disturbed character. His capacity to miraculously appear in one place and then vanish is given a fairly simple narrative explanation: in the years since the death of his mother, Jason has constructed a network of tunnels underneath Camp Crystal Lake, allowing him to haunt the facility undetected. In Nispel's film, one of the female characters, Whitney, is kidnapped and held captive for weeks on end, finding certain resonances with torture porn conventions. "The original Jason," Kevin Wetmore reminds us, would have simply "killed her," but he presumably holds her captive because she looks like his mother.[32]

Rob Zombie's 2007 *Halloween* similarly attributes to Michael human characteristics. A significant amount of screen time is dedicated to Michael during his childhood, raised in a dysfunctional home: the paternal figure (Michael's stepfather) is abusive, drinks, and is out of work, while Michael's mother does her best to support the family, working as a stripper in a seedy nightclub. Set in this impoverished environment, the parental unit is incapable of providing proper supervision, too busy working to make ends meet, or willfully neglects their responsibilities, and subsequently they sow the seeds of wickedness. Michael's parents do not recognize the signs of trouble—the elder teenage daughter openly flaunting her sexuality (egged on by her stepfather no less) and Michael's violent behavior (e.g., killing his pet rat, getting into trouble at school). Brought to a boiling point on Halloween, Michael duct tapes his inebriated stepfather to a chair (a typical torture porn trope) and slits his throat, watching him slowly bleed out, and dispatches his elder sister and her boyfriend. Michael punishes his elder sister for not taking him trick-or-treating and electing to have sex with her boyfriend instead.[33] When Michael's mother returns home later that night, after finishing her shift at the nightclub, she finds Michael on the front porch with his baby sister (Laurie Strode) in his arms.

Committed to an institution, Michael slowly retreats into himself. And it is there that he develops a relationship with Dr. Samuel Loomis. Michael's withdrawal into himself is manifested in an increasing obsession with masks, until he is nothing but a mask. Eventually, Michael refuses to speak and retreats behind the mask altogether. Similar to the more mundane Jason in Nispel's feature, Zombie's monster, Michael, is given a substantive biography, making him less a supernatural boogieman and lending him characteristics that make him more human.

Zombie's *Halloween* takes the evolution of the final girl even further. In the climactic moments of the film, Michael abducts Laurie and returns to the long-abandoned Myers house. As in Carpenter's original film, Dr. Loomis arrives and attempts to save Laurie, but in Zombie's film, he is more inept. In keeping with the conventional final girl, it is ultimately up to Laurie to vanquish the monster when the figures of authority repeatedly fail to. The incapacitated Loomis yields his gun to Laurie, and she acquires the phallic instrument intended to restore order to the narrative.

The Myers house is the site of trauma, the site where monsters are born. The (haunted) house is a common trope in the horror genre, and Zombie mobilizes it to elicit the uncanny, a place both familiar and strange. Michael returns Laurie to the poisoned womb, the site of sexual trauma and death.[34] And more than this, Laurie is not just inside the home but literally crawls into the bowels of the house, hiding in a wall, before finding her way into the attic space. In an effort to locate Laurie, Michael repeatedly thrusts a two-by-four into the bowels of the house. The repeated thrusting begins to resemble the sexual act, and this act has incestuous connotations in terms of both his sister's presence and the corresponding relation to the house and his mother's body—Michael is a mother fucker.

The association between the house and the womb is made all the more explicit in the reference to Tobe Hooper's 1982 film *Poltergeist*. Dianne Freeling enters the netherworld through a vaginal-like portal to retrieve her child, Carol Anne. A tether straddles this world and the beyond, allowing Dianne to navigate between dimensions, and when she emerges from the nether regions, a portal in the ceiling opens, from which Dianne falls, clutching her child. The umbilical cord/tether is undone, severing the line between inside and outside, between the nether region and earthly bounds. Steven Freeling takes his wife and child in his arms to the awaiting bathtub, smearing away the bloody mucus covering Dianne and Carol Anne, all the while pleading, "breathe, damn it, breathe." Suddenly, Dianne takes a gasp of air as Steven lovingly caresses his wife, saying, "Baby."

The ceiling portal in the Freeling house corresponds quite closely with Laurie's fall through the ceiling in Zombie's *Halloween*, absent the paranormal element, though. The birth-like passing from the nether regions into this world witnesses Dianne and Carol Anne caked in bloody mucus; Laurie, too, is covered with debris—dust, cobwebs, splinters of wood, plaster—and blood. Just as in *Poltergeist*, Laurie is "born again," and when she is ejected from the bowels of the house, she stumbles—like a gangly newborn foal—to her feet, gun in hand. When Michael finds her, she still has not quite found her balance but manages to raise the gun to fire, but Michael drops his phallic two-by-four and lunges for her before she gets off a shot. The pair fall from a second-story window. When Laurie comes to, she is on top of her brother, astride him.[35] She

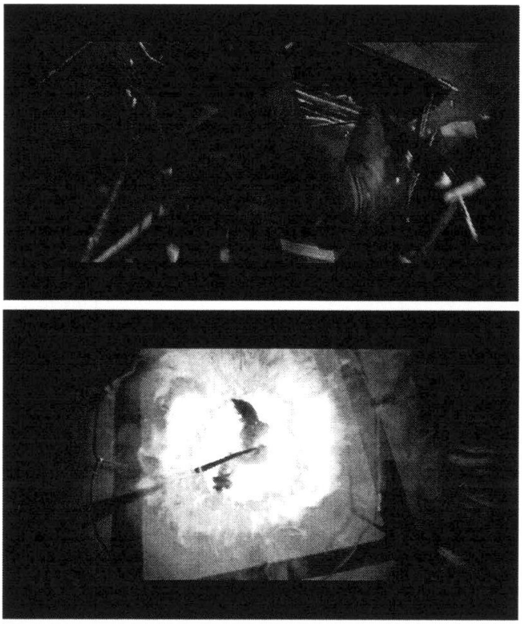

3.1 The ceiling portal in *Poltergeist* (Tobe Hooper, 1982) finds affinities with Rob Zombie's *Halloween* (2007).

reaches for the gun and points it point-blank at Michael's head and pulls the trigger. Nothing happens, just the click of the hammer slapping down on an empty barrel of the revolver. This happens three times, before Michael grabs his sister's forearms, when she pulls the trigger again, finally getting off a shot. It is unclear what Michael's intentions are: does he attempt to stop his sister, or is he steadying her hand?

Whatever the case might be, the return to the house/womb has given birth to a new monster—in which the conflation of the final girl and the monster is made flesh. Laurie is made a monster in her traumatic rebirth. Although she does not appropriate Michael's tools as such, she nevertheless wields a weapon and uses it with deadly force. Echoing the conclusion of Carpenter's film, the fall from the second-story window further places Laurie in the monster's company. And though she sustains severe injuries—she is covered in blood and struggles to muster the strength—she exhibits some of the near superhuman strength that the monster does. Zombie's Laurie might not be as zealous as Sidney, but she proves to have the mettle and does what it takes to vanquish the monster, her blood kin.[36]

Alexandre Aja's 2003 film *High Tension* (*Haute Tension*) reimagines slasher tropes as well. The film is, like *Scream*, highly self-aware, but without the meta-cinematic elements that we find in Craven's film. For instance, when Marie, the final girl, hides in a bedroom closet from the grotesque portly "monster," she hides in a closet with white slatted doors; this is almost identical to the closet in which Laurie Strode hides from Michael. In the climactic chase, in which the "monster" pursues Alex, another female character, through the forest, "he" does so with a gasoline-powered circular saw, resonating with Tobe Hooper's 1974 film *The Texas Chain Saw Massacre*. Most significantly, though, like Zombie's film, the final girl and the monster are intimately bound together—in fact, in *High Tension*, the final girl and the monster are one and the same (hence my use of scare quotes around the masculine pronoun and the term "monster").

Similarly, in the opening moments of *Scream*, many of the identifiable torture porn tropes are laid bare: a character gagged and bound to a chair, the game motif, and finally the oft-repeated question "Why are you doing this?" *Saw* appears to draw directly from the game motif most specifically, as characters bargain for their lives by playing games. Jigsaw, the pro(an)tagonist of the *Saw* series, also initiates his victims with "I want to play a game . . ." In addition, the mediated delivery of the game and the associated rules are quite similar too. In both cases, the perpetrators disguise their voices using a voice modulator, lending something of a mechanical and dissonant character to the voice. The voice is further mediated through technology. In the *Saw* series, Jigsaw delivers the rules to each game through a video or audio cassette. With *Scream*, on the other hand, the killers use the telephone to bait their victims. Where these films part company is that in *Scream*, the games are "unwinnable"; regardless of whether a victim answers a question correctly, he or she still dies. In the *Saw* series, victims, no matter how slim their odds, still have a chance to escape with their lives. We might find additional affinities between the final girl and Jigsaw. Like the final girls that populate slasher films, Jigsaw is modest in disposition and incredibly resourceful—think specifically of Nancy in *A Nightmare on Elm Street*, who prepares traps for Freddy.

Whereas slasher films are preoccupied with sexual mores and engage with inward introspection, in the wake of the 9/11 terrorist event, what spawns dread is people: a hijacker armed only with a box cutter, a suicide bomber, or even a CIA agent in the extraordinary rendition program. This is not to suggest that sexuality is absent from torture porn, but the governing angst driving these films is quite distinct from slashers. Nevertheless, the seeds of this motif—characterizing the monster as human, rather than a supernatural boogieman—were sown in the *Scream* series. This evolution in the slasher genre—drawing close affinities between the monster and the final girl—also prepared the ground for pro(an)tagonists such as Dexter, Jigsaw, and even such characters as Jack Bauer.

The conflation of sex and violence and the emphasis on gore in torture porn films clearly find their heredity in exploitation cinema. The medicalization of torture porn gore owes a debt to the character motifs found in exploitation cinema, namely, the Mengele motif. It is also drawn more generally from the traditions of Naziploitation films that frequently incorporated medical experimentation into their narrative—offering a narrative alibi for the exhibition of naked and tortured bodies. The sadistic disposition of characters in torture porn also draws from these tropes found in exploitation or films such as *Salò*. Additionally, the motif of confinement is associated with the sadistic disposition. Sadism in its clinical form demands strict adherence to a code of conduct and that violence be sequestered in hermetic spaces. While these characteristics are not wholly consistent with the exploitation genre (many of the characters are colloquial sadists), the basic elements of confinement and the sequestering of violence is—the torture chamber within the prison, the medical lab in the concentration camp. The path leading to torture porn is long and meandering, but as we can clearly see, its antecedents are found in the traditions of representing sadism, as well as in the cinematic legacy of exploitation and slashers.

4

The *Saw* Franchise

Videogames and the Sadistic Pro(an)tagonist Jigsaw

It Came from Out Back . . .

James Wan's 2004 film *Saw* is one of the progenitors of the torture porn genre, and at present, the franchise now includes seven films. Torture porn is a distinctly American genre, and the *Saw* franchise is certainly emblematic of it. There is only one small problem with this, though: Wan and his close collaborator, screenwriter Leigh Whannell, are Australians. Wan was actually born in Malaysia, of Chinese ancestry, but was raised in Perth on the western coast of Australia and went to school at the Royal Melbourne Institute of Technology. Wan and Whannell met in film school in Melbourne and collaborated on the nine-minute short *Saw* (2003); Whannell plays the central character, David. Whannell also stars as Adam Faulkner-Stanheight, the photographer, in the original 2004 feature film. Wan and Whannell produced the subsequent sequels to the original feature.

Victims in the *Saw* series are compelled to play "games" in a bid to save their own skin. John Kramer, whom the police dub "Jigsaw" because his victims have a jigsaw shape excised from their skin as a trophy, ostensibly is the antagonist of the series, and yet through the course of the series, we come to identify with him. He is more appropriately the pro(an)tagonist of the series. He is dead for half of the series, but he appears in all of the films, returning in later films in flashbacks. He is terminally ill with a brain tumor and is profoundly cognizant of the preciousness of life. In addition to being terminally ill, when his pregnant wife is assaulted—resulting in a late-term miscarriage—he determines to exact justice after the conventional legal system fails. The animatronic puppet that delivers the rules of Jigsaw's elaborate games is an avatar of his deceased son.

Jigsaw was a successful engineer in his prior life, and as a consequence, his traps are elaborately designed. Despite his demise, he sets in motion intricate plans that are to be executed even after his death, and in the later years of his life, he acquires disciples—survivors of Jigsaw's traps who find a new appreciation for life and carry on his work. Jigsaw never kills his victims but rather places them in situations where they are compelled to make choices. If a "player" makes "good" choices, the victim lives—although usually not without profound consequences (e.g., killing or maiming another "player" or enduring some grievous bodily injury him- or herself). Jigsaw is a sadist par excellence. The spectator effectively roots for Jigsaw, who, for instance, in Kevin Greutert's 2009 film *Saw VI*, subjects a health insurance executive to his "deserved" punishment for being scandalously callous, more concerned with the bottom line than his clients' care.[1] Much in the same way that we root for Dexter (the title character for the Showtime program) or Jack Bauer in *24*, we are more inclined to sympathize with Jigsaw than with the pitiful individuals in one of his traps.[2]

The box-office success of the first *Saw* film—an amazing feat for first-time filmmakers—speaks to the resonance of the film. Although coming from Australia, the first *Saw* film, and the subsequent franchise, tapped a nerve in the American market (and abroad). Whannell speculates that *Saw* (and other films like it) satisfied a desire for a more visceral type of horror film. And, if only obliquely, the films approached the political environment in 2004—"The Iraq War had just started. There was a lot of doom and gloom," Whannell reminds us. "People were being accused of torturing . . . prisoners of war," and he adds, "maybe the public—not just in North America but around the world—was . . . reacting to this stuff they were seeing on the news every night by somehow venting in the theater."[3] Matt Hills views the *Saw* franchise in a similar light: "The *Saw* films can be read as recodings of U.S. political debates," Hills observes. "Neither allegories nor metaphors for U.S. foreign policies leading to and following 9/11, the *Saw* movies are nonetheless not wholly divorced from post-9/11 contexts, especially since debates over whether the United States' treatment of 'prisoners of war' can be construed or defined as torture, along with media coverage of Abu Ghraib. As torture porn, these movies circle thematically around contemporary political controversies, without quite being 'about' them."[4] While film critics of the Vietnam era bemoan the supposed pointless nihilism of torture porn,[5] many fail to see that as much as George A. Romero's 1968 film *Night of the Living Dead* is about one generation cannibalizing another in the grind mill of the Vietnam War, torture porn exhibits the existential crisis of a new world (dis)order in the wake of 9/11.

The success of the *Saw* franchise is as much an accident of historical happenstance—being at the right place at the right time—as it is by design. Whannell cites *The Blair Witch Project* (Daniel Myrick and Eduardo Sánchez, 1999) as an inspiration; premised on "real" experiences, *The Blair Witch Project* was shot in the spirit of cinema verité. This particular strategy did not necessitate a large production budget—no supernatural elements requiring expensive special effects—and while in no way is *Saw* shot in the tradition of cinema verité, Whannell and Wan were particularly pragmatic in their approach to the film. In addition, to keep costs relatively low and to make the screenplay marketable, Whannell set a significant part of the film in a single location—a bathroom. Supremely cognizant that the film could not rely on expensive cinematic thrills (and there was no expectation per se of launching a franchise), Whannell made every effort to develop a tight screenplay that delivered a surprising twist.[6] While the sequels increasingly relied on the spectacle of the individual traps and the grisly exhibition of bodies being ripped apart, the first film is truly more akin to psychological thrillers such as Jonathan Demme's 1991 film *The Silence of the Lambs* and David Fincher's 1995 film *Se7en*.[7]

In fact, many of the rudiments of *Se7en* are present in the first *Saw* film. Both films draw extensively from the police procedural as an armature on which the core narrative is structured but add elements of gore and horror to invigorate the well-worn genre. They both feature African American cops who are in some fashion obsessive and psychologically damaged—Morgan Freeman plays Detective William Somerset in *Se7en*, while Danny Glover plays Detective David Tapp in *Saw*. And they also both have startling twist endings that do not necessarily lead to satisfactory narrative closure in the conventional cinematic sense.[8]

The visual and audio design of these films shares certain affinities too. Many of the victims in *Se7en* are found in squalid conditions—apartments that are dimly lit and soaked in dank, earthen hues (various shades of gray, brown, and green), walls covered in peeling paint, and dog-eared, dingy wallpaper. The bathroom in *Saw* shares many of these traits but is more industrial in character and bathed in the sickly greenish-blue hue of fluorescent lighting. The industrial lighting array in the *Saw* bathroom suffuses the room's tone with an eerie hum, and when the lights are first thrown on, there is the nondiegetic high-pitch squeal of scratching metal. Though *Se7en* is more conventional in its diegetic and nondiegetic sound design, it does employ dissonant metallic strings that begin to approach the deeply embellished soundscape in *Saw*—for instance, when Victor (the Sloth) is discovered. The opening title credits for *Se7en*, interestingly, feature the song "Closer," by the industrial-inspired

Nine Inch Nails, and it just so happens that Charlie Clouser—who played with Nine Inch Nails from 1994 to 2001—composed the original score for *Saw* and all the subsequent sequels.[9] (I address the sound design of *Saw* in more detail later.)

The antagonists of these films are also quite similar: John Doe in *Se7en* and Jigsaw in *Saw* are both clinical sadists. In *Se7en*, an unknown killer exacts his form of justice based on the seven deadly sins. While Detective Somerset's fiery partner is quick to label John Doe a lunatic, Somerset is more measured in his assessment. Reviewing the evidence, and specifically recalling the Sloth case, Somerset recounts, "Imagine the will it takes to keep a man bound for a full year to sever his hand and use it to plant fingerprints, to insert tubes into his genitals. This guy is methodical, exacting, and worst of all, patient." The characters Somerset and John Doe are mirror reflections of each other; Somerset is also meticulous and keeps reminding his passionate partner, "He's playing games. We have to divorce ourselves from emotion." John Doe is in fact characterized as sadistic, and the detectives track him down by pulling records from the public library. An individual listed in the library records as "Jonathan Doe" has checked out books by the Marquis de Sade and Saint Thomas Aquinas, who wrote on the seven deadly sins—the detectives, without any other leads to go on, decide to question this "Jonathan Doe." John Doe, executing his own brand of justice, targets individuals who have each violated one of the seven deadly sins. All of his violence—with the possible exception of the climax—happens in hermetic spaces adhering to John Doe's methodically executed scheme. Jigsaw, too, likes to "play games," to carefully craft traps in hermetic spaces that dispense justice—particularly to individuals who take life for granted. (Later I address at length Jigsaw's sadistic disposition.)

While *Se7en* dictates a relatively clear roadmap for the first *Saw* narrative, other plot elements have an Australian source. In the first film, two characters—Dr. Lawrence Gordon and Adam Faulkner-Stanheight—awake to find themselves in a large bathroom in a sewer treatment plant that has apparently fallen into disrepair; each character at opposite ends of the room is chained by the ankle to rusting pipes. This basic plot element is taken from the Australian film *Mad Max* (George Miller, 1979), in which the title character handcuffs the antagonist, Johnny the Boy, to the undercarriage of a wrecked car. Johnny begs for mercy, but Mad Max coolly explains, "The chains in those handcuffs is high-tensile steel. It would take you ten minutes to hack through it with this," holding up a hacksaw. "Now if you're lucky, you can hack through your ankle in five minutes," Mad Max says, dropping the hacksaw at Johnny's side and hobbling away, leaving Johnny to his fate. The basic plot element in *Saw* of giving a character a choice—you cut through either the chain (which would take too long before the car is set to explode) or your ankle—is drawn from this scene. In addition, the rudiments of the cinematic antihero are also retained from *Mad Max*. In sum, *Mad Max* is a revenge narrative, in which the title character takes justice into his own hands in a world where all social order is turned on its head. Jigsaw, in the *Saw* series, likewise dispenses justice as he sees fit, though he proclaims that he is more interested in rehabilitation than vengeance. In fact, he rarely has any personal stake in a victim. And as much as we might be repulsed by Jigsaw, in the end, we are encouraged to identify with him, perhaps even to sympathize with him.

Recent trends in extreme cinema, particularly from Korea and Japan, have left their mark on torture porn too. Gary Ross's wildly popular 2012 film *The Hunger Games* is an anemic knock-off of Kinji Fukasaku's 2000 *Battle Royale*. This Japanese film achieved cult status and is quite influential. Similar to its American counterpart, in *Battle Royale*, a group of adolescents are compelled to play a game—a battle to the death, with the winner being the last person standing. There are certain shared affinities between *Battle Royale* and the *Saw* franchise. When the students in *Battle Royale* are drugged, abducted, and secreted away to an isolated island, they wake up to find themselves in an abandoned school. The school is bathed in washed-out earthen hues, the air seems to hang heavy with dust, and the fluorescent lighting occasionally flickers on and off—which is not all that different from the dilapidated bathroom found in the first *Saw* film. The rules of the game are delivered through a prerecorded videotaped message, similar to Jigsaw, but delivered in that particularly perverse *kawaii* (cute) manner. One of the boys asks Kitano, who is overseeing the orchestration of the game, "Why are you doing this?" echoing that commonly heard torture porn refrain. Interestingly, in the latter moments of the film, Shogo Kawada, poised to be the sole survivor, says, in English no less, "Game over." The color scheme, the hermetic containment of violence, the signs of decay, and the various plot elements make for an interesting comparison between the two films. While *Battle Royale* is pat in its conventional arc—locating spectator identification with the least violent, most heteronormative couple—the film baits its audience into expecting, perhaps even wishing, for the next kill.[10] Who is next, and in what way might he or she meet a grisly end? Something similar happens within the *Saw* franchise. So not only might we identify with Jigsaw, but these narratives—the *Saw* franchise and torture porn in general—titillate us with the promise of violence.

On the surface of things, this titillation appears to be one of torture porn's gravest violations in the eyes of film critics who beat the drum of moral outrage. David Edelstein, who coined the term "torture porn," ponders the trend of extreme violence in post-9/11 cinema, observing that "the issue of where the spectator's sympathies lie at violent movies has always been a complicated

4.1 Like the *Saw* franchise, the rules of the game in *Battle Royale* (Kinji Fukasaku, 2000) are delivered through a prerecorded videotaped message.

one. But there's no doubt that something has changed in the past few decades." Whether we are speaking of John Doe, Jigsaw, or Dexter, Edelstein opines, "Serial killers occupy a huge—and disproportionate—share of our cultural imagination: As potential victims, we fear them, yet we also seek to identify with their power."[11] Edelstein's position that our identification lies with serial killers is hardly enough to flippantly dismiss the torture porn genre, though. Film noir is populated with accidental heroes of questionable moral fiber that nonetheless capture our imagination. Think, for instance, of the serialized private eye Mike Hammer, who would stop at nothing in the pursuit of truth, acting as judge, jury, and executioner. Less-than-scrupulous characters are not alien to the cinematic narrative; what is really at stake, and *Saw* exemplifies this, is not narrative content (and the characters that populate it) so much as narrative form.

Indeed, from the omnipresent point-of-view shot and wandering camera in slasher films—compelling the spectator to identify with the vigilante monster—to the seductive allure of Jigsaw, who only wants to put the world right, the cinema traditionally encourages an identification with agents that effect change, even when that agent is monstrous. Carol Clover argues, though, that our identification in the slasher film is complicated. That identification might vacillate between various perspectives, even with the killer's, but at the end of the day, it is the figurative position of the final girl with which we identify, because so much narrative and cinematographic real estate is given to her. Clover takes issue with nonhuman perspectives, whether it is the shark in *Jaws* or the birds in Hitchcock's film *The Birds*: it "would seem to suggest either that the viewer's identificatory powers are unbelievably elastic or that point-of-view shots can sometimes be pro forma."[12] Though Clover dismisses the nonhuman agent, I would suggest that identification *is* considerably "elastic," because the fact of the matter is that we identify less with any one agent in the *Saw* films and rather with what Jigsaw *does*. We identify with his games, not his character per se. Identification need not be with a character, let alone a human being, nor does it have to be reduced, as Clover guardedly does, to the equation "point of view = identification."[13] Clover appears to presuppose that a point of view is assigned to a (human) character. Finally, the *Saw* films, and other torture porn films, encourage fluid identification, though not simply with literal and figuratively gendered characters, as envisioned by Clover, but also with a nonhuman agent—the gamic camera and the sadistic disposition (discussed further later).

As mentioned before, the *Saw* films do in fact have fairly complex narratives (and this is particularly true of the first installment), but nonetheless what critics and film scholars bemoan is the episodic nature of the *Saw* series, which in its intervallic structure resembles the pornographic genre. Viewed through this lens, torture porn, then, is little more than a series of violent vignettes loosely tied together with a narrative that offers little or no motivation for the exhibition of carnage. Drawing from Cynthia Freeland, Matt Hills compares the spectacle of the *Saw* traps to another cinematic attraction, the musical: "The traps of the film series are significantly akin to what Cynthia Freeland terms horror's 'numbers' in an analysis of the *Hellraiser* movies. By 'numbers,' Freeland is likening moments of horror spectacle to the song-and-dance numbers in a musical. These represent points where the narrative is somewhat displaced in favor of displaying grand set-pieces."[14] Take, for instance, David Hackl's 2008 film *Saw V*, in which five characters are subjected to a series of tests. As the group progresses through each "game," one character is eliminated—meeting a grisly end.[15] In a structure very much like pornography (or even the musical), each test echoes the sexual number in porn, building tension until it is finally released in the rending of a body—analogous to the climactic cum shot. Each torture number is framed by narrative elements to offer the appearance of motivation and progression. In fairness to the Australian filmmaking team, the original 2004 Wan/Whannell feature film is in fact largely narrative driven (its success or failure is a different matter); the reputation of the franchise, though, certainly precedes it, if not completely overshadowing that fact.

Game Over: Videogame Discourse and Audio Design in the *Saw* Franchise

> As s(t)imulating machines, video-games enable active participation, encourage the mastery of various skills, and translate those into spectacular and instantaneous screened events. They obviously produce intense pleasure and allow for momentary and imaginary empowering experiences. As socializing agents, they might offer more pleasure than television-watching and might thus displace it as a site/practice of ideological communication.
> —Simon Gottschalk, "Videology"

James Wan and Leigh Whannell are well versed in the tradition of cinematic horror, and the gaming discourse in the series owes some debt to the *Scream* films. (This is discussed at greater length in chapter 3.) The killer(s) in *Scream* goads his victim over the telephone, "I wanna play a game," much in the same way that Jigsaw does via a recorded audio or video message. It is also interesting to note that Randy, a cinephile, leaves his final warning on a videotape message in Wes Craven's 2000 film *Scream 3*. And just like Jigsaw, Randy's message comes from beyond the grave; he is killed in *Scream 2*. There are other instances of videogaming in the horror genre. Though distinctly campy and referencing an earlier generation of gaming, Rachel Talalay's 1991 film *Freddy's Dead: The Final Nightmare* features a sequence in which one of Freddy's victims is lured into a videogame landscape and manipulated by Kruger.[16]

While many torture porn films are typically framed within the debates about torture and the critical discourse of post-9/11 cinema (and certainly the *Saw* franchise can be approached in this way), one of the features that distinguishes the *Saw* series from other films in the genre is its explicit appropriation of videogame syntax, rhetoric, and visual/audio aesthetics. As mentioned at the beginning of this chapter, *Saw* largely adopts the conventional narrative traits of the police procedural—bearing the hallmarks of predictable storytelling tropes, psychologically motivated characters set in a diegetic cause-and-effect trajectory—while at the same time integrating videogame elements.[17] Characters in the series are required to solve riddles, to navigate through spaces, and to follow a set of rules. Characters might have to either work together or plot against one another in a bid to survive (i.e., win); failure to do these things has lethal consequences. For instance, Jigsaw's audiotape left for Dr. Lawrence Gordon explains,

> Dr. Gordon. This is your wake-up call. Every day of your working life, you have given people the news that they are going to die soon. Now you will be the cause of death. Your aim in this game is to kill Adam. You have until 6:00 on the clock to do it. There's a man in the room with you. When there is that much poison in your blood, the only thing left to do is shoot yourself. There are ways to win this hidden all around you. Just remember: "X" marks the spot for the treasure. If you do not kill Adam by 6:00 then Alison [Lawrence's daughter] and Diana [Lawrence's wife] will die, Dr. Gordon. And I'll leave you in this room to rot. Let the game begin.

The audio recording, like the expository introduction to many videogames, dictates the objective, "to kill Adam," and initiates the countdown.

Most explicitly, the parlance of the films also evokes the discourse of videogames. Jigsaw, for instance, ends the first film by saying, "Game over," leaving a character for dead before the screen fades to black. This becomes a catchphrase for the whole film series. Additionally, when victims are first introduced to their specific challenge, an audio or video recording typically begins with, "Hello, [player's/victim's name], I want to play a game," and the recorded message frequently ends with "Let the game begin."[18] And it comes as absolutely no surprise that the film spawned a videogame, *Saw: The Video Game*—released in 2009 for the Playstation 3 and Xbox 360 platforms—which capitalizes on the motifs already present in the film franchise. The following year saw the release of another videogame—*Saw II: Flesh and Blood.* While I read these video messages through the lens of the sadistic gaming discourse, others have read them as part of Jigsaw's "moralistic crusade. Like the Islamic extremists his work imitates, he sees Western society as decadent."[19] Either way, the discourse of gaming clearly informs the narrative structure and the aesthetics of the *Saw* franchise—and this is perhaps one more impediment to critics and scholars applying conventional critical narrative paradigms to the series.

In the sequels to the original *Saw*, a player/victim traverses passages, moving from room to room. The character (or group of characters) is meant to accomplish one test after another, effectively adopting videogame discourse by moving from one "level" to another. The movement between spaces has some of the hallmarks of first-person shooter (FPS) games—but without adopting the distinctly characteristic point-of-view shot.[20] Rather than employing the point-of-view shots associated with the FPS aesthetic, in certain instances, the films replicate the free-floating, disembodied camera-eye that hovers above the gaming landscape. The disembodied camera-eye developed in tandem with dual-toggle controllers, allowing the player to maneuver the perspective in three-dimensional space; the first game to incorporate this disembodied view was probably the *Lara Croft: Tomb Raider* series (1996–2010). This particular perspective is fairly ubiquitous now and is evident in a whole host of

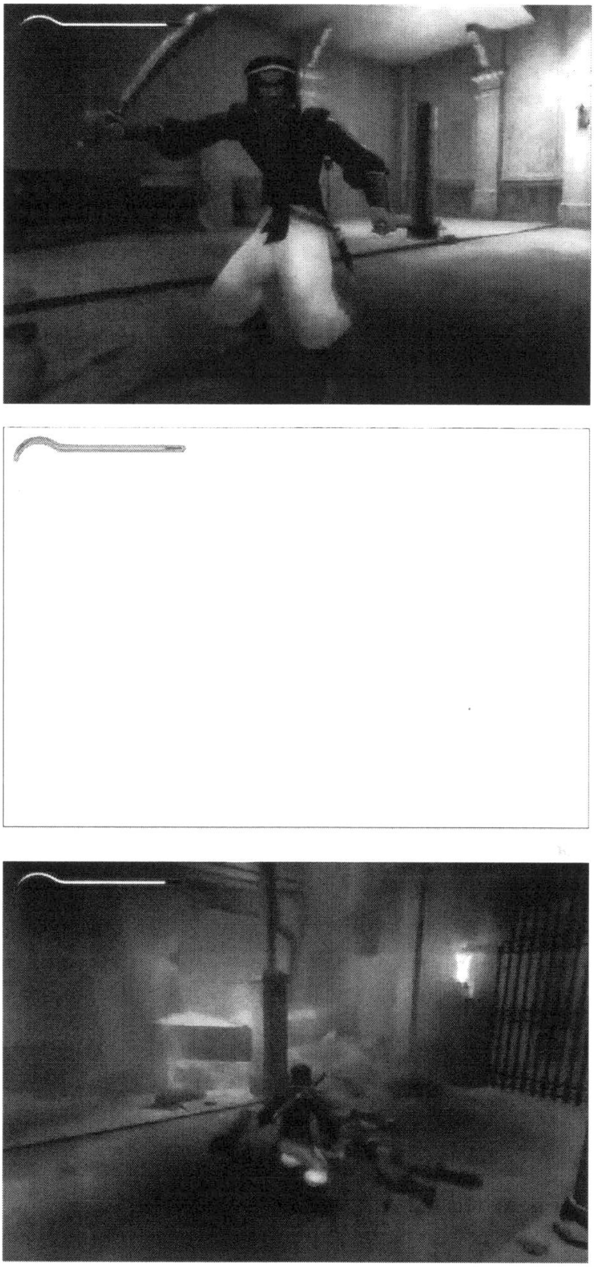

4.2 The "editing" in the videogame *Prince of Persia: The Sands of Time* (2003) is similar to what is found in the *Saw* films.

games including *Hitman* (2001–2013), *Batman Arkham Asylum* (2009), *God of War* (2005–2012), *Diablo* (1996–2012), and *Prince of Persia* (1989–2010).[21]

The latter two are particularly interesting. The expository prologue for *Diablo II* (2000), titled "The Calling," unfolds in a distinctly cinematic manner and includes a number of shots in a cell, hovering above the central character, that call to mind some of the shots in the *Saw* bathroom. In *Prince of Persia: The Sands of Time* (2003), at various points in the game, such as when the character moves from one room to another, the equivalent of a cinematic cut is marked by a flash of white coupled with the nondiegetic sound we might associate with a sword being unsheathed—the characteristic scraping sound of metal that trails off. (These "cuts" actually mark points where the player momentarily surrenders control to the game, where the game effectively "cuts away" to a "flashforward" providing the player with a tutorial on how to complete the next challenge.) The white flash and the nondiegetic sound correspond quite closely to the editing techniques found in the *Saw* series. In addition, when a player reaches a climactic point (a save point) in *Prince of Persia* and is "transported" to the next sequence in the game, the "camera" (similar to the opening moments of *Saw*, discussed later) zooms in on the central character as he is enveloped in a beam of light. The screen is suffused in a series of hot white flashes and nondiegetic sound, though more embellished than the simple "cuts" mentioned previously; in this case, the scraping metal sounds are accompanied by an otherworldly ghostly babble and a winding drone. Between the flashes of white, "flashbacks" highlighting the action of the completed level are shown in rapid succession, and the coupling of white flashes and flashbacks shares distinct affinities with the *Saw* franchise. In the climactic moments of *Saw III*, for instance, Jigsaw reveals that he has been testing his disciple, Amanda, all along. "This was your test, your game," Jigsaw says, confirmed with a series of flashbacks, set in a brisk volley of shots, partitioned by blown-out hot whites. In the use of nondiegetic sound design, editing, and cinematography, the likeness of the *Saw* franchise and the *Prince of Persia* game is quite uncanny.

In the opening moments of *Saw*, after the lights in the bathroom have been thrown on, the perspective cuts from an objective shot of Lawrence, his back up against the wall, to what we first imagine to be his visual perspective. The camera, deviating from the conventions of the shot/reverse-shot formation, though, is disembodied. In a single shot, the camera pulls back, tilts downward to reveal a corpse (the victim of an apparent self-inflicted gunshot to the head) at the center of the room, and then spins around a full 360 degrees, in what Alexander Galloway calls the "*gamic camera*."[22] This disembodied hovering camera-eye, which freely moves through space and above the scene, demonstrates "*that the camera can be subjective with regards to computerized space.* If computers have a gaze of their own, it is this."[23] Indeed, the subjective shot here is severed from Lawrence's visual perspective and is given over to the game that Jigsaw is playing, embodied in the dizzying excess of the gamic camera. Counter to Clover's assumption that cinematic identification is aligned with (human) characters, in this case, we find the "elastic" potential for identification, and not even with a "thing" as such but with a system—Jigsaw's game.

The gaming aesthetic is relatively consistent across the franchise. The films generally adhere to the conventions of police procedurals, using flashbacks to reveal information (e.g., how a trap was set, how a player was abducted), cross-cutting to build Hitchcockian suspense; the camera conforms to the principles of conventional cinematic syntax and, when placed in movement, is typically quite restrained.[24] These shooting and editing techniques are set in contrast to when a game is being played; the videogame aesthetic is generally reserved for when a "player" discovers him- or herself ensnared in a Jigsaw trap. And with the gamic camera, the subjective view does not belong to the victim but is from the perspective of the game itself. These subjective shots—detached from characters as such—are not simply about looking but about inhabiting and moving through space. "The subjective camera doesn't just look at a scene," Steven Shaviro posits. "It moves actively through space. It gets jostled, it stops and starts, it pans and tilts, it lurches forward and back. It follows the rhythms of the whole body, not just that of the eyes. This is a presubjective, affective and not cognitive, regime of vision."[25] Galloway reads this "affective regime of vision" as characteristic of the gamic camera, and this is precisely what we find in the *Saw* films.

The sound design of the *Saw* films might very well echo the visual schema. Charlie Clouser, who played with the industrial-inspired Nine Inch Nails (as well as Prong, Marilyn Manson, and White Zombie), is responsible for the soundscape in the *Saw* franchise, and he explicitly describes incorporating sound sources that could potentially be diegetic (e.g., scraping metal) but really have no discernable diegetic source, blurring the boundaries between these registers. In fact, he generated some of the sound elements by bowing large metal sculptures.[26] Assessing the *Saw* sound design, K. J. Donnelly observes, "The convergence of music with ambient sound and sound effects contravenes the film tradition of solid demarcation between such elements." He continues, "This has led to a more aesthetic rather than representational conception of sound in cinema."[27] The inability to precisely locate a referent—be it audio or visual—is what commonly creates a sense of unease, eliciting the sensation of abjection; the "lack of synchronization in this equation adds up to a degree of mental uncertainty, emphasized by the film for the purposes of horror."[28] This slippage in aural signifiers also corresponds to the cinematic syntax that unbounds itself from characters grounded within the narrative diegesis and is instead attributed to Jigsaw's ghostly (non)presence in the game. That is to say that some shots that might be read as subjective are detached from human agents.

Clouser's sound design was not immaculately conceived. The shrill sound of metal scraping on metal resonates with a number of sources and is placed in a continuum of diegetic and nondiegetic conventions in the horror genre. To begin with, the dissonance of the characteristic metal scraping sound in *Saw*[29] finds antecedents in Bernard Herrmann's classic horror riff featured in Alfred Hitchcock's 1960 film *Psycho*. Herrmann's shrieking violins, played as Norman repeatedly stabs Marion to death in the shower, shares affinities with the shrill call of birds of prey. Norman is, of course, associated with birds via his hobby—taxidermy. In the realm of diegetic sound, Freddy Kruger in Wes Craven's 1984 film *A Nightmare on Elm Street* runs his knife-fingers along metal, producing a similar grating sound to what we find in the nondiegetic design of *Saw*. Japanese and Korean horror films too—at least since the release of the Japanese film *Ringu* (Hideo Nakata, 1998)—have profoundly influenced the audioscape of horror, particularly in the design of nondiegetic sound. (The influence of Japanese and Korean films is discussed at greater length in chapter 5, specifically in reference to the *Hostel* films.)

The nondiegetic sound of scraping metal reverberates and echoes through Clouser's haunting soundscape, and by no accident, the reverberant character of the sound corresponds with the sound of a table saw (or some other power saw—a band saw, a circular saw) ripping through material. The winding up and the trailing off of the sound source is woven into the haunting nondiegetic design. And this twanging whirr bears some similarities to Tobe Hooper's 1974 film *The Texas Chain Saw Massacre*; in the nondiegetic design of Hooper's film, the synthetic rapping on metal in some fashion evokes the industrial clamor of the slaughterhouse, while in the diegetic sound design, Leatherface violently throws open the metal door to his workshop, and of course there is the roaring drone of his chainsaw.

There are clear affinities between *Saw* and the sound design of Japanese horror as well. Take, for instance, the climactic sequence of Takashi Shimizu's 2002 film *Ju-on*, in which Rika, one of our primary female characters, discovers that she is the conduit of evil. When she passes before a mirror in the haunted house, she sees, out of the corner of her eye, not her own reflection but rather that of a specter. She returns to the mirror, studies her reflection (now normal), and then is suddenly bombarded with a series of flashbacks. The flashback is bookended by a grainy, blown-out image, coupled with a highly charged nondiegetic drone (1:24:05) mixed with a modulated scream. A similar editing and audio strategy is employed just a couple of minutes later in the final moments of the film. Likewise, the opening moments of *Ju-on* rely on an embellished audio design to convey the dread of the scene. Images are on screen for a very short period of time and in tight close-up. The visual field is presented in fragments—a man with a blood-spattered face, a dead woman with her eyes wide open, the man nibbling his own blood-soaked fingers, the (off-screen) killing of a cat with a utility knife. These fragmentary images lead to the main title card, which is accompanied by a nondiegetic audio element—a reverberant metallic, twanging screech, reminiscent of the *Saw* films, mixed with the high-pitched shrill of violins, the airy, heaving breath hailing from the nether regions, and a discordant piano riff so characteristic of the horror genre.

Saw's theme song, "Hello Zepp," with the characteristic hammered dulcimer sound, which (in some variation) is featured at the end of all the films in the series, has a decidedly strange pacing to it.[30] In the conventional sense, a film follows an upward arc, reaching a peak before it winds down, and presumably the scoring should match; there should effectively be a definable climax from which the score eases downward. The *Saw* theme song does not really do that, though; in fact, it seems to do just the opposite. The rhythm suggests a perpetual ratcheting up of tension, and this is particularly striking because as much as any of the films find a resolution (e.g., we learn who Jigsaw is at the end of the first film), overall, the individual films, and the series in general, never really come to a proper close. There is no wider resolution; Jigsaw, and his worldview, exists "out there" completely beyond the grasp of figures of authority. Jigsaw is never brought to justice, and it is unclear exactly how many disciples he has. This leads one to wonder, will his work go on in perpetuity? There is nothing that suggests otherwise. In fact, in Darren Lynn Bousman's 2007 film *Saw IV*, Jigsaw lies dead on an autopsy table, his stomach cut open to reveal an audiocassette, which proclaims, "I promise that my work will continue. That I have ensured. By hearing this tape some will assume that this is over. But I am still among you. You think it's over just because I am dead? It's not over. The games have just begun."

Terrorism too is endless—hydra-headed. The United States has systematically killed (or detained) top-ranking members of Al-Qaeda (how many times have we heard, "Al-Qaeda's number 2 has been killed in a drone strike"?), but this brings little comfort. The Bush administration, in the wake of the September 11 attack, rather than directing the rhetoric of war toward the organization that carried out the attack, decided to wage a war on a tactic instead. Its absurd phrasing "War on Terror" effectively placed the United States in a state of perpetual war. "Unlike many other iconic horror monsters," Matt Hills observes, "Jigsaw's 'evil' is propagated as a belief system. His 'deviant' beliefs, within which the United States is corrupt, decadent, immoral, and in need of punishment, are inculcated in others who have undergone his testing. In short, Jigsaw's role as a horror villain is not merely embodied: he has converts to his way of thinking who carry on his campaigns against the unworthy."[31] It is not Jigsaw the personality as such that is the driving force of the *Saw* narratives but the sadistic disposition. I am not inclined to read Jigsaw as an embodiment of a terrorist (though some people do—including Kevin Wetmore); however, in this particular case, that reading seems quite apt. Although the United States conducted a daring mission to kill Osama bin Laden, the threat of terrorism did not end with his demise. Likewise, while Jigsaw lies dead, the "games have just begun." Furthermore, Jigsaw is utterly fearless precisely because, like the suicide bomber, he is already dead; Jigsaw has come to terms with being terminally ill and throws off all the shackles of the mundane world. The suicide bomber, the committed Jihadist, or terrorism writ large share to one degree or another a similar transcendent view, making for an enemy that is effectively impossible to kill—how does one kill what is already dead? In part, this is probably what Jean Baudrillard means by the "spirit of terrorism."[32] And this is what makes the "War on Terror" so absurd—which then finds analogs not only in the narrative content of the *Saw* franchise (e.g., Jigsaw and his devoted disciples) but also in the nondiegetic score that seems to endlessly spiral upward in tension, never finding its resolution.

Clouser cites György Ligeti as an inspiration, specifically referencing the single-note piece in Stanley Kubrick's 1999 film *Eyes Wide Shut*, when Dr. William Hardford is commanded to remove his mask during the meeting of the secret society; Clouser describes it sounding "like someone pounding on a piano with a hammer, the same note over and over again in dead silence."[33] The *Saw* theme song seems to echo this piece, endlessly ramping up in the tension in its cyclical riff. A soundtrack that "goes nowhere" is precisely what nondiegetic audio tracks in videogames tend to offer; they merely ratchet upward as the levels become increasingly more difficult or sustain the gamer's long effort to master the logic of the game.[34]

Unlike conventional narrative cinema that relies on the tradition of clear linear narrative arcs, videogame discourse unfolds in a series of loops. In the constant intertextual exchange between cinema and gaming, Will Brooker associates the eternal loops in videogames with the "Tarantino effect," in which films exhibit networks of hypertextuality—generating endless references to other films. And this is also evident in the pastiche of cinematic references that populate the *Saw* series, from *Scream* to *The Blair Witch Project*, from *Psycho* to *Salò*, from *Se7en* to *Mad Max*; the metacinematic references are set in a seemingly endless loop. *Saw* loops not only in its cinematic references but also in its repetitive structure; audiences came to expect serial repetition of audio/visual and narrative motifs, and the "looping [of] mini-narratives and retelling of the same story with variations" are, as Brooker explains, "like repeated attempts [in videogames] at the same level."[35] The spectacle of Jigsaw traps is set in an endless repetitive loop; spectators wait with baited breath for the next ingenious exhibition of bodies being ripped apart.

Videogame discourse shares affinities with the cinema of attractions. "On a broad aesthetic level," Brooker observes, "the term 'video game' is used to connote spectacular, showy displays of effects at the expense of subtext and character."[36] The orgiastic exhibition of rending bodies, particularly in the *Saw* sequels, caters to the tastes of the largest moviegoing demographic: adolescent boys and young men, many of whom are also intimately acquainted with the discourse of videogames. Whereas the original *Saw* is in fact largely driven by the principles of conventional narrative progression[37] (though some critics were unable to get beyond wagging the finger of moral indignation to see it), the later films increasingly rely on spectacles of violence, frequently adopting in these instances the highly frenetic gamic camera and editing accompanied by a decidedly embellished gaming audio design. Accordingly, then, in the *Saw* franchise, the attraction is seamlessly woven into its appropriation of videogame discourse. And there is something potentially quite troubling about this, because the discourse of videogames effectively eroticizes the execution of rules and relieves the player of ethical considerations. The player is rewarded for carrying out the rules of the game, not for acting judiciously, and in this sense, gaming resembles the sadistic disposition.

Jigsaw (or his disciples) sets traps that demand a strict adherence to rules. As found in many videogames, violence for the most part plays out within a hermetic space—an abandoned shuddered-up home (which is the case for Darren Lynn Bousman's 2005 film *Saw II*) or some secluded industrial site. Jigsaw's games unfold within chambers, enclosed devices, rooms; and more than this, these insular spaces are frequently housed within a larger complex—again typically an industrial site. As with videogames, victims are frequently given an allotment of time to complete a challenge, to figure out a riddle, to figure out how to extricate themselves from a device; failure to do so within the prescribed time—or within the parlance of videogames, "to lose"—has lethal consequences. In addition, rooms or chambers are also frequently armed with automated locks, and again, if victims are unable to complete their challenge within a given time, they might well be entombed within the hermetic torture chamber forever. The rules associated with each game and trap or traps—sometimes characters are subjected to a series of tests—require scrupulous adherence. The gaming discourse—the hermetic spaces and the execution of challenges within an allotted time and within prescribed rules—resonates with the sadistic disposition.

The very discourse of videogames elicits the sadistic disposition. "Video games possess 'an excess of visual and aural stimuli' but also 'the promise of reliable rules.' These rules, which are reliable in that they are systematic and unambiguous (for they are unencumbered by morality or compassion), constitute the video game's environment, or location, which is not restrained by the laws of the physical world."[38] Rather than locating pleasure in the ultimate objective—for instance, completing the "final level," which effectively spells the end of the game and a general loss of pleasure—gamers instead locate ecstasy in the mastery of rules, or "deciphering the game's logic."[39] Recalling the experience of coin-operated arcade games, and the same might be said of home-console games as well, Simon Gottschalk observes that "the essence of 'video pleasure' consists in outsmarting it, if only for a while, and in extending the game to long sessions so that a single coin gives as much pleasure/time as possible."[40] The sense of immersion into the universe of the game "may alter the user's state of consciousness and lead to a momentary loss of self."[41] And it is precisely the ecstasy in executing the internal logic of the game, which potentially leads to "loss of self," that allows a player to divorce him- or herself from the burden of ethics, conforming to the sadistic disposition. The sadist eroticizes the execution of rules, and this is precisely where Buckland locates pleasure in the videogame: "Video pleasure, created by a user's addiction to and immersion in a game, is therefore not simply a matter of a heightened stimulation generated by high quality graphics, audio and animation, but is also—and, I would argue, primarily—a function of these rules, of the user's success at mastering these rules."[42] The sadistic disposition, then, is woven not only into plot elements found in the *Saw* franchise, Jigsaw being the grand master of sadism, but also into the very structure of the series's narratives and its cinematic syntax appropriating the discourse of videogames.

The *Saw* Franchise, or How I Learned to Stop Worrying and Love Jigsaw

David Hackl's 2008 film *Saw V* includes a scene that is particularly illustrative of Jigsaw's sadistic disposition. Early in the film, we find a man, Seth, strapped to a table and cut in half with a swinging pendulum; the grisly murder is erroneously attributed to Jigsaw. The culprit, though, as we discover later, is Detective Mark Hoffman, who in previous films pursues Jigsaw. Familiar with Jigsaw's patterns, Hoffman executes the man who raped and killed his sister and gives the act the hallmarks of a Jigsaw crime.

As it turns out, Jigsaw is aware of Hoffman's scheme and abducts him to submit him to a test. Hoffman is strapped to a chair and has a double-barrel shotgun mounted between his legs and pointed straight at his head. When Hoffman comes to, we find Jigsaw casually sipping tea from a Japanese earthenware cup. Jigsaw—the Zen master of sadism—intends to either eliminate Hoffman or make his transformation complete, turning him into one of Jigsaw's disciples. Jigsaw's icy disposition hardly ever wavers, even in emotive moments, but at the end of the day, he sympathizes with Hoffman's intent to set the world right. Jigsaw quizzes Hoffman and plays "a little game" with the

4.3 The memento mori and the death pact in *Saw V* (David Hackl, 2008).

detective to see if he has what it takes. Jigsaw applauds Hoffman's compulsion to mete out justice but is appalled by his method. Hoffman, the novice sadist, is overcome with emotions and lambasts his captor, exclaiming that the man who killed his sister deserved to die. Jigsaw responds, wagging the finger of discontent, "Killing is distasteful—to me." The dark master of sadism leans in to whisper to reassure his novice pupil that there is another way.[43]

The formal lesson of sadism begins here, though; as Hoffman is strapped to the chair, Jigsaw sits down and places his finger on the trigger and asks, "What do you see?" Jigsaw punctuates the question with a sharp command—"Look!"—and repeats, "What do you see?" Full of fear, Hoffman chokes out, "Tell me what you want!" Returning to his measured voice of reason, Jigsaw asks, "I want to know if you have what it takes to survive." Trembling with fear, Hoffman gasps for air—the nondiegetic audio design all the while ramping up the tension. Hackl cuts between a two-shot—Jigsaw's inquisitive face paired with Hoffman's angst-filled expression—to a close-up of Jigsaw's finger on the trigger. Finally, Jigsaw pushes down on the trigger, causing the cocked hammer of the shotgun to slap down. But the shotgun, as it turns out, only has one of its barrels loaded, the hammer coming down on the empty barrel.[44] Exasperated, Hoffman turns to Jigsaw: "Fuck you. Fuck you."

Capitalizing on the lesson, Jigsaw coaches Hoffman on refining his techniques, saying in a gentle tone, "You see. It's a different method I'm talking about. If a subject survives my method, he or she"—Jigsaw waving his hand as if a magician—"is instantly rehabilitated." Jigsaw then poses to his pupil, pointing a straight razor at Hoffman as a teacher might a pointer, "Now, you want a chance?" Hoffman nods affirmatively. Jigsaw stands up before the mirror and gazes into it, staring at Hoffman through the reflected image, and says, "I am the man you call 'Jigsaw.' It's your duty to bring me in. But I know who you are. And I know what you've done." In between the reflected image of both men is a human skull, which is placed on a work table at the back of the room—a memento mori akin to the distorted figure found in Hans Holbein's 1533 painting *The Ambassadors*, it also signifies the death pact that will bind the men through the rest of the film series.

Hoffman naturally rejoins, "So this is blackmail?" Disappointedly, as if his new pupil has not heard a word of what he has said, Jigsaw responds, "No, no, no. This is redemption," as he cuts Hoffman from his restraints with the straight razor, placing the blade atop the newspaper with the pendulum-murder headline—the perfection of the straight razor's tempered steel set in contrast with the substandard pendulum utilized by Hoffman, the sadistic interloper. Hoffman weighs his options; a subjective shot from Hoffman's perspective—seeing the unattended straight razor—though, offers another route, and Hoffman blurts out, "Or I can kill you right now." Seated in a chair, Jigsaw calmly explains that contingency plans are in place should Jigsaw die at Hoffman's hand. Jigsaw inspects the chambers of the shotgun to reveal that one of the chambers was in fact loaded. As with all his victims, Jigsaw finally arrives at the conclusive point: "How would your sister feel? We're at a crossroads, detective. Make your choice." Hoffman closes the straight razor, tosses it on the table, and without a word assumes the role of Jigsaw's disciple.

The contrast between Jigsaw's stoic disposition and Hoffman's emotionally driven violence is what sets the pair apart. Without ever stating as much, the philosophy that Jigsaw subscribes to is that of libertinage. He is governed strictly by reason, and he executes his "games" dispassionately. The traps and the games are explicitly designed so that players/victims can extricate themselves if they precisely abide by the rules. And this is Jigsaw's lesson for Hoffman—to remove ethics and emotion from the execution of justice. As an aside, Hoffman's vengeance, which will be channeled into his sadistic conversion, might be read through the lens of the rape-revenge narrative.[45]

Similarly, one of Jigsaw's other disciples, a survivor from the first film, Amanda Young, is also prone to emotional outbursts. And, like Hoffman, as we find in Darren Lynn Bousman's 2006 film *Saw III*, Young also designs traps that are impossible to escape, violating Jigsaw's rules of conduct. She is prone to jealous fits and is quick to lose her temper. Young abducts a surgeon to care for the terminally ill Jigsaw, who is inflicted with a brain tumor. During a surgical procedure, Jigsaw dreams that he rejoins his former life partner in romantic bliss. (The operation, cutting away part of the skull to relieve pressure, is maximized for gore to appease the fans of the genre.) When he recovers consciousness, groggily he imagines that the surgeon is his beloved and grabs her arm and says, "I love you." Seeing this, Young is wracked with jealous rage and unable to contain her emotions; she directs her angst inward and resorts to cutting herself. As much as Jigsaw invests in Young, making her a disciple of sadism, she is at the core a masochist; she is not a novice cutter, nor is this a completely capricious act, as she has a kit stored away for these sorts of occasions.[46]

The treatment of Young's character reminds us that the misogynistic legacy of the horror genre is alive and well in torture porn. Playing to age-old patriarchal values, wherein the arbiter of reason is Jigsaw, the father figure, the film shows that Young, despite everything that the paternalistic sadist teaches, is governed by emotions. Even when Young executes violence, it is at her master's bequest. In the third installment of the franchise, Young is cast as Jigsaw's caregiver, so even as she supervises Jeff's deadly game, she is still the "nurturer." (Jeff's child was killed in a traffic accident, and he is consumed by fantasies of revenge; Jigsaw constructs a series of games that allow him either to fulfill his fantasies or to let go of his anger and forgive those who have wronged him.) And finally at the end of it all, after repeated and violent tests, Young never lives up to Jigsaw's expectation, and it is a male character at the end of the series that assumes the sadist's throne.

Jigsaw's project is pedagogical, but it is also paternalistic. Throughout the *Saw* franchise, Jigsaw proclaims that his mission is to rehabilitate his victims so that they might find a new appreciation for life, to cherish it, in effect to be reborn. Jigsaw himself comes to this realization following a failed suicide attempt—emerging from the experience with a newfound appreciation for life. As Madeline Smith observes,

> The association of Jigsaw with rebirth is heightened by womb-like and birthing imagery evident in the *Saw* franchise. In *Saw* for instance, Adam (Leigh Whannell) awakens in a bathtub full of dirty water and falls from it, coughing and spluttering, onto the floor. Similarly in *Saw III*, Jeff (Angus Macfadyen) is encased in a small, dark and entombing box that he is violently ejected from, head first. Such imagery strongly aligns Jigsaw with the figure of the "archaic mother," presenting a masculinized reworking of the role in creation, birth, and potentially death.[47]

In the role as Victor Frankenstein, Jigsaw is placed in the "maternal" position, giving form to new life and "instructing his offspring in the proper ways of the body."[48] While all his acolytes apparently fail in the end, save Dr. Gordon, Jigsaw makes efforts to—almost in a biblical sense—sculpt protégés in his own image. It is perhaps no small coincidence, then, that the first character that we see in the series is Adam.

The father/daughter, student/pupil relationship between Amanda and Jigsaw echoes the relationship between the detectives David Mills and William

4.4 Wrestling with emotions in *Se7en* (David Fincher, 1995) and *Saw III* (Darren Lynn Bousman, 2006).

Somerset in David Fincher's 1995 film *Se7en*. The elder Somerset, on the verge of retirement, routinely lectures his younger colleague on the virtues of protocol, rationality, divorcing himself from emotion, and even when bending the rules, knowing how to do it, so as not to jeopardize the integrity of the criminal case. Detective Mills, on the other hand, like Amanda, finds it difficult to contain his emotions. Even down to some of their gestures, the similarities are quite striking. Take, for instance, the climax of *Se7en* when Mills discovers that John Doe has had the detective's pregnant wife's severed head delivered to him. Mills is overcome with emotion, tearfully wrestling with the devastating revelation. Somerset begs Mills to restrain himself, but Mills summarily executes John Doe. (Mills completes John Doe's mission, with Mills enacting the last deadly sin: wrath.) Amanda, in the climax of *Saw III*, tearfully contends with her anger, at one point holding her gun much in the same way that Mills does, before she abruptly discharges it, killing the captive surgeon who is treating Jigsaw.

The traps are in themselves neutral and merely follow the laws of physics, and in that respect, Jigsaw removes human mores from the "games," consequently subjecting players/victims to the laws of the natural world. A compressed spring necessitates an eventual discharge of energy; a particular gear ratio delivers a specific amount of torque relative to the amount of force applied; human bones are capable of withstanding only so many pounds per square inch before they break—these are the laws of nature, divorced from human values. There is a degree of liberation afforded the viewer, too, because victims/players have been placed beyond mundane human values and yield instead to the sublimity of the natural order. The sadist appropriates the laws of nature, replicating nature's will, cutting the moorings to any human sentimentality.[49] By abdicating human ethical responsibility—foisting everything on the laws of nature—the sadist is liberated from any sort of emotional or ethical concerns.

Furthermore, all of the players/victims in the *Saw* series "deserve" their fate in Jigsaw's eyes; all of them have transgressed social/cultural or legal bounds of one kind or another—adulterers, sexual predators, embezzlers, liars, drug dealers and addicts, racists, or individuals who simply do not value life. This makes sympathizing with the players/victims difficult,[50] and it offers a narrative motivation for their punishment. As addressed earlier, the sadist is not an anarchist (in the colloquial sense). He or she does not advocate the abolition of laws; to the contrary, the libertine revels in the strict application of laws. The players/victims, then, are fair game, and the audience derives pleasure in the spectacle of their punishment and the execution of rules.

See, Seeing, Saw: Voyeurism in the *Saw* Franchise

The title of the film says it all: *Saw*. What was seen? Was missed? Or hiding in plain sight? *Saw* references not only the device cutting through chains, or cutting through flesh, ligaments, and bones, but the past tense of "to see."[51] "Jigsaw is not just a cutter, he is an observer," Kevin Wetmore notes. "The film concerns watching people being tortured to see if they change their ways, or if they reveal information."[52] So much of the franchise's plots revolve around Jigsaw and surveillance: whether it is Jigsaw himself surreptitiously watching people for his reeducation program (much of which might only be implied in the narrative), the surveillance monitors that track a player's performance in a game, or the spectator's implication in the cinematic syntax of the pornographic regime. As much as the *Saw* franchise "is about torture," Wetmore observes, it is also "about watching."[53]

Voyeurism is an important feature of the *Saw* franchise—capitalizing on the spectacle of tortured bodies. It is featured in the very first film and the very first victim. In the opening moments of *Saw*, after Adam retrieves the audiocassette player from the "dead man" at the center of the room, he plays the tape intended for him. This is the first time that we hear Jigsaw, and what is particularly fascinating is that Adam is of course played by Whannell, the screenwriter. "Rise and shine, Adam," Jigsaw begins. "You're probably wondering where you are. I'll tell you where you might be: you might be in the room that you die in. Up until now, you simply sat in the shadows watching others live out their lives. What do voyeurs see when they look into the mirror? Now I see you as a strange mix of someone angry and yet apathetic—but mostly just pathetic. So are you going to watch yourself die today, Adam? Or do something about it?" It is no accident that Adam is a shady photographer-for-hire, a voyeur par excellence; Whannell makes himself and the film complicit in the voyeuristic thrill of violence.

There is also a cinematic source for this device. In order for people to play Jigsaw's little games, they must be abducted first. When Adam finally recalls how he came to be locked away in the dank bathroom, he remembers awaking in his apartment to discover that the lights do not work—perhaps the circuit breaker needs to be flipped? As Adam searches for a flashlight (the batteries turn out to be dead), he hears someone in his apartment. He grabs his camera and snaps a shot to trigger the flash. "I can hear you," Adam calls out as he triggers the flash again; the snap of the aperture and the whirr of the flash charging up pierce the dark, eerie quiet. The series of flashes break the darkness, finally illuminating—in a frightening flash—the prowler (presumably Jigsaw) in his pig's-head disguise, who lunges out from a darkened closet. Deploying the camera flash in this way calls to mind two of the most famous cinematic voyeurs: Mark Lewis in Michael Powell's 1960 film *Peeping Tom* and Jeff in Alfred Hitchcock's 1954 film *Rear Window*. In both cases, in the climax of these films, the voyeuristic photographers use the camera flash as a weapon—similar to its use in *Saw*.[54] The photographic flash, and the highly distinctive whir following the discharge, is also traceable to the opening of Tobe Hooper's 1974 film *The Texas Chain Saw Massacre*. Though the scene is not explicitly voyeuristic as such, the Hitchhiker, as he is named in the credits, digs up graves, plunders body parts, forms sculptures, and apparently snaps photographs of his own handiwork. The Hitchhiker then constructs necrophilic scenes of desire that he captures with his camera. Whannell aligns his screenplay, himself, and his character with these cinematic voyeurs—an intertextual cinematic gesture that acknowledges the film's complicity in the spectacle.

4.5 The letter "A" hovers over the voyeuristic eye in the short film *Saw* (James Wan, 2003).

This self-referentiality also materializes in the visual design of the film, which acknowledges—without ever being navel gazing—the role of the cinematic apparatus and its capacity to elicit pleasure from the sadism of the voyeuristic gaze. Take, for example, one instance when the detectives David Tapp and Steven Sing inspect Jigsaw's handiwork—a room lined with seemingly random numbers written in red. In flashback, a device that is used frequently in the series, Wan cuts to the trap when it is first sprung. "Hello, Mark," Jigsaw begins, "if you're so sick, then why do I have so many photos of you up and about?" As it turns out, Jigsaw hired Adam to conduct surveillance on people, and apparently Mark has called in sick one too many times. "Let's put your so-called illness to the test," Jigsaw taunts. "Right now, there is a slow-acting poison in your veins. The antidote is inside the safe. The combination to the safe is written on the wall. Hurry up and program it in. But watch your step." The floor is covered in broken glass. The room is dimly illuminated, and a lit candle is the only source of light that allows Mark to read the numbers on the wall. But Jigsaw cautions Mark, "By the way, that's a flammable substance smeared on your body. So I would be careful with that candle, if I were you—or all the people you've burned with your act just might have their revenge." The investigating officer at the scene explains to detectives Tapp and Sing, pointing to a hole in the wall, "There was someone standing outside here watching through this peephole." The peephole motif has been present from the very

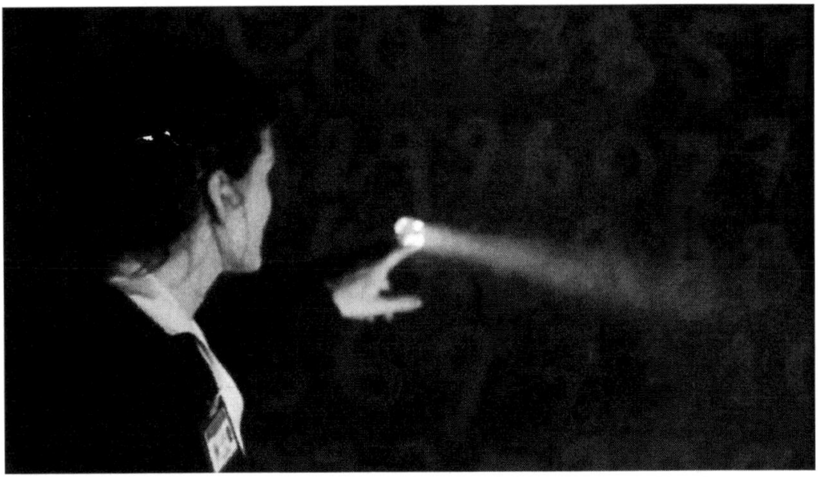

4.6 Dina Meyers points to a shaft of light resembling a cinematic projection in *Saw* (James Wan, 2004).

inception of the *Saw* narrative; in fact, the original nine-minute short ends precisely on this point. At the very end of the short, the camera tracks forward in a dank bathroom—similar to the one featured in the original full-length film—and a tile falls away from the wall to reveal an eye peering through a rough-cut hole in the wall. The title, "SAW," is superimposed on the shot, the "A" hovering over the eye, while the distinctive hammered dulcimer theme begins to play.

The peephole in Mark's trap, which as the investigating officer, Dina Meyers, points out to Tapp and Sing, resembles a cinematic projection. Emerging from the peephole is a shaft of light, cutting through the dimly lit space. "Looks like our friend Jigsaw likes to book himself front-row seats to his sick games," Meyers notes, adding that the investigation of another site—Paul's trap—found a peephole too, suggesting a pattern. The booking of a "front-row seat" to the performance calls to mind any number of examples in cinema: Norman watching Marion getting undressed in *Psycho* or the "opera seating" at the climax of *Salò, or the 120 Days of Sodom*.

Earlier, Adam discovered a pair of hacksaws in the toilet cistern; while Adam and Lawrence attempt to cut through their respective chains, Adam's saw breaks. Incensed, Adam throws his broken hacksaw against the adjacent wall, shattering part of a mirror. Later, frustrated and scared, Adam begins to rail against Lawrence, imagining that he had a hand in the situation. Adam picks up a shard of glass from the broken mirror and threatens Lawrence: "Now you either tell me what is really going on, or I'll cut you with this. You hear me? I'll cut—" Adam stops midsentence when he realizes that the mirror is actually a two-way mirror. Adam finds an object to throw at the mirror, and when the mirror shatters, he discovers a closed-circuit camera mounted in the wall. Wan cuts to the grainy black-and-white image of the surveillance camera, and the camera pulls back to reveal that we are actually watching a security monitor—and we are led to believe that Jigsaw is the owner of the gaze (one of the carefully crafted narrative conceits of the film). Many of the films include surveillance equipment—used to monitor the games, emphasizing the voyeuristic thrill of the violent spectacles. Taken broadly, this surveillance might be associated with the predatory vision found in slasher films. As Catherine Zimmer observes, the use of closed-circuit cameras seems "to be simply a televisually technologized version of the sadistic voyeur killers with whom horror film has long been familiar."[55] Gone are the days of the wandering I-camera associated with the slasher genre, and what comes in its place is surveillance video. This trope is not evident in every installment of the *Saw* franchise, but it is a discernable trope nonetheless. And there are certainly 9/11 implications here: most of us experienced that day as a mediated event through the utter saturation of news reportage, events incidentally caught on security cameras and amateur footage.

In no small part, the success of the *Saw* series is predicated on the elaborate traps that victims must extricate themselves from; audiences are lured to the films by the promise of intricate devices that exact grievous bodily harm. Indicative of this is Kevin Greutert's 2010 film *Saw 3D: The Final Chapter*, which is perhaps the least interested in narrative content and is clearly invested in the spectacle of tortured bodies. Though the film ostensibly crowns Jigsaw's legitimate heir, the film, which is shot in 3D, largely celebrates the Grand Guignol aesthetic at the expense of narrative concerns. Following the credit sequence, the opening scene of the film begins with a nod and a wink acknowledging its shameless revelry in the spectacle of gore. Completely detached from any narrative element, and quite uncharacteristic of any previous trap, we find three individuals restrained within a glass kiosk—visible to a public square filled with people. Horrified witnesses gather to watch the struggle, with many mediating the event through their mobile devices. This is unique among Jigsaw's traps, staged for public exhibition, but it nevertheless remains within the realm of libertinage as the glass case maintains a border between inside and outside—preserving the requisite hermetic containment of violence.

Two men, Brad and Ryan, find themselves strapped before circular saws, while their two-timing girlfriend, Dina, facing downward, is strapped to a contraption mounted to the ceiling—her body mounted just a couple of feet away from a third circular saw. The animatronic puppet associated with Jigsaw pedals into the space on a child's tricycle and begins with Jigsaw's characteristic narrative exposition:

> Hello, Brad. Hello, Ryan. I'd like to play a game. The same woman has played each of you for a fool, manipulating your love for her, and causing nothing but pain. Her fun and games pushed you both to break the law to fulfill her material needs. She is toxic, and today all of your transgressions will be made public. Now you must choose who will drop out of this triangle, for within sixty seconds, one of you must die. If you wish to save her, then the saws must be pushed all the way to one side or the other, sparing her while proving for good who is indeed the alpha male. Are you both strong enough to walk away from what is destroying you, or will you fight one more time for the heart that binds? You have sixty seconds to decide. Live or die. Make your choice.

Following Jigsaw's standard discourse prior to a game, establishing the reason the victims/players have been chosen and setting down the rules of the game, the three saws suddenly begin to spin. The two men struggle, pushing the interconnected device toward their "opponent," while the saw mounted below Dina correspondingly moves away from her bound body as the contraption moves to one side or the other. As Dina pleads, Ryan finally heeds Jigsaw's admonishing words and tries to reason with Brad: "Is the chick that fucked me in your bed two days ago worth one of our lives?" As the men decide to sacrifice Dina to save their own skin, Dina screams at Ryan, "What are you doing, you fucking asshole?" To which he responds, "I think we're breaking up with you, Dina!" The men let the center circular saw rest in the upright position and watch as the remaining seconds on the clock count down, allowing the saw to cut Dina in half.

The slasher genre, to the exclusion of almost anything else, focused intently on issues related to gender and sexuality—and more specifically the anxiety associated with female sexuality. Torture porn, on the other hand, generally focuses less on gender and sexuality. However, as the opening of *Saw 3D* abundantly demonstrates, this is not to suggest that these issues are altogether absent. Dina's body is highly fetishized—she is bound in Jigsaw's trap like a BDSM (bondage/domination/sadism/masochism) contraption, her wrists are restrained, and the body harness that suspends her from the ceiling emphasizes her buxom figure. The narrative situation is also fueled by overripe misogynistic tropes—the two-timing girlfriend, the gold-digger, the bitch. In the end, and presumably Jigsaw would concur, the two men make the "correct" choice in allowing Dina to die. Moreover, it is no mistake that the men are placed in a position to determine the characters' fates, whereas Dina (aside from vocal protest) is helpless to do anything. Whereas the men are active, Dina is acted on. The patently misogynistic exhibition of female bodies is relatively anomalous for the franchise, though.[56]

One might read this opening trap—placing it in a center of commerce, and its overwrought misogyny—as a form of self-criticism; after all, the entire film franchise has capitalized on the voyeuristic spectacle of bodies being ripped apart. And to read this scene generously, it is possible to locate affinities between the critique of the voyeuristic spectacle and the closing moments of Pasolini's *Salò*. The torture and humiliation at the Château de Silling in *Salò* culminates in an orgy of violence within an enclosed courtyard. Perched in a room overlooking the spectacle and seated in a Mackintosh chair, as if at the opera, each libertine takes his turn to revel in the exhibition of tortured bodies. Most notably, the Duke watches the spectacle through opera glasses, and Pasolini cuts to his subjective shot—as viewed through the opera glasses. In one instance, the Duke even flips the opera glasses wrong way around, distancing us from the display of torture in the courtyard and effectively laying bare the cinematic apparatus. Despite our moral indignation, Pasolini mobilizes cinematic syntax that encourages us to identify with the libertines, and the subjective shots as viewed through the opera glasses—in these climactic moments of violence—render us complicit to one degree or another in the spectacle of violence. The opening trap in *Saw 3D*, in its explicit voyeurism and contextualization within the center of commerce, might share in this metacinematic critique.[57]

Without discounting this possibility, I posit that the *Saw* series (and torture porn in general) figuratively pulls back the curtain to reveal the veiled exercising of American power abroad and the sadistic disposition intrinsic to it. There is a morbid fascination associated with the execution of American power in its so-called global War on Terror. While extraordinary rendition and CIA black sites—facilities located in undisclosed locations outside the United States—conceal the delivery of enhanced interrogation techniques, torture porn films appear to appease our morbid curiosity—what exactly happens in these black sites? Kevin Wetmore similarly observes that Jigsaw never sullies his hands with torture, strictly speaking. Rather, Jigsaw uses surrogates, much in the same way that the United States hands over terrorist suspects to other countries to do our "dirty work." This tactic of using "surrogates to torture suggests America's policy of extraordinary rendition, in which third parties do the actual torturing. Yet the question Jigsaw asks is at the heart of America's torture policy: will you harm others, perhaps even innocents who have done no wrong, in order to protect and save yourself?" Wetmore continues, noting that although we might condemn characters for vile acts, even when they are compelled to do so as "players" in a Jigsaw trap, the fact remains that American foreign policy justifies the use of torture (directly or through a third party) to keep us safe.[58] And the *Saw* franchise depicts the execution of American power, including torture, in its naked form.

Michel Foucault demonstrates that the history of punishment has been an incremental sequestering of disciplinary action. In times past, the sovereign exercised his (or her) power as the "right to make war on his enemies."[59]

Foucault, for instance, understands the public exhibition of capital punishment "not only as a judicial but also as a political ritual. It belongs, even in minor cases, to the ceremonies by which power is manifested."[60] The opening scene in *Saw 3D: The Final Chapter* explicitly returns us to when the gallows were set up in the public square. And this appears implicit throughout the *Saw* franchise and torture porn generally; these films return to the visible world what has been denied to us—the visible evidence of exercised power. What is denied to public eyes is the demonstration of American power that supposedly keeps us safe. Enhanced interrogation is not disciplinary in nature, but rather it reaffirms American power.[61] If the 9/11 attacks "emasculated" American prowess, the *Saw* series exhibits the naked power harbored within the American sadistic disposition.

Power in the Foucauldian register is frequently ascribed to those who see, versus those who are seen. Of course, this is most evident in Foucault's much-cited discussion of the panopticon. While Foucault's account, as Catherine Zimmer observes, "emphasizes the production of 'docile bodies' through a shift *away* from torture, *Saw*'s narrative use of surveillance within a torture film as a tool and form of confinement, control, and power has notable resonance with the Foucauldian account."[62] And to add to this, one of the things that was largely overlooked in the rancorous editorials and the Bush administration's media campaign to minimize the damage over the Abu Ghraib photographs is that the (photographic) image itself is torture. Indeed, one of the threats against the detainees in Abu Ghraib was that the images of them in humiliating poses, engaging in what would be viewed as indecent acts (e.g., masturbating, simulating or in fact engaging in homosexual acts), would be disseminated to their families—forever sullying their reputation. As Catherine Soussloff insists, "To participate in the negation of the events of torture that are shown to have taken place by using euphemistic terminology—including the insidious 'prisoner abuse'—is to deny the actual wounding power of the photographs."[63] It is not just what those images depict but the images themselves that are part of the regime of torture. Though Jigsaw does not "take pictures," as such, his incessant need to see seems to reacquaint Foucault's panopticon vision, which produces "docile bodies," with physical brutality.

Jeremy Morris also finds affinities with the spectacle of torture in the *Saw* franchise (as well as other films—*Se7en* and *The Last House on the Left*) and the public exhibition of punishment. Morris observes that "the appeal of torture-horror is not unlike that offered by the carnival atmosphere of public executions, common until the last century."[64] Morris specifically locates this pleasure in narratives of retribution. What Morris fails to recognize, though, is that it is not the deliverance of "just punishment" on display per se but rather an exhibition of power. If 9/11 wounded American prowess, the execution of the War on Terror is less about getting the bad guys and more about restoring American power.

There, of course, is a long tradition of public executions. Some of the most striking images of torture, and especially those captured in the photographic (or moving image) medium, are captivating precisely because they make institutionalized torture visible (a relative rarity in the modern era). Take, for instance, Georges Dumas's photographs of Fou-Tchou-Li—an image that is central to Pascal Laugier's 2008 extreme film *Martyrs*. Found guilty of murdering Prince Ao-Han-Ouan, Fou-Tchou-Li was sentenced to die by Leng-Tch'e—what in colloquial terms we call "a death by a thousand cuts" but in the Chinese is called "Hundred Pieces." In Beijing on April 10, 1905, the condemned man—given opium to withstand his torture and to prolong his death—was executed by literally being cut into pieces. In a public space, bound to crossed wooden poles, the condemned was sawed apart. In the execution of state power, torture is just one tool that can be applied to the supple body and perpetrated without moral reservation because the state sanctions it. Torture porn renders this power visible.

In the wake of 9/11, the fallacy of a Manichean world crumbled before our very eyes, and what these films do is to exhibit in full view the morass of moral ambiguity. As Catherine Zimmer observes, the *Saw* franchise posits that no character is wholly innocent.[65] Sade was critical of the revolution because it refused "to recognize that it lives only through evil and claims to exist for the sake of the good,"[66] which equally applies to the brazen claims that enhanced interrogation techniques do not amount to torture and that they are being deployed to keep us secure. While the content of these films might be far removed from the existential realities of American foreign policy, they nevertheless render the sadistic disposition bare—demonstrating how legal reasoning might excuse the application of violence. Sade's project is pedagogical in nature; he demonstrates the ways in which rational discourse might be corrupted. And so "it is not Kant who was a closet sadist," as Slavoj Žižek concludes; "it is Sade who is the closet Kantian."[67] More than we would care to admit, we certainly still have a lot to learn from Sade and, dare I say it, from Jigsaw.

5

The *Hostel* Films

Consuming Bodies

> No matter what I put in a movie there is nothing worse than what's going on in New Orleans [and the aftermath of Hurricane Katrina in 2005]. I mean, I can put the most violent stuff in a film and people know it's fake—they are paying for a fantasy. . . . What gets people desensitized is when there are school shootings every week, when we say, "Oh, another ten people were killed in Iraq." . . . George Bush and Dick Cheney kill people for real. . . . That is what gets people desensitized, when people turn on the TV and they've seen that New Orleans has completely fallen apart, and people are screaming for help and people are shooting each other, and raping each other, and it takes the US Army *five days* to show up! That's what gets people desensitized; it's not movies or videogames—that's a reaction to that.
> —Eli Roth

Introduction: Intertextual Cinema

Whereas the *Saw* films have fairly complex plots, Eli Roth's 2005 film *Hostel* is straightforward: American travelers Josh and Paxton, along with their Icelandic buddy, Oli, sow their wild oats while touring Europe and are lured to Slovakia with the promise of available beautiful women. Of course, this is merely a ruse, and the Elite Hunting syndicate, which caters to the sadistic taste of its exclusive clientele, abducts them. Syndicate clients pay thousands of dollars to torture and kill abductees in an abandoned Slovakian factory repurposed as a complete in-house torture facility. *Hostel: Part II* (2007) starts where the first film ends, and the plot is effectively the same; however, rather than a group of American college-aged men, this film features three American women. In 2011, Scott Spiegel directed the straight-to-video *Hostel: Part III*, which also follows the basic Roth formula (Roth is listed as one of the cowriters) but this time sets the action in Las Vegas. Here, I address elements of *Part III*, but my focus is largely trained on the two Roth films.

The two American male characters in *Hostel*—Josh and Paxton—are indicative of contemporary American attitudes. They are both book smart and are presumably off to graduate school in the near future. Paxton, the more adventurous of the two, urges Josh to take advantage of the opportunities afforded them. Hooking up with women and indulging in all manner of vice as they tour Europe, Josh and Paxton are the epitome of the American sense of entitlement, and they trade in the currency of American exceptionalism. When Josh accidently spills a local Dutchman's drink, thus prompting a physical altercation; Josh and his mates are thrown out of the club by a bouncer. Josh protests, "I'm an American. I got rights!" Assuming that his American privileges preempt local jurisdiction—a belief quite indicative of the American disposition—Josh confuses the privilege of consumption (entry into a nightclub) with his constitutional rights (e.g., free speech, fair trial). Purchase power opens up certain opportunities; it affords access to goods and services—it is not a right. And in a sense, this very issue permeates the entire *Hostel* narrative—where those who have purchase power command the ability to do whatever they want to another human being. Their money supersedes everyone else's rights—even the right to live. Josh and Paxton, joined by Oli, are clearly privileged and arrogant and believe the world is theirs for the taking—and more specifically that European women are theirs for the taking. Despite all of this, and no matter how book smart they are, they are not particularly attuned to their environment. Catering to the sadistic taste of rich patrons, Elite Hunting serves clients who pay thousands of dollars to do anything they want to another person. Clients pay $5,000 for a Russian, $10,000 for a European, and $25,000 for an American. In the second film, victims are auctioned off to the highest bidder.

"Why are you doing this?" is a question that is frequently asked during the course of a torture porn film. After being drugged, Josh finds himself hooded and strapped to a chair in a dark and dingy room equipped with a vast array of tools and surgical equipment. Once his torturer enters the room and unhoods him, he pleads for answers: "Who are you?" and "Where the fuck am I?" and then also "I didn't fucking do shit to you. What the fuck!" and "Please, I didn't fucking do anything." (In Eli Roth's 2007 film *Hostel: Part II*, Whitney pleads, "What did I do wrong?") Josh, the smart and "responsible one," as Paxton refers to him, is utterly bewildered by his situation. Many of the other victims in the *Hostel* films ask similar questions of their torturers. All this pleading distinctly resonates with that post-9/11 question "Why do they hate us so much?" Josh's predicament—hooded, drugged, and secreted away—also shares affinities with the CIA rendition program.

In the slasher film, the final girl brings about the conditions that allow for the restoration of order; a resolution, though, is rarely found in a torture porn film. The first installment of *Hostel* (and *Saw* for that matter) invited speculation that we might witness the rise of the "final boy," but no such trend in the end materialized. Nonetheless, our "final boy" in *Hostel*, Paxton, manages to escape—even inflicting some "righteous" vengeance along the way—but he ultimately never brings about the conditions that suggest that the world has been set right. The infrastructure of Elite Hunting is very much left intact, and in fact Paxton in the opening of *Part II* is petrified, for good reason, that Elite Hunting will eventually track him down, which is precisely what happens. In the first film, he nonetheless exacts revenge in the spirit of *The Last House on the Left*.

After Paxton makes his getaway on a train out of Slovakia, he by chance hears the Dutch torturer on the train (the same man who killed his friend Josh). Stalking him like prey, Paxton kills him in a train-station bathroom in a capricious act of revenge. Paxton is deliberate in his vengeance, though—while struggling with his German-speaking torturer, Paxton loses two of his fingers, and he retaliates in kind by severing two of the Dutch businessman's fingers with a scalpel. Looming over the Dutchman, Paxton grabs the businessman by the hair, pulls his head back to expose his neck, and while reflected in a chrome fixture, slashes the man's throat. Earlier in the film, the Dutch businessman dispatched Josh in virtually an identical fashion—with the Dutchman and Josh reflected in a broken mirror.[1] The nondiegetic score now emphasizes Paxton in the role of torturer, with a track that is similar to the scoring in the torture chamber.[2] This capricious act of vengeance sets Paxton apart from the torturers, though, as they are sadistic in the clinical sense and are governed by a set of rules (i.e., the syndicate's code). Paxton, on the other hand, is driven by emotions. Paxton is set in a long tradition of cinematic characters in the thriller/horror genre that, like the Collingwood parents in Wes Craven's

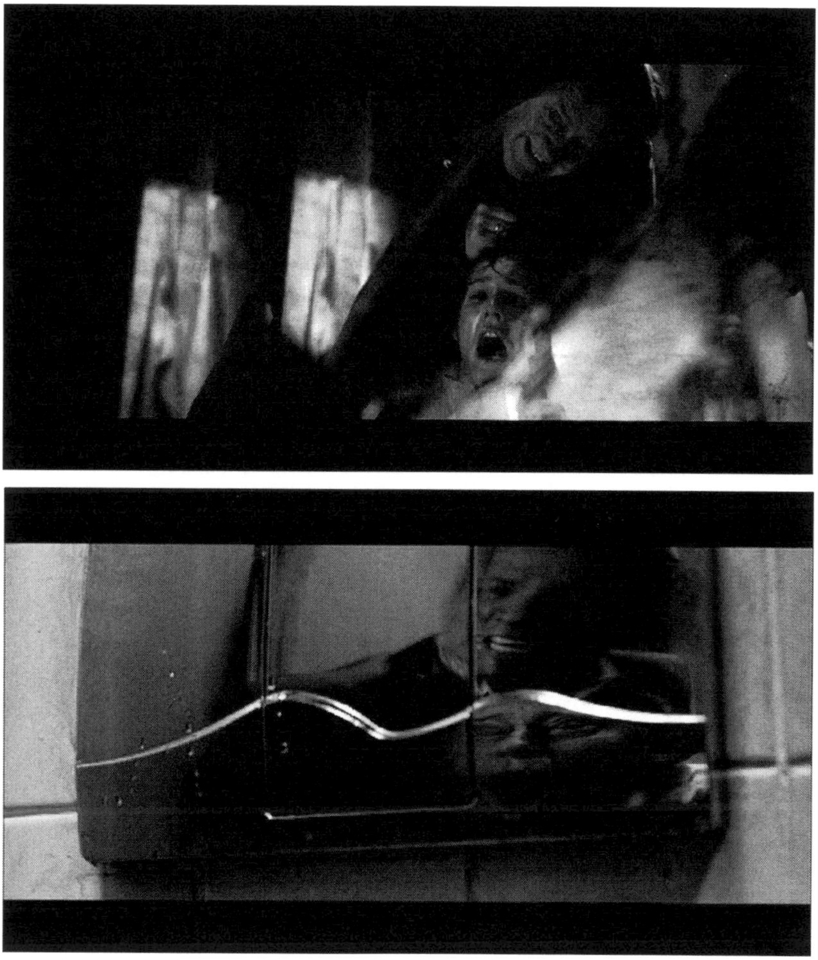

5.1 Tit-for-tat violence in *Hostel* (Eli Roth, 2005).

1972 film *The Last House on the Left*, exact revenge in the latter part of the narrative.

The reversal in which the tortured becomes the torturer, which Jeremy Morris identifies as a key trope of torture porn, is also analyzed in Jason Middleton's article on *Hostel*.[3] Similarly, Adam Lowenstein identifies a series of parallels in the *Hostel* films.[4] Josh, Paxton, and Oli in the first *Hostel* film exercise their "power and privilege" but have this turned back against them, as they change "from subjects seeking to consume to objects to be consumed."[5] Middleton reads this reversal as the thematic rehearsing of "American economic and political power, power whose misuse has led to a broadly unfavorable worldwide view of the nation."[6] While *Hostel*, at least initially, "constructs its protagonists' attitudes and actions to evoke the American cultural arrogance that underlies such abuses of power," in the end, the film "distances its surviving protagonist from these flaws."[7] *Hostel* legitimizes Paxton's violence as the surviving protagonist, Middleton subsequently argues, and "resonates with neoconservative perspectives on the justness and necessity of American aggression within a dangerous world."[8] Without dismissing this position, and fully appreciating that what becomes manifest in a film and what a filmmaker may intend might be two radically different things, I would suggest that Roth views "righteous vengeance" as tawdry, jingoistic, and morally bankrupt. The allusion to *The Last House on the Left* plot, if nothing else, already points to a strong sense of cinematic self-awareness and to the fact that the "revenge fantasy" is exactly that—a fantasy. Unlike Middleton, I posit that the overwrought action/thriller genre conventions in the latter third of the film are more farce than an affirmation of a "conservative vision of American violence as sometimes justifiable and necessary," as Middleton concludes.[9]

Eli Roth and Quentin Tarantino are kindred spirits—they consume cinematic bodies. The affection that Tarantino holds for Brian De Palma and Sergio Leone is self-evident in his films, as is his appreciation for a whole host of lesser-known foreign and exploitation filmmakers. Like Tarantino, Roth also makes nods to other filmmakers. The affinities between Roth and Tarantino run deep, with the latter being the executive producer of the *Hostel* films, and Tarantino cast Roth as Sergeant Donny Donowitz in his 2009 Holocaust revenge fantasy *Inglourious Basterds*.[10] In 1994, Roth received a Student Academy Award for his NYU thesis film *Restaurant Dogs*, a take on Tarantino's 1992 film *Reservoir Dogs*.

Tarantino is no stranger to extreme violence; the infamous ear-cutting scene in his heist movie *Reservoir Dogs* bears some of the hallmarks that we now associate with torture porn. When a heist goes bad, Mr. Pink, Mr. White, and Mr. Blond (Blondie) take a cop hostage (later we learn that his name is Marvin Nash). The cop is bound to a chair with duct tape, similar to Josh in the first installment of *Hostel* and so many other unfortunate characters that populate torture porn. The setting is quite spare—a functional warehouse space, bathed in a dingy pale green. Although the warehouse is adjacent to a residential area, it contains the violence, keeping it within a hermetic space. Other accents in the mise-en-scène evoke contemporary horror, including chains hanging from the ceiling and a toilet at the back corner of the warehouse, which is fully exposed and is not all that different from the industrial bathroom found in *Saw* (James Wan, 2004). The color scheme is quite similar to that of *Saw*, too.

What sets this scene apart from torture porn conventions is the use of interrogational torture. The spoiled heist suggests that the cops were tipped off somehow. Nice Guy Eddie Cabot arrives on scene and finds Mr. White and Mr. Pink using Nash as a punching bag. Nice Guy Eddie asks, "Why you beating on him?" Mr. Pink replies, "Maybe he can tell us who the fuck set us up." In an almost prophetic gesture, as if to anticipate the debates about the efficacy of torture in the post-9/11 era, Nice Guy Eddie admonishes, "If you fucking beat this prick long enough, he'll tell you he started the goddamn Chicago fire. Now that don't necessarily make it fucking so! Come on, man, think!"

After Nice Guy Eddie, Mr. Pink, and Mr. White leave, Blondie is left alone with the bound cop. Unlike Mr. Pink and Mr. White, who intend to get information from Nash, Blondie has no such interest, and more in keeping with torture porn, his violence is noninterrogational, torture for the sake of it. "Look, kid, I'm not going to bullshit you, okay?" Blondie says to the bound cop. "I don't really give a good fuck what you know or don't know. But I'm going to torture you anyway, regardless. Not to get information. It's amusing to me to torture a cop. You can say anything you want 'cause I've heard it all before." Reinforcing his noninterrogational interest in violence, Blondie then proceeds to duct tape the cop's mouth. Blondie then adds, "All you can do is pray for a quick death, which you ain't going to get." Blondie pulls out his gun, pointing it at the bound cop, who violently squirms. Blondie chuckles at the sight of his terrified victim; he walks away, places his gun aside, pulls a straight razor from his cowboy boot, and asks, "You ever listen to K-Billy's Super Sounds of the Seventies? It's my personal favorite." Blondie turns on the radio and tunes it, and "Stuck in the Middle with You" plays. Blondie begins to dance with the popular tune and slashes the cop in the face (similar to Dexter Morgan's ritual of cutting his victims' cheek to extract blood for his trophy). Blondie, astride his bound victim, commands him, "Hold still!" while the camera tilts upward and pans to the left, leaving the violence just offscreen, and Blondie cuts off the cop's right ear with the straight razor. Much is left to the imagination, as there is very little explicit gore, which makes this scene more in line with the soft-core horror that we find on television (a subject discussed in chapter 7). Nevertheless, the elements of torture porn—the setting, the chair, the bound victim, the noninterrogational torture—are evident and certainly inform the exhibition of violence in the *Hostel* films.

Like Tarantino, Roth finds the Grand Guignol spectacles associated with exploitation films, especially those from the 1970s and '80s, thrilling. And this certainly seeps into the aesthetics and the content of torture porn. David Edelstein bemoans this abject seepage: "Explicit scenes of torture and mutilation were once confined to the old 42nd Street, the Deuce, in gutbucket Italian cannibal pictures like *Make Them Die Slowly*, whereas now they have terrific production values and a place of honor in your local multiplex."[11] It is not simply that this material exists—recall that Edelstein says he made peace with the horror genre long ago. Rather, what is disturbing is that this brand of excessive gore and violence has crept into the mainstream. (Truth be told, though, the *Hostel* films are nowhere as gory as critics such as Edelstein make them out to be—there is little explicit gore.) Roth in interview after interview recites the cathartic value of the horror genre. In a world rocked by terrorism, the cataclysmic Hurricane Katrina (and the inept and racist-tinged response to it), and (now) more than a decade of war, the extreme nature of real-world violence demands a proportional response in the fictional world.

Despite claims that the *Hostel* films do not offer narrative contextualization for the exhibition of violence, Roth is, in fact, a competent visual storyteller. Take for instance one of the most vivid exhibitions of violence in *Hostel: Part II*. Lorna, the mousy virgin, is strung upside down, hanging above a large bathing basin lined with candles. A woman, perhaps in her midforties, without ever uttering a word, enters the torture chamber, disrobes, lies in the basin, and proceeds to cut Lorna's skin with a scythe. This image of a woman bathing in the blood of a virgin is clearly drawn from the legend of Hungarian Countess Elizabeth Bathory, who supposedly bathed in the blood of virgins to keep her youthful appearance.[12] Bram Stoker's *Dracula* is largely premised on this historical sixteenth-century countess. Roth makes no bones about it; this particular scene conflates sexual satisfaction and violence. Indeed, doused in Lorna's blood, the female figure heaves in ecstasy, caressing her body and masturbating.[13] Censors, critics, and self-appointed morality police claim that this scene, and others like it, is gratuitous and that there is no narrative contextualization for it. What so many appear to miss is how this particular scene is literally framed—immediately prior to the Bathory scene and immediately following it, Roth shows Lorna's friends bathing in therapeutic natural hot springs. Cutting directly from the Bathory scene back to the spa, the wafting smoke of a candle snuffed out with blood matches with the succeeding shot of steam rising from the natural hot spring—visually emphasizing the (narrative) link between the two diegetic spaces. At the spa, the camera tilts down, and in the background, to the right of the screen, an elderly couple enjoys the soothing waters, before Axelle's figure enters and commands the frame. (Axelle, like Alex in the first film, is the sultry figure that lures the American women to Slovakia.) Wearing a black bikini, she is a fetishistic spectacle, an embodiment of the very convention of beauty, a youthful nubile body. Roth gives the audience enough credit to make a connection *visually* between pursuit of youth and beauty in the Bathory legend and the Slovakian spa. It is no accident that the film cuts from the Bathory scene to the spa, where we see an elderly couple followed by the femme fatale, Axelle—a young Bathory in the making. Urging Beth—one of the American women lured to Slovakia—to "relax," Axelle caresses her back, pulls her hair aside, and moves in, kissing her neck as if she were a vampiress. Through editing, the act of brutal violence is thus given narrative context, but Roth relies on spectators' intertextual knowledge and their capacity to consume the narrative as a visual spectacle.[14]

5.2 The Bathory sequence in *Hostel: Part II* (Eli Roth, 2007).

Earlier I spoke of the negative critical reception of torture porn as a disguised prejudice against spectacle-driven films and posited that this was the result of a critical paradigm not altogether capable of addressing the emphasis on visual and audio design. The emphasis on visual storytelling in the Bathory sequence is a case in point, but there is something else potentially at work in the negative reviews, without the critics explicitly saying as much—a failure in genre. Like Tarantino, who might slip between war movie, heist movie, spaghetti western, revenge fantasy, and spy thriller in a single film (*Inglourious Basterds*), torture porn does not necessarily conform to the conventions of horror—especially as it has been conceived over the past thirty to fifty years either in its more psychological form (*Psycho*, *Rosemary's Baby*, *Carrie*) or its form as body horror that makes spectators jump in their seats, lurch, perhaps even laugh (*Halloween*, *Friday the 13th*, *Alien*, *Scream*). The *Saw* films, and this is especially true of the first installment, are in some respects closer to police procedurals and thrillers than to horror—recall that *Saw* draws heavily from *Se7en*. The *Hostel* films, on the other hand, straddle any number of genres—bro-com, thriller, exploitation.

Critics, then, unable to contextualize torture porn films within an existing genre, presume that the films are incoherent—a compendium of brutality lacking any organizing principle. Torture porn's violation is not its crass content, though some critics focus on this as something of a MacGuffin, but rather its perceived failure to conform to the conventions of what is understood as "mainstream" horror—torture porn, then, is a trespasser, an impersonator, in the hallowed halls of our local multiplex. Kaleem Aftab sums it up: "Narrative development is a mere inconvenience in" the splatter/exploitation films of the 1960s, "but at least these films knew their place in B-movie theatres."[15] David Edelstein is not that harsh and is not afraid to admit that *Hostel*, on its own terms, is a fairly good film. "It's actually not a bad little thriller, if you can live with the odd protracted sequence of torture and dismemberment."[16] The backhanded compliment, nevertheless, makes it clear that the bleeding of one genre into another is not kosher. Critics unable to contextualize these films project onto them their own failure to break free of calcified genre regimes. Rather than reflecting on the evolution of genres or their own assumptions about a genre, the critics instead cast aspersions on the filmmaker—it is not my fault (that I cannot contextualize this film); it is the filmmaker's fault (for making a film that does not conform to decades-old conventions).

Hostel, much in the way that Tarantino utilizes multiple genre tropes, can be partitioned chronologically into three discrete sections, each with its own distinctive genre hallmarks. (Analogously, *Hostel: Part II* might be partitioned into thirds as well.) The first part of the film unfolds as a bromance, in which Josh, Paxton, and Oli, in the spirit of fraternity high jinks, drink to excess and try to hook up with local women or fellow travelers.[17] The median segment of the narrative, in which Elite Hunting ensnares the young men, satisfies the horror constituency. Paxton's escape unfolds as a classic Hollywood thriller, akin to John Schlesinger's 1976 film *Marathon Man* (I discuss this film at some length later in the chapter). The color and lighting schemes generally correspond to their respective genres—the thriller and bromance segments tend to use natural lighting or, when set within an interior space, high-key lighting. The horror segment is decidedly darker in color palette and favors low-key lighting. Likewise, the nondiegetic and diegetic audio design conforms to the respective genres; dialogue is "naturalistic" in the bromance and thriller segments, whereas the horror segment is more reverberant, with voices echoing through concrete industrial spaces. Nondiegetic scoring in the first segment is largely rock driven and coupled with diegetic club music. The horror segment is richly textured with drones and wailing string instrumentation and is accented with a vast array of diegetic elements—dripping water, screams, crying, rattling chains, power tools, creaking, and slamming doors. The thriller segment is shockingly conventional, dominated by brass instruments and textured with racing strings.

Like Tarantino, Roth is an informed filmmaker self-aware of genre conventions. In the end, though, Roth could never match the real-world horrors visited on humanity. The *Hostel* films are not obscene; they reflect what is. What is obscene is the violence that human beings perpetrate against one another. What is obscene is that the president of the United States, "George [W.] Bush doesn't care about black people," as Kanye West stated on live national television in the aftermath of Hurricane Katrina.[18] The *Hostel* films, and torture porn, while clearly informed by our post-9/11 experience, at the same time address the American economy of violence.

I'm Going to Go Medieval on Your Ass . . . or Japanese or Korean or . . .

I imagine that Kaleem Aftab had Eli Roth in mind when he stated, "Torture porn is possibly the worst movement in the history of cinema."[19] Who could have thought up such ghastly acts, right? The fact is, though, that history is littered with the corpses of tortured bodies, and the implicit question "Who thinks up all this sick stuff?" very well might give Roth far too much credit. Even within the diegesis of the first *Hostel* film, Roth reminds his viewers of this fact (again, something that the critics conveniently forget), when Josh and Paxton visit the "Museum Tortury." Roth presents us with the ghoulish historical instruments of torture—the miniature guillotine used to "punch" visitors' tickets, the eighteenth-century Witch's Chair, the hanging cage, the hooded henchman—if nothing else, the filmmaker demonstrates just how staid the torture in the *Hostel* films is.[20] Or seen in a more flattering light, Roth predicts the wagging finger of moral discontent, and the exhibition of medieval torture devices set in a post-9/11 world demonstrates just how little we have progressed—so that the euphemism "enhanced interrogation" quickly runs up against, as Cullen Murphy observes, the sixteenth-century Roman Inquisition's "*rigoroso esamine*, or 'rigorous examination.'"[21] The truth of it is that the vehement moral indignation is nothing but show, a hollow and tawdry gesture, and disavows any stake in the violence that is being perpetrated on our behalf.

The history of human violence is something that Roth certainly draws on, but so too is the wealth of cinematic violence. One should not be seen wholly separate from the other—there is a distinct interplay between fictional torture and real-life torture. Inexperienced interrogators drew from the Fox Network's *24* for examples on how to interrogate detainees at the Guantánamo Bay facility.[22] Likewise, fiction films, such as exploitation films from the 1970s, have drawn from popular accounts of torture. For instance, Don Edmonds's 1975 film *Ilsa: She-Wolf of the SS* includes a scene in which a female subject is exposed to rapid decompression—gleaning from the historical record, the Nazis actually conducted experiments to determine how much the human body could tolerate, for instance, when being subjected to the sudden loss of air pressure in an aircraft.

Along with exploitation cinema, Italian *giallo* films, and proto-slashers (e.g., *Pieces*, *Torso*), Roth enthusiastically acclaims the relatively recent trend of extreme cinema in Asia, as well as more conventional horror films coming out of Korea and Japan, respectively known as K-horror and J-horror. Roth's films are an interesting confluence of cinematic history. Roth particularly admires Japanese filmmaker Takashi Miike, known for his extreme films (for instance,

Audition, 1999, and *Ichi the Killer*, 2001), and cast him in a small part in *Hostel* as an unnamed syndicate client.

With respect to audio design, in particular, we might take J-horror as something of a transition between the slashers, ending with Wes Craven's 1996 film *Scream*, and torture porn. Using Takashi Shimizu's 2002 film *Ju-on* as an example, when Rika, one of the primary female characters, drops in on a social service client, she is spooked by the house, as underscored by a nondiegetic synthesizer (3:50) that suggests the presence of the uncanny. Alone, the visual image is quite banal; it is the audio that informs us of the dreadful things that lurk there. The synthesizer, more metallic or "inorganic" than a common analog instrument (e.g., piano, violin), can be viewed as a bridge between the nondiegetic scores associated with American slasher films such as *Halloween* and *A Nightmare on Elm Street* and what emerges in the audioscapes of torture porn.

Although torture porn does not include supernatural elements, the films nonetheless trade heavily in the aesthetic tropes associated with ghost stories—which J-horror films invariably are. Narratives featuring haunted houses (and this is distinctly evident in *Ju-on*) utilize squeaky doors, stairs, and floorboards; the rattling of chains (or some household fixture—in the case of *Ju-on*, a chandelier; 4:40); the sudden slamming of doors or windows; the howl of the wind whistling through the house. Many of these stock audio devices associated with the horror genre are also found in the *Hostel* films. *Ju-on* replaces the stock horror cliché of howling wind with a synthetic drone (5:15), and it produces a similar effect. However, whereas wind is woven into the fabric of the diegetic sound design, the synthetic drone such as we find in *Ju-on* straddles the diegetic and nondiegetic register. As an audio source in between, without a category, unhinged from the diegetic realm, it evokes abjection. Roth's film prior to the first *Hostel* film, *Cabin Fever* (2002), is closer to the slasher tradition or to films such as *The Evil Dead* (Sam Raimi, 1981). Nathan Barr, the composer for Roth's 2002 feature who also did the original scoring for the two *Hostel* films, explains that for *Cabin Fever*, he and Roth "experimented with musical effects that were almost sound effects": "We did that, for example, in the opening titles, where you can't really tell if it's sound effects: Is it musical effects? What is it? It sort of takes on this other, completely eerie quality."[23] This happens frequently in torture porn—screams, for instance, might originate within the diegetic environment but then, using an effects processor, be abstracted and modulated to such a degree that they are unbounded from the narrative space and stitched into the fabric of the nondiegetic environment. This audio strategy is also evident in J-horror. During a flashback in *Ju-on*, for instance, Rika's scream (1:24:06), which is asynchronic to begin with, is difficult to locate. Is the scream understood as the reemergence of a past scream into the diegetic space? Is it internal diegetic (an imagined scream)? Or is it simply a nondiegetic element? Its wispy character dissolves into the nondiegetic score, straddling the diegetic/nondiegetic audioscape.

Early in *Ju-on*, when Rika discovers a boy trapped in an upstairs closet, she is confounded (the boy is actually a ghost). She returns downstairs to quiz the elderly woman she is attending to, but the woman is nearly catatonic and unhelpful. Rika then calls her associate at the social service office but gets no answers and is still unsure of what to do. The low rumbling drone, more physical in its "bassiness," something felt more than heard, suddenly crescendos (13:09) with a crashing twang—along the lines of an industrial warehouse's metal roller door slamming shut.[24] This audio element is the synthetic equivalent of the sudden clap of thunder at the discovery of something frightful. And this is precisely how this explosive audio element is used. The bassy drone accompanies Rika as she mounts the stairs—the stairs *of course* creak as she does this—and when she finds the child peering through the stairway banister above her, the startling moment is accompanied by this nondiegetic eruption. The synthetic nondiegetic audio elements all have a metallic timbre, and this particular metallic quality is distinctly evident in the torture porn audioscape as well. Just as in *Ju-on*, in *Hostel* and other torture porn films, we find highly embellished sound designs, dressing the audioscape with an array of reverberant sounds—rattling chains, locks or latches clicking into place, doors slamming open or shut, rusty hinges creaking. Sound design is supremely important in the horror genre in general—it is one of the most significant elements that determine a film's affective charge. And Roth is keenly aware of this; he would never submit a version with a finished audio track of his film to the MPAA, the American film ratings board. "If you submit your movie with all the sound effects," Roth says, "it's going to be more horrific."[25]

Korean films, and most especially Chan-wook Park's vengeance trilogy—*Sympathy for Mr. Vengeance* (2002), *Oldboy* (2003), and *Lady Vengeance* (2005)—have also been highly influential for Roth. These films are not horror films but rather are more in keeping with dramatic thrillers; these films nonetheless include elements of extreme violence. In relation to *Hostel*, Roth speaks about the influence of Asian extreme cinema, specifically Takashi Miike and Park, saying, "They aren't exactly pure horror movies. . . . There is a wave of these ultraviolent films that are much more horrific than scary. . . . It's about real people, doing real things, and it's just horrifying and disturbing. And that's the type of film that I really wanted to make."[26] This "realistic" element is a key trope found in torture porn—real people doing terrible things to others. While Park's films are unapologetically violent, they are not shoddy—visually, his films are patient, perhaps even meditative, and undeniably lavish in their cinematography and color. Certainly nowhere as contemplative as Park, Roth nonetheless is a gifted visual storyteller, and a number of critics, if begrudgingly, acknowledge this.[27] From the more implicit tone to more explicit nods—the severing of Josh's Achilles tendon is taken directly from Park's *Sympathy for Mr. Vengeance*, for instance—Korean and Japanese films have left their mark on the *Hostel* films.

Oldboy exhibits many of the tropes of torture porn. Dae-su Oh, the primary male character, is held in captivity for fifteen years. In an apartment building repurposed as a detention facility, Dae-su is kept in solitary confinement in a small studio apartment. His only contact with the world is a television and his speechless captors, who shove trays of food through a small slot at the base of the apartment door. The studio is rigged with surveillance equipment monitored by the captors. A bank of monitors reveals that this is a sophisticated network; Dae-su is just one of many detainees. When his captors need to enter the studio, a gas, accompanied by a disturbingly chirpy domestic chime, is pumped into the small apartment (the gas, as we learn, is the same that the Russians used during a Chechen terrorist hostage situation). The repurposed apartment shares certain affinities with the retrofitted Slovakian factory in the *Hostel* films or the postapocalyptic depiction of limbo in Aleksander Nordaas's 2008 nine-minute short *In Chambers*.[28] We also learn that Dae-su's captor is merely a "gun for hire" and, like Elite Hunting, is simply providing a service to a rich client, Woo-jin Lee, who has a score to settle with Dae-su. The retooled apartment building as a detention facility (like a CIA black site), the sophisticated network catering to rich clients, the surveillance equipment, the link to terrorism—all these elements in some form materialize in the *Hostel* films.

When Dae-su is finally released, completely ignorant of his offense, he lives only for vengeance. Tracking down the syndicate responsible for detaining him for fifteen years, Dae-su tortures the syndicate owner to determine who orchestrated his incarceration. Dae-su "persuades" the syndicate owner by pulling out his teeth with a claw hammer, extracting one tooth for every year of captivity. With duct tape, Dae-su straps the syndicate owner to a chair, immobilizes his head, and pries his mouth open. The use of involuntary dental work places *Oldboy* in a continuum of films that influenced the *Hostel* films, namely, *Marathon Man* and *The Last House on the Left*. Finally confronting the antagonist of the film, Woo-jin says, "It's a game," giving Dae-su five days to figure out the riddle. Without giving anything away, Woo-jin sets in motion a highly complex and intricate plan that would make Jigsaw marvel. Although self-interested, Woo-jin, like the *Saw* pro(an)tagonist, seeks justice and achieves his objective by "playing a game," introducing both the game motif and a countdown into the *Oldboy* narrative similar to what we find in the *Saw* franchise. The retributive element in *Oldboy*, if not the whole vengeance trilogy, is most clearly aligned, though, with the basic plot of the *Hostel* films, in which a character escapes and reaps revenge—Paxton in the first installment, Beth in the second, and Scott in the third.

Lady Vengeance, like *Oldboy*, is also quite influential. Wrongly convicted Geum-ja Lee serves a thirteen-year prison term for kidnapping and murdering a child. Geum-ja, the lady vengeance of our story, devises an elaborate plan to bring Mr. Baek to "justice"—it is Baek who kidnaps children, holds them for ransom, and in the end kills them. Geum-ja seeks vengeance not only for her own peace of mind but also for the other families that have lost children to

5.3 An example of a violent flashback mediated through video in *Lady Vengeance* (Chan-wook Park, 2005).

Baek. Like other films at the periphery of torture porn—*Wolf Creek*, *A Serbian Film*, *Caché*—Park uses a video camera (plugged into a television monitor) as a device to enter a flashback, and to mediate violence, where we witness Baek's treatment of his young abductees. Geum-ja assembles the families touched by Baek's crimes at an abandoned school in a remote rural area. The school, with its institutional character, shares some of the hallmarks of the Slovakian factory in the *Hostel* films. Not only does the classroom where Baek is held, bound to a chair (of course), resonate with the Slovakian torture facility, but the floor, which is lined with heavy plastic sheeting, is also quite similar to what we find in Dexter's kill rooms. The affinities between Park's vengeance trilogy and Roth's films are fairly transparent. What sets the *Hostel* films apart is that not only are the proper channels of authority corrupt, but justice is never fully satisfied. Individual characters might "get what they deserve," but the infrastructure of Elite Hunting remains unscathed.

Holocaust Contours

Quite a number of torture porn films follow the contours of Holocaust visual culture—as established by documentaries (e.g., *Night and Fog*, *Memory of the Camps*), dramatized accounts (e.g., *The Pawnbroker*, *The Night Porter*, *Salò, or the 120 Days of Sodom*), and even patently tasteless exploitation films (e.g., *Salon Kitty*, *Ilsa: She-Wolf of the SS*). To be clear, torture porn films are not necessarily drawing from the historical event per se but more specifically from the ways in which it has been represented. Perhaps owing to Roth's own biography—descended from a European Jewish family—the *Hostel* films bear the most distinctive traces of Holocaust imagery in the torture porn genre.

While watching Eli Roth's 2005 film *Hostel*, I was suddenly captivated by the image before me, and it had very little to do with the grim exhibition of torture—Josh's torturer drilling holes into his hapless victim. Rather, the sparse concrete room reminded me of something, but what? Then it came to me in an instant, what Roland Barthes calls the "punctum."[29] I had seen this space before, I had walked through it, or at the very least I had been in a space very reminiscent of what I was seeing in *Hostel*—Crematorium I in the Main Camp of Auschwitz. While visiting the archives of the Auschwitz-Birkenau State Museum, I explored the Auschwitz complex. Of course, one of the most charged sites in the Main Camp is the gas chamber and crematorium, the only one remaining intact (the gas chambers and crematoria at Birkenau were all destroyed). What is perhaps most striking about the site is its sparseness—the bare concrete exhibiting the distinct patina of age. For me personally, a small detail caught my attention, a roughly chiseled-out square opening (actually I am not even sure what its function was—or if it was a postwar artifact), and I was startled to find it in *Hostel*. Like Crematorium I, the torture chamber in

5.4 Uncanny similarities between Auschwitz Crematorium I and Josh's torture chamber in *Hostel* (Eli Roth, 2005).

Hostel is decidedly sparse; the walls bear the characteristic wear of age, even a rectangular centrally placed window and that uncanny roughly carved-out square opening.

While this small detail in the set is particularly uncanny (at least for me), there are numerous other elements that connote the visual culture of the Holocaust. One of the very first lines of dialogue in the initial film includes a Holocaust reference, as Paxton and Oli debate whether to smoke pot or go to the red-light district in Amsterdam. Josh suggests instead, "Hey, I think the Anne Frank house is around here." The *Hostel* films draw not only from the signifiers of victimization but also from those of the perpetrators. In the first installment of the series, we discover that the emblem of the torture syndicate is a bloodhound. All the torturers—and all members of the syndicate,

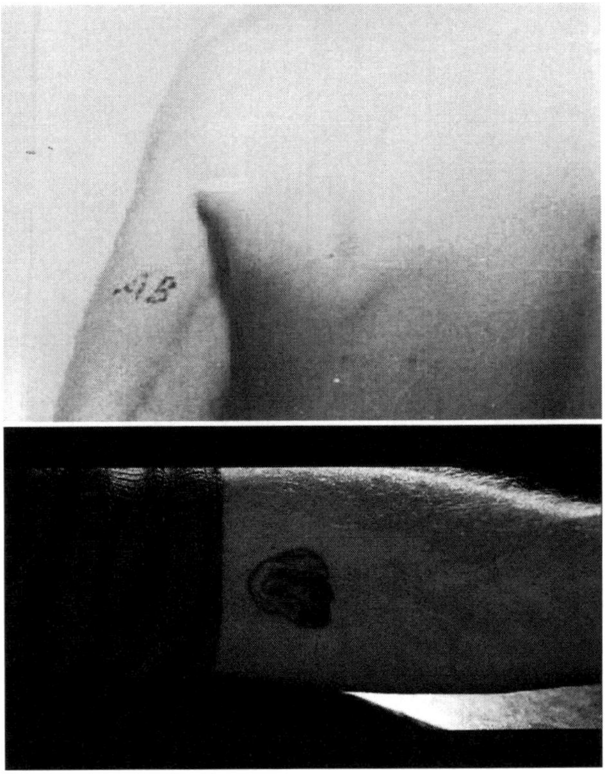

5.5 The blood-type tattoo of SS officers finds affinities with the tattooed bloodhound emblem of Elite Hunting in *Hostel* (Eli Roth, 2005).

all the employees—have the syndicate's tattoo. Our first encounter with the tattoo is when Josh sees it on the Dutch businessman's left arm. At first glance, the insignia in itself is nothing special; however, this tattoo implicitly relates the members of the syndicate to the SS, many of whom also had tattoos on their left underarm, indicating their affiliation with the Waffen-SS and the individual's blood type. Adopting the *blood*hound (on the left arm) as the syndicate's tattooed emblem corresponds with the tattooed *blood* type of the SS (on the left underarm).

Mastering the industrialization of death posed certain challenges for the Nazis—the discreet disposal of thousands of human bodies. To solve this problem, the engineers of genocide incorporated crematoria into their factories of death. One of the most potent images in both the *Hostel* films is the factory furnace used to cremate bodies. The abandoned Slovakian factory, retrofitted as a torture facility, is topped with a large smokestack, which echoes the profile of the concentration camp, where the crematoria smokestack—belching smoke and human ash—loomed large over the landscape infected with death and suffering. With armed men in black fatigues guarding the exterior gate of the facility, the concentration-camp imagery is more pronounced in *Part II*. In what is perhaps beefed-up security following Paxton's escape, the gate is more substantive, and guards command vicious German shepherds. When the clients have sated their bloodlust, Elite Hunting staff clean up, and a large hunchbacked undertaker hauls bodies (or in some instances body parts) into a room where they are then butchered into smaller pieces and unceremoniously tossed into an oven.

The mise-en-scène of *Hostel* is remarkably similar to Tim Blake Nelson's 2001 film *The Grey Zone*, set in the Auschwitz-Birkenau crematoria and gas chambers. Nelson's film dramatizes the Sonderkommando uprising in Auschwitz-Birkenau.[30] Composed of Jews in an isolated area of the camp, the Sonderkommando (the special work detail) conducted the most gruesome business in Nazi death camps: they led deportees into the undressing rooms, collected valuables (including the hair shorn from women), directed them into the "shower" where they were gassed en masse, removed the corpses, cleaned the gas chamber, and finally burnt the bodies, disposing of what remained. In one specific instance, we can track closely aligned sequences in *The Grey Zone* and *Hostel*: in *The Grey Zone*, when Hoffman, a member of the Sonderkommando, discovers an adolescent girl miraculously still breathing after a gassing, he attempts to save her. The audio design elicits the sensorial experience of disgust—sorting through corpses, the sloppy-slippery sounds of bodies slathered in human waste of all kinds, and water (after hosing down the gas chamber), as well as the Sonderkommando's footsteps on the wet concrete floor (49:28). The audio design, more than anything we see, emphasizes the gruesome nature of the task. Pulling the girl's body from a heap of corpses, Hoffman throws the limp, unconscious girl over his shoulder and places her in a freight elevator leading to the crematorium, stacked with other bodies. Hoffman bounds through the dark concrete halls to meet the elevator on the upper level and sees her body hurled across a cart. After reviving the girl, with the assistance of a doctor, a handful of Sonderkommando strategize in a locker room—what are they going to do with this girl?

This sequence of events in *The Grey Zone* closely follows Paxton's escape from the Slovakian torture facility in *Hostel*—Paxton, like the girl, escapes certain death. After dispatching his *German*-speaking torturer,[31] Paxton makes his way through a corridor; the industrial, bare-cement construction finds clear affinities with the functional architecture in the re-creation of the Auschwitz crematorium found in *The Grey Zone*. Hiding in a room, Paxton is compelled to play dead when the large undertaker comes to collect a heap of bodies stacked up on an industrial cart, almost identical to the one found in *The Grey Zone*. While on the cart passing through the halls, Paxton sees the facility in operation—a torturer presumably on his way to his torture cell flanked

5.6 Striking visual similarities found between *The Grey Zone* (Tim Blake Nelson, 2001) and *Hostel* (Eli Roth, 2005).

on either side by Elite Hunting security, a torture chamber being hosed down (strikingly similar to an earlier shot in *The Grey Zone*). The undertaker finally comes to a stop, rolling the cart of bodies into an industrial freight elevator. The elevator stops and is apparently adjacent to the undertaker's workshop (or butcher shop more like) and the facility's furnace. Paxton eventually finds himself in the locker room, where Elite Hunting clients suit up. Paxton meets an American client wearing standard-issue torture gear (red long-sleeve jumpsuit, leather smock, rubber cap, and surgical mask) in the locker room; luckily for Paxton, though, the American assumes that Paxton is just another client. The aprons worn by Sonderkommando in *The Grey Zone* resemble the butcher smocks worn by the torturers in the *Hostel* series. The cart of dismembered bodies pushed by the undertaker in *Hostel* evokes the industrialized killing and disposal of bodies as seen in *The Grey Zone*. The dingy, dark tones of the industrial setting, the locker room, the elevator that finally leads to an oven—all these things are common to both films.

The oven, the smokestack, and the piles of mutilated corpses are hard, if not impossible, to separate from the images that we associate with the Holocaust. The furnace is precisely where Roth's 2007 film *Hostel: Part II* begins; an unseen undertaker rummages through a victim's belongings, setting aside valuables and casting other personal possessions—clothing, a diary, photographs, and postcards—into the flames, which resonates with the Nazis' plundering of loot collected from deportees. This is very reminiscent of the early scenes in Ka Tzetnik 135633's Holocaust novel *House of Dolls*, which also includes

5.7 Hosing down the gas chamber in *The Grey Zone* (Tim Blake Nelson, 2001) closely matches the hosing down of a torture chamber in *Hostel* (Eli Roth, 2005).

descriptions of Nazis discarding photographs, letters, and other personal items, while retaining anything of monetary value.[32]

Roth's films specifically and the genre of torture porn in general also evoke an earlier thriller, John Schlesinger's 1976 film *Marathon Man*. In many ways, the content and the mise-en-scène of Schlesinger's thriller set the stage for the torture porn genre some thirty years later by pitting an innocent character against a clinical sadist. The primary male character, Babe, is a young graduate student in the History Department at Columbia University, writing a dissertation on tyranny. Babe's elder brother, Doc, is enmeshed in a world of international intrigue and inadvertently gets his young brother involved. The antagonist of the film, Christian Szell, has amassed a huge collection of diamonds confiscated from Jews during the Second World War, and Szell believes that Doc, before dying, has divulged information about the diamonds to his younger brother. Babe is genuinely innocent and knows nothing of the diamonds, but Szell has to be certain of this. Babe, then, functions much in the same way that the victims in torture porn do, and figuratively speaking, Babe could have fathered either Josh or Paxton—they are cut from the same cloth. Like Josh and Paxton in *Hostel*, Babe is book smart, attending graduate school, and despite this, not especially worldly. Josh is potentially coded as Jewish—after the group is thrown out of a club, Oli says to Josh, "I thought you were a Jew, man. This guy's a fucking Israeli!"[33] Babe—whose name is actually Thomas Levy—is coded Jewish as well.

Set against Babe—his name even connotes innocence—is the sadistic antagonist: Christian Szell, a Nazi war criminal. We learn that in Auschwitz, he was known as Der Weisser Engel (the White Angel) on account of his stark white hair. A character that obviously trades in the currency of the historical figure of Josef Mengele, the Angel of Death, Szell ran an experimental medical camp at Auschwitz. Arranging safe passage for Jews for substantive payments in diamonds, Szell also extracted gold fillings from Auschwitz internees before sending them off to their death. This plunder eventually ended up in a safety deposit box in New York City, managed by Szell's brother, while Szell himself is in hiding in Uruguay. When Szell's brother suddenly dies in a fiery car wreck, Szell, at great risk of capture, arrives in New York to recover his plundered treasure.

A dentist by trade, Szell approaches his work clinically. In terms of narrative content and form, a critical scene in which Szell employs his dental trade to torture Babe establishes a clear lineage between *Marathon Man* and the genre of torture porn. When Szell, with his two accomplices, enters the room where Babe is confined, he moves with purpose, opening his briefcase and placing his tool kit matter-of-factly on a worktable. Szell is clinical in manner and speech, never once losing his temper or letting his emotions get the better of him. Dressed in a three-piece suit, he retreats to the back corner of the room where there is a sink, removes his coat, and washes his hands as any professional doctor would. Szell then asks, "Is it safe?" Of course, Babe is utterly unaware of the saga unfolding all around him and is confused by the question. As Szell repeatedly asks, "Is it safe?" Babe searches for the answer that he wants to hear. Walking back over to the worktable, all the while calmly asking, "Is it safe?" Szell unfurls his tool kit, revealing an assortment of dental tools. Taking a pick and a dental mirror, Szell proceeds to examine Babe's teeth, but not before some resistance and fidgeting from the reluctant patient. Poking about, Szell finally asks, "That hurt?" Babe manages, "Uh-huh." "I should think it would," Szell admonishes. "You should take better care of your teeth. You have quite a cavity here." And then abruptly Szell asks again, "Is it safe?" Babe begins to answer before Szell firmly launches into the cavity with his pick, causing Babe to lurch and scream in pain. Convinced that Babe knows something, Szell calmly applies some clove oil to Babe's tooth. "Isn't that remarkable?" he says with a gentle smile. Babe feels instant relief. Szell steps back, holding the bottle of clove oil and the pick, and begins, "Life can be that simple. Relief, discomfort. Now which of these I next apply, that decision is in your hands, so take your time and tell me, is it safe?"

True to the sadist disposition, everything is meticulously planned. After this first round of dental procedures are over, Babe is dragged off to another room, where he is allowed to rest. One of Szell's accomplices nurses Babe, administering more clove oil to relieve the pain. A government agent, Janeway, surreptitiously enters the room, dispatching one of Szell's accomplices with a knife, gunning down the other, and springing Babe from the clutches of the former Nazi. In the getaway car, in an overwrought tone, Janeway reveals the plot—telling Babe about Szell's treasure and that Doc worked as a courier. He asks if Doc said anything before he died. Still, of course, Babe is clueless; he knows nothing of this international intrigue. The whole escape turns out to be a ruse, however; when the car comes to a stop, Babe finds himself exactly where he started and back in the hands of Szell's accomplices, who are very much still alive. In the true meaning of sadism, which is more about power and intellectual mastery, even the "escape" was intended to pump Babe for information. Babe once again finds himself in Szell's makeshift dentist's chair. This time, though, Szell brings out his electric drill and purposefully drills into a healthy tooth to inflict intense pain. He is finally assured that Babe knows nothing and instructs his accomplices to "get rid of him." It is no accident, then, that a power drill is used for the first torture scene in *Hostel*. While the drill in this instance is a household power drill, the affinities between Szell and his dentist's drill and the Dutch businessman (whose denied life ambition was to be a surgeon) are evident. (There is also an allusion to *Marathon Man* in the opening moments of season 3 of *Dexter*, in the premier episode, "Our Father.")

The mise-en-scène of this scene is very significant and illustrates the intimate link between the genre of torture porn and the representations of the Holocaust. Although it goes relatively unnoticed during the *Marathon Man* torture scene itself, in its aftermath, it is clear that Babe is wearing a robe and white-and-gray-striped pajama bottoms, evoking the attire associated with concentration-camp internees. At the beginning of the torture scene, Babe finds himself in a dark room, immobilized, confounded, and struggling to get his bearings, a situation remarkably similar in many respects to Josh's predicament in the first *Hostel* film. Suddenly, a single industrial light is turned on, and we discover that Babe is alone in a dingy room; his arms are strapped to the arms of a chair, and likewise his feet are strapped to the legs of the chair. The room is relatively small and sparse, an office in a larger warehouse. Though

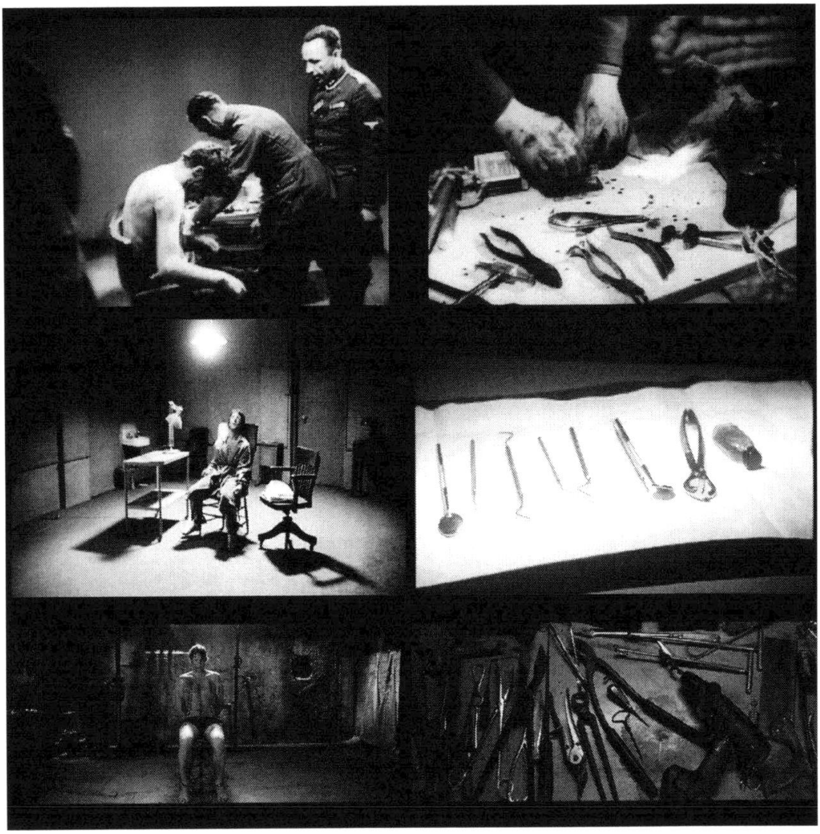

5.8 The heritage of torture porn tropes found in *Rome, Open City* (Roberto Rossellini, 1945), *Marathon Man* (John Schlesinger, 1976), through *Hostel* (Eli Roth, 2005).

modest by torture porn standards, Szell's collection of dental tools is laid across the makeshift worktable, and their display is intended to provoke anxiety not only in Babe but in the spectator as well. Shots panning across the instruments of pain are used in torture porn films too, much to the same effect, arousing an anxious anticipation in the viewer and in the hapless victim usually strapped to a table or chair. An earlier film that resonates with this trope but predates these films is Roberto Rossellini's 1945 film *Rome, Open City*, which exhibits many of the same characteristics: a Nazi torturer, a sparse room, a tortured subject strapped to a chair, ordinary household tools transfigured into instruments of torture.

The banality of the space, the decor, and the instruments displayed before the victim are charged with dread. The everydayness of the objects is recontextualized within the discourse of torture, designed to destabilize the order of things.[34] The dentist-torturer is not simply spawned by the commonly held dread of regular oral hygiene but is rooted in historical accounts of torture. As already cited in chapter 2, Elaine Scarry observes, "Reports of torture from prisoners in the Philippines include references to 'unwanted dental work.' . . . In Brazil, there were forms of torture called 'the mad dentist' and 'the operating table.'"[35] The topsy-turvy universe of torture is itself a weapon transforming "common domestic objects" into instruments of pain and suffering. And this is no mere accident; after all, as Scarry reminds us, "so much of our awareness of Germany in the 1940s is attached to the words 'ovens,' 'showers,' 'lampshades,' and 'soap.'"[36] The figure of Mengele (and the characters that are derivatives of him, including Szell) then also fit in this topsy-turvy universe, as the acts of a man of science, of medicine, whose pledge to "do no harm" is radically turned on its head. Here, then, is yet another example of inversion, a critical trope in torture porn.

Whether in life or in art, the environment that the tortured subject inhabits "is limited to the room and its contents; no other concrete embodiments of civilization pass through the doors."[37] The signature enclosed space in torture porn films corresponds to the sadist's reliance on a hermitic universe, where within a strictly defined space, nothing is abject. And from this perspective, it is possible to see how the torture chamber in torture porn films is an overdetermined site, alluding to representations of the concentration camp, to the libertine's universe in Sade's novels, and to earlier cinematic depictions of torture and post-9/11 imagery. While the space where pain is administered in *Marathon Man* is relatively sterile, albeit a bit dingy, what distinguishes it from its torture porn progeny is that in torture porn, the torture chamber typically exhibits symptoms of abjection. The torture chamber in the torture porn genre is frequently a dank, dark, damp space—walls and pipes seep, water (or some other fluid) drips, surfaces are discolored or stained, colored in the various shades of fecal matter. And in the fecal palette, the torture chamber in torture porn approaches the conceptualization of the concentration camp, which some people referred to as *anus mundi*—the asshole of the world.[38] Most of *Saw*, interestingly enough, takes place in a bathroom.

"This Is Business": Pornography and Sadism

> People that come to see *Hostel: Part II* they want some of the fun, and they want some of the sex, and they want some of the humor. But they want to see some gnarly shit happening to people; they want to see people gettin' fucked up bad.
> —Eli Roth

There is a strong sadistic current that runs through the *Saw* franchise, in the clinical sense. (I addressed this issue in the previous chapter.) Many of the sadistic elements materialize in the gaming motif in the *Saw* films, and what the game allows for is the abolition of civil mores. While it is true that Jigsaw and his disciples spring the traps, once a game begins, it is entirely up to the player/victim either to scrupulously follow the rules of the game and win/live or to flout the rules and lose/die. Completely divorced from any human sentimentality and governed strictly by the rules of a game, Jigsaw ensures that violence is "appropriately" channeled through the sadistic regime.

The gaming motif is also evident in the *Hostel* films—particularly in the second and third installments of the series. Whereas in the first film, different nationalities sell apparently for a fixed rate, in *Part II*, victims are auctioned to the highest bidder. The competitive bidding is framed as a sport, wealthy bidders jockeying for position and attempting to outbid one another. Todd, the winning bidder, interestingly enough is about to tee off, evidently playing a round of golf with visiting Japanese businessmen. While Todd and Stuart, Todd's friend, wait for Elite Hunting to notify them that their torture chamber is ready, they entertain themselves at a local brothel, but Todd—unsatisfied with sexual conquests—toasts, "To the next level," evoking the videogame vernacular. And as the pair enters the venue, he adds, "Let the games begin."[39]

Part III is set in Las Vegas, which by virtue of its location, already points toward the gaming motif. The main floor of the Las Vegas Elite Hunting franchise is arranged as part theater, part casino. Well-dressed and bejeweled Elite Hunting clients lounge at tables; scantily clad women serve drinks, and at the front of the room, behind thick glass and a red velvet curtain, scenes of torture are enacted on a stage. Clients play the "Wheel of Misfortune," placing bets on the outcome of the staged scenarios—Will the victim plead with the torturer, "I have children"? Will the victim attempt to bargain with the torturer with the promise of money, "I can pay you"? At the end of the Grand Guignol theater, the clients applaud the performer.

The staging here actually comes very close to Sade's scenario in *The 120 Days of Sodom*. Just as the storytellers are commanded to provide salacious tales to fuel the four libertines' imagination in Sade's dirty little novel, the staged performances aim to captivate the spectators in *Part III*. Sade explains in *The 120 Days of Sodom* that the libertines assembled in a circular room every day to hear one of the four storytellers' episodes; they each sat in recesses that faced the center of the room. The storyteller, set as if on a stage, sat in the center. Sade tells his readers, "in this position she was not only well before the four niches intended for her auditors, but, the circle being small, was close enough to them to insure their hearing every word she said, for she was placed like an actor in a theater, and the audience in their niches found themselves situated as if observing a spectacle in an amphitheater."[40] Roland Barthes, addressing the theatrical nature of Sade's scenario, observes, "In this theater everyone is actor and spectator."[41] And this is particularly true in *Part III*, as the clients/spectators wager on (that is, act on) the fate of the victims/players (and in that sense "actors").

Unlike the *Saw* franchise, in which the sadistic disposition rests within the game motif, sadism is found elsewhere in the *Hostel* films: business. Elite Hunting maintains a strict code of conduct, its underlying principles governed by the application of the most stoic form of free-market capital. Untethered from any sentimentality, the syndicate replicates the will of nature, applying the Darwinian doctrine that only the most (financially) fit survives. Surrendering all ethical accountability to the will of market forces releases the syndicate client from any basic obligation to civil principles. Fraternity, goodwill, compassion, any recognizable form of humanity are utterly meaningless within the syndicate's universe.

Take, for instance, the climactic moment of *Part II*. Beth—Stuart's intended victim due to her uncanny resemblance to his wife—manages to get the upper hand of the situation and demands to negotiate with Sasha, the president of Elite Hunting. Beth has chained Stuart to the torture chair and is poised to castrate Stuart with a pair of pruning shears. Assuming that Beth is of no significant stature, Sasha orders the Elite Hunting security to kill both Stuart and Beth. But Beth insists, "Wait! I want to buy my way out of here." Sasha scoffs at the idea, "You can't afford it." Beth forcefully returns, "Don't tell me what I can't afford. There's nothing I can't afford. I could buy and sell everyone in this room." With a sarcastic smirk, Sasha snidely asks, "You going to call your parents for money?" Beth angrily entreats, "No, motherfucker, it's my money. Just get me a PDA, a SWIFT number, and a recipient name. I have accounts in Switzerland, Luxembourg, and the Isle of Man. Just name your fucking price! Trust me, I got it." Sasha, in a more agreeable tone, gestures for his henchmen to lower their weapons, and he steps in closer: "Okay, we negotiate." Stuart feels betrayed and protests, "This is bullshit!" But Sasha corrects him, "This is business."

Although the negotiation between Beth and Sasha is purely a financial exchange, there still is more to the contract than simply money. Stuart does not have the financial wherewithal to compete with Beth's capital (Todd, as it turns out, paid for both himself and Stuart); the contract stipulates that no one can leave the facility without killing. Stuart, still trying to angle for any sort of leverage, berates Beth, "They're still going to kill you, you fucking stupid cunt." Beth turns to Stuart, "What did you say to me?" He replies, "You're a stupid fucking cu—" as Beth clamps down on the pruning shears and castrates Stuart. Beth grabs Stuart's penis, throws the severed member to the dogs, and marches out of the torture chamber with commanding authority, saying, "Let him bleed to death." In the succeeding shot, we see Beth having the bloodhound tattoo placed on her lower back.

Stuart is emasculated at home and eventually in the marketplace. Up to the climactic moment in *Part II*, Stuart's anger and frustration experienced within the domestic space finds outlets in the marketplace—his purchase power (or, in truth, Todd's purchase power) affording him the ability to subjugate the body of another, what he could never do at home, first in brothels around the world and now in the Slovakian torture factory. Maisha Wester seems to agree: "Social mandate requires him to suppress such violent impulses, yet success with the market allows him renewed access to them in extreme ways." Stuart figures as the waning image of "patriarchy since his privileges are up for sale to the highest bidder. Indeed, as illustrated in his demise, his penis can be figuratively and literally bought." The fact that Beth emasculates him, both literally and figuratively, signifies the erosion of men's special relationship to patriarchal power and marks the ascension of women (or perhaps just the reaffirmation of market capital?). "What compounds Stuart's frustration is the betrayal he suffers at the hands of other men in deference to capitalism."[42] As Roth observes in a radio interview with Elvis Mitchell, Americans do not value education or cultural innovations of any kind; what Americans prize the most is the capacity to generate wealth.[43] Nothing speaks louder than money. But more than this, what distinguishes Beth from Stuart is the former's ability to fulfill the contractual obligations agreed on by Elite Hunting and the clients it serves. Not only does Stuart not really command the capital that is required by the contract, but also he hesitates and requires coaxing to fulfill his end of the agreement. Beth, when it really counts, never wavers at the terms of the contract—unlike Stuart, she has no problem with the cost of the service; she dispatches Stuart, hardly batting an eye, and gets the bloodhound tattoo without any apparent equivocation.[44] Stuart, on the other hand, equivocates at every turn—unable to pay, uneasy with the idea of killing, and resistant to getting the bloodhound tattoo.

Whether Beth retains genuine agency in *Hostel: Part II* is subject to debate. Like Jennifer, the protagonist in the rape-revenge narrative *I Spit on Your Grave* (Meir Zarchi, 1978; Steven R. Monroe, 2010), Beth castrates her abuser. Beth gains the upper hand when she offers herself to Stuart, but her servile posture is a feint.[45] At the end of the day, it is her inherited wealth that finally saves her. Jason Middleton argues, though, that "any radical potential contained in the actions of the female protagonists in rape-revenge films like *I Spit on Your Grave* is here undermined, because Beth's power remains that of a consumer. She does not truly claim power from the patriarchy because she does not belong to the system of globalized capital as a *generator* of wealth."[46] Perhaps not yet. Likewise, Josh and Paxton in the first installment too have yet to embark on their careers, and whatever privilege they enjoy (and assuredly they are privileged) is not fully revealed. Furthermore, in the clear parallelism that Roth builds into his *Hostel* narratives, Josh, Paxton, and perhaps even the goofy Oli are torturers in the making. In the locker room when Paxton puts on a suit and tie, as Middleton observes, he is "in disguise as Paxton's future self, based upon the life path he has established."[47] And more than this, the fellow American client that mistakes Paxton as another Elite Hunting client addresses him "as an equal and confidant," which then casts Paxton's earlier "innocent" sexual indulgences in the brothel as a prelude to torture.[48] If Middleton presumes that Paxton occupies a (future) position of authority, why not Beth? Despite American mythos regarding the "self-made man," the fact remains that wealth and social privilege are largely inherited. This is not to suggest that Beth's character is necessarily progressive—a female character with agency—rather that in the matrix of global capital, it just so happens that she commands a good deal of wealth and can buy her way out of the situation. This is not a sign of virtue but a sign of fortunate privilege.

Pornography is big business—indeed, sex sells, and the industry is fully aware of the cinematic patterns (editing, pacing, composition, and cinematography) that keep customers coming back for more.[49] And perhaps the financial success of torture porn rests in its assimilation of pornographic strategies. The shooting regime in torture porn replicates the patterns found in pornography; take, for instance, the scene in which Paxton is tortured. The episodic numbers in mainstream heterosexual pornography in many instances, if there is any semblance of a narrative at all, contain two or more characters that find themselves together (e.g., the plumber arrives to fix a broken pipe, a teacher is tutoring a student), thus precipitating the sexual encounter. (Many pornographic films that abandon narrative pretense altogether use a theme—amateur, anal sex, babysitter, cheerleader, MILF, porn star, squirting—as the organizing principle that ties the individual episodes together. The shooting regime, though, generally remains the same.) Initial shots tend to be long or medium long to emphasize the body of the female performer before she is "cut up" into smaller fetishistic close-ups. Depending on the specific niche that the film serves, preliminary banter, before sexual contact, might range from erotic "sweet nothings" to outright misogynistic diatribes. Banter usually establishes something of the female character's disposition—she is shy and needs some coaxing, she is a naughty student that needs to be taught a lesson, she is a dirty bitch. In most cases, pornographic scenes build sexual tension; once the preliminary narrative motivations and sexually charged banter is dispensed with, sexual contact initiates with foreplay (heavy petting, teasing), kissing, perhaps the introduction of sex toys, oral sex, before culminating in vaginal penetration. These initial acts, prior to penetration, witness the first exchange of bodily fluids. During the sexual encounter, medium shots tend to dominate, cut with a bounty of forensic close-ups, known as meat shots, to establish proof of penetration. The climax of the episode crests with the money shot, with the male character(s) ejaculating, in many instances on the female actress's face—the facial cum shot—her heaving breath and expression of ecstasy coupled with ejaculate displaces the visible signs of male orgasm onto the invisible female orgasm.[50] The (facial) cum shot is the grand finale and the definitive exchange of fluids.

When the young men in the first *Hostel* film book into the Slovakian hostel, they meet the Sirens of the narrative—Natalya and Svetlana, syndicate agents. After Josh and Oli mysteriously disappear, Paxton locates Natalya and Svetlana and demands to know where his friends are. Natalya obliges him, escorting him to the torture factory. Immediately prior to entering the torture chamber, Paxton turns to Natalya, realizing that he has been duped, and exclaims, "You fucking whore. You fucking bitch. You fucking bitch!" Natalya simply laughs, saying, "I get a lot of money for you, and that make you my bitch." Here Paxton is figured as the female character in the pornographic regime. Seized by Elite Hunting security, Paxton, flanked on either side, writhes in terror, screaming, and just as in the pornographic convention, he is seen in long shot. Once within the torture chamber, the majority of the shots are medium shots (or medium close-ups), with close-ups that detail the fetishistic accouterment of torture—Paxton's hands are cuffed behind him, and his feet are shackled to the chair. Though he is no longer visible—as Paxton sits alone in the pitch-dark torture chamber—we can hear him sob. When Paxton's torturer arrives on scene, he is escorted by a hulking syndicate security figure, who demands, "Talk." Confused, Paxton exclaims, "What the fuck do you want me to say?" The Elite Hunting security guard gestures to the German-speaking torturer, "American." Paxton protests, insisting that he is not American, but over Paxton's shoulder, we see the security guard showing the torturer Paxton's passport. This exchange has affinities with the banter in pornography, confirming that Paxton is a sniveling "dirty little American" just waiting to be "fucked (up)."

Satisfying the perfunctory motivations for the scene, the German-speaking torturer wants to fuck (up) an ugly American. Or, seen from another perspective, this naughty little American is ready for his punishment, thus setting the stage for foreplay to begin—many of the shots now in medium close-up or close-up. The torturer wields a formidable pair of scissors, running the blades down Paxton's cheek, snapping them together in the air, snapping them over and over inches from his face, before clipping a sample of Paxton's hair, which he places in a small plastic ziplock bag as a trophy. Paxton squirms, begging, "don't, don't," while the torturer becomes visibly aroused, seemingly restraining the clipping/foreplay so that he does not climax prematurely. This is precisely Todd's problem in *Part II*—during "foreplay," when he taunts Whitney with a circular saw, he accidentally gets too close, effectively scalping her, and his interest in her wanes. The spewing of blood amounting to premature ejaculation, he leaves the torture chamber deflated, uninterested, and impotent.

Back to the scene in the first *Hostel* film, the torturer "toys" with Paxton; brandishing a three-pronged claw, he gives Paxton a couple of quick jabs.

The first signs of blood drawn by the torturer find affinities with the initial exchange of fluids in pornography. Paxton thrashes about and begs his assailant to stop, but the torturer, in German, commands Paxton to stop talking. Hearing this, previously unaware that his torturer is German speaking, Paxton now pleads in German, saying, "If you kill me, it'll destroy your life. Every time you close your eyes, you'll see me. I'll be in your nightmares every night, your whole life. I will ruin it." This shatters the torturer's fetishistic vision of fucking (up) an ugly American. Incensed, the German-speaking torturer slaps Paxton across the face, stomps out of the torture chamber, and beckons for the Elite Hunting security. The hulking figure returns and places a ball gag in Paxton's mouth, making it impossible for him to speak (the ball gag, of course, is more commonly a trope of BDSM than torture porn per se). Capable of speaking German, Paxton is no longer the ugly American but, in the torturer's universe, a sentient being. Having his subject gagged and unable to speak allows the torturer to reconnect with his fetishistic fantasy to proceed with his encounter. He places a pistol between Paxton's eyes, and Paxton's body quivers in terror. But this proves unsatisfying to the torturer, who sets the pistol aside and returns with a chainsaw. (This is fairly similar to Blondie's taunting of Nash with a gun before he brings out his straight razor in *Reservoir Dogs*.)

Raising the roaring chainsaw above Paxton's head, the torturer taunts him. Now the shots are tighter, near extreme close-ups of Paxton's eyes gripped in terror. Paxton's body convulses with so much fear that he vomits—the equivalent of squirting in pornography.[51] The torturer is enthralled at the sight, sets the chainsaw down, and attempts to "finger the wet hole." Paxton snaps at the torturer, who pulls back, dreading the displaced vagina dentata, and picks up his chainsaw, severing two of Paxton's fingers (in a meat shot) but at the same time freeing Paxton from his cuffs. The torturer lunges for Paxton but slips on the pool of blood, causing him to fall backward, and the chainsaw cuts into his thigh. "Gendered" roles switch here; the German-speaking torturer is now the docile "female" body uncontrollably quivering on the floor, blood pulsing from his severed limb—now he is the "squirter." Paxton eventually breaks free, commandeers the pistol, and shoots the torturer in the head—gray matter and blood ejecting out the back of his head. The climax of the torture number culminates with a facial cum shot of another kind, in which the viscous red spray displaces the milky white ejection of cum in the pornographic genre. Interestingly, when Roth cuts to the corridor, where the Elite Hunting security guard is posted, the lumbering figure is watching porn on a portable DVD player—another instance of Roth's competence in visual storytelling, fully aware of the parallels between the spectacle of torture and the sexual number in pornography.

Middleton makes similar observations regarding the parallels drawn between acts of violence and the pornographic (or the sex trade within the

5.9 Appropriating the pornographic regime in *Hostel* (Eli Roth, 2005).

diegetic narrative). In the first third of *Hostel*, the film depicts sex tourism (in Amsterdam) and how it relates to the torture tourism offered by the Slovakian Elite Hunting. Furthermore, Middleton keenly observes that the long hallway in the Amsterdam brothel is highly suggestive of the Slovakian torture facility—bearing close visual affinities. "In the brothel, translucent doors present the activity in each room to the characters and viewer in the form of silhouettes."[52] Middleton adds that further parallels are drawn "between these two spaces in which people pay for sex or for torture through a sight gag."[53] In the brothel hall, Josh "hears smacking and moaning . . . and sees in silhouette what appears to be a person beating another."[54] Alarmed that someone is in distress, Josh barges into the room and discovers instead a consensual BDSM scenario, in which the paying client is being subjected to "abuse" by a dominatrix. The prostitute bitterly chides Josh, "You watch! You pay!" Roth establishes a series of parallels and, in so doing, "sets up a future inversion," as Middleton notes; "in the acts of torture depicted later in the film, the paying customer is now the torturer, not the tortured, and the paid-for object is not the torturer but the tortured." He continues, "This inversion foregrounds the slipperiness of the idea of 'consent.' Despite being in the 'top' role, the prostitute here remains the purchased object; the film's visual and narrative parallelisms and reversals suggest that legal prostitution and illegal human trafficking exist more on a continuum than in two separate spheres."[55] In addition to the poignant concomitance between pornography and the spectacle of violence, between human trafficking and (legal) prostitution, between BDSM and torture, there is also in Roth's filmmaking a clear predilection to emphasize visual storytelling and visual parallelism.

The shooting regime associated with the pornographic genre, which is largely informed by the discourses of epistemology, predate cinema itself—Linda Williams pursues this subject in great depth in her seminal volume *Hard Core: Power, Pleasure, and the "Frenzy of the Visible."* In Eadweard Muybridge's protocinema, which ostensibly is about physiology, each gender is treated differently, as Williams demonstrates. No sooner had the moving image been invented than it was employed to render the body, to subjugate it to regimes of knowledge, and to compel it to reveal "truths." The moving image delivered the "ability to induce and photograph a bodily confession of involuntary spasm," and so "Muybridge's prototypical cinema arrives at the condition of possibility for cinematic hard core," Williams observes.[56] Nevertheless, the application of this (proto)cinematic image was not gender neutral; while "the male movements require props, these props are always simple, such as a saw and some wood for carpentry. But when the women require props or tools, these are not only more numerous but often do not even serve the activity being illustrated."[57] Whereas Muybridge's men usually are doing something (wrestling, boxing, running), his women are shown frequently in domestic scenarios (cleaning, bathing, lying down). Williams cites John Berger's influential work *Ways of Seeing*: "*men act* and *women appear*."[58] The women, then, are fetishized in a manner that male models are not. While there is no question that Roth capitalizes on the fetishistic economy of the female body (and this is especially true of the femme fatales—Natalya and Svetlana in *Hostel* and Axelle in *Part II*), what is particularly intriguing is the manipulation of the male body and how it is compelled to submit to the pornographic regime. Utterly gripped with terror, for instance, Paxton's body "confesses" in its convulsions and vomiting.

Whether male or female, victims in the *Hostel* films are treated with a relative abundance of props and set within a fantasy scenario. Josh and Paxton are each strapped to a chair and confronted with variants on the Mengele motif.

Miroslav, Whitney's boy toy, is strapped to a table and eaten alive (the cannibal is played by none other than Ruggero Deodato, director of the 1980 film *Cannibal Holocaust*).[59] Lorna is strung up; candles light the room for the ritualistic bathing in the virgin's blood. Whitney is "tarted up" for Todd; she is presumably playing the role of all the "sorority girls" who rejected him. Beth plays the part of Stuart's wife.

Muybridge strove to capture the body in motion—walking, pouring water, ascending or descending stairs, and sometimes quite violent actions: men wrestling, exercising, or doing some industrious work. But of particular interest to us is plate 545 of Muybridge's *Animal Locomotion: An Electro-Photographic Investigation of Consecutive Phases of Animal Movements*, which is captioned, "Artificially induced convulsions, sitting."[60] There are two series of images on plate 545; the top series consists of twelve images set straight on, while the bottom set, also composed of twelve images, is seen in profile. The top series is centrally framed in long shot, the set of twelve still images capturing a nude woman convulsing in a chair. When this series of still images is animated and set in a loop (the actual animation only lasts about a second), it appears that

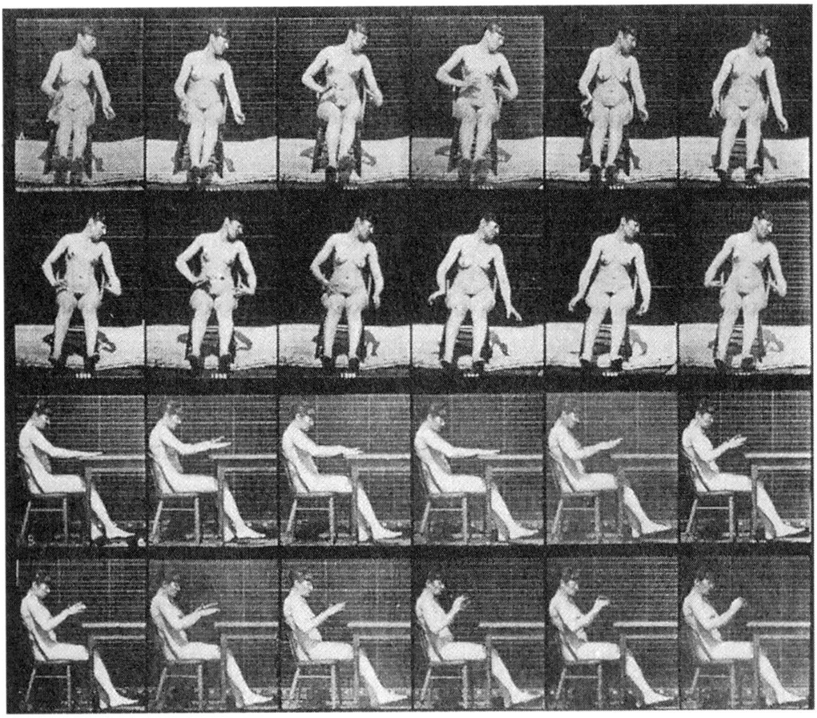

5.10 Plate 545 in Eadweard Muybridge's *Animal Locomotion: An Electro-Photographic Investigation of Consecutive Phases of Animal Movements* (1887). The plate is captioned, "Artificially induced convulsions, sitting."

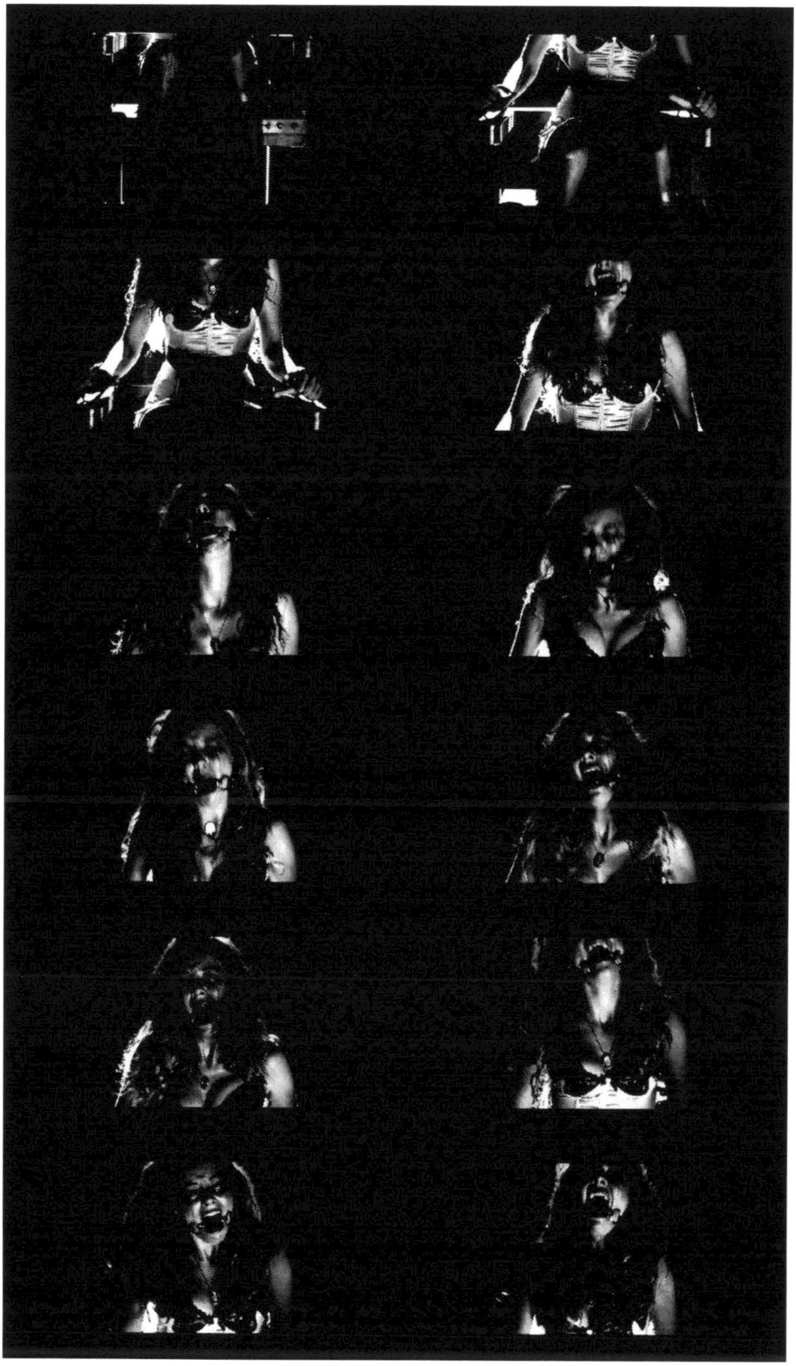

5.11 Similar to Muybridge's figure, Whitney convulses in *Hostel: Part II* (Eli Roth, 2007).

the woman writhes in her chair uncontrollably and unabated. Compare this, for instance, to the image of Whitney strapped to a chair—as the camera tilts up, scanning her body, resting at a medium shot, she too convulses "hysterically," writhing in her chair absolutely gripped with terror.

The male characters, though, are not immune to the epistephilic fascination of the pornographic gaze. All the tortured male characters after all are "fucked (up)." This is particularly true of Josh—he is feminized, his sexuality is under suspicion, and his torturer, who just wants to "play doctor," drills him. Though Roth capitalizes on the fetishistic exhibition of the female form, offering "prolonged shots of [women's] naked bodies," Maisha Wester observes, "the women in the sex scenes are largely silent." Wester argues that "our attention is split between" the erotic display of female bodies and the men, who comparatively writhe and heave in ecstasy. Josh "in particular . . . sighs, groans," and contorts his face in "orgasmic . . . expressions."[61] The history of the pornographic genre could be said to be the sustained pursuit to make the female orgasm visible,[62] and so this compulsion to make the body "speak," to compel it to offer up its secrets, is usually reserved for the female body. But here Roth also trains the pornographic camera on men. Earlier scenes in which the male characters in *Hostel* engage in sex, and again most specifically Josh, set the stage for the male characters to be positioned "as pornographic objects in the torture chamber as we are allowed prolonged views of their bodily traumas, gross reactions to pain, and inarticulate screams and sobs." Josh—as he pleads, cries, gyrates, and quivers, echoing the earlier sex scene—occupies within the pornographic regime the position of woman.[63] While protocinematic imagery of the body is "ostensibly scientific discourse on the human body," it nevertheless "immediately elicits surplus aestheticism in the fetishization of its women subjects."[64] While this is most certainly evident in the *Hostel* films, with its surplus of scenarios and props, the fluidity of gender roles appears to be contingent and complex.

The intimate relationship between pornography and the horror genre is not new. Carol Clover identifies, at least within narrative regimes, similarities in the slasher genre: "violence and sex are not concomitants but alternatives, the one as much a substitute for and a prelude to the other as the teenage horror film is a substitute for and a prelude to the 'adult' film (or the meat movie a substitute for and prelude to the skin flick)."[65] And of course, Linda Williams finds affinities between the genres as well, placing horror, pornography, and even melodrama under the larger umbrella of body genres.[66]

The assimilation of pornographic regimes in torture porn, and specifically here in the *Hostel* films, cuts any number of ways: (1) it merely replicates the fetishistic/sadistic gaze (in the tradition of feminist film theory), (2) it functions as a critique of the commodification of the body, or (3) some complex combination of these. Whatever conclusion that we might arrive at, through the depiction of the buying and selling of human beings in the *Hostel* films—whether in the context of the sex trade or of the torture trade—Roth invites a critique of capital. In the *Hostel* films, money can buy characters anything they want—a prostitute, the life of another, or in Beth's case, in the climactic moment of *Part II*, freedom. While Paxton and Oli urge Josh to be more adventurous and go with a prostitute, he timidly rebuffs, "Thanks, but paying to do whatever you want to someone isn't a turn-on." The Dutch businessman whom the group meets on the train bound to Slovakia, nostalgic with envy, seeing the band of young men full of vitality, says, "You can pay to do anything. *Anything*."

Torture porn not only critiques the (American and western European) presumption that money can buy you anything but also argues that we inhabit private worlds governed by alienation—alienated from the bodies of others and even alienated from our own bodies. Seeing the Dutchman eating with his hands, Paxton asks, "Do you need a fork there, chief?" The Dutchman explains that he prefers to eat with his hands, to retain some relationship with the living thing that died so he will not go hungry. The Dutchman insists that it is only human nature to consume the flesh of other animals, but Paxton, a vegetarian, returns, "Well, I am human, and it's not in my nature." The Dutchman turns to Josh, placing his hand high on his thigh: "Tell me, what is your nature?" Josh violently recoils, demanding, "Woah, don't touch! Don't fucking touch me!" Startled by Josh's violent rejection, the Dutchman excuses himself from the young men's compartment. With both Josh and Paxton, there is a denial of bodies (despite their hedonistic pursuits), a denial of intimacy. The Dutchman's violation, then, is not simply that he touches Josh—breaking through the protective shield of alienation and the social mores governing personal space—but that he wants to know his true nature, that is to say, to be intimate.[67] Later, when the Dutchman tortures Josh, he explains that he went into business because he was unable to be a surgeon—his true passion—on account of his shaky hands. "But business is so boring," he says, continuing, "You buy things, you sell them. You make money, you spend money. What kind of life is that? A surgeon," he explains in an excited tone, "he holds the very essence of life in his hands." Whether we are speaking of the *Hostel* films, the *Saw* franchise, or any number of films in the torture porn genre, there appears to be a desire to "know" the body, to become intimate with it. (Knowing the body is also an important feature of *Chained*, discussed in the following chapter.)

The *Hostel* films reacquaint audiences with the body, its fragility and vulnerability, and this resonates with the post-9/11 "passion for the Real," as Žižek calls it. The American preoccupation with safety, with health and well-being, in one stroke necessitates intimacy with the body but in the same instance encourages a denial of the body—for instance, a diet regime or medical procedure that proclaims one need not sweat to obtain a healthy body.[68] Or, seen from a more conceptual frame, American exceptionalism is figured as a false sense of "immunity." Torture porn taps into the "passion for the Real," a compulsion to intimately feel the body, and not the body as a concept (a vessel of the subject) but the body as raw meat, bypassing sentiency—as if hardwired directly into the sensorial economy. It is not only that torture porn resonates with the post-9/11 experience but also that torture porn refamiliarizes us with our bodies. While many people referred to the 9/11 experience as if it were a movie, Žižek positioned it as "snuff pornography."[69] To "get it," to "comprehend" the 9/11 experience, necessitates the assimilation of the pornographic regime to apprehend the "snuff-like" character of 9/11 visual culture—to get into the very sinews of tissue, the flesh as flesh, the body without organs (as Deleuze might have it).

Like the uncanny, which is a return of the repressed, Roth's films feature a revolt of the flesh, its sudden insistence to "be heard"—"the sighing of the beast."[70] Prior to the *Hostel* films, Roth released in 2002 *Cabin Fever*, a clear homage to *The Evil Dead*, in which a group of twenty-somethings go to a remote cabin in the woods and contract a skin virus. The premise of the film is partially inspired by Roth's own personal experience when, while an exchange student in Iceland, he contracted a flesh-eating virus—in a number of interviews, he describes shaving only to discover that as he dragged his razor across his face, he was peeling skin away. Working on the visual effects of the film, Roth and his crew drew inspiration from artists, most particularly Francis Bacon, whose paintings, as Gilles Deleuze says, "dismantle the face," or body in general, "to rediscover the head"—that is to say, the very sinews and muscle it is composed of—and to make it "emerge from beneath the face."[71] Bacon revered meat, loved its texture and its rich color, even comparing the abattoir to images of the crucifixion. Bacon exorcizes the semiotic traces of the body in his renditions of wide gaping mouths—a wracked figure in the middle of a scream. What is at stake, as Tomas Geyskens observes, "is not so much how to paint a sound, but how to make visible forces that otherwise remain invisible."[72] And does this not share affinities with what Williams identifies as the underlying agenda of the cinematic hardcore—an effort to make the body give up its secrets? Roth in his own way participates in this project—bodies rent asunder and transformed into meat, torture chambers in a fecal palette lathered in abject ejections. Roth, like Bacon, refamiliarizes us with our own bodies.

6

"I Think We Took a Wrong Turn . . ."

The more remote or exotic the place, the more likely we are to have full frontal views of the dead and dying.
—Susan Sontag, *Regarding the Pain of Others*

Reading Signs and All the Others

Paxton narrowly escapes in Eli Roth's 2005 film *Hostel* in part because he is bilingual, able to speak English and German. In *Hostel: Part II* (Eli Roth, 2007), Beth possesses the disposition of the financial elite, being capable of speaking Sasha's "language," the language of "high rolling" and "high-stakes" business. And in many respects, the films in the present chapter have to do with a character's ability or more commonly their inability to read the local signifiers of danger or to mobilize the local signifying system to their own advantage. Josh and Paxton, in the first *Hostel* film, typify the characters found in these films as they make a fateful error and end up taking some sort of wrong turn. En route to Spain, Josh and Paxton (and even Oli, their Icelandic buddy) are blinded by their quest to hook up with hot, young, available women and get led astray by Alex telling them, "You have to go east my friend—this is where the best girls are, the best." And very much like Josh and Paxton, while the characters in wrong-turn films tend to be college educated, at the same time, they are not especially worldly or observant; they are arrogant, are Euro-American-centric, and trade in the currency of exceptionalism.

In a foreign context, the "ugly American" in a wrong turn film is the definitive victim, and a stone's throw from this character trope in a domestic setting is the self-absorbed urbanite (regardless of nationality). In either case, characters frequently have to reconcile their position of privilege when coming face to face with the (colonized) other. The characters are placed in the center of the colonized landscape—whether it is the hills of Appalachia, the dense jungles of Brazil, or Iraq. Uncanny, strange, yet intimately familiar, these colonized zones make urban life possible, the spaces from which energy (coal/oil) or raw materials are drawn.[1] Disoriented characters find themselves lost in these spaces, sometimes literally a foreign place (that is to say, foreign for the character in peril) or a space that is coded as "savage"—it is off the beaten path, an unsanctioned "shortcut" in between civilized centers, a rural backwater, a place not on the map. Being "lost" is relative, though; waxing philosophical, Lewis proclaims in *Deliverance*—clearly a model for many wrong-turn films—"Sometimes you have to lose yourself before you can find anything."[2]

These heterotopic sites in wrong-turn films are populated with foreigners with nefarious schemes or "uncivilized" compatriots—inbreds, hillbillies, mutants. Characters are bewildered in these spaces in between, spaces that shatter a character's coordinates. Characters vocalize their disorientation in lines such as "Where am I?" or "What is this place?" Many of these films are not only "out of place," in the sense of being in the wrong place or being "nowhere," but they are "out of time," a place where "time stood still," a so-called primitive space.

Those who are familiar with the horror genre will surely recognize that the films discussed here owe a debt to Wes Craven's 1977 film *The Hills Have Eyes*—the kernel of nearly all wrong-turn plots find affinities with the Craven film. When conducting research for *The Hills Have Eyes*, Craven discovered the legend of the Sawney Bean family. Originally from East Lothian, the Scotsman Sawney Bean and his wife left their home and took up residence in a cave at Bennane Head along the Asyshire coast. The Beans had children, and their children bore children—as legend has it, the inbred clan reached a population of about thirty members altogether. They survived by preying on unsuspecting travelers, stealing their possessions and consuming the victims.[3] When the authorities were alerted, after a victim managed to escape, the clan was brought to Edinburgh and tortured to death—the punishment proving to be as barbaric as the Beans themselves. This latter inversion, in which the representatives of civilized society prove to be just as savage as the perpetrators, is highly characteristic of Craven narratives—Craven dubs this the "Kosovo Effect," in which peaceable people might under certain circumstances suddenly, and violently, turn on one another.[4]

In Craven's 1977 film, the Carter family, traveling from Cleveland to California—from one civilized point to another—take the scenic route through the desert to visit an old silver mine that they inherited years ago. While they fill up at a lonely desert gas station, a curmudgeonly attendant—the gas station and the curmudgeon now stock figures in horror films—warns the family that the silver is long gone and that there is nothing to see now, and as the family pulls away, the attendant yells out, "You folks stay on the main road now, you hear!" The gas station is a heterotopic site—akin to the airport or the train station—it is a transitional site, a space in between a point of departure and a destination. In these films, and *The Hills Have Eyes* is emblematic of this trope, a curmudgeonly figure, "off his rocker," sometimes nefarious in appearance, is nevertheless in his own eccentric way wise—intimately familiar with the region. This stock character probably has its roots in the western; think of Mose Harper in John Ford's 1956 classic *The Searchers*.[5]

Of course, Big Bob Carter, the paternal figure in *The Hills Have Eyes*, has no such intention of staying on the main road and does not heed the old man's warning, turning off the main road and driving deeper into the desert. Things from this point go from bad to worse—naturally, Bob crashes the car, stranding the family in the middle of the desert, and little do they know, but *the hills have eyes*. A family of mutants—exposed to radioactivity from a nearby military bombing range and nuclear testing site—live in a cave and prey on folks, like the Carters, who pass through this remote part of the desert. Big Bob Carter, a retired cop, complains that thugs on the streets of Cleveland have nearly killed him, but none have come closer, as he says, "than my own God damn wife and her God damn road maps and her *wrong turns* and her

6.1 The curmudgeonly gas station attendant in *The Hills Have Eyes* (Wes Craven, 1977).

God damn hysterical screaming and her—" Ethel Carter, Bob's wife, holding their granddaughter, interrupts, saying softly, "Watch your language." Bob and his son-in-law, Doug Wood, set out on foot in an effort to locate help, while the Carters' youngest son (about sixteen years old), Bobby, is left to protect the family—Ethel, Brenda Carter, Lynne Wood, the baby Catherine Wood, and two German shepherds, Beauty and Beast. Things do not end well—Bob is crucified and burned alive, Ethel and Lynne are shot, Beauty is disemboweled, the baby is abducted and nearly ends up dinner for the mutant family. Bobby and his sister Brenda work together to combat the mutants, as does Doug, the previously self-absorbed whiner, who steps up and becomes a "real" man, along with the trusted family dog Beast, to reap revenge and save his daughter from the clutches of the mutants.

Alexandre Aja's 2006 remake of *The Hills Have Eyes* leaves much of Craven's elements in place. While neither Craven's 1977 film nor Aja's remake meets the criteria for torture porn—mutants already ventures into the realm of science fiction and bumps uncomfortably close to the supernatural—the latter film nonetheless is certainly informed by the post-9/11 experience and draws from torture porn aesthetics. The Parisian Aja wrote and directed the acclaimed *High Tension* and is frequently associated with the so-called Splat Pack, a group of directors/writers who produce films that emphasize gore and graphic violence.[6] It is important to note, however, that while Splat Pack filmmakers emphasize gore and graphic violence, Splat Pack films are not necessarily torture porn—which, as I am arguing in the present volume, is a very specific brand of horror with very specific tropes. The updates that Aja makes to *The Hills Have Eyes* in most instances are consistent with the aesthetics of torture porn, keeping its intimate relationship with the post-9/11 experience intact. Big Bob Carter, as in Craven's film, is a retired cop, but in this case, he intends to launch a private security firm—a huge business in the wake of the invasion of Iraq, where security for personnel was largely privatized, with highly lucrative contracts awarded to (now infamous) companies such as Blackwater.[7]

The feminization of Doug is more pronounced in Aja's film, which makes for a more distinct character arc than in the 1977 version. He is coded Jewish, given the surname Bukowski instead of Wood, and is figured as a shlemiel—inept and somewhat feminine.[8] When Bob and Doug are about to go on their expeditions to locate help, Bobby taunts Doug with a gun, but the senior Carter jokingly chides his son, "Leave Doug alone. He's a Democrat; he doesn't believe in guns." Later, Bobby in a fit of rage calls Doug a "pussy." When the surviving family members are able to commandeer a walkie-talkie used by the mutants, Doug pleads pathetically, echoing the familiar torture porn dialogue, "Why are you doing this to us? Why are you doing this? You hear me? Give me back my baby. What the fuck do you want from us? What do you want?" In the face of grave danger, and fueled by revenge, the liberal urbanite Doug casts all his values to the desert wind and takes up arms against the mutants. And might this be how the world views the American Left (such as it is)—as a bunch of "pussies" that kowtowed to the Bush administration and its pandering of patent lies, tripping over themselves to jump onto the war bandwagon to fight in another far-flung desert?

When Bob returns to the gas station, after hiking back out of the bush, he finds the place deserted and discovers photographs and newspaper clippings pinned up on a board. Using jump cuts and other abrupt editing techniques, rapidly cutting from one shot to another, the sequence places a contemporary spin on the expository montage, in which twirling newspaper headlines flash across the screen, a technique found in so many classic Hollywood films.

6.2 Using newspaper clippings as an expository narrative device in *The Hills Have Eyes* (Alexandre Aja, 2006).

The nondiegetic audio design underscores the rapidity of the cuts, which are accentuated with hot white flashes. The newspaper headlines relate to nuclear testing in the area, the miners who used to populate the place, and stories of disappearances, succinctly compressing the history of the setting and the evolution of the mutants into a pithy, stylized sequence. This is not a flashback in the conventional sense, but it nonetheless functions in much the same way. And more than this, like a number of examples from torture porn, the flashback, such as it is here, is mediated through technological devices (though they are hardly cutting-edge): newspapers and photographs. One of the last photographs we see is of a family of four, a nuclear family of a different type, suggesting that these are the people who sowed the seeds of this new "nuclear Sawney Bean family."

In addition to the caves, Doug discovers a ghost town populated with mutants. The town is "frozen in time," stuck in the era of the "Old West" but also with vestiges of the Cold War as well—1950s-era cars, televisions, mannequins (left over from the test blasts) dressed in vintage clothing, and the like. In the context of the post-9/11 experience, the mutants set in this heterotopic space resonate with the colonial and racially tinged rhetoric that conservative pundits and the Bush administration used to describe Al-Qaeda and the Taliban. President Bush, for instance, while addressing reporters shortly after 9/11, stated that the terrorists might be hiding, "but we're going to smoke them out." He proclaimed, "I want justice," and added, in his own peculiar colloquial tone, "And there's an old poster out West that says, 'Wanted: Dead or Alive.'"[9] The rhetoric is clear here: Bush attempts to make Al-Qaeda/Taliban play Indian to our cowboy. Running parallel to conservative efforts to transpose the cowboy-and-Indian narrative over the War on Terror narrative, wrong-turn films, such as *The Hills Have Eyes*, play on an analogous evolution in cinematic history. Carol Clover recognizes that "the settler-versus-Indian films of the thirties and forties bear an astonishing resemblance to" the films of the '60s and '70s, "not only in plot structure and in political and economic sensibility, but in fine details of appearance, character, and behavior. The difference, of course, is that the redskins have become rednecks, the white settlers city vacationers, and the cavalry the corporation—the 'power company,'" with Clover referencing *Deliverance* in this latter instance.[10] Fast-forward thirty more years, and we discover Indians now in the guise of Al-Qaeda (though thinly veiled as cave-dwelling hillbillies/mutants or vengeful foreigners).

Aja ends his version of *The Hills Have Eyes* striking a similar chord, but with an ironic nod. At the climax of the film, Doug emerges from the hills as the righteous hero, steeped in the swelling of triumphant nondiegetic music, as the remaining family members are reunited. Woven into the nondiegetic score is the slight twang of a guitar clearly drawn from the western cinematic genre (1:43:45), suggesting that Doug—the deputized figure of authority, having thrown off the yoke of liberal values, embodying the romantic vision of the lone cowboy—has vanquished the marauding hordes and tamed the savage outback. And presumably this is exactly what the public craves? In this light, we might view pro(an)tagonists such as Jigsaw, Dexter, and Jack Bauer as a contemporary take on the cowboy—lone figures on the fringes of society prepared to do the dirty work required to weed out things that might disrupt civil society.[11] Aja, the Frenchman, caters to this American sensibility for a brief instant but then pulls the carpet out from under us. The fantasy of a "happy ending" is quickly undermined when the camera zooms out, placing the surviving family in extreme long shot, the screen now matted to suggest that this final shot is a subjective shot as viewed through the lens of a mutant's binoculars, implying that this is not over and maybe never will be.

In addition to the conservative rhetoric associated with the romanticized image of the cowboy—the rugged individual, gun at the ready, prepared to do whatever it takes to tame the wild West—politicians and conservative pundits frequently framed Al-Qaeda and the Taliban as "primitive," with all the associated connotations of the term: uncivilized, barbaric, backward, cave-dwelling Neanderthals. Conservative commentator George Will characterized the post-9/11 conflict as "pitting the world's mightiest industrial nation against a cave dweller."[12] And yet at the same time, as Frank Rich from the *New York Times* and so many others repeated, Osama bin Laden might be a "cave dweller, [but] we keep being rudely reminded, [he] is no caveman."[13] Similarly, on the Sunday program *Meet the Press*, Tim Russert helped to peddle the administration's wares while interviewing the secretary of defense, Donald Rumsfeld. Russert asks the secretary about the search for Osama bin Laden: "There is constant discussion about him hiding out in caves, and I think many times the American people have a perception that it's a little hole dug out of a side of a mountain." Rumsfeld simply shrugs, "Oh, no." Russert then continues, cutting to an illustration of an elaborate cave:

> The *Times of London* did a graphic, which I want to put on the screen for you and our viewers. This is it. This is a fortress. This is very much a complex, multitiered, bedrooms and offices on the top, as you can see, secret exits on the side and on the bottom, cut deep to avoid thermal detection, so when our planes fly to try to determine if any human beings are in there, it's built so deeply down and embedded in the mountain and the rock it's hard to detect. And over here, valleys guarded, as you can see, by some Taliban soldiers. A ventilation system to allow people to breathe and to carry on. An arms and ammunition depot. And you can see here the exits leading into it and the entrances large enough to drive trucks and cars and even tanks. And it's own hydroelectric power to help keep lights on, even computer systems and telephone systems. It's a very sophisticated operation.[14]

In one fell swoop, Osama bin Laden, Al-Qaeda, and the Taliban are at once barbaric and uncivilized, cowardly hiding in caves and at the same time are highly sophisticated and dangerous, with the capacity to inflict harm. Here, either in the fabrication of intelligence or in the passing off of unreliable intelligence, we have another instance of misreading—or misleading.

At many junctures along the way, there have been failures in reading signs: the 9/11 Commission referred to the failures in intelligence as a failure in imagination,[15] there was the apparent failure in the sharing of intelligence, there was also a failure in listening (Colin Powell's apparent reservations about instigating a war with Iraq, invoking the Pottery Barn rule—you break it, you buy it), and friendly governments such as France were skeptical of the intelligence. Surely, or at least one hopes, the Bush administration was mindful of all these "misreadings," because either it was frankly inept and really failed to read the signs, or it ignored these admonitions and consciously offered this obfuscated reading to grant itself license to pursue a broader geopolitical strategy. The films in the present chapter do not necessarily reflect the dubious framing of the War on Terror but rather feature the failures in reading or the outright manipulation of signs.

Films discussed in this chapter also exhibit elements of other genres—namely, the slasher genre and the road movie. Some of the traits associated with Tobe Hooper's 1974 film *The Texas Chain Saw Massacre*, for instance, are distinctly evident in Rob Zombie's films. Rob Schmidt's 2003 film *Wrong Turn* is clearly indebted to the slasher genre—twenty-somethings wandering around in the woods and ambushed by monsters—but nevertheless bears some of the trademarks of the torture porn genre. In many cases, wrong-turn films might share certain affinities with the road movie, but invariably travelers are sabotaged, have their car break down, or (oddly enough) take a wrong turn. And the intersections of these other genres necessitate a renegotiation of a critical torture porn trope—the insular space where violence occurs. Rather than relying on fixed and confined spaces—such as we find in the *Hostel* films or the industrial sites where Jigsaw sets his traps—wrong-turn films recontextualize the heterotopic spatial field as a vast open space: the backwoods of West Virginia in the *Wrong Turn* films, the jungles of Brazil in *Turistas*, the lonely roadside motel in *Vacancy*, the isolated highway rest stop (appropriately enough) in *Rest Stop*, the shuddered-up home set within the vast prairies of the Midwest in *Chained*.[16]

Led Astray

Being "lost" or even inadvertently taking a "wrong turn" is to one degree or another subjective. What in one instance might constitute "being lost" might in another amount to wandering, discovering, or exploring. Being led astray, however, is something altogether different, because this suggests a power relationship between parties, one who knows more relative to another who is operating at a deficit. (And certainly given what we know today, the Bush administration led the American public and the world astray when plotting the War on Terror.) Being led astray implies manipulation—Alex in *Hostel* and Axelle in *Part II*, for instance, manipulate characters in their narratives—and there are a number of other films that similarly string characters along: *The Final*, *Captivity*, *Steel Trap*. These films in particular play on characters' fears, insecurities, and/or narcissism.

"You're the only one that loves me, Suzie," Jennifer complains to her overly pampered lapdog toward the beginning of *Captivity*. Jennifer is "trapped" in her life as a celebrity/fashion model, little more than a prop—although her body is the object of constant attention (seen by millions in advertisements and television appearances, primped and fussed over by photographers and advertising agents), as a person, she is utterly alone. When she does finally hope to make a "real" interpersonal connection, meeting a friend for a drink at a club named Façade—appropriate given her profession and the shallow nature of her relationships—she gets a text: "Sorry babe, something came up. Call you soon." Jennifer orders an apple martini while the antagonist of the narrative, having stalked Jennifer for a good part of the day—at a fashion shoot earlier and now at the club, catching her every move on a concealed DV cam—laces her drink with a drug.[17] What we soon come to realize, however, is that the scheduled meeting at the club was all a ruse—the meeting and the subsequent text canceling the appointment were all intended to lead Jennifer astray and into the clutches of the antagonist. The meeting also preys on Jennifer's loneliness.

Once Jennifer is captive, the games begin. Jennifer awakes to find herself in a torture chamber—dull concrete walls, a video monitor (or projection) for a simulated window. Torture chambers—cut off from the civilized world—are heterotopic spaces, and this is certainly the case here; but this space is particularly confounding for Jennifer, because it is modeled after her own apartment and even filled with her belongings. In this uncanny space—at once familiar and in the same instance completely alien—Jennifer screams, "Where am I?" Jennifer rails against her unseen captor before a gas is introduced into the room, sedating her (a clear nod to *Oldboy*).

After the gas is introduced into the room, Jennifer loses consciousness. She wakes to find herself strapped to a dentist's chair in a large cage with the hooded perpetrator. Jennifer is forced to watch a video (sharing certain affinities with Jigsaw's videotaped messages or Alex's reconditioning in *A Clockwork Orange*). A woman on the video monitor, presumably an earlier victim, pleads with her captor, saying that she is sorry and that she promises not to disobey. Soon thereafter, Jennifer, parroting the video, also begins to plead as she watches the woman, showered in acid, writhe—her face severely burned and disfigured. Jennifer continues to parrot the video she has just seen, beseeching her captor, "I'll do whatever you want. Anything!" But her captor, without so much as a word, silently continues with the procedure, and Jennifer is showered in what we are led to believe is acid. Jennifer awakes to find herself back in her cell, with blood-stained bandages covering her face. She removes the bandages to discover that this too has been a ruse—her face is flawless. Inspecting herself before a mirror, she does find a "wound" on her face, only to realize that it is just a bit of "movie magic," a special effects appliance, which she peals off. From the plotted abduction and the torture chamber modeled after Jennifer's own apartment to the staged video depicting the acid shower, the antagonist reveals a distinct sadistic disposition—crafting elaborate games that are seemingly more about mental mastery than about inflicting harm. Additional elaborate games are played, some of which are timed, that appear to threaten Jennifer with physical harm (though in actual fact she is never in grave peril), demonstrating—at least in the elaborate staging of games—clear affinities with the *Saw* films.

There are a number of references to the post-9/11 experience in *Captivity*—including an intertextual reference regarding Jennifer, who is played by Elisha Cuthbert and was also cast in the Fox Network series *24* as Kim Bauer, Jack Bauer's daughter. Jennifer is tortured in a number of different ways, some of which are drawn from the trove of tactics euphemistically known as "enhanced interrogation techniques." Jennifer, for instance, is given a leather corset and leather skirt and expected to put them on, but when she refuses, her torture chamber suddenly blisters with blinding lights and an excruciating high-pitch sound. This is similar to the treatment of prisoners at Guantánamo Bay and other facilities, where prisoners were shackled to the floor and hammered with strobe lights and throbbing music (this is depicted in Michael Winterbottom and Mat Whitecross's 2006 hybrid documentary *The Road to Guantánamo*). Although it is unclear if the Bush administration ever approved, the CIA nonetheless "sought permission to utilize 'mock burials.'"[18] This has a distinctly Sadean element to it—the theatricality of "staging" a burial is all about mental manipulation of the target subject. Jennifer is sedated (again), placed in a glass box, and rudely awoken with sand pouring in from the top of the enclosed vessel. Jennifer struggles and pleads for help as the sand all but fills the vessel. Outside, in the larger torture chamber, a video monitor feeds a recording of Jennifer answering questions in a television interview and an image from an advertising campaign featuring Jennifer seductively sprawled across the advertised product with the Great Pyramids of Egypt in the background (Egypt, of course, being one of the destinations for individuals subject to rendition and in all likelihood torture). Jennifer is nearly buried alive when another captive, Gary, from an adjacent cell, hearing her pleas, comes to her aid at the very last second. The antagonist sits before a bank of surveillance monitors and watches this all unfold as he sips a glass of red wine.

The pair make a daring escape creeping through the crawlspace—the space between an ordinary suburban home and the subterranean torture chambers beneath—eventually making their way to a room where they find the corpse of the woman scalded with acid (or is it simply a lifelike movie mannequin?). When Gary turns on the lights, a reel-to-reel tape recorder (something that we might find in the *Saw* franchise) is heard: "'Why do bad things happen to good people?' you ask. That's the mystery." The recording is slightly modulated (again something that is associated with the *Saw* films, as well as the *Scream* series). When the pair finally find a car (supposedly in a garage), Gary manages to get the car started and crashes through the garage door, only to have something stop them in their tracks—a gas is pumped into the car (pouring through the vents), causing the pair to go unconscious. Later, after waking and finding themselves back in their individual chambers, Jennifer laments that they will never escape. Gary insists that there is always a way: "You just have to think like him. Anticipate—" Jennifer interrupts him midsentence, "The way he anticipated us? . . . He's making it impossible to get out of here, but we can get through the vents. . . . The car—he's playing with us, showing his power." Without explicitly using the term, Jennifer finally realizes the true nature of her captor—a sadist par excellence. Indeed, we eventually discover that Gary is the perpetrator's brother and that the brothers are working together in an elaborate scheme. In retrospect, the escape attempt and the getaway car all turn out to be a highly choreographed hoax, finding antecedents in *Marathon Man*.

Dean Lockwood also views the gaming element as central to the genre of torture porn and to *Captivity* in particular. He posits that "torture porn films also can be understood as allegories of control." Linking the game motif to contemporary trends in so-called reality television, he continues,

> The basement room in which Jennifer is kept captive in *Captivity* is an environment (accessed by her captors by means of codes and swipe cards), which, like the *Big Brother* house, is subject to constant adjustment and surveillance. Initially, it resembles a comfortable living space, containing a picture window, TV, clothes rack, lamps, and flowers in vases, but it is soon revealed to be, in effect, a laboratory designed to assist study of her tolerances. Metal drawers slide open without warning, containing messages and items—perhaps a garment she is instructed to wear. If she fails to follow instructions she is punished—knockout gas is introduced into the room, sudden and abrasive metallic noises occur, accompanied by an assaultive bright white light. At intervals, excerpts from television interviews she has conducted burst onto the TV screen. Escape routes and companions are introduced at various junctures, but these ultimately amount to further test procedures.[19]

What Lockwood cites as an allegory of control—highly staged, scripted episodes—I would characterize as the distinctive hallmarks of sadism. Sadism is, of course, also an allegory of control.

In keeping with the sadistic enterprise, we discover that Gary is a plant. He is collaborating with his brother, Ben, the shadowy figure orchestrating the various scenarios. The violence that the brothers perpetrate stems from childhood trauma. The compulsion to repeat, to act out, is symptomatic of a traumatic experience, and it appears that everything that the brothers devise is a "replaying" of an abusive childhood. Jennifer is only one among a long line of other victims, playing a role in a well-rehearsed drama. Gary is cast as the figure to save the girl—playing the hero who never came to save him and his brother, Ben, from the clutches of a junkie mother who inappropriately says, "I like touching you" on a grainy eight-millimeter home movie. Whereas Gary is more prone to emotion, his brother is a truly stoic sadist. Ben is a portly man but sophisticated in manner, cultivated (we see him, for instance, delicately preparing sushi); he listens to classical music and keeps the brothers' shared home orderly. There is also another intertextual reference: the brothers' surname is Dexter—an all too obvious nod to the Showtime program. The systematic abduction and torture of a victim is a well-scripted event, but Gary wonders if the drill is becoming too predictable. In a revealing exchange, Gary demonstrates a degree of dissatisfaction, but sternly Ben marches to his brother's side, giving him a slap upside the head: "You stop playing the game before it starts playing you." In a firm but loving manner, Ben says, "What do I always tell you? Play them—" "Not with them," Gary finishes. Ben reminds Gary of the trove of videos and scrapbooks they have assembled as trophies: "It's the tapes and the books that make it better, make it last forever, right?" But Gary is too enamored with Jennifer, too emotional, and stabs Ben in the chest, ending their game and causing everything to unravel. (Like the *Saw* films, *Captivity* demonstrates how the gaming motif corresponds to the sadistic disposition.)

It is rare that a victim survives in a torture porn film; *Captivity* is different in this respect. Jennifer emerges as the final girl, and as discussed in chapter 3, the final girl, particularly later in the slasher-film cycle, adopts the characteristics of the monster, even in some cases discovering that they are blood kin. A good number of torture porn films open with a gruesome set piece (this is a feature of the *Saw* franchise), and in some instances, the opening number turns out to be a flashforward (this is true of *Turistas*, *Severance*, and *Captivity*). The opening of *Captivity* begins with the torture and death of a man strapped to a rusted bedframe. It is not revealed until the conclusion of the film that the perpetrator in this case is Jennifer wearing a black wig. Learning from her captors—Gary and Ben Dexter—she stalks and kills those who have escaped the criminal justice system, rightfully inheriting the perpetrators' surname. She operates like Dexter Morgan in the Showtime series, a serial killer who stalks and kills other serial killers, delivering swift justice.

Like *Captivity*, which plays on Jennifer's insecurities leading her astray, *Steel Trap* plays on its characters' narcissism and insecurities. Whereas Jennifer is led astray by an invitation for drinks at a club, in *Steel Trap*, characters are presented with special invitations to an exclusive party. The film is laced with the stylistic and narrative tropes of torture porn—embellished editing and cinematography similar to what we find in the *Saw* franchise, as well as games, traps, countdowns, and surveillance. The perpetrator—who is hiding in plain sight the whole time (just like Jigsaw in the first *Saw*), within the ranks of the group—is reaping revenge for being tormented during her high school years. Each victim receives a degree of poetic justice—a female character, for instance, with a heartless disposition has her still-beating heart ripped out from her chest.

Similar to *Steel Trap*, Joey Stewart's 2010 film *The Final* features a small band of tormented high school students reaping revenge. The popular kids are led astray with private invitations to an exclusive costume party; on account of their narcissism and insecurities, no one wants to miss it. As in *Captivity*, the drinks served at the party are laced with a narcotic that causes the partygoers to lapse into unconsciousness. They awake to blaring music and are shackled to the floor, like terrorist suspects being broken by interrogators at the detention facility at Guantánamo Bay. Dane, the ringleader of the small band of outcasts, dressed in an SS uniform and wearing a gas mask, says in a modulated voice, "Get up, sleepy heads." (In this case, the modulated voice seems to be drawn from Jigsaw recordings, the *Scream* films, and perhaps even Darth Vader.) As the students come to, Dane explains, "There is some good news and some bad news. The good news is we don't plan to kill you. The bad news is you will wish we had. Some of you will be spared, but you will all bear witness to the horror just as you did in the hallways, just as you sat idly by as pain was inflicted upon us. What you fail to understand with reason you will with wrath." While the film follows many of the conventions of the revenge-fantasy film, *The Final* is one of the more transparent approaches to the post-9/11 experience, the nerdy kids playing the part of Al-Qaeda suicide terrorists. (The nerdy crew has entered a suicide pact; they intend to terrorize the popular kids for the night and then kill themselves.)

When one of the shackled students asks, "Why us?" Dane returns, "Why us? You know, that's the same question we've been asking ourselves for years. Why us? Why us always on the receiving end of your taunts, your laughter, and your childish cruelty? Now it's your turn to ask, 'Why us?'" Dane, echoing the disenfranchised Jihadist, in one fell swoop demonstrates just how telling that post-9/11 question really is—"Why do they hate us so much?"—and how easily this exact question might be turned around, because the

Palestinian in a refugee camp, the unemployed Arab, the innocent Yemeni killed by an American cruise missile or drone might ask the very same question. "I want you to think real hard and ask yourselves," Dane adds, "'Where did all this evil come from? What did I do to make someone hate me so much to go to these lengths?'" Again, the shackled students need only to look in the mirror to answer this question.

The film also includes a number of set pieces that are similar to the numbers found in torture porn films or are explicit nods to other influential films. Like the opening of *Saw IV*, where two characters are pitted against each other, in *The Final*, certain characters are compelled to make choices and commit acts of violence against others to save their own skin (literally and figuratively). When Bridget apologizes to Emily, Emily rewards her by promising not to hurt the popular girl, but for this gesture of goodwill, Bridget has to amputate all of Bradley's fingers—Bradley is a star football player, and this will mean the end of his sporting ambitions and, more importantly for him, the adoration that he so desperately craves. Bridget refuses: "I can't do this. I can't hurt anyone." Emily returns, recalling all the times that she has been tormented at school, "Sure you can. You hurt me, without even blinking an eye." When Bridget refuses to play along, all bets are off, and Emily gives Bradley a chance. Either way, someone is going to lose fingers; the only question is who. Eventually we find Bridget in the dentist chair, placed at the front center of the room for all to see; Bradley is forced to his knees as Bridget pleads with him, and he in turn tries to "shush" her, insisting, "I have to." Bradley cuts off two fingers, and Emily asks Bridget if she wants him to stop, saying that all she has to do is to inflict pain on another. Finally, Bridget relents and agrees to Emily's terms—but at the end of the day, she still cannot follow through.

Although Bradley saves his fingers, it is all for naught, as Dane severs his spinal cord, rendering him a quadriplegic. Everything that his life is about—playing sports, having sex—all this is gone in an instant. Bradley is simply a "head on a stick," as Mick, the antagonist of *Wolf Creek*, says when he performs a similar operation. Emily is dressed in fetishistic gear with a creepy "nonface," a mask that is an abstraction of a classic Japanese beauty. We presume that Emily's costume is generic, but when she mounts a prone, incapacitated jock, the cinematic reference becomes self-evident—Emily reenacts the climactic scene in Takashi Miike's 1999 film *Audition*. Playing the part of Asami, Emily performs a twisted version of acupuncture, inserting long needles under the jock's eyes, saying all the while in a playful little-girl voice, "Deeper, deeper, deeper."

Whereas *Captivity* and *Steel Trap* focus more on the victims, Jennifer Chambers Lynch's 2012 film *Chained* is a profoundly disturbing portrait of how monsters are made. When the producers of the film, Lee Nelson and David Buelow, first approached Lynch to direct the film, she was initially puzzled because Damian O'Donnell's original script for *Chained* was so clearly written as a torture porn film. Without dismissing the genre, Lynch had no interest in making a film of that kind. Lynch is known for making dramatic thrillers with an edge—*Boxing Helena* (1993), *Surveillance* (2008)—and the producers wanted to see where she might take the script.[20] Lynch preserved O'Donnell's core scenario—Bob, a taxi driver and serial killer, abducts female victims in his cab and takes them to his remote home, where he abuses the victims and dispatches them.

The producers of *Chained* were not misguided in thinking that Lynch might be a good candidate to direct a torture porn film. An analysis of Lynch's 2008 thriller *Surveillance*, for instance, reveals some basic torture porn tropes. Moreover, recall the intimate relationship between *Saw* and *Se7en*—the thriller/police procedural has been a close associate of the torture porn genre. In *Surveillance*, the FBI is called in to take over an investigation of a brutal home-invasion murder in a small midwestern town. There are certain affinities between the home invasion in Lynch's picture and that of Bryan Bertino's 2008 film *The Strangers*. The two agents set up monitoring equipment in the small-town police headquarters to interview witnesses, including one of the cops, whose partner was killed by the masked killers. During the course of the investigation and the questioning of the witnesses, the narrative slips into flashbacks, some marked by the hot white flash of a crime-scene camera. Contrary to what the surviving cop says during his testimony, the pair of officers are far from "the best and the finest." They abuse their power, shoot out motorists' tires out of boredom, play good cop/bad cop with motorists whom they have pulled over, berate and sexually harass motorists, and become sexually aroused by the execution of their power. The narrative leads us to believe that the corrupt cops are actually the killers, but it turns out that the FBI agents are imposters, as the real FBI agents are later found dead in a hotel room. The pair of killers tie one of the female witnesses to a chair, execute everyone in the police headquarters (save one little girl), and drive away, unscathed and unpunished. The surveillance equipment mediating narratives, the use of flashbacks, the exhibition of sadism, the manipulation of the killers posing as FBI agents—effectively "toying" with everyone, playing a little game—tying the female witness to a chair: all these various elements, and more, bear the hallmarks of torture porn.

Whereas the original script for *Chained* apparently focused more on the violent episodes, Lynch instead offers insights into Bob's psychology, as well as that of a nine-year-old boy whom he enslaves—the child is the son of one of Bob's many victims. Bob names the child "Rabbit"; the narrative quickly leaps ahead many years later (probably another nine years) to see that the child is now a young man—still literally chained to the house and still cleaning up after Bob.[21] Rabbit is obliged not only to keep the house in order but to clean up Bob's torture chamber and to bury his many victims in the basement. Much of Lynch's focus is on the relationship between Bob and Rabbit, which in its own perverse way is quite tender—not in the sense of being compassionate but rather in the way that it follows the general outline of the paternal. There is no question that this relationship is abusive, obviously, but there might be some affinities between these characters in *Chained* and the father-son relationship in the Showtime series *Dexter*. Over the years, Rabbit, with Bob's help, teaches himself anatomy and internal medicine. Bob brings home books on the subject, and there is no shortage of specimens to study. And similar to Dexter's father, Harry, Bob eventually initiates Rabbit in the regime of killing, bringing Rabbit a girl of his own to victimize and dispatch.

Rabbit resists becoming a monster to the bitter end, but like some Greek tragedy, his fate is already sealed. In a surprising twist (which apparently was also in the original O'Donnell script), it turns out that Bob is Rabbit's uncle; Brad, Rabbit's father, paid his brother to get rid of his wife and child. Brad, having dropped off his wife and son at the movie theater, insists that they take a cab home rather than taking the bus. What appears to be a sign of protectiveness turns out to be a calculated statement intended to lead the two astray—and into Bob's cab. As they drive past their off-ramp, Rabbit's mother casually informs the driver, "Um, excuse me, that was our exit." Eventually, as it becomes increasingly clear that this was no accident, that they are now in peril, Rabbit's mother discovers that there is no cellphone service this far out of town. Rabbit, learning the truth, eventually kills Bob and confronts his father to discover, in a fate perhaps worse than being chained up for years on end, that his father rejects him. "I don't even want to look at you," he says, pushing Rabbit toward the door. "Goddamn, disgusting piece of shit," Rabbit's biological father continues, but his new wife intercedes, pleading with Brad to stop. Brad turns abusive toward his wife, slapping her, the violence triggering for Rabbit flashbacks that erupt in lightning-fast bursts. Rabbit yells, "Don't hurt her!" and hits Brad across the back of the head with a solid glass candleholder. Now astride his father, Rabbit lands a deadly blow to the head. In the final shot of the film, we find Rabbit returning to Bob's remote home, now the inheritor of Bob's monstrous kingdom.

Bob's kingdom is a heterotopia. It is "in the middle of nowhere." The film was shot in Moose Jaw, Canada, a setting that evokes the lonely ranch-style homes amid the great prairies of Oklahoma or the Dakotas. There is at once claustrophobia in the vast flat expanse of the surrounding landscape and at the same time something sublime in its oceanic scale—finding close affinities with Michel Foucault's description of the ship as a heterotopic site par excellence, a site "that is closed in on itself and at the same time is given over to the infinity of the sea."[22] There is "nothing" for as far as the eye can see, just the fallow farm fields. Shortly after Rabbit's abduction, the youngster attempts to escape—but all the windows are sealed shut with sheet metal. Managing to make it to the attic, Rabbit kicks out an air vent, only to find Bob waiting for him. "I know every move that you make," Bob admonishes. Rabbit desperately screams, "Help!" but Bob, in a pedagogical and taunting tone, adds, "Everything you do I let you do! Go ahead, let it out." Indeed, the paradox of the vast expanse is revealed here—at once an open space and at the same time entirely shut out from the civilized world, a cage without bars, a prison without walls. Bob, nonetheless, takes the added measure of shackling Rabbit's ankle to a long, heavy-gauge chain.

Bob's kill room, like the torture chambers in the Slovakian factory found in the *Hostel* films, is very spare and bathed in dark, earthen hues. If Bob's home is in the middle of nowhere, his torture chamber is the absolute center of "nowhere," a black hole that swallows up his victims never to be seen again. Rabbit's routine includes cleaning the torture chamber. We see, for instance, Rabbit on his hands and knees with a scrub brush and bucket, washing away blood and finally disposing of the body. In Rabbit's routine, there might be certain affinities with the Sonderkommando—commissioned against their will to participate in the practice of murder, to clean up the kill room, and to dispose of the bodies. Adjacent to Bob's torture chamber, and apparently down a few feet, a small door opens to the final sanctuary of Bob's victims. Rabbit buries each body in a shallow grave, covers the body with lime, and decorates each grave with a small trinket that belonged to the victim; Rabbit has also strung up a string of colorful Christmas lights, turning this unholy site into a mausoleum, affording the victims a modicum of dignity in death.

Bob is a stone-cold killer—divorced from emotions, he is utterly incapable of empathy. A sadist, he is seemingly quite intelligent, despite his workaday job as a taxi driver. He appears to command extensive medical knowledge. When Rabbit asks why he must learn, Bob tersely explains, "Because without an education, you're fucked." In a moment of affection, though not without perverse intentions, Bob admits, "I mean, you've seen some things. I've showed you some things for sure, but you haven't understood them." Bob then takes a different tact: "You ever do a puzzle? You know, the kind of puzzle that has the picture on the outside of the box?" Rabbit nods affirmatively. "That's what people are," Bob states flatly, "pictures on the outside, pieces inside." Pointing to a book on anatomy, which Rabbit flips through, Bob adds, "This book is about the human puzzle. You study this, you learn it, and you know how to take people apart, put them back together, understand them." Rabbit softly acknowledges, "Oh." Bob continues to suggest that if Rabbit studies hard, he might be able to win some freedom and, because he is older now, even, as Bob says, "have a taste of a woman real soon." But Rabbit refuses, setting the anatomy book aside: "I won't take the puzzles apart. I won't kill them." (The idea of people as puzzles might be a reference to Juan Piquer Simón's 1982 film *Pieces*.)

This infuriates Bob, not because Rabbit has violated some rule but because he has rejected a gift—the gift of sadism. Bob views women as a sum of parts, to be assembled and disassembled, utterly divorced from ethics—clearly illustrative of the sadistic disposition.

Insofar as torture porn attempts to reacquaint us with the body—frequently exhibited in terms of medicalized gore—here in *Chained*, medicalized gore is "institutionalized," so to speak, within the discourse of anatomy and thus neutralized. As Julia Kristeva says, the corpse seen outside of God or science is utterly abject.[23] On the other hand, if the corpse is contained within the shroud of religious ritual or the stoic discourse of science, the (dead) body is made approachable. Indeed, as brutal as *Chained* is, what is on exhibition here is the social face of the abject—bodies are never "felt" as such in the film; they are only puzzles that can be taken apart and put back together.

Bob is a creature of habit and, according to the sadistic disposition, adheres to a strict regime. When Rabbit first arrives, Bob lays down the law, explaining when Rabbit is allowed to eat, what can and cannot be done, and the various chores that are expected of him. Among his chores is very neatly clipping out stories from the newspaper about the women whom Bob has murdered—usually appearing as a missing-person story. These clippings are then placed into a scrapbook, figuring as part of Bob's trophy collection.

Lynch's film is most interested in the psychology of a monster, so the film relies less on the spectacle of violence. There are no elaborate traps, as we find in the *Saw* films, or Grand Guignol set pieces, but the film nonetheless pulls no punches. Like many torture porn films, *Chained* uses flashbacks to reveal the trauma that sowed the seeds of its pro(an)tagonists' monstrous behavior. One of Bob's fares is a father and son; it is abundantly evident that the son has done something that gravely disappoints the paternal figure. Bob watches in his rearview mirror as the paternal figure lashes out at the teenager, slapping him across the head. The abusive behavior, and the crack of the slap, triggers a flashback. The flashback is accompanied with a nondiegetic drone, the sound of rattling metal, as the crack of the slap slips between the diegetic space of the cab and Bob's flashback—Bob, as a teenager, beaten by his father and forced to have sex with his mother. (The trauma being rooted in incest gives *Chained* certain affinities with *Captivity*.) The traumatic scene, as in so many torture porn films, is partitioned by the sudden eruption of hot white light and dizzyingly fast edits. The decor of Bob's house, in light of the flashback, suggests a man stuck in time, as if the man-boy never left his parents' home. While modest and orderly, Bob's shuddered little fortress—a ship floating in the vast expanse of the prairies—is nonetheless dingy and frozen in time. The furniture, the appliances, and the wallpaper suggest a heterotopic arresting of time—as if time stopped here in 1960.[24] The ghosts of Bob's trauma, of parental abuse, haunt this place, and this uncanny affect is generated through the mise-en-scène. Claire Bueno, interviewing Lynch at the Film4 FrightFest and the UK premiere screening of *Chained*, observes that the film is saturated with dingy yellow and sepia tones, to which Lynch affirms that the palette was intended to evoke a sense of "homey nausea—I love scary stuff that happens in broad daylight."[25] And as much as Lynch pushes her narrative toward suspense and away from torture porn, is this not precisely what makes torture porn so frightening, at least conceptually: where the ordinary—household objects, mundane rational human beings—is corrupted in the service of violence? The insistence on "reality" in torture porn is not that far removed from Lynch's idea of "homey nausea."

The Return of the Colonial Repressed

John Guillermin's 1976 remake of *King Kong* is strangely prophetic when viewed through the post-9/11 lens. An expedition team sets sail in the hope of discovering an untapped petroleum source; recall that only a few years earlier, in 1973, OPEC brought American gas-guzzling drivers to their knees with an oil embargo, and as a result, this particular plot element would have resonated with a contemporary audience. The expedition team does not find any marketable petroleum but does find Kong and brings the giant ape back to New York. Whereas the great ape makes its last stand atop the Empire State Building in the 1933 Merian Cooper and Ernest Schoedsack original, in Guillermin's film, Kong mounts the newly constructed Twin Towers of the World Trade Center. The return of the colonial repressed is central to the Kong narrative (and speaks to its lasting resonance), but with the 1976 film, some twenty-five years prior to the 9/11 plot, this film forges specific affinities between the Western world's insatiable thirst for oil and the WTC site as the nerve center that governs the circulation of global capital. It is hard to fathom the "failure of imagination" in the intelligence community in the face of such a vivid fantasy.

King Kong is by no means a torture porn film, but there are a few post-9/11 horror films that negotiate the return of the colonial repressed. "Films such as *Turistas*, *The Ruins* and *The Last Resort*," Kevin Wetmore observes, "all show young American tourists enjoying themselves in Latin America and being tortured and killed as a result."[26] The latter two films, however, include supernatural elements, precluding them from the genre of torture porn. They nonetheless all share certain characteristics with the genre. The protagonist/antagonist regime in these films does not wholly correspond to the tidy paradigms of good/bad; rather, protagonists are not completely innocent, being so self-absorbed and Euro-American-centric that they are utterly blind to the ramifications of their actions. Likewise, antagonists are not evil as such—they are not governed by the devil—they might, however, be ruthless, cold, or even in a perverted sense altruistic. Torture porn generally dispenses with the Manichean worldview, and wrong-turn films feature victims who are unintentionally impertinent but, despite their benign intentions, offend locals, and perpetrators (if we can even call them that) are either operating within a (ritualistic) system or redressing the colonial imbalance as a matter of business.

Many of these films feature Americans, their coalition partners—Brits, Australians—or characters from other developed countries backpacking in remote "exotic" lands. We find Swedes, Brits, an Australian, and Americans traveling through Brazil in *Turistas*. Greeks, Germans, and Americans enjoy Mexican sites in *The Ruins*. Characters find themselves lost or venture outside sanctioned tourist circuits, thus allowing for "unscripted" encounters with "natives" that prove dangerous. Anthropologists refer to these sites as contact zones, where the colonizing and colonized subject might encounter one another. Mary Louise Pratt defines the contact zone as "the space of colonial encounters, the space in which peoples geographically and historically separated come into contact with each other and establish ongoing relations, usually involving conditions of coercion, radical inequity, and intractable conflict."[27] While power is commonly assigned to the colonizing subject, in a film such as *Turistas*, it is the Brazilian who subjects the Euro-American travelers to "conditions of coercion," divorcing them from their privileged position of mobility and placing them into a position of "radical inequity." And although the "colonial frontier" might be viewed as synonymous with the contact zone, Pratt is careful to note that "within a European expansionist perspective (the frontier is a frontier only with respect to Europe), 'contact zone' is an attempt to invoke the spatial and temporal copresence of subjects previously separated by geographical and historical disjunctures, and whose trajectories now intersect."[28] Rather than a "foreign" space, contact zones consider "the relations among colonizers and colonized, or travelers and 'travelees,' not in terms of separateness or apartheid, but in terms of copresence, interaction, interlocking understandings and practices, often within radically asymmetrical relations of power."[29] The title credits of *Turistas*, for instance, feature a collage of maps, currency, medical illustrations of organs, fetishistic tourist photographs (images of the exotic Brazilian body and poverty porn), and an American passport—encapsulating the network of mediated encounters between "travelers and 'travelees.'"

Carter Smith's 2008 film *The Ruins* is not torture porn. It does, however, intersect with a number of critical tropes (e.g., medicalized gore) and themes (e.g., negotiating the post-9/11 American experience) that are associated with the genre. At a Mexican resort, a resort being another heterotopic space,[30] Americans and Europeans excessively indulge in carnal delights; like Josh and Paxton in the first *Hostel* film, all of the twenty-something characters are poised to achieve success in lucrative careers or postbachelor study. Mathias, a German national, has not heard from his brother, who left with a woman—an archeologist—exploring a Mayan ruin, and wants to investigate the site to ensure that he is safe. The German invites his new American friends to come along. "So what do you guys think," Jeff, the straight-laced American asks his friends, "ancient Mayan temple off the beaten path?" For good reason, the temple is not on any map; it is not within the sanctioned circuitry of tourist travel, and this initiates a series of missteps and misreadings that ultimately prove to be fatal. A vine covers the Mayan pyramid and infects living creatures, using the body as a host. Local Mayans salt the soil surrounding the pyramid to keep the vine contained.

When the band of Americans, along with their German and Greek buddies, arrive at the pyramid, an older man on horseback, a Mayan, yells at them. The bearded figure, in well-worn, light, earth-toned clothes, has affinities with the gas station attendant found in so many other wrong-turn films. Like his Appalachian kin, the older Mayan man, though rough on the surface, is actually warning the group of their imminent peril—but the band of foreigners misread the signs. First they imagine that he wants money, and Jeff goes for his wallet and tries to pay him off—a typical American response. In the meantime, two other Mayans arrive on horseback and strike a threatening pose. The Mayans show no interest in Jeff's money, and all the while, Amy—vine underfoot—has been taking pictures. Still unable to discern what has raised the ire of the Mayans, the group imagines that they want the camera—playing on the tired idea that indigenous people view the camera as a "soul catcher"—Dimitri, a Greek, takes the camera from Amy and offers it to the men. But as he approaches the men, gesturing to take the camera, a Mayan archer shoots Dimitri, and the older bearded Mayan then shoots the Greek in the head with a revolver. Scared and confused, Amy grabs the vines at her feet, tearing tendrils away, and throws them toward the growing crowd of Mayans. The plant hits a young boy; the older Mayan stoically turns to the boy and shoots him dead. The travelers retreat up the steep steps of the pyramid still puzzled, prompting a variation on that all too familiar torture porn refrain, "Why are they doing this?"

Eventually the group pieces enough details together to realize that they are being quarantined—left there to die. Jeff, the smart and rational one in the group, about to enter medical school, insists, invoking the currency of exceptionalism, "This doesn't happen! Four Americans on a vacation don't just disappear!" The group has left Dimitri's friends, fellow Greeks, behind at the resort—still passed out from a night of excessive drinking. Confident that Americans do not just disappear, Jeff continues, "Somebody—the police, our parents, the Greeks, somebody—somebody is going to find us. We just have to be alive when they do." The Mayans make a concerted effort to contain the abject monstrosity of the vines, but the Americans (and their European counterparts) bring about violence everywhere they go. In the closing moments of the film, all are dead except Jeff and Amy; Jeff distracts the Mayans, allowing Amy to escape. Jeff is killed at the base of the pyramid, and although Amy manages to escape, she is infected, carrying the seeds of monstrosity outside the bounds that the Mayans have so diligently patrolled.

Kevin Wetmore reads the vines as the seeds of terrorism; I would add that they signify the pent-up rage fermenting in the developing world. "The Americans themselves are innocent and naïve and believe that their incursion into the pyramid is nothing serious." And while the Americans, and their "European associates, are not evil," they are utterly unprepared and have no sense that their actions have consequences. The self-absorbed characters have no ill intentions; as Wetmore adds, while "ignorance is no excuse, it is not malevolence."[31] (This might not be an altogether satisfying argument, but what I might stress is that characters are not acting on evil intentions.) And does this not encapsulate the inequities built into the globalized economy, where the people of the Northern Hemisphere (by and large) enjoy the bounties of the Southern Hemisphere and, while meaning no ill will as such, are completely oblivious to the consequences of their consuming habits and how they impact local communities?[32] And does this not also illustrate how this asymmetrical relationship potentially foments resentment—a potential breeding ground for violence? An explosive violence that potentially materializes as terrorism? And we really still need to ask, "Why do they hate us so much?"

Where "counterhistorical" films (such as *Beyond Rangoon* and *Salvador*), as Elizabeth Swanton Goldberg posits, present Western subjects that are "safe, superior, and separate from the rest of the world,"[33] torture porn films, such as *Turistas*, do no such thing. Counterhistorical films place Western characters in the position of "outside" observer—photojournalist, tourist—immune to the extremities of violence. Victims in *Turistas*, on the other hand, are selected precisely *because* they are Westerners. And while they might plead, apologize for any offense they might have caused, and insist on exceptional status, the Western body does not go untouched. What torture porn films share in common with Goldberg's counterhistorical narratives is that they are told from the perspective of a privileged Western body. Counterhistorical films work "ultimately [to] consolidate a (white) Western identity at the expense of other cultural and national identities, leaving the stories 'behind' international and domestic torture and terror in the background, as yet untold."[34] Torture porn films might share certain affinities with the counterhistorical film insofar as they are both not about the cultural other and the other's supposed penchant for violence, but—and here is where they might part company—torture porn reveals far more about the American disposition than anything else, even if it is geographically displaced.[35]

John Stockwell's 2006 torture porn film *Turistas* (alternatively titled *Paradise Lost*) opens, like *Captivity*, with a flashforward, though we only understand this in retrospect. Highly characteristic of the torture porn genre, the film opens with the screen washed in a scalding-hot white, diegetically motivated by a surgical lamp, and a nondiegetic drone and electrified screech. The opening episode of the third season of *Dexter*, "Our Father," begins in virtually the same way, blinding light thrown from a lamp, though whereas the reverse shot in the Showtime series reveals Dexter at the dentist for a regular checkup, in *Turistas*, we discover a woman on a surgical table. A highly stylized series of frenetic cuts offer forensic details—an IV needle inserted into a vein, blood running through a surgical tube, shots of surgical equipment, a scalpel running across the woman's abdomen, and the pooling of blood in her navel—while the woman pleads, "You don't have to do this. Not like this. No, you can't. Please!" Screams and nondiegetic metallic elements mix together, all of which—the graphic content of the images, the editing, and the audio design—are highly indicative of the *Saw* franchise. The frenetic editing, the pulsating shots, and the grating audio design build to a fever pitch as the woman continues to plead, "Por favor! I am so sorry. Oh, God, I want to go home," as the screen cuts to black with a nondiegetic clank.

Following this blood-soaked prelude, we find our characters on a ramshackle bus (not that far removed from the beat-up vehicles found in the Appalachian films), driven by a scruffy man. Alex, the responsible one, has come along on this Brazilian trip to keep an eye on his sister Bea. Tightly gripping the rail of the seat in front of him, Alex asks his sister, "Am I the only one having a problem with this?" as the bus quickly screeches around corners on a narrow mountain road. "I guess they're used to it," Bea says to her overly protective brother. Alex abruptly yells out, "Would you slow the fuck down!" Embarrassed, Bea turns to Alex, "Jesus Christ, relax! You're such a tourist." Rounding a bend in the road, the bus comes upon three young men (tourists perhaps) carrying surfboards. The bus driver swerves to miss them, sending the bus off the road—everyone manages to escape the precariously perched bus before it topples down the mountainside.

As everyone collects their things from the wrecked bus, Finn and Liam, a pair of British tourists, meet Alex, Bea, Bea's friend Amy, and Pru, an Australian tourist. As the group sorts out their options, Finn and Liam discover that they have been heading the wrong direction the whole time. Finn declares, "We got on the wrong fucking bus!" And adding insult to injury, there is no cellphone reception. The passengers, waiting for the next bus to come along, congregate at the roadside. Bored, Bea snaps a couple of pictures of a Brazilian girl; the girl's father, turning to see Bea, becomes utterly incensed. Pru, the only one in the group who speaks Portuguese, tries to calm the situation and tells Bea that you need to ask permission first. (There might be some similarities here with *The Ruins*, playing on the idea that the camera is a "soul catcher.") Bea, clinging to her innocent ignorance, wonders how she was supposed to know that. By chance, a pair of locals carrying drinks in coconuts (a fetishistic fantasy image) pass by, and Pru asks where they got them. The pair gestures down the hill, where there is a small bar on the beach. The group, rather than waiting for the bus at the roadside, elect to go to the beachside bar—one more fateful error, taking them further off the sanctioned circuits for travelers.

Traveling by herself, Pru, an experienced world traveler, is the most astute at reading local signs—having at least a working knowledge of the language and being culturally informed. Like George Sand, the French writer who assumed a male persona "to move freely in the city, to experience the gendered freedom of the flâneur,"[36] Pru never disavows her gender, and if anything, she mobilizes her sex to her advantage. Nevertheless, she, like Sand, commands enough cultural (and no doubt monetary) capital to move with relative ease through the traveler's circuit. The gender politics associated with travel are central to the film and come into sharper focus as the peril becomes amplified. From the conventional viewpoint, women should not travel—in the end, it is Alex, the ugly American, who protects his sister Bea and saves Pru. "'Good travel' (heroic, educational, scientific, adventurous, ennobling) is something that men (should) do," James Clifford observes. "Women are impeded from serious travel."[37] Although Pru is far more worldly than Alex, who thinks that Brazilians speak Spanish, it is his gender (manifest as brute force) at the end of the day that saves them.

The group is ecstatic when they emerge from the densely forested slopes and arrive at a beautiful beach. Whooping and hollering, the travelers cast off their clothes and plunge into the ocean, before heading to the beachside bar. The bartender, Camila, after serving the group drinks, calls Zamora, a Brazilian doctor, telling him, "More gringos arrived." He asks how many. "There are eight of them now"—the group that narrowly escaped death on the bus and two Swedes—and she adds, "They're all yours." Zamora thanks her for the "Christmas gift." As in the *Hostel* films, the local venue that caters to tourists serves as the conduit for a crime syndicate. Whereas Elite Hunting in the *Hostel* films abducts backpackers to cater to the tastes of its rich patrons, Zamora is more altruistic—he harvests the organs of tourists to help needy Brazilians.

After a day of play and drinking, the night brings the locals and tourists together—sensuously dancing at the beachside bar to Brazilian hip-hop. A beautiful local woman seduces Finn. Hailed to her side, he asks her name. "Arolea," she responds; after a couple of botched attempts, he pronounces her name correctly, and she rewards him with a kiss. The beautiful young woman leads him away to a room, which prompts a group of boys to erupt in laughter. Finn imagines that the encounter is mutually amorous, asking if she wants to "come back to London." But as the sexually spent Finn lies on the bed, Arolea casually walks over to his discarded clothes, takes out his wallet, and takes his cash. Finn whines, "It's not like that," but Arolea in Portuguese says, "É assim" (It sure is). "But I thought you liked me. No?" Finn gripes, but Arolea simply replies, "No," collects her things, and leaves. The eruption of the boys' laughter suddenly comes into focus. Finn, like so many in *Turistas* and other films discussed in this chapter, fails to read the signs, is incapable of reading them, or (perhaps even willfully) misinterprets them.

Disappointed but undaunted, Finn returns to the bar to find the Swedes passed out; he imagines that they have drunk too much, but we learn that the group was drugged. The Anglophone characters awake early in the morning to discover that they have been robbed, left with nothing but the shirts on their own backs. The Swedes, on the other hand, are in a tougher fix—gagged and bound, toted through the jungle on a pole by nefarious Brazilian characters, at least one of whom is coded as indigenous. The iconography is clearly drawn from the colonizer's nightmare: the image of the headhunter. The Swedes seize an opportunity to escape but die. The group walks to a small town in an effort to find the authorities, but they find it "lawless." First they find the Swedes' motorcycle, then a local kid wearing Alex's hat—their belongings redistributed to the local population. Liam, with the others trailing behind, tries to chase the kids down but is quickly ditched and then pelted with a small rock. The kids, like the Roma kids in the *Hostel* films, taunt the desperate tourists. The Brit, in pursuit, throws a rock at the youngster's head, knocking him to the ground. Soon a trivial crime—the theft of a cheap hat—begins to escalate into a major incident. A growing angry crowd begins to form, but a local young man, Kiko, intercedes and directs the hapless group away from the town and away from trouble, leading them deep into the jungle to his uncle's house.

Like gender, race also plays a part in the *Turistas* narrative. Kiko, an Afro-Brazilian, leads the group into the jungle; his character is plucked straight from the pages of colonial-era travel literature. "Victorian bourgeois travelers, men and women," James Clifford observes, "were usually accompanied by servants, many of whom were people of color. These individuals have never achieved the status of 'travelers.'"[38] Kiko is not a servant, but he is not a "traveler" either—though he commands intimate knowledge of the local environment, he is not afforded the same privileges of mobility beyond this space that the Brits, Australian, and Americans are. Clifford continues, "Racism certainly has a great deal to do with this. For in the dominant discourse of travel, a nonwhite person cannot figure as a heroic explorer, aesthetic interpreter, or scientific authority."[39] Kiko, like the real and fictional characters before him, is precluded from the paradigm of "traveler." And in the end, his exclusion is justified in the narrative because he is working with Zamora—guiding the group to this remote facility so that the doctor can harvest the travelers' organs. Though Kiko is clearly enamored with the group, he is nevertheless bound culturally and economically to Zamora, being constrained by the colonial politics governing this space.

Like the torture factory in *Hostel* and the industrial sites in the *Saw* films, Kiko's "uncle's house" is a remote heterotopic space—apparently designed specifically for the purpose of harvesting organs from gringos. When the group arrives, Alex discovers passports from former victims and wonders, "Who the hell are these people?" But he still fails to read the danger signs all around. Alex also discovers a bank of surveillance monitors, a trope associated with the torture porn genre, and unable to sleep, he posts himself before the video monitors, unaware that he has already missed signs of peril. The sound of baying dogs and the whir of a helicopter approaching suddenly get his attention and awake the rest of the group. Zamora and his small army, carrying in supplies, suddenly swarm the place. One of Zamora's assistants asks in English, "You guys Americans?" Bea and Alex nod. "Cool. I've been one time to New York." Initially seeming like a casual encounter, the woman abruptly continues, "Go. Run." Alex does not comprehend: "What do you mean?" The woman insists, "Run right now. This guy has plans for you and your friends—and his plans are pretty fucking elaborate and pretty fucking fucked. So if I were you, I'd just run." Spoken in clear English, the signs of peril could not be more explicit, and yet like deer in the headlights, the group is paralyzed. Soon the group is restrained. Amy finds herself strapped to a surgical table, with Finn waiting in the wings, and the rest of the group are placed in small cages—similar to the ones found at Camp X-Ray at Guantánamo Bay.

Echoing the opening shots, Amy's face is shown in tight close-up, and the presence of the surgical lamp affirms that the earlier scene was in fact a flash-forward, as Zamora prepares to harvest the American's organs. Adopting the Mengele motif, Zamora reassures the anesthetized but still semiconscious Amy, "If it makes you feel any better, please know that I'm doing this for a good cause." He continues to explain that there is a waiting list for organs and that it can take years—seven years in America and even longer in Europe. "So if a rich gringo needs a kidney, what does he do? Wait and get sick and die like the rest of us? No. He comes here to Brazil to take advantage of our bounty and of our poverty." He pauses to give instructions to his assistant and then continues, "The whole history of our country is you taking from us and our land—rubber, sugar, gold. And from our bodies—for slaves, for sex. And now, for—our insides. But I have had enough." Zamora continues to offer motivations: "It sickens my heart, this combination—your greed and our weakness. And so I am thinking, maybe there is something I can do to even the scales just a little—to help you find a way to give back." Zamora calmly explains, "Today I am to take the organs of all of you and give them to the People's Hospital in Rio. Counting down from right now, I have about twelve hours to get your liver and your kidneys and the livers and kidneys of all your fucking *amiguinhos* into that helicopter and back to the city. I'd take your hearts too, your corneas—even the skin from your lily-white asses," he chuckles, "but they don't travel too well. You can only keep a heart outside the body for six hours. But I want that. I want a heart—a heart of some arrogant gringo tourist, pumping life back into the veins of a little *Brasileiro*. But that's gonna take more planning." Finished with Amy, he sighs and says to Finn, "Your turn."

In line with the conventions of the torture porn genre, the twenty-something Anglo characters have not committed any significant transgression (save perhaps overindulging in alcohol and perhaps illicit sex in Finn's case). These characters are effectively innocent. It is not that they have personally done anything wrong as such; rather, they are selected as victims solely because they are gringos. Terrorism tends to employ the same logic—no one specific individual is usually targeted, but rather the very tactic of terrorism relies on its randomness. This sense of randomness is central to *The Strangers*, which was discussed earlier (in chapter 2), in which the victim implores one of the intruders, "Why are you doing this to us?" to which the masked stranger simply responds, "Because you were home." Rodrigo Cortés's 2010 film *Buried* similarly features Paul Conroy, a truck driver, who wakes up to find himself in a coffin. Conroy's convoy in Iraq is attacked, and he is held for ransom. The truck driver pleads for help from the authorities via his cellphone, but all is for naught as he slowly suffocates. The entire film is set within the coffin as it slowly fills with fine Iraqi desert sand, save one shot mediated through Conroy's phone—the killing of a colleague by his captors, sent to him as a video message. He is compelled to make an Al-Qaeda-like ransom video, as well as a video of him cutting off his own finger as a gesture of attrition to his captor. The unseen antagonists have nothing against Conroy, the individual, but he is an American in the wrong place at the wrong time. *Buried* is not torture porn as such; it is far closer to the thriller genre. But as Kevin Wetmore observes, the "ending is very nihilistic,"[40] and this is a trope that we commonly associate with torture porn. From *Turistas* to *Buried*, in these films, we witness "ordinary Americans" or our "ordinary" coalition partners subject to abuse not for what they have individually done per se but because of who they are.

Appalachia and the "Other" Americans

> For a new generation subject to oppressively normative conceptions of what it means to call oneself a citizen of the United States, hillbilly horror thus offers its audience a means of critically engaging with the nation's territorial ambitions, allowing for both an interrogation of the implications of President Bush's Orientalist demonization of the terrorist as deviant other, and the ability to ask the most shocking questions: whether, in the age of the propagandistically named Patriot Act, the concentration camp that is Guantanamo Bay, and the judicially sanctioned form of kidnap and torture that is "extraordinary rendition," Americans retain the right to speak of liberty at all.
> —Linnie Blake, "'I Am the Devil and I'm Here to Do the Devil's Work'"

While the geeky crowd in *The Final* plays the part of the Jihadist, it is the stock cinematic figure of the inbred hillbilly that begins to approach the displaced figure of Al-Qaeda in films considered here. And at first glance, this might seem like a strange coupling—the hillbilly and the terrorist—but if you accept that the Afghan-based Jihadist is the product of our own excesses, as Slavoj Žižek posits,[41] then the correlation begins to come into focus. It is not that hillbillies are the product of the excesses of the more "cultured urbanites"—the "proper" collective "us"—but rather that they constitute an abject "them," that thing that we would prefer to disavow, to eject from the social body, but is nonetheless a part of us. The hillbilly, the backwoodsman, the rural prefigures the terrorist in the American imagination, but Linnie Blake situates the American other "as a means of negotiating the increasingly traumatic disjunction between the aspirations of a 'civilized' society, and the acts of savagery perpetrated in its name."[42] I suggest that we proceed with caution here, though, because if we figure Al-Qaeda as our progeny, we run the risk of denying the terrorist agency, and this verges on a different topsy-turvy colonial enterprise, colonizing the 9/11 terrorist attack (as if to say, the 9/11 attacks were only possible because we made it possible, and not in a conspiratorial sense but because it is through us that they possessed the knowledge and the means). The point, however, is to acknowledge that as alien as "we" make Al-Qaeda or hillbillies out to be, they are our kin.

At the risk of undoing the nuance I hope to encourage here, there are, nonetheless, certain affinities between the people of Appalachia (or, more accurately, their cinematic representations) and Al-Qaeda Jihadists. Appalachia, which is a large swath of land that stretches from the western edges of the New England states into the South, is a region rich in coal and other natural resources. Kathleen Stewart refers to the southwestern area of West Virginia as a "hard-core Appalachian coal-mining region" that "constitutes an 'Other America' not because it is somehow 'outside' or marginal to 'America's' cultural landscape but because it has, through a long history of exploitation and occupation"[43] by the coal industry and unremitting narrativization, been framed as our other—situating the Appalachian as the proverbial "them" to the (sub)urban "we." Mercilessly, the people of Appalachia are figured as "uncultured" backwater simpletons or worse. And for better or for worse (probably more of the latter), the horror genre contributes to the project of narrativizing the Appalachian other—the *Evil Dead* films, the *Wrong Turn* films (there are currently five), Eli Roth's 2002 film *Cabin Fever*, Neil Marshall's 2005 film *The Descent*, among others. Appalachians have experienced "a long history of exploitation and occupation" in the quest to extract coal to fuel the (post)industrial economy, and does this not echo the sentiments of the disenfranchised people in the Arab world, the vast majority of whom do not share in the proceeds from the extraction of oil? If 9/11 was a movie featuring the return of the colonial oppressed—after all, it was "just like a movie"—these horror films that figure the Appalachian as the terrifying other imagine the uncanny reemergence of the repressed social other.

The fantasy of the Appalachian other is complex, though, because the other elicits not only dread but also fascination—an object of taboo desire.[44] The hill people in the popular imaginary are "more in touch" with an authentic (American) culture—closer to the Earth, living off it, and making a living in it by working in the mines, self-sufficient, radically independent, seemingly unburdened with the (sub)urban rat race, and in this respect, closer to God. At the same time, the Appalachian is viewed as embodying a bacchanal fantasy—disregarding taboos and social mores. Is this not precisely why the figure of the inbred hillbilly is such a potent trope of the Appalachian holler folk—signifying the erasure of the incest taboo? The popular image of the Appalachian man is a figure soiled with grease and grime, unshaven, matted hair, and blackened and/or missing teeth. Social mores regarding the clean and proper body are seemingly cast aside, communing with all sorts of abject filth—animal carcasses, snakes, bones, butchered mountain game or domesticated live stock, and detritus of all manner. Loafing on a ramshackle stoop, distilling moonshine, drinking, chewing tobacco, the Appalachian does not yield to the demands of the reality principle and postponing gratification. Idleness, squandering time, inebriation, the Appalachian indulges in the transgressive, and in this sense the figure is invested with a complex and contradictory emotional charge.

Whereas a number of films feature displaced figures akin to the Appalachian other—the Texan redneck in *The Devil's Rejects*, the backward eastern European in *Severance*—Rob Schmidt's 2003 film *Wrong Turn* dispenses with the thinly veiled disguise and situates the narrative in the heart of Appalachia: Greenbrier Backcountry, West Virginia. Chris Flynn, the primary male character in *Wrong Turn*, is an impatient urbanite, traveling in his vintage 1967 Ford Mustang on his way to Raleigh. A jackknifed truck, spilling its load, has brought traffic to a complete standstill. Chris, anxious to keep his 7:00 p.m. appointment, turns off the main highway and onto an unpaved country road.

Chris's vintage Mustang is a sign of affluence. Whereas Appalachians litter their properties with the corpses of rusting vehicles or drive rambling heaps—vehicles kept in service long past their life expectancy—Chris's Mustang, on the other hand, while old, is nearly in mint condition. Not only is the Mustang literally an instrument of mobility, in its pristine condition, it also suggests the ability to traverse the temporal dimension as well. The ramshackle vehicles of the hills—grotesque in nature, pieced together with spare parts from scavenged material—are not intended for "travel" as such, because the "traveler, by definition, is someone who has the security and privilege to move about in relatively unconstrained ways," as James Clifford observes, adding, "This, at any rate, is the travel myth."[45] Chris is a "traveler," but established social circuits bind even the most privileged "traveler." Drawing from Mary Louise Pratt, Clifford adds that "most bourgeois, scientific, commercial, aesthetic, travelers moved within highly determined circuits."[46] And it is the spaces outside the "highly determined circuits" that potentially harbor danger, and whether by design or by accident, deviating from these sanctioned conduits amounts to a "wrong turn" and invites the possibility of a perilous encounter.

The lonely roadside gas station usually marks the border between the "civilized" and the "uncivilized" worlds in the horror film. On the fringes of either end of the spectrum (more often than not leaning toward the uncivilized), the attendant of the gas station, a curmudgeonly figure, straddles these two different worlds, monitoring the border separating these realms. The attendant negotiates encounters between the inbred monster and the traveler, who never really means to stop (save for gas) or stay in the area but is instead always just passing through, traveling from one civilized point to another. In *Wrong Turn*, Chris hopes that he might be able to find a way around the main highway to bypass the jackknifed big rig. Stopping at the rural gas station, he asks the haggardly attendant—missing teeth and drinking Pepto-Bismol straight from the bottle like it is water—if he can use his phone. The attendant asks, "Long distance?" Chris looks over his shoulder toward the overgrown landscape: "What isn't long distance from here, right?" The contingent nature of the linguistic shifters "here," "there," and "long distance" or the coordinates of "backwater"—to what?—all come into sharp focus. The attendant is offended and says, "That'n there is my only phone," gesturing to the broken pay phone. Looking at a tacked-up map, Chris runs his finger along the unpaved (read: unsanctioned/uncivilized) Bear Mountain Road: "It looks like it runs into the highway about fifteen, twenty miles. Is that right?" The attendant shrugs unconvincingly: "If you say so." (Here is an instance of misreading—both the map and the attendant's reticent warning.) Chris, desperate to make his appointment in Raleigh, says to himself, "It could work," thanks the attendant, and says as he leaves, "You take care, okay." The unkempt attendant mutters to himself, "You're the one gonna need to take care," as he watches the Mustang pull away. The shot immediately following this is an aerial view of the vast verdant landscape coupled with an ominous score—as if to swallow Chris up as he enters the heterotopic no-man's-land.

Distracted while driving, Chris does not see a Range Rover parked at the side of the road and crashes into it. He is dazed but manages to walk away from the wrecked Mustang. He and the group in the Range Rover have no other choice but to hike to the nearest civilized point. From here, *Wrong Turn* adopts fairy-tale tropes. Like the story of Hansel and Gretel, who get lost in the forest and imprisoned by an old hag who intends to eat the children, in *Wrong Turn*, three bearish, inbred hillbillies discover Chris and the others

6.3 The curmudgeonly gas station attendant in *Wrong Turn* (Rob Schmidt, 2003).

snooping around their ramshackle cottage, and the travelers all manage (at least initially) to escape the hillbillies' dinner table.

The succeeding *Wrong Turn* films dramatically increase the gore factor. Characters are caught in mutant hillbilly traps—the deformed holler folk compelled to cannibalism because all the forest game is gone. Whether it is contestants on a reality television program (*Wrong Turn 2*) or twenty-somethings on a canoe trip that come upon a prison chain gang (*Wrong Turn 3*), characters are hunted like prey—snared in a trap, shot through with a bow and arrow, or hacked to pieces with a hatchet. Some traps slice characters into pieces; others impale them—all emphasizing gore. In *Wrong Turn 4*, the inbred hillbillies are "running the asylum"; they have taken up residence in an abandoned sanitarium, and this offers some motivation for more *Saw*-like set numbers and medicalized gore. The inbred mutants in *Wrong Turn 5* are able to come out of the woods and hide in the crowd on Halloween—everyone presuming that the deformed figures are just wearing costumes. Mutant hillbilly compounds—either a shack in the forest or some abandoned facility (for instance, an old paper mill in *Wrong Turn 2*)—are "off the grid" heterotopic spaces, out in the middle of "nowhere"; inside and out, they are cluttered with all manner of things waiting to be repurposed for some abject function. Human remains are strung up as trophies or hung to cure like wild game. The mutants are feral, only nominally speak, and are more likely to grunt, cackle, or howl.

Whether we are discussing the *Wrong Turn* films or some other hillbilly horror, the hill people—or inbred mutants—who populate these films are scarred, their clothes stained, stitched together from this and that. This is true in the *Wrong Turn* films as well as in *The Hills Have Eyes*, films all drawn from the image of the Appalachian man that tinkers with his truck, the men who, as Kathleen Stewart observes, "are *like* the trucks—scarred and welded together out of a history of accidents"—and like "the old women [who] fondle the quilts they have stitched together out of torn fragments of their relations' old clothes."[47] The appearance of the inbred hillbillies in *Wrong Turn* follows this regime carefully; their clothes are well worn, stained, faded, and mismatched, while the deformed faces of the backwoodsmen are cleft, scarred, seemingly assembled from disparate parts—animal and human.

The graveyard of cars or the vehicle assembled from scavenged materials—especially tow trucks—is a common feature in a number of wrong-turn films.

6.4 The tow truck as a trope, from *Deliverance* (John Boorman, 1972) to *House of 1000 Corpses* (Rob Zombie, 2003), *Wrong Turn* (Rob Schmidt, 2003), *Wrong Turn 3: Left for Dead* (Declan O'Brien, 2009), and *Wrong Turn 5: Bloodlines* (Declan O'Brien, 2012).

One can find these tropes in *Deliverance*, *House of 1000 Corpses*, *Wrong Turn*, *Wrong Turn 3*, *Wrong Turn 5*, and *Rest Stop*. The vehicles driven are monstrous not simply because of their excessive wear but because of their Frankenstein assemblage, fabricated outside conventional industrial means, signifying a resistance to participate in the sanctioned economy. The DIY tow truck is an imposing and threatening site/sight not only in its tarnished physicality but also in that it easily slips into the realm of abjection—here is a vehicle that is designed to "save," to "rescue" hapless souls, but is commissioned for more nefarious tasks.

In Stewart's ethnographic survey of Appalachia, she observes that yards and homes are littered with all manner of things just waiting to be repurposed, with the people using "washing machine parts as truck parts to see what will happen." She notes that holler folk "pile up objects ceaselessly and without goal in an 'insane collection' that values objects for themselves and not for their place in a systematic, 'collectable' order of things."[48] These characteristics of the Appalachian domestic scene materialize in horror films. Think of the Firefly homestead in Rob Zombie's films *House of 1000 Corpses* and *The Devil's Rejects*—clearly drawn from *The Texas Chain Saw Massacre*—bones assembled into light fixtures (another Ilse Koch reference; see chapter 3), decapitated dolls littering the mise-en-scène, a baroque assemblage of stuffed animals, and a multitude of other things. Stewart's description of the Appalachian home bears an uncanny resemblance to Zombie's sets:

> Picture the porches piled high with couches, chairs, plastic water jugs. The yards filled with broken toys, washing machines, scrap metal and salvaged wood, cars and trucks on blocks or belly-up being dismembered piece by piece. All the living room walls crowded with signs of absent presence: the pictures of kin who have left and the dead in their coffins, the paintings of the bleeding Sacred Heart of Jesus with the beautiful longing eyes. All the mantels and tabletops covered with *what nots* and shrines. The newspaper clippings of deaths and strikes.[49]

The dizzying collection of odds and ends that line the Firefly homestead is very much an outward projection of the family's internal psychology—chaotic, an unrestrained id—offering an image that is at once remarkably fascinating and at the same time deeply unsettling.

Zombie's film *The Devil's Rejects* effectively picks up where his earlier film *House of 1000 Corpses* left off. Like the slaughterhouse family in *The Texas Chain Saw Massacre*, the Firefly family preys on passersby. And similar to Hooper's film, when the group of twenty-somethings stops to pick up a hitchhiker—the seductive Baby Firefly, a Siren in another guise—this initiates a series of grave missteps. It is abundantly clear that Zombie's films, as Linnie Blake correctly observes, "pay self-conscious tribute to their generic

6.5 A baroque assemblage of things as a signifier of the American other in *House of 1000 Corpses* (Rob Zombie, 2003) and *The Devil's Rejects* (Rob Zombie, 2005).

precursors—Otis Firefly's penchant for wearing the faces of his victims, his brother Tiny's deformity, their charnel house of a homestead, the implication of incest and inbreeding, their insatiable taste for blood, and their penchant for hunting their prey down to the last woman—all echoing Hooper's and Craven's films of the 1970s."[50] Like Leatherface in *The Texas Chain Saw Massacre*, Otis has a workshop: a shack (appropriately a smokehouse) around the back of the house, a chapel of torture. Having abducted several cheerleaders, Otis has chained up the young women, incising into their chests phrases such as "Go team!" When the police finally come to investigate, prying the shack doors open, the women are all dead. One positioned at the center of the shack is hung in a cruciform (echoing the iconic Abu Ghraib photograph?),

6.6 Like Leatherface's workshop, Otis has his own torture chapel—appropriately a smokehouse—in *House of 1000 Corpses* (Rob Zombie, 2003).

with multiple antlers and a deer skull mounted above her head. The gruesome discovery prompts a nearly seamless slip into a flashback (set in slow motion), in which we see the women, strung up but still alive, writhe in agony. Mother Firefly entertains Sheriff George Wydell in the house parlor; when Wydell realizes that there is trouble at the back side of the house, Mother Firefly shoots him point-blank in the head. Like Eli Roth, Zombie is keenly aware of exploitation cinema and the multiple machinations of the horror genre, and he appropriates the fetishistic and sadistic treatment of female characters from them. And while Roth might from a certain perspective interrogate or perhaps even turn these conventions on their head, Zombie, on the other hand, in the spirit of Russ Meyer, lavishes the screen with unapologetic fetishistic/sadistic treatments of his female characters.

In *The Devil's Rejects*, Sheriff John Quincy Wydell, George's brother, aims to get revenge. After police descend on the Firefly homestead, Wydell orders the family to come out, but the Fireflys, outfitted with makeshift body armor, instead engage in a massive shoot-out with the police. Mother Firefly is captured, while Otis and Baby slip into the basement (notably lined with Guantánamo-like prison cells) and into a secret subterranean passage. Wydell, hell-bent on revenge, has already tortured Mother Firefly to death in her prison cell, in a manner reminiscent of torture scenes found in *24*, before apprehending Captain Spalding (a close associate of the Firefly family), Otis, and Baby to deliver "righteous" retribution. Drawn from that common Craven inversion, the figure of authority proves to be just as vicious as the Firefly family. Though he couches his actions in terms of "justice," the sheriff nevertheless

6.7 Sheriff Wydell tortures the Firefly family in *The Devil's Rejects* (Rob Zombie, 2005).

becomes the very thing that he is fighting. With the three Fireflys bound to chairs back at the homestead, the Sheriff begins, "You know, I got to thank you all—for helping me to understand what my heritage is. Now, my granddaddy, he rode with the likes of Tom Horn, killing scum like you for a living. We've always been devil slayers." Wydell—like the Jihadist or the American right-wing warmonger—invokes the divine to justify violence. Wydell proclaims that he tried to apply conventional law enforcement tactics, walking the line, but says, "I realize that there is no line. We here, we are playing on a level that most will never see." Zombie, on the DVD commentary, suggests that this statement sums up the film: "good and evil don't matter anymore." And does this not capture the very spirit of our time? With the utter collapse of the Manichean worldview? Where torture is viewed as a legitimate tool in the so-called War on Terror? And does not Wydell's personal heritage in some fashion correspond to the history of American violence—particularly in the project of "taming the Wild West"?

Linnie Blake similarly observes how "the dividing line between civilization and savagery, between the moral authority of the state and the amoral excrescence that is the Firefly clan, collapses as Wydell (avenging the death of his brother and some seventy other posited victims) tortures his victims with the enthusiasm of a madman."[51] Indeed, Wydell not only believes that he is carrying out justice (in the eyes of God); he revels in delivering pain—stapling forensic photographs of Otis's victims to his chest, doing the same to Baby, using an electric cattle prod on Captain Spalding, driving a large nail through each of Otis's hands, evoking, with Otis's Christ-like long, stringy hair and beard, the image of the stigmata. The prolonged vicious torture of the Firefly family has a curious emotional effect, because if the audience did not before, they very well might now shift their sympathy to the Fireflys despite the fact that they are on "the wrong side of the law" and are themselves ruthless killers.[52] Hillbilly horror, and Zombie's films in particular, Blake concludes, offers a countermemory to the conventional narratives that we tell ourselves.[53] And this is also evident in the next chapter, in which television programs wrestle with the post-9/11 narrative.

7

Soft-Core, and Beyond Torture Porn

Soft-Core Torture Porn

The Fox Network series *24* premiered November 6, 2001, predating torture porn. If we elect to crown James Wan's film *Saw*, which was released October 29, 2004, as the first torture porn film properly speaking, which I am inclined to do, then, *24* precedes it by three years. From a certain perspective, *Saw* might be viewed as the hardcore version of *24*. And it is interesting to note that Tobin Bell, the actor who plays Jigsaw, is also cast as Bauer's nemesis, Peter Kingsley, in the second season of *24*. Although *Saw* does not include elements of international intrigue, it nevertheless bears some of the hallmarks of the police procedural, which of course, in a nutshell, is what *24* is. One of the mainstays of the Fox program is the ticking-time-bomb scenario, lifting from Alfred Hitchcock's formula for suspense, as outlined in a famous conversation between him and the French filmmaker/critic François Truffaut. Hitchcock explains that if a bomb goes off in a film, it might give an immediate shock, but it does not offer suspense. The audience has to be made aware that the blast is imminent; as the Master of Suspense says, "In the first case we have given the public fifteen seconds of surprise at the moment of the explosion. In the second we have provided them with fifteen minutes of suspense." Hitchcock concludes that the audience needs to be made aware of the peril.[1] The coup of the *24* series is that it does not sustain the suspense for a mere fifteen minutes but for an entire season. And one of the ways it does this is through its constant references to time, effectively making viewers watch the time countdown on the imminent ticking time bomb. The *Saw* franchise uses this tactic too, frequently in the form of a digital readout similar to the typeface found throughout the *24* series. While a great number of lives are at stake in *24*, counting down to the imminent destruction of a city, or some such thing, in the *Saw* franchise, typically it is a solitary individual, or at most a handful of "players," racing against the clock before the "player's" body is rent asunder. As we found in the analysis of *Saw*, there are certain affinities between the countdown and the discourse of videogames. Bauer and his Counter Terrorist Unit (CTU) team, in a similar arrangement, are in a race against the clock to solve the riddle and "win" the game. And it is little wonder, then, just like the *Saw* films, that the Fox program spawned a videogame based on the series—*24: The Game* (2006).

The set pieces in *Saw* that exhibit the rending of a body or the vignettes in *Hostel* within the Slovakian torture factory, as discussed in previous chapters, evoke the shooting and editing strategies associated with hardcore pornography. The ratcheting up of tension in a torture number typically climaxes in the expulsion of bodily fluids; sequences include close-ups or extreme close-ups to offer gory forensic details akin to the meat shot in pornography. Television, on the other hand, even cable networks such as Showtime, target a much wider audience than the relatively small horror niche, and this consequently demands less explicit content—in a word, soft-core.

In "The Art of the Sp(l)atter: Body Horror in *Dexter*," coauthors Simon Brown and Stacey Abbott, without stating as much, appear to argue that *Dexter* is erotica or soft-core horror. The Showtime series as an example of soft-core programming "protects the audience from seeing the full horror of what Dexter actually does by framing the murders so that they are concealed from view. The sounds of his power tools and his victims' screaming, along with the occasional glimpse of blood, make it clear what he is doing but do not risk breaking the identification by having the audience see too much."[2] Whereas the soft-core obscures vision in one form or another, as Linda Williams views it in her *Hard Core: Power, Pleasure, and the "Frenzy of the Visible,"* the "hardcore tries *not* to play peek-a-boo with either its male or its female bodies. It obsessively seeks knowledge, through a voyeuristic record of confessional, involuntary paroxysm, of the 'thing' itself."[3] In addition—and I suspect this is perhaps even more significant than what is seen or hidden from view—whereas the hardcore tends to be more episodic, a string of vignettes, the soft-core is usually nested within a narrative.

There is no question that the graphic nature of sex and violence is veiled in television—visual fields are obscured by objects in the scene, camera angle, editing, mise-en-scène, and the like. Acts of violence on the small screen are typically more compact, taking up less narrative real estate. Violence on television tends to be given more context, which is precisely what so many film critics and scholars believe is missing from cinematic torture porn. Sex on television is tempered all the more compared to violence. It has been said more than once that Americans are far more comfortable with depictions of violence than they are with sex. This seems to be confirmed in the displacement of sex for violence in torture porn; cinematic torture porn presents a near negation of sex. The soft-core, in its hesitation to exhibit graphic sexual content, relies more on violence and dramatic tension. Truth be told, though, the graphic nature of cinematic torture porn is overstated. For any film to receive the coveted R-rating and to win theatrical distribution (which for the time being is still the standard distribution model), it must limit what it shows. And even when we consider that more graphic elements are offered as a "bonus" for the "uncut" DVD release, the amplified nature of the violence is still overstated.

We might presume that television programming, supposedly the pale shadow of its cinematic kin, is tame by comparison. While by certain measures this might be true, we should consider other factors. It is self-evident that the graphic nature of the violence (and the sexuality) on the small screen is more tempered, though some premium cable programs have been pushing boundaries. What is different is the intensity of the violence. What do I mean here? The intensity of the violence is fueled not so much by what is depicted immediately in the visual field (though that is part of it, no doubt) but by the fact that it is contextualized, framed within narrative motivations, be they for ill or for good. And here I might deploy David Edelstein's argument against itself: the violence might be more intense in television precisely because of its narrative framing, its motivations. Violence *is* motivated in television—Jack Bauer tortures to circumvent a terrorist plot, and Dexter kills to rid the world of scum. And with narrative motivation comes identification; the intensity of that violence—and dare I say it, the thrill associated with it—is rooted in our sympathy for the characters committing acts of violence, and perhaps this even renders us complicit. "Clearly, though, no one wants a Torture Channel added to their cable or satellite systems," Douglas Howard observes, "just as no one wants to be complicit in their own homemade Abu Ghraib, and, in order to alleviate any guilt that we might openly feel in endorsing this behaviour, *24* clearly couches its cruelty within the context of a timed crisis that makes it all morally acceptable."[4] Situating torture within a narrative, thus offering character motivations, if anything seems more dubious than the most gratuitous violence exhibited in torture porn, which makes little effort to contextualize it. The latter might even be more honest than the former.[5]

Moreover, while graphic violence is exchanged for amplified intensity, this might be the result of greater intimacy between the characters in television programs. Dexter's tactile relationship with his victims and his personal investment in dispatching them and Bauer's in-your-face interrogations and his compulsion to save America again and again from catastrophe—these inter-character relationships appeal to the viewing spectator's emotions. And to be precise here, emotions are a response to narrative content, such as character arcs or motivation, while the hyperstylized numbers of torture porn appeal more to our senses—along the lines of what is discussed in chapter 1. Many film critics/scholars seem to confuse and/or to conflate the two. Perhaps more than we do with Jigsaw, we identify with characters such as Bauer and Dexter; we want them to do terrible things, and there is distinct satisfaction when they accomplish their objectives. In fact, it seems that spectators are more enamored with what Jigsaw *does* (i.e., the execution of the sadistic disposition) than who he is. With Bauer and Dexter, while there is no denying that we find what they do thrilling, we are also invested in who they are and the successes that they might enjoy.

And perhaps when discussing the genre in the context of television, I should throw scare quotes around the term "torture porn," which I am inclined to do for films from abroad as well that share some of the traits of torture porn but are spawned by other cultural anxieties—*The Human Centipede*, *Martyrs*, *Wolf Creek*, *A Serbian Film*, *Kinatay*, *Funny Games*, *Inside*, *Cold Fish*, *Cut*. In both these cases, we find films from abroad or television programs trading in the currency of torture porn tropes without necessarily being torture porn properly speaking. While *Dexter*, as Brown and Abbott identify, might well qualify as soft-core horror, it is in actual fact far closer to a police procedural or thriller. Fox's *24*, with its international terrorist plots and espionage, has far more in common with *Taken* or *Marathon Man* than it does with *Hostel*. These television narratives form part of the soul-searching discussions spawned by revelations of enhanced interrogation techniques, the efficacy of torture, issues of culpability, and the like. Despite the differences, these programs either draw on or share close affinities with torture porn tropes.

In addition to *24* and *Dexter*, torture porn tropes have seeped into a wide range of television programs. The popular HBO series *Game of Thrones*, especially in the third season, exhibits elements of torture. Sadistic characters enact elaborate games—even allowing a character to "escape," for instance, only to discover that it was all a ruse, very much in the spirit of *Marathon Man* or *Captivity*. A wide range of programs incorporate elements of torture or extreme violence. The award-winning Showtime program *Homeland*, for instance—which is more in the spirit of *24* or *Syriana*—has viewers waiting with bated breath for the next dose of torture or scenes of extreme violence, and when it does not happen, there is a resounding cry of disappointment. The FX Network's *American Horror Story: Asylum*, a rare example of the horror genre on television, as opposed to programs that "nest" horror elements within other genres, includes medicalized horror that we associate with torture porn. ABC's *Revenge* is at its core a melodramatic soap opera, only a stone's throw from *Desperate Housewives*, but the underlying violence and the revenge plot that drives the narrative are not that far removed from the trope of retribution found in torture porn and its association with an inversion—the tortured becomes the torturer. Another ABC program, *Scandal*, features Olivia Pope, the White House communications director, who attempts to fix the public image of politicians. Violence is introduced into the plot in a number of ways, but of particular note is the explicit exhibition of torture, including waterboarding. The figure of the serial killer apparently continues to fascinate us, and this is certainly true of NBC's *Hannibal*, which for television includes some fairly gruesome imagery, frightful eruptions, stylized editing, and an embellished audio design that recalls torture porn. The spy thriller *The Blacklist* on NBC is peppered with scenes of extreme violence, medical gore, and torture.

The program that has most thoroughly assimilated the elements of torture porn is Fox Network's *The Following*—the inaugural season ran during the winter-spring prime-time lineup of 2013. Kevin Williamson, the *Scream* screenwriter, created *The Following*. While Williamson and others associated with the program are at pains to distinguish themselves from the "gore-fest" of torture porn, *The Following* nevertheless could be envisioned, like *24*, as a soft-core version of the *Saw* franchise. It is a police procedural/dramatic thriller with a bit of an edge to it. Joe Carroll is an extremely charismatic figure—a professor of American literature, specializing in Edgar Allan Poe—and he develops something of a following (hence the title). As it turns out, Carroll is also a serial killer. An FBI agent, Ryan Hardy, tirelessly pursues the killer and eventually is instrumental in his capture, all depicted within the pilot episode. In the climactic moments immediately prior to Carroll's capture, the serial killer manages to stab Hardy in the chest, nearly killing the agent and necessitating that he be fitted with a pacemaker. Although lauded for apprehending Carroll, Hardy leaves the FBI and writes a book on the serial killer.

Like Jigsaw, who orchestrates elaborate plans and little games, even after his death, Carroll, while in prison, initiates a complex scheme with the assistance of his acolytes. Many of the traps or set pieces in *The Following* are premised on Poe, and actually, in retrospect, we might recognize Poe in the *Saw* franchise. Think, for instance, of David Hackl's 2008 film *Saw V*, in which we find a man, Seth, strapped to a table and cut in half with a swinging pendulum; the grisly murder is erroneously attributed to Jigsaw but is Detective Hoffman's handiwork. Regardless of who set the trap, of course, it calls to mind Poe's story "The Pit and the Pendulum." In the reliance on violent numbers, there are seemingly built-in affinities between the film franchise and the television program.

One of the things that motivates Carroll's character is his effort to reunite with his family—his wife, Claire Matthews, and his young son, Joey Matthews. Carroll does in fact manage to escape from prison, and he finds refuge in a large rural estate occupied by his followers. During Hardy's initial investigation (and we learn this through flashbacks, another torture porn trope), an amorous relationship developed between Claire and the FBI agent. The animosity between Carroll and Hardy runs deep, then, and the triangulated relationship manufactures dramatic tension—something that Williamson is well known for.

Jigsaw is also motivated (at least in part) by the breakup of his family. His wife loses their child during an assault. This loss forever embitters Jigsaw, souring his relationship with his wife, and prompts his general contempt for people—especially those who take life for granted. Jigsaw's animatronic puppet, which is sometimes seen riding a child's tricycle, is an avatar of his son, killed in utero. Although Joey does not die in *The Following*, Carroll feels that his boy has been taken away from him, which further fuels his rage.

Carroll's disciples are numerous, and they are given particular assignments. Jacob Wells and Paul Torres pretend to be a gay couple and live next to a woman who survived an assault at Carroll's hand. Jacob and Paul, for a couple of years, function as a sleeper cell, waiting to be called into action—and when activated, the pair abduct their neighbor and deliver the woman to Carroll so that he might finish what he started. Emma Hill works as a sleeper cell too; she works as Claire's nanny, watching Joey. And at the appointed time, she abducts Joey right under the watchful noses of the police and FBI agents. Another triangulated relationship—Emma, Jacob, and Paul—ensures that more dramatic tension is built into the program. And just as in the *Saw* franchise, rivalries emerge. Emma's character, for instance, in her steadfast adherence to Carroll's project—murder as art—and her clear affection for him, shares certain affinities with Amanda and her relationship with Jigsaw in the *Saw* films.

Stylistically, there are some similarities between *The Following* and the *Saw* films. While there are limits to what can be aired on broadcast television, *The Following* pushes the envelope—screening fairly explicit gore and including startling jump-out-of-your-seat moments. In certain instances, I would even suggest that *The Following* is scarier than the *Saw* films, which rely more on gore, the choreography of the pornographic regime, and suspense. Carroll toys with the FBI, invoking the gaming motif that we associate with the *Saw* films. The television program also relies heavily on flashbacks to illustrate, for instance, how an acolyte became a Carroll follower. Although the program does not use a searing-hot white flash as a transition between the narrative diegetic space and the flashback, more often than not, a cut to a flashback is accompanied with a nondiegetic whooshing sound—effectively the audio equivalent of a hot white transition. As witnessed in *The Following*, television, clearly, has opened a space for the emergence of soft-core torture porn. Now let us consider *24* and *Dexter* in further detail and examine the qualities of soft-core torture porn.

Jack Bauer in *24*, or Jesus, Is That You?

Soft-core torture porn has always shadowed its hardcore cinematic cousin and perhaps even laid the foundation for it. Fox's *24*, as previously stated, was already in production when Al-Qaeda launched its 9/11 plot, and the tremendous popular success of the program suggests that it resonated with an anxious public. Conservative pundits, lawmakers, high-ranking American officials shaping the War on Terror narrative (including John Yoo),[6] American interrogators,[7] and even the Supreme Court justice Antonin Scalia[8] have all drawn on the program to justify the application of torture. The line of argument that begins, "What if, like in *24* . . ." is hyperbole—indeed, a fiction. And yet repeatedly, the refrain stands as if it were a self-evident argument, denying the reality and the complexities of interrogation. What many people fail to consider in the application of *24* logic is that when Jack Bauer tortures a terrorist subject, he knows that he is breaking the law and takes responsibility for it.[9] Bauer does not "get away with it"—he accepts the responsibility, sacrifices himself, even in the season 6 prequel donning a Jesus beard, bearing the cross so that we might carry on blissfully unaware that Armageddon has just narrowly been averted (or at least mitigated). The opening of the seventh season, for instance, begins with Senate hearings; Bauer sits before a panel of senators, and despite a vehement admonishment from the chair of the committee, Senator Blaine Mayer, Bauer refuses legal counsel, fully aware of the consequences.

Bauer is more than a hero; he is a martyr. "Torture is the modus operandi of personal discovery, rediscovery, and physical reformation, enacted by an alternating, shadowy figure whom we can only identify as a primal antagonist, be it the scenario's theoretical villain or presumptive hero. The *24* protagonist/antagonist Jack Bauer . . . , like Barnes (in *Syriana*) and V [in *V For Vendetta*], is victim as much as victimizer, transformers of lives, and loci of Christ-like suffering and rejuvenation."[10] Bauer knows exactly what he is doing and that it is wrong, but he does it for the greater good; he sacrifices himself (morally) for us, because the terrorists leave him no other choice.[11] While it is Bauer who breaks fingers and tortures his own brother to death, as much as his subjects suffer, Bauer bears the burden of it, and in the end, it is Bauer who is viewed as the victim.

There is an inversion that takes place here, because it is really the terrorists' "fault"—inversions, of course, being a common torture porn trope. In Bauer's refrain, "Damn you for making me do this!" there is also an inversion. Lindsay Coleman notes,

> The high priest of the CTU [Bauer] suffers with his victims. In this respect the agents of torture, clearly, cannot apply their methods without some masochistic tinge. This self-flagellating contemporary trend in the depiction of torture may

> be detected in the *Saw* films (Wan 2004; Bousman 2005), which like *24* deal with explicit torture as an important narrative element. Just as Bauer seeks to draw the truth of his victims' actions from them, so does the serial killer Jigsaw seek, through punishment, to educate his victims in their hypocrisies and misdeeds.[12]

The oscillation between victim and victimizer is part of what Jean Baudrillard refers to as the "mental hygiene" of post-9/11 violence: Bauer's acts of violence are warranted because he—personally and as an agent of the U.S. government—is the victim.[13] In the second season's twelfth episode, "Day 2: 7:00 PM–8:00 PM," Bauer arranges for the mock execution of the son of Syed Ali, a terrorist, and in his characteristic appropriation of victimization, he says to Ali, "I despise you for making me do this." The narrative logic of the victim absolves Bauer and the viewer of responsibility for the violence, or as Douglas Howard says, "Not only does *24* give us our weekly dose of sadism, then, but it also painlessly reconciles it for us before our consciences ever kick in."[14] For every film critic and scholar who laments the absence of narrative contextualization, here is perhaps another way to view it: narrative context justifies barbarity.

The lie that the Fox program peddles season after season, episode after episode, is that torture works—"I stopped that attack from happening!" Bauer harangues during the Senate hearing in the premier episode of season 7. Despite evidence to the contrary, *24* panders this fiction. Veteran interrogators refute this claim—an individual subjected to torture is likely to say

7.1 Jack Bauer arranges for the mock execution of Syed Ali's son in the second season of *24*, "Day 2: 7:00 PM–8:00 PM" (Frederick King Keller, Fox Network, February 11, 2003).

anything to make the suffering stop; the veracity of statements made under duress is always suspect. "But Jack Bauer's torture not only elicits the truth," Dahlia Lithwick observes; "it does so before the commercial."[15] The conceit of the dramatic program, nevertheless, supports the right-wing delusion that torture, or torture by another name—enhanced interrogation techniques—has prevented a repeat of 9/11. The truth is that the viewing public wants the world to be this simple—Jack Bauer is never wrong, he always interrogates the right person, he always gets actionable intelligence vindicating his actions, no matter how egregious, and the violence visited on the tortured subject expedited the delivery of vital information to avert the terrorist plot. Indeed, as David Edelstein notes, "Our righteousness is buoyed by propaganda like the TV series *24*, which devoted an entire season to justifying torture in the name of an imminent threat: a nuclear missile en route to a major city. Who do you want defending America? Kiefer Sutherland or terrorist-employed civil-liberties lawyers?"[16] When framed in this highly simplified way, lacking any nuance, the choice is clear.

The aesthetic tropes of torture in *24* are not that far removed from torture porn. The torture of Syed Ali (season 2, episode 12), like many of the other torture scenes in the series, takes place in a subterranean site—in this particular case, the basement of a mosque. The walls are bare, the set lightly dressed—and nothing ornate, a functional table, a chair, some free-standing industrial-grade lights—the space bathed in a pale, dingy yellow color palette, similar to the colors found in the *Hostel* films. The use of practicals—lights within the scene itself, rather than conventional studio lighting—makes for a low-light environment, sharply accented by the lights supposedly brought in by Bauer's team. The spare mise-en-scène is quite indicative of the torture porn aesthetic. Interesting, too, is the inclusion of audio elements that suggest the "subterranean," namely, the sound of dripping water (at 4:13 and again at 14:13). There is no apparent source for this audio element, and it appears to be used solely for effect. From Stephen Gaghan's 2005 thriller *Syriana* to *24* and even Errol Morris's 2008 documentary *Standard Operating Procedure*, it is striking, as Lindsay Coleman observes, how frequently torture is set within subterranean environments—invoking the heterotopic. "The dimly lit CTU, Abu Ghraib harsh walls, the black corridors of the CIA—all are spaces outside the public realm." These spaces, though, by no small coincidence are aligned with the sadistic demand to sequester violence within a hermetic space. Coleman continues, "These spaces and their associated realms, be they lonely streets or some distant cell in a land far from the narrative's center, are chambers of transformation. Like perverse catacombs, they are venues of renunciations of faith and womblike parturition."[17] The function of the space is to isolate, to remove the violence from the public sphere, and this is also indicative of torture porn.

Among the enhanced interrogation techniques that the CIA employs is mock executions,[18] which of course are featured as a tactic to try to break Ali. Not only does Bauer beat Ali and break his finger, in an effort to get him to talk, but Ali is also made to believe that his eldest son has been executed on Bauer's orders. The conceit of the mock execution is delivered through a video feed. The grain of the video, the motion of the handheld camera (held presumably by an American operative), the momentary blurring of the image associated with a consumer-grade video camera with an autofocus, the "amateurish" framing—all emphasize the "reality" of what is seen on the video monitors. This is similar to a scene in Darren Lynn Bousman's 2005 film *Saw II*, when Detective Eric Matthews has Jigsaw in custody. A bank of surveillance monitors feeds video from within a house where one of Jigsaw's games is being played out. The static view (characteristic of a surveillance camera) and the grain of the image, similar to what we find in the *24* episode, lend the video image veracity. Among the seven "players" is the detective's son, Daniel. What Detective Matthews does not know is that what is presumed to be a live video feed is in fact a recording; while Detective Matthews imagines that time is running out, analogous to the ticking-time-bomb scenario in *24*, in fact, he only needs to wait and be patient. Ali and Matthews, both goaded by threats to their sons, are manipulated through the use of (surveillance) video. The mediation of violence through video is also a common torture porn trope.

Inversion is used with frequency in *24*; the intended function of medical technology is turned on its head. And this is true of friend and foe alike. Abu Fayed in season 6 hooks Bauer up to an EKG machine to monitor his vital signs to ensure that he does not die—at least not too quickly. And as Michael J. Lewis observes, "Fayed also uses crude medical instruments as means of causing pain."[19] Bauer and the CTU are just as likely—actually even more likely—to employ medical technology to inflict pain. In the episode in which Bauer is compelled to torture his own brother, a CTU agent monitors a bank of computer screens to register the subject's vitals while administering a drug that produces pain. In another instance, a national security adviser, Roger Stanton, in season 2 is tortured using a defibrillator. Whereas the medical instruments that Bauer and the CTU use are "top of the line," the same cannot be said of Fayed's, which are "crude and rusted," but in all cases the torturers are "perverting their intended use," as Lewis notes. "Instead of being tools of healing they are tools of pain."[20] The bald face of abjection is here, for the very things that are "supposed to save me from death"[21] are repurposed as instruments of destruction.

The twenty-first episode of season 8 of *24*, "Day 8: 12:00 PM–1:00 PM," has one of the most explicit examples of torture in the series. In an effort to unravel a complex international plot involving the Russian mob and a peace treaty to be signed between the United States and the fictional Middle Eastern

Islamic Republic of Kamistan (clearly modeled after Iran), Bauer tortures Pavel Tokarev, a Russian assassin. In an earlier episode, Tokarev kills Renee Walker, a CTU agent and Bauer's love interest; though a veteran assassin with a high-powered sniper rifle and a clear shot, Tokarev purposefully ensured that Walker died a slow, painful death. Bauer, in this case, not only has obligations to his country but also has a personal stake in reaping revenge.

In this torture scene, the color palette is much cooler than in the mock execution discussed earlier; in this case, the set is dressed in cold steel-blue/green, closer to the color scheme associated with the *Saw* franchise. Once again, torture is set within a cavernous space—perhaps a large commercial space under renovation or a warehouse. The walls are bare and exhibit signs of age—peeling paint, exposed concrete beams, bare concrete floor, and cyclone fencing that partitions the space.

The good/evil dichotomy is reinforced in the nature of the violence in *24*. Jack Bauer and the terrorists (of all stripes) all employ violence. Bauer does it "as a reluctant hero," while the terrorists are motivated by selfishness or other self-centered reasons.[22] Bauer tortures because he has to; the terrorists (or other nefarious characters) torture because they want to. While there might be some overarching political reason for terrorist actions, without fail, the terrorists are ultimately motivated by selfish ambitions, perhaps hijacking a political cause to serve their own personal gain or to settle a personal score.[23] There is also a racial dimension to the antagonists that populate the *24* series. Bauer, the golden-haired American, is set in contrast to a cast of national/racial others. There is nothing inherently wrong with this per se; the *24* plots are about international intrigue, after all. In many instances, of course, fueled by our experience in the post-9/11 world, terrorists are frequently cast as Arabs. As Tung Yin observes, "The problem with the depiction of Arabs as terrorists in *24* lies less in that Arabs have in fact been cast as the villains. Rather, the problem lies in the one-dimensional nature of the Arab terrorists as nihilistic ciphers—they are essentially dehumanized, which in turns makes the torture inflicted upon them by Bauer more palatable than if they were seen as persons."[24]

Yin approaches the *24* series through the legal lens and notes in the opening of his article that Bauer "is, by any reasonable measure, a criminal. He routinely violates laws against torture, murder, aggravated assault, armed robbery (including carjacking), airplane hijacking, burglary, and making false statements to government officials (usually his superiors)."[25] And this is a man that Justice Scalia and other American officials laud as a hero? This is a man that current interrogators hope to emulate? The Fox program clearly supports the neocon contention that enhanced interrogation techniques are legitimate tools. From a slightly different perspective, perhaps an overly optimistic one though, Coleman concludes about the series, "through television and further revelations of improper conduct, the viewing public seeks, perversely, to learn more of its own nature through their prolonged voyeuristic engagement with both fictional and real-life proxies."[26] Sade's casts of libertines were examples of what not to be; the *24* narratives, on the other hand, are perhaps not extreme enough to be read in these pedagogic terms.

Dexter: Our Hero, Our Monster

Jack Bauer might be a martyr, but Dexter Morgan, the title character of the Showtime series, is a superhero. Jigsaw is also a superhero. Like Batman, Jigsaw's superhero persona is spawned from a traumatic event, he pursues vigilante justice, and he leads a secret double life. (And I suspect that the sharp increase in darkly toned superhero films in the wake of 9/11 plays to anxieties similar to those that fuel torture porn narratives.) Jigsaw does not wear a mask, but he wears a hood and cloak (or robe). He is exceedingly resourceful and intelligent and creates fabulous machines that execute "justice." The same might be said of Dexter; he is also a superhero. In "From Silver Bullets to Duct Tape: Dexter versus the Traditional Vigilante Hero," Stan Beeler approaches the character of Dexter in these terms as well. Superman is "an alien pretending to be the human Clark Kent,"[27] he observes, and Batman hides his identity to assist the police. In "The Dark Defender," the fifth episode of the second season of *Dexter*, a comic-book illustrator, Denny Foster, depicts the mysterious vigilante killer that is dubbed the Bay Harbor Butcher as a superhero. Unbeknownst to Foster and the other characters, the Bay Harbor Butcher is none other than Dexter. An associate of the now-deceased Foster explains that the comic-book illustrator had the ambition to adapt the Bay Harbor Butcher news story into a graphic novel, *The Dark Defender*: "stalker of the night, his blade of vengeance turns wrong into right" is Foster's tagline. Although Dexter is captivated by a poster bearing his avatar, he explains in an interior monologue, "I never really got the whole superhero thing, but lately it seems we have a lot in common: tragic beginnings, secret identities, part human, part mutant, archenemies." Dexter is enamored with the superhero vision and even dreams of himself dressed as The Dark Defender saving his mother from a grisly death, but he sardonically dismisses it: "The Dark Defender—nah, Miami is too hot for all that leather."

Casting these characters as superheroes is a rhetorical exercise obviously; Jigsaw and Dexter—no matter which way you cut it—are murderers. David Edelstein posits, "Something has changed in the past few decades. Serial killers occupy a huge—and disproportionate—share of our cultural imagination: As potential victims, we fear them, yet we also seek to identify with their power." He continues by observing, "A key archetype is Will Graham in Thomas Harris's *Red Dragon*—a genius serial-killer tracker because he can walk through grisly crime scenes and project himself into the killers' heads. He's

7.2 Dexter imagined as The Dark Defender in season 2 of *Dexter*, "The Dark Defender" (Keith Gordon, Showtime, October 28, 2007).

both the instrument of justice and the empathic consumer of torture porn."[28] These words could easily describe the pro(an)tagonist of *Dexter*, which ran from 2006 to 2013, following the rise and fall of the torture porn cycle.

Dexter is a serial killer, but he only selects victims who "deserve" to die—other murderers. He works in the forensics department of the Miami Police Department, as a blood-spatter expert—Dexter, like Graham, "can walk through grisly crime scenes and project himself into the killers' heads." And while Graham, a legendary FBI agent, dispenses justice through legitimate channels, Dexter delivers justice through the judicial system and through extrajudicial means. Though Dexter is certainly a consumer of torture porn, he is also a producer of it. (Dexter might be considered a consumer of torture porn insofar as he finds pleasure in gruesome crime scenes or marvels at another killer's work. Dexter's veiled pleasure, in fact, is what prompts the detective James Doakes to becomes suspicious of Dexter.) As with most serial killers, Dexter keeps trophies of his kills: a drop of blood on a glass slide. (Though there are a few exceptions when Dexter cannot, for whatever reason, go through his full ritual.) His sister works along side him, working through the ranks as the series progresses and eventually, but reluctantly, functioning as his accessory in season 7. Dexter follows a strict code dictated by his adoptive father, Harry Morgan, a veteran cop. Like Jigsaw, Dexter is the pro(an)tagonist of the series; we identify with him and his capacity to effect change. Dexter dispenses "justice" quickly and definitively—no drawn-out trials, no chance that a subject might get off on a technicality, no avenues to an appeal. Despite the fact that Dexter is a murderer, we are rooting for him; we desperately want him to dispatch scum, to "clean up" the world, to do the business that the conventional criminal justice system for whatever reason has failed to.

Dexter is a monster, and he knows it. As a young boy, three years old, Dexter (and his elder brother) watched their mother, Laura Moser, get hacked to bits by a chainsaw-wielding murderer inside a large shipping container. Harry found Dexter and his brother and eventually adopted the younger boy. During his teenage years, Dexter begins to exhibit the traits of a budding serial killer, such as killing animals. In "If I Had a Hammer," the sixth episode of the fourth season, Dexter confesses to the audience in his characteristic voice-over (and this device is used a lot), "I was born of primordial ooze." He continues, explaining, "I crawled out of my own mother's blood. I hid amongst the humans, hoping not to be seen. But somewhere along the way, I grew legs, stood upright. I became a husband, a father. I had to evolve. It was the only way to survive." It is Harry, in part, that is the catalyst for Dexter's evolution. Harry advises Dexter against familial trappings, though, as he realizes that Dexter cannot give a partner enough attention, shepherd a child (or children), and tend to his "Dark Passenger," as Dexter calls his compulsion to kill, all at the same time.

Harry, an accomplished detective and mindful of Dexter's traumatic past, attempts to channel Dexter's need to kill for "good." When Harry confronts Dexter, realizing that something must be done, he has a little heart-to-heart with the teenager. Finding dried blood on Dexter's knife collection, Harry demands an explanation. "Animals—I find animals, that's all," Dexter insists. "Okay, so we can't stop this," Harry concedes, "but maybe we can do something, to channel it, use it for good." The youngster throws back, "How could it ever be good?" The seasoned detective shares, "Son, there are people out there that do really bad things—terrible people. And the police can't catch them all. Do you understand what I'm saying?" Dexter answers in schoolboy obedience, "You're saying—they deserve it." The master-pupil relationship starts here, and a nondiegetic drone signals the conception of a monster, as Dexter's father responds, "That's right, but of course you've got to learn how to spot them, how to cover your tracks. But I can teach you." Suddenly burdened with this tremendous realization and responsibility, Dexter shows signs of anxiety, but his father reassures him, "It's okay, Dex, you can't help what happened to you. But you can make the best of it. Remember this forever: you are my son, you are not alone, and you are loved." Counter to the tenderness and the genuine love expressed between a father and son, the nondiegetic drone gestures toward the inherent perverted articulation of law, order, system—the abject monster that Harry has conceived.

From the inaugural moments of the series, Harry is already dead. He, like Jigsaw, repeatedly returns from the dead in flashbacks or more commonly as a conversant vision—a spectral incarnation of Dexter's superego. Harry frequently returns to Dexter at moments of high tension or critical junctures when Dexter is faced with some sort of choice. He is there to chide Dexter when his son—to his eyes—is about to make a poor choice, to coach and counsel him, but he is also there as a loving and proud father. The spectral Harry undergoes a transformation as the series progresses; convinced that his son is a monster through and through, he offers the Code of Harry not just to execute "justice" but to keep his son out of the electric chair, the first rule being "Don't get caught." Harry is forced to reconsider his position when he recognizes human qualities in his son. In the ninth episode of the fifth season, "Teenage Wasteland," Dexter beats up an abusive father to protect his stepdaughter, Astor, and her friend. When Harry appears following the incident, Dexter expects to be given a lecture, but instead Harry commends him, even saying, "I'm proud of you." Harry continues, "I underestimated you—assumed you were a monster, when you were capable of so much more [i.e., of being human]. If only I had seen it, I wouldn't have led you down this path." It is interesting, if not ironic, that Harry views this act of violence as a sign of genuine humanity.

For all Harry's good intentions and genuine affection, there is something quite dubious about him and the way he has channeled Dexter's compulsion to kill. "Harry is really more Victor Frankenstein than Ward Cleaver," Douglas Howard observes, "where the sins of the creator are revisited upon the creation and give birth to a different kind of monster."[29] Howard's comparative analysis between Mary Shelley's classic novel and *Dexter* is superbly persuasive. Howard observes that in *Frankenstein*, "the creature becomes Victor's symbolic attempt to resurrect or recoup the loss of his mother,"[30] and this finds affinities with Dexter, because Harry's molding of the youngster into a neat monster is born out of the death of Dexter's mother. Harry is the creator and, like Victor, envisions his son as the grand arbiter of justice. Dexter and his sister initially idolize Harry, viewing him as an infallible figure, the God-like creator,[31] but as the series develops, they learn that their father was not as virtuous as they made him out to be. We learn, for instance, that Harry was having an adulterous affair with Dexter's mother, who was working with him as a confidential informant, possibly shedding new light on Harry's earlier declaration, "Remember this forever: *you are my son*, you are not alone, and you are loved." This might also explain why Harry adopts Dexter but not his elder brother. As Dexter learns more about Harry, he begins to realize that he has been molded into Harry's "own personal vendetta machine," as Dexter says in "Our Father," the opening episode of the third season. And when Dexter, "like Shelley's creature," discovers in Harry "a significantly flawed creator, a man prone to temptation and weakness, a liar, a cheater, and a manipulator,"[32] his faith in the God-like creator is shaken. We learn, however, in the eighth season that a psychiatrist, Dr. Evelyn Vogel, played by Charlotte Rampling, is the architect of the Code; she counseled Harry on how to channel Dexter's compulsion. The Frankenstein motif is explicitly addressed early in the eighth season; while Dexter laments that Dr. Vogel has created a monster, she instead views him as sheer perfection.

Harry's faith is shaken, and he grows unsure of what he has created (and this is expressly detailed in season 8). In "There's Something about Harry," the tenth episode of the second season, in a flashback, Harry, as if catching his young boy with pornography, discovers Dexter (at about eighteen years of age) in the family garage, dismembering a body. "Hey, Dad," Dexter says, searching for approval, "look what I did. It's Juan Rainez, the pimp who killed that girl. I finally got him for you." Speechless, horrified at the sight, Harry turns away and throws up. Concerned, Dexter, who is wearing a clear vinyl raincoat, covered in blood, innocently asks, "Dad, what's wrong? Are you okay?" Gasping and disgusted, Harry responds, "Just stay away. Please, stay away." Three days later, Harry kills himself, disgusted by what he has created. Victor turns away from his monster too, disgusted by the sight of it.[33] While Dexter's faith in the Code of Harry might falter, it remains a guiding principle throughout. Harry certainly has created a monster in Dexter, but Dexter, unlike the monster in *Frankenstein*, never completely disavows his creator. The Code of Harry comes into question at certain instances, but at the end of the day, Dexter returns to it—and the same goes for the spectral Harry; he never abandons his son.

While Dexter and Harry, monster and creator, come to terms with each other, ultimately, "Dexter is," as Howard observes, "only a more advanced form of artificial life, a bizarre cross between Robbie the Robot and Michael Myers or Mr. Data with a butcher's knife, and, for all of Harry's instructions, he still lacks the feelings that would make him whole."[34] Dexter is all too aware of his nature; he knows what he is, and in order to survive, he must feign human feelings. Dexter and Harry (at least in his spectral incarnation) take ownership of the monster that has been spawned. But the question remains, does the spectator? Subtextually, the series is about culpability and appears to ask this question: To what extent are we willing to go in the name of security? Are we prepared to take responsibility for the monsters that we have created? Do we in the end want Harry's little monster out there "cleaning up" the streets? Is Dexter our hero or our monster or even both?

The inaugural episode of the series exhibits many of the characteristic conventions associated with the torture porn genre. Take, for instance, Dexter's stalking of Jaworski—a man who videotapes himself raping and killing women and then posts the footage on his hardcore sadomasochism website, "Scream, Bitch, Scream." Torture porn frequently mediates violence in some fashion—video cameras, surveillance monitors—and in this specific instance, violence is mediated through Dexter's computer screen. As Dexter clicks his way through Jaworski's site, we witness Jaworski raping a woman, her mouth covered with tape, her hands shackled to a pipe. The violence is set in a hermetic space: a sparse, confined room with cold, dank cement walls, dimly lit and furnished with nothing more than a dingy mattress. When Dexter recognizes a distinctive tattoo on Jaworski's right arm—confirming his identity beyond the shadow of a doubt—Dexter says in his characteristic voice-over, "Now it's just a matter of time before he becomes a drop of blood in my glass-slide collection." Dexter, as he is saying this, is bathed in blood-red light. Dexter continues, "But I have to wait," as the camera pulls into a tighter shot; "I have to be careful and follow the Code of Harry." Using a graphic match, we are suddenly flung into a flashback, the image of Dexter's face consumed by a naked, burning-hot white lightbulb. In many instances, torture porn uses an unmotivated hot white flash as a transition between the diegetic narrative and a flashback; in this particular case, though, the hot white finds the glowing lightbulb in the Morgan family's shed (or garage) as its motivating source—leading directly into the illuminating scene in which Harry first confronts Dexter about his insatiable desire to kill and Harry's determination to channel it. Many of these elements are on screen only for a split second, but nonetheless, many of the conventions of torture porn are on exhibition here: mediating violence through a form of technology, a bound victim, a sparse torture chamber, a flashback, and hot white light used as a transitioning device.

Some of the most explicit torture porn conventions are found in the fifth season. Dexter pursues Boyd Fowler, a serial killer by night, dead-animal sanitation worker by day. Clouded by emotions and too anxious to move on from Rita's death (his wife and the mother of his child, killed in the final moments of season 4), Dexter does not use his standard overabundance of caution and nearly botches the kill. In fact, his first attempt to kill Fowler goes horribly wrong, necessitating a hastily constructed kill room in Fowler's home. What Dexter does not know is that he is being watched. Just after plunging a knife into Fowler's heart, Dexter hears shuffling feet from behind a ventilation grate on the door leading to the attic. Dexter discovers a woman, Lumen Ann Pierce, locked in the attic—whip marks cover her back, and she is dirty and frail. Had Dexter been more methodical, he would have discovered that Fowler was really little more than a custodian for a network of torturers—Lumen is only the latest victim in a string of tortured and slain young women. This season quickly begins to resemble the rudiments of the *Hostel* plots. Fowler's attic and a remote summer camp take the place of the Slovakian factory, and the circle of torturers in the fifth season echoes the Elite Hunting syndicate.

Reluctantly at first, Dexter trains Lumen in the tricks of the trade, teaching her the Code of Harry. The pair hunt down the circle of men led by Jordan Chase, a motivational speaker, who torture and kill women. Before Dexter agrees to help Lumen, she strikes out on her own. Her first kill does not go well, and she has to call Dexter to help her clean things up. Later, at his home,

Dexter finds Lumen in the bath, echoing the pose of his murdered wife, Rita. Lumen uses Rita's towels to dry off and her robe; when Dexter goes to drain the tub, he is suddenly stricken with a flashback—marked with an explosive hot white and a surge of nondiegetic sound (season 5, episode 6, 44:54)—cutting back to the bloody scene of Rita's murder. Lumen's gesture, the donning of Rita's robe, and the tub all spark the violent return of the repressed, which is represented in a manner so characteristic of the torture porn genre.

Flashbacks also haunt Lumen. In "Circle Us," the seventh episode of the season, when Dexter and Lumen return to Fowler's home in an effort to remove any evidence that Lumen was there (they need to ensure that the police will not connect Lumen, and consequently Dexter, to an open homicide investigation), she is assailed by flashbacks. As soon as Dexter slides the bar lock to the attic door leading to the Chase circle's torture chamber, the diegetic sound of the lock (28:16) mixes with a scraping metallic sound verging on a scream, inaugurating a series of shots in rapid succession. This is highly indicative of the flashbacks found in the *Saw* franchise. While there is no hot white transition in this case, the metallic nondiegetic sound design, coupled with the lightning-fast series of shots, finds clear affinities with torture porn.

Indicative of *Dexter*'s soft-core status, images in Lumen's flashback are partially obscured and remain onscreen for only the blink of an eye—the sparse torture chamber with its naked wood framing, a rope coiled on a soiled twin-sized mattress mounted on a simple metal frame, Lumen's foot and calf hooked around her rapist as she is presumably being violated, a man's dress shoe, and Lumen's arm gripped tightly by one of the assailants (these individual shots are only intelligible by going frame by frame). Despite the brisk editing and the compositions that partially obstruct our view, when the images are taken together and joined to the nondiegetic audio, we are given a frightful vision of Lumen's torment. In the torture chamber itself, Lumen is presented with still more flashbacks—at least two male figures grip her body, her arms are shackled to the metal bedframe, she is blindfolded, and at least one of the male figures unbuckles his pants. All the while, the audio channels are flooded with screams, modulated for effect.

Using the door lock as a triggering device for a flashback is also quite indicative of the torture porn genre. In torture porn films, doors or locks might trigger a flashback or some sort of dreadful revelation—things are not going to end well—and in many cases, this is followed by highly stylized editing or camerawork. In the *Hostel* films, doors and locking mechanisms creak and clang, reverberating throughout the torture facility. In the *Saw* franchise, doors slam shut; think, for instance, of the closing shot in the first installment, clearly drawn from *The Texas Chain Saw Massacre*, in which Leatherface slams the sliding metal door to his workshop. Doors are set to timers, slamming shut after a player has "lost," and keys open locks, initiating the game or becoming

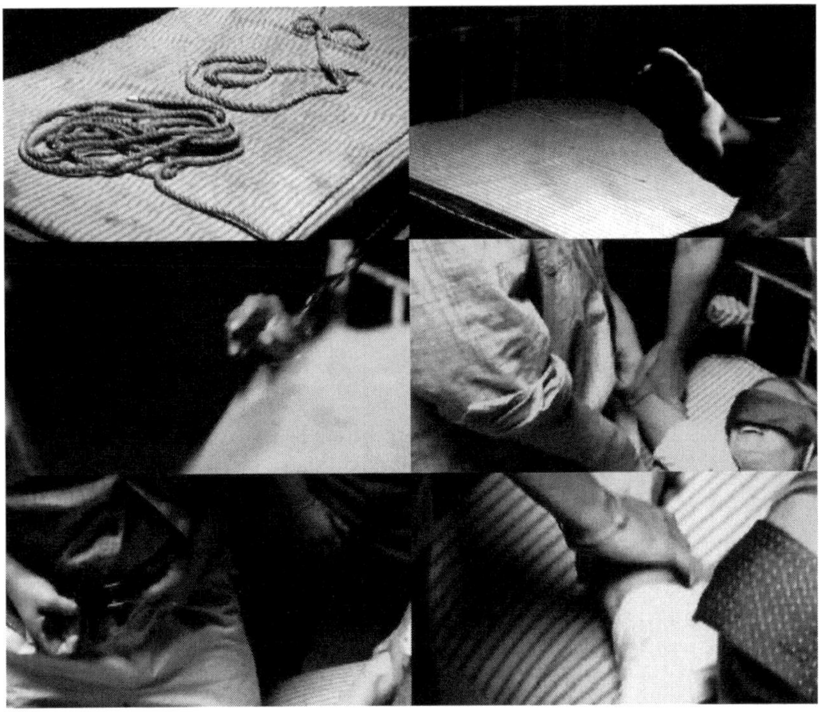

7.3 Stylistically similar to the *Saw* films, traumatic memories assail Lumen in the fifth season of *Dexter*, "Circle Us" (John Dahl, Showtime, November 7, 2010).

the object of a game. Amanda, for instance, has to locate the key in her drug dealer's stomach to unlock her reverse bear trap.

In the final episode of the fifth season of *Dexter*, Dexter and Lumen find themselves bound and strung up in the abandoned summer camp, River Jordan Camp, from which Jordan takes his name (his real name is Eugene Greer). This is where Jordan and his circle first developed their taste for torture. The abandoned summer camp has the hallmarks of a torture porn heterotopic site—bathed in a sickly yellow light, dingy walls and floors, hooks, metal fixtures that exhibit the patina of age, a spare metal bed frame, plain light fixtures, grimy tiles, begrimed shower fixtures, and worn metal tools and chains exhibited on the wall for effect. (The summer camp, though, also evokes slasher films.) The tide turns, though, and Dexter and Lumen manage to finally get the upper hand. Improvising, Dexter straps Chase to a gurney with dingy canvas straps and worn leather bindings—all found at the site, presumably, and in a stroke of poetic justice, used in the torture of past victims.

In some cases, Dexter (and the proper authorities) are confronted with a perpetrator who creates elaborate tableaus. The "Doomsday Killer," Travis Marshall, for instance, in season 6 sets up a trap for the police. When the

7.4 Torture porn mise-en-scène found in the fifth season of *Dexter*, "The Big One" (Steve Shill, Showtime, December 12, 2010).

police arrive at a crime scene, they discover a female victim suspended and bound but still alive; when an officer unsuspectingly triggers a trip wire, the victim falls into a cruciform, arms outstretched with angelic white wings, and the device punctures her jugular, causing her to bleed out and die. This trap in particular is something that Jigsaw might marvel at.

In certain instances, the elements of torture porn are exhibited in jest. In the opening episode of season 3, for instance, "Our Father," we are presented with images that are expected to elicit dread. The very first shot (following the opening title credits) is a large medical lamp, which when turned on is coupled with diegetic electrical static (an audio embellishment for sure) and a nondiegetic thud, all highly characteristic of the *Saw* franchise. The lamp, nearly filling the frame, emits a blinding hot white light. Dexter's characteristic voice-over begins to ruminate as a man (we presume Dexter) snaps on surgical gloves. This is followed by the exhibition of a highly polished metal surgical tray with an assortment of medieval-looking surgical instruments; this shot too is coupled with a nondiegetic audio element—the twang of a knife being sharpened. A drill whirring close to the camera and a syringe, which follows the chilling display of surgical instruments, embellish the scene further. The image of the syringe is coupled with the stock shrill of violins, a cliché of the horror genre. This is all very reminiscent of the opening of *Turistas*. In the

7.5 A trap that would have Jigsaw marvel, as found in the sixth season of *Dexter*, "The Angel of Death" (S. J. Clarkson, Showtime, October 30, 2011).

absence of any establishing shot, we presume that we have found Dexter with his latest catch, but when the camera does give us a wider shot, we find Dexter in a dentist's chair, receiving regular dental care. The shots and the audio elements, on their own, gesture toward the conventions of torture porn, as well as a host of other films—*Rome, Open City*, *Marathon Man*, *Hostel*—but in the mundane setting of "good oral hygiene," they are a metacinematic quip.

Dexter is a clinical sadist second to none. In the inaugural episode of the series, simply titled "Dexter," the title character says in voice-over, "Harry was a great cop here in Miami. He taught me how to think like one; he taught me how to cover my tracks. I'm a very neat monster." Dexter is very neat in everything he does, from doing thorough research to ascertain the guilt of his target to methodically planning his kill, setting the ritualized kill within a hermetic space, and meticulously disposing of the dismembered subject. Clinical sadism goes by a different name in the series: the Code of Harry.

We are first introduced to the Code of Harry in the first episode, framed between a planned kill and its execution. During the planning, Dexter says in voice-over, "Preparation is vital. No detail can be overlooked," and Dexter adds—surveying the blueprints of a building where the kill is to take place—"and the ritual is intoxicating." Adding to the idea that it is ritual that most excites him, Dexter finds no satisfaction in sex, especially early in the series. He feigns human interactions and sexual interest to cloak his true self. The planning, the preparation, the hunt, and the highly choreographed and ritualized kill—that is what gratifies him, what he finds "intoxicating." Libidinal energy

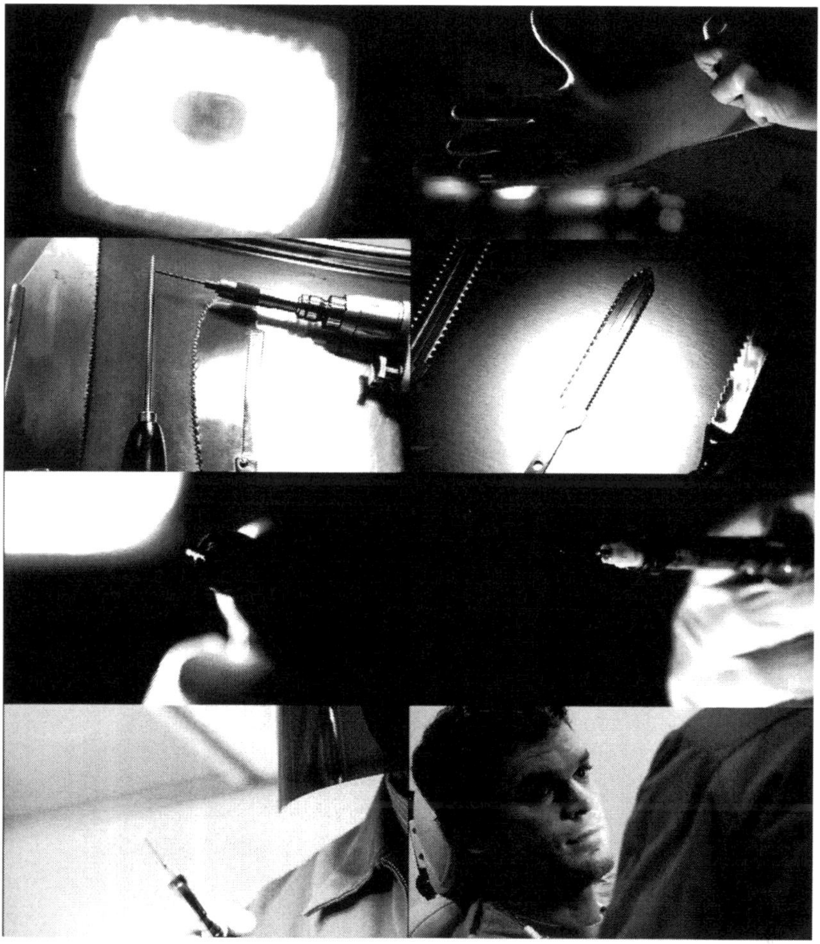

7.6 The ruse of torture porn tropes as found in the third season of *Dexter*, "Our Father" (Keith Gordon, Showtime, September 28, 2008).

does not find "normal" outlets but instead is sublimated in the eroticization of law and its execution, that is to say, the execution of the Code of Harry.

Arguably, it is not until season 5 that Dexter expresses any genuine emotion or erotic feelings. While hunting down the members of Jordan Chase's circle, Dexter develops feelings for Lumen. This is made possible not out of pity for Lumen but because she also develops a taste for sadism. When Dexter incrementally allows Lumen to participate in the killing of the Chase circle, the affection that develops between the two directly corresponds to how much Lumen knows about and finally can execute the Code. In her character's transformation, Lumen exchanges the heteronormative libidinal channels of eroticism for the execution of the Code of Harry. In the eighth episode, "Take It!," when her ex-fiancé, Owen, arrives in Miami unannounced and asks her to go around the world with him (literally, he has purchased "around-the-world tickets"), she chooses the Code over romantic love. Earlier in the same episode, Dexter gives Lumen a shopping list to set up a kill room. Lumen is a bit shaken, and Dexter asks if she is okay. She is, but Lumen adds, "A few months ago, I was shopping for a wedding dress, and now I'm shopping for thirty yards of polyethylene sheeting. It's crazy, isn't it, how quickly you can get used to the supremely weird?" The signifiers of heteronormative love (a wedding dress) are exchanged for the tools of sadistic violence (thirty yards of polyethylene sheeting). It is true that Lumen's eroticization of the Code of Harry is fueled by revenge, that is to say, an emotional impulse, but she nevertheless sublimates all emotions and channels them into the rationalistic discourse of the Code to achieve her objective: to kill those who abused her and other women.

Dexter prepares the kill room for Cole Harmon, Chase's head of security, in a hotel room immediately adjacent to the target. While Lumen assists Dexter—buying the materials for the kill room—insofar as the kill was conceived, she was not intended to be present. (Dexter was going to meet Lumen a few blocks away to pick up the supplies.) Sitting at the edge of the hotel bed, Lumen tells Dexter about Owen's proposition but confides in Dexter, "This is the only part of my life that makes sense anymore." Dexter inquires, "What about Owen?" Lumen responds, "He's leaving. . . . Tomorrow." Dexter abruptly entreats, "Stay the night." The context—the discussion of Owen, the hotel room, the bed, and the connotative associations with sexuality in all these—along with Dexter's "Stay the night," witnesses the channeling of normative courtship into the ritual of killing. Dexter clearly has feelings for Lumen, and "Stay the night" is certainly sexually charged, but this is really more a screenwriting coup than a sexual overture, because when Dexter says, "Stay the night," this refers to the modified plan to kill Cole in Lumen's presence; Dexter has no sexual motives.

Interestingly, when Dexter and Lumen hear Cole enter the adjacent room, shortly thereafter, they hear a woman scream. Both imagine the worst, and Dexter goes to investigate. He discovers Cole roughly fucking a woman—at least one of her hands is restrained, tied to the bedframe; while the sex is relatively rough, it is apparently consensual. Here too we find sadism, in its colloquial manifestation, and sexuality conflated, echoing the budding relationship between Dexter and Lumen. The scene is highly reminiscent of *Hostel*, in which Josh confuses the sounds of BDSM for that of malicious violence.

In the concluding moments of episode 10, "In the Beginning," Lumen makes her first kill. When Lumen kills Alex Tilden, one of her torturers, she mounts the kill table and plunges the knife into his heart as Dexter watches. The sexual connotations—the penetrating knife, the way that Lumen mounts the table and her victim, the almost fetishistic plastic gear that she wears, her heaving breath—are tinged with eroticism. Here is the complete sublimation of the libidinal drive into the ritual of killing, where Lumen too finds satisfaction not just in the kill but also in the execution of the Code. Returning to Dexter's apartment, Lumen enters, and her shoulders relax, as if a burden has lifted or as if in postcoital surrender. Dexter is putting his tools away when Lumen, without saying a word, approaches him and takes off her shirt. Dexter rises silently, and she pulls off his shirt—for a moment, his shirt shackle his wrists, echoing the gesture of rough sex in "Take It!" The pair make love—there is here not only a consummation of the relationship but also a consummation of the Code.[35]

Dexter's kills, in keeping with clinical sadism, are typically highly scripted events.[36] Dexter usually furtively stalks and then tranquilizes his targets (he uses M99, an animal tranquilizer), partially wraps their body in plastic, and places them on a table in a previously constructed kill room. Kill rooms are usually lined with plastic, and in many cases, Dexter will set up photographs of the subject's victims. Dexter forces his subjects to confront the lives that they have destroyed. Some subjects are contrite, others are not, but regardless, they all die. Before dispatching them, Dexter, usually with a surgical scalpel,

7.7 Channeling libidinal energy into the Code of Harry in the fifth season of *Dexter*, "In the Beginning" (Keith Gordon, Showtime, November 28, 2010).

cuts each subject's right cheek, collects a small blood sample, and places it on a glass slide as a trophy.

As in Sade's universe, nothing within the Code is abject. Sade's universe is methodical, governed by a set of principles that contain all "excess" within a defined space. "Sade's scene integrates," Julia Kristeva says; "it allows for no other, no unthinkable, nothing heterogeneous. Rational and optimistic, it does not exclude."[37] Everything within the Code is accounted for. Everything within Dexter's kill room is contained, scripted, preordained, controlled. When Dexter kills, it is usually very clean; blood does not spray but is contained within the plastic that wraps the subject. Bodies are dismembered and placed in heavy-duty black garbage bags. There are no remainders, nothing left behind. Perfectly contained within the kill room, nothing abject leaks out.

"The corpse," Kristeva says, "seen without God and outside of science, is the utmost abject."[38] Dexter has this covered on both counts: (1) Harry, the creator, and his word, his Code, is tantamount to the word of God; (2) the ritualization of the Code and the act of murder echo the contours of the sacred (ritual sacrifice/murder); and (3) Dexter approaches the body through the discourse of science, namely, forensics. Once again, everything approached through the lens of the Code, or through the discourse of forensics, is accounted for—making the body, even the body in parts, approachable. The Code, the ritual, and forensics neutralize the abject. Like the surgeon, who can within the scientistically coded space of an operating room approach and even transgress the body's boundaries, Dexter can kill and dismember within his contained plastic shell. This particular element corresponds to the medicalization of contemporary horror.

And this neutralization of the abject has frightful implications for our post-9/11 world, because it demonstrates how easily torture and extrajudicial practices can be rationalized. Like Sade's expansive universe that accounts for all "perversions" within a prescribed space, the "Torture Memos" render torture within the bounds of law and thus "legitimate." In "Neoliberal *Dexter*?," Michele Byers interrogates the politics of the Showtime series, observing that a number of programs that engage with post-9/11 politics "end up entangled, producing narratives that ultimately reify the very systems they purport to critique."[39] Dexter's unilateral actions are framed "as vigilante justice that serves the people (and saves them from the failures of the state)[.] Dexter and his crimes become not only comprehensible, but somehow laudatory [just like Jack Bauer]. That's what makes him 'work' as a hero in the narrative: ostensibly he does what *we* understand needs to be done."[40] The neoconservative vision of citizenry—the self-reliant, self-made (white) "man"—matches up with Dexter's disposition; "Dexter now . . . [has] responsibilities, including cleaning up the state's mistakes, on one level by filling its holes—by dispensing vigilante forms of justice—but also by cleaning up the broader problems created by the erosion of traditional systems of privilege and power—by purifying the public sphere of Others."[41] In a world where people of color and women are responsible for the community's security—and this is precisely the face of the Miami Police Department as it is represented in the series—it necessitates a solitary white man, a cowboy in disguise, to come in and do the work that they have failed to. The truth of the matter is that we are rooting for a mass murderer. That is what Dexter is. The conclusion of the first season ends with a fantasy sequence—Dexter imagines himself bathing in the glow of adoration: people cheer; red, white, and blue confetti streams down; an EMT gives a masculine nod and says, "Way to take out the trash. Thanks, buddy"; a woman gleefully shouts, "All right Dexter, protecting our children!" Dexter closes with his characteristic voice-over, "Yeah, they see me. I am one of them—in their darkest dreams."[42] The politics of *Dexter* very well might support the neocon agenda—maybe even despite the program's intention. Regardless, it prompts us to ask, "What do we really want?" and "What are we prepared to accept in the name of security?"

The Corpse of Torture Porn

The fourth chapter of Steve Jones's impressive survey of torture porn takes issue with the historical allegory—cinematic narratives of torture that correspond to the Bush administration's foreign policy. If torture porn appeals to broader concerns—that is to say, if it is to remain relevant in the future—Jones argues that it must be viewed through the deontological lens. Jones prefers to unshackle torture porn from the historical allegory. I am amenable to Jones's proposition; however, as I have illustrated throughout the present book, while torture porn responds to the War on Terror, at the same time, it speaks to a deep-seated culture of violence. The analog of this in the slasher genre might be the women's liberation movement, which served as a catalyst, but slashers themselves ultimately revealed an underlying set of fears and desires that supplied it with its themes and motifs. Torture porn has broader appeal because it reflects our (namely, American) penchant for violence. In the wake of Auschwitz, Günter Grass said, "Finally we know ourselves."[43] In the face of the War on Terror—the rendition program, CIA black sites, enhanced interrogation techniques, and the abuses at Abu Ghraib and Guantánamo Bay prison—we, too, "know ourselves." Jones is absolutely correct in his insistence that torture porn addresses "moral issues, not just the War on Terror."[44] Stopping at the historical allegory is, indeed, insufficient, because, after all, the Bush regime required willing parties to formulate and execute the War on Terror. Torture porn reveals the American sadistic disposition that not only made the War on Terror possible but also desired it.

While I have attempted to outline the boundaries of the torture porn genre, the simple fact is that any category that we might establish, no matter how rigidly defined it might be, is almost invariably porous, subject to exception and evolution. Whether we are speaking in historical terms (torture porn is situated from 2004 to 2010—from the first installment of the *Saw* franchise to its last) or conceptually (a taxonomy), at the borders of the genre, there has always been something of a gray zone, where definitions begin to fray. As I stated at the opening of this volume, the torture porn cycle is almost certainly dead, but there is little doubt that it has changed the landscape of the horror genre and our visual and media culture in general. Jason Middleton posits the same in the opening of his article on the *Hostel* films, noting that there has been "an ebbing in critical attention, and an increase in high-profile horror films that return to more supernatural themes," which "suggest that the disappointing box-office returns of *Hostel II* marked the cresting of the wave."[45] During the torture porn cycle, it seems that the soft-core and the cinematic hardcore entered a feedback loop, one feeding into the other. And regardless of the precise origin of torture porn, it has changed and continues to shape the media.

As we have seen, torture porn, at least in specific cases, found its way into television. While there have been a number of films that have come out in recent years that restore the scare factor back into the horror genre, many of which films we might categorize as ghost stories, there are other films that exhibit some of the elements of torture porn and lean toward the thriller genre. *American Mary* (Jen Soska and Sylvia Soska, 2012), which slowly evolves into a rape-revenge film, features a promising medical student, Mary, who makes cash on the side by performing unconventional body modifications. The surgical elements afford time for medicalized gore, and this sets up a strange parallel between those who pay Mary to perform body modification procedures and her rapist—who serves as her unwilling body-modification test subject. Less gory and more of a straightforward rape-revenge thriller, Austin Chick's 2012 film *Girls against Boys*, like *American Mary*, also includes traces of the torture porn genre—for instance, the double amputation of a rapist with a power tool. Torture porn is even evident in comedies, such as Larry Charles's 2012 *The Dictator*, featuring Sacha Baron Cohen as a Middle Eastern autocrat, which includes a torture scene that is dressed and lit very much in the style of torture porn. The assimilation of these tropes in the comedic genre points to its demise.

Torture porn elements have crept into some of the most unlikely places in television. Take, for instance, a recent Woolite commercial directed by Rob Zombie—someone has to pay the bills, right? Indeed, torture porn has gone mainstream. Not only has it found its way into your local multiplex, but vestiges of it can also be found in popular television programs and even

7.8 Someone has to pay the bills—Rob Zombie's 2013 commercial for Woolite.

commercials selling household cleaning products, no less—strange, given torture porn's propensity to engage with all manner of abject filth.

The punch that we used to associate with the torture porn genre has been by and large tamed, assimilated into mainstream culture. "Wherever there is independent representation," Guy Debord laments in his *Society of the Spectacle*, "the spectacle reconstitutes itself," assimilating and neutralizing its political potential.[46] I certainly would never suggest that torture porn was ever revolutionary—that window has seemingly closed (if it ever was open to begin with)—however, for whatever it is worth, torture porn did in certain instances speak truth to power, to reveal the naked truth of our violent and sadistic disposition. It is ironic, then, that it is a domestic cleaning product that illustrates that torture porn has been "cleaned out" of its never fully realized political potential. This is not to suggest that torture porn is utterly vacant. There is no need to "throw in the towel" and concede to film critics and scholars, "You were right all along; torture porn is meaningless nihilism." From Jigsaw to Dexter, these figures confront us with our complicity in the sadistic disposition. Whether we consider soft-core torture porn on television or its more hardcore cinematic cousin, we arrive at an uncomfortable conclusion, and perhaps in this instance Edelstein was correct: "Fear supplants empathy and makes us all potential torturers, doesn't it?"[47]

Notes

Chapter 1 Torture Porn: From 9/11 to the Multiplex

1 These accounts of John Walker Lindh and Maher Arar are based on passages from Jennifer Harbury's book *Truth, Torture, and the American Way* (Boston: Beacon, 2005), 5–6.

2 Dana Priest and Barton Gellman, "U.S. Decries Abuse but Defends Interrogations," *Washington Post*, December 26, 2002, http://www.washingtonpost.com/wp-dyn/content/article/2006/06/09/AR2006060901356.html.

3 Cullen Murphy, *God's Jury: The Inquisition and the Making of the Modern World* (Boston: Houghton Mifflin Harcourt, 2012), 215.

4 John Rizzo, a senior CIA general counsel, similarly recounts, "If all my years and experience at the CIA taught me anything, it's that virtually every secret doesn't stay secret forever, and that the shelf life of new secrets is getting shorter all the time." John Rizzo, *Company Man: Thirty Years of Controversy and Crisis in the CIA* (New York: Scribner, 2014), 6.

5 Jason Middleton, "The Subject of Torture: Regarding the Pain of Americans in *Hostel*," *Cinema Journal* 49, no. 4 (Summer 2010): 9.

6 Elizabeth Swanson Goldberg, "Splitting Difference: Global Identity Politics and the Representation of Torture in the Counterhistorical Dramatic Film," in *Violence and American Cinema*, ed. David Slocum, 245–270 (New York: Routledge, 2001).

7 Jeremy Morris, "The Justification of Torture-Horror: Retribution and Sadism in *Saw*, *Hostel*, and *The Devil's Rejects*," in *The Philosophy of Horror*, ed. Thomas Fahy, 42–56 (Lexington: University Press of Kentucky, 2010), 44–45.

8 Murphy, *God's Jury*, 92.

9 Ibid., 94.

10 Steve Jones notes that fourteen years earlier, "Jane Caputi . . . similarly used the term 'gorenography' to denigrate popular horror film." Steve Jones, *Torture Porn: Popular Horror after "Saw"* (New York: Palgrave, 2013), 132. See Jane Caputi, "Advertising Femicide: Lethal Violence against Women in Pornography and Gorenography," in *Femicide: The Politics of Woman Killing*, ed. Jill Radford and Diana E. H. Russell, 203–221 (New York: Twayne, 1992).

11 David Edelstein, "Now Playing at Your Local Multiplex: Torture Porn," *New York* 39, no. 4 (February, 6, 2006), http://nymag.com/movies/features/15622/.

12 Ibid.

13 Ibid.

14 There still is significant work to be done on the subject of the "final boy," but a case can be made for it. The "final boy" is mentioned in passing in Evangelos Tziallas's article "Torture Porn and Surveillance Culture," *Jump Cut* 52 (Summer 2010), http://www.ejumpcut.org/archive/jc52.2010/evangelosTorturePorn/. Gabrielle Murray also uses the term in her article "*Hostel II*: Representations of the Body in Pain and the Cinema Experience in Torture Porn," *Jump Cut* 50 (Spring 2008), http://www.ejumpcut.org/archive/jc50.2008/TortureHostel2/. James Fenimore Cooper wrote an master's thesis on the subject, "From Bates to Bush: The New Slasher Film" (master's thesis, Oklahoma State University, 2011), ProQuest (1501027).

15 Will Self, "The American Vice," in *Screen Violence*, ed. Karl French, 71–81 (London: Bloomsbury, 1996), 75–76, emphasis in original. I accept Self's argument at face value, but I do not quite understand his "confusion" about the subjective shots; it seems pretty self-evident to me.

16 This idea is not new: Carol Clover commented on spectator identification and the ways in which it might vacillate in her *Men, Women, and Chain Saws: Gender in the Modern Horror Film* (Princeton, NJ: Princeton University Press, 1992), and Edelstein is certainly aware of this issue too. If he is not familiar with Clover's text, as a veteran film critic, he is cognizant of how identification functions in the cinematic text.

17 Tom Gunning, "The Cinema of Attraction[s]: Early Film, Its Spectator and the Avant-Garde," in *The Cinema of Attractions Reloaded*, ed. Wanda Strauven, 381–388 (Amsterdam: Amsterdam University Press, 2006), 385.

18 Ibid., 384.

19 Adam Lowenstein, "Spectacle Horror and *Hostel*: Why 'Torture Porn' Does Not Exist," *Critical Quarterly* 53, no. 1 (2011): 50.

20 Edelstein, "Now Playing at Your Local Multiplex."

21 Lowenstein, "Spectacle Horror and *Hostel*," 49. In this case, Lowenstein is discussing the reenactment of the execution of Mary, Queen of Scots, in Alfred Clark and William Heise's 1895 film *The Execution of Mary, Queen of Scots*, but it equally applies to the torture porn genre, which one might argue (and that is certainly what I am doing) is in part a reenactment of the War on Terror.

22 Alfred Hitchcock, quoted in Linda Williams, "Discipline and Fun: *Psycho* and Postmodern Cinema," in *Reinventing Film Studies*, ed. Christine Gledhill and Linda Williams, 351–378 (London: Arnold, 2000), 353.

23 Ibid., 354.

24 Ibid.

25 Ibid., 356.

26 Cynthia A. Freeland, *The Naked and the Undead: Evil and the Appeal of Horror* (Boulder, CO: Westview, 2000), 266. Also see Matt Hills, "Cutting into Concepts of 'Reflectionist' Cinema? The *Saw* Franchise and Puzzles of Post-9/11 Horror," in *Horror after 9/11: World of Fear, Cinema of Terror*, ed. Aviva Briefel and Sam J. Miller, 107–123 (Austin: University of Texas Press, 2011), 114.

27 Linda Williams, *Hard Core: Power, Pleasure, and the "Frenzy of the Visible"* (Berkeley: University of California Press, 1989), 130.

28 Ibid.

29 Ibid., 134.

30 Dean Lockwood similarly observes, "Just as in porn, where there is nothing beyond the wish to arouse and all is staged for this purpose, in horror everything is pared back to foreground the fearful expectation of suffering. Torture porn, it seems, is

just more honest and full on than previous horror, more blatantly akin to its pornographic cousin." Dean Lockwood, "All Stripped Down: The Spectacle of 'Torture Porn,'" *Popular Communication* 7, no. 1 (2009): 41.

31 Middleton, "Subject of Torture," 6.

32 Kevin Wetmore also finds affinities between the games in the *Saw* franchise and the games played on reality television programs: "Between reality shows that eliminate one or more contestants each week (the repeated use of the words 'eliminate' and 'elimination' in talking about people on such programmes is also highly suggestive of horror films, in which a group gets smaller each period with the 'elimination' of one of the group—there is a fine line between *Halloween* and *Hell's Kitchen*, between *Alien* and *America's Next Top Model*)." Kevin J. Wetmore, *Post-9/11 Horror in American Cinema* (New York: Continuum, 2012), 78.

33 Edelstein makes a similar comparison to pornography: "Unlike the old seventies and eighties hack-'em-ups (or their jokey remakes, like *Scream*), in which masked maniacs punished nubile teens for promiscuity (the spurt of blood was equivalent to the money shot in porn), the victims here are neither interchangeable nor expendable. They range from decent people with recognizable human emotions to, well, Jesus [Christ, in Mel Gibson's 2004 film *The Passion of the Christ*]" ("Now Playing at Your Local Multiplex").

34 For an excellent accounting of the pornographic genre set in contrast with torture porn, see the third section, chapters 7–9, of Jones's book *Torture Porn*.

35 For a succinct discussion of the term "torture porn," and specifically the labeling of the genre as "porn" or "pornography," see Steve Jones, "The Lexicon of Offence: The Meanings of Torture, Porn, and 'Torture Porn,'" in *Controversial Images: Media Representations on the Edge*, ed. Feona Attwood, Vincent Campbell, I. Q. Hunter, and Sharon Lockyer, 186–200 (Basingstoke, UK: Palgrave Macmillan, 2012), 186–200. Also see Jones's book-length study of the genre, *Torture Porn*; he takes issue with the term "torture porn."

36 Lowenstein, "Spectacle Horror and *Hostel*," 42.

37 Ibid.

38 Lockwood, "All Stripped Down," 47.

39 Murray, "*Hostel II*."

40 Lockwood, "All Stripped Down," 40.

41 Ibid., 47.

42 Ibid., 47–48.

43 Morris, "Justification of Torture-Horror," 43.

44 Wetmore, *Post-9/11 Horror in American Cinema*, 101.

45 Morris, "Justification of Torture-Horror," 48.

46 Ibid.

47 Ibid., 49.

48 Ibid.

49 Christopher Sharrett, "The Problem of *Saw*: 'Torture Porn' and the Conservatism of Contemporary Horror Films," *Cineaste* 35, no. 1 (Winter 2009): 32.

50 Christopher Sharrett, "Genocidal Spectacles and the Ideology of Death," in *Bad: Infamy, Darkness, Evil, and Slime on Screen*, ed. Murray Pomerance, 65–78 (Albany: State University of New York Press, 2004), 72. Also see Christopher Sharrett, "The Idea of Apocalypse in *The Texas Chainsaw Massacre*," in *Planks of Reason: Essays on the Horror Film*, ed. Barry Keith Grant, 255–276 (Lanham, MD: Scarecrow, 1984). For a "redemptive" reading of earlier horror films, see Robin Wood's book *Hollywood from*

Vietnam to Reagan (New York: Columbia University Press, 1986). As for generational differences, see Jones's book *Torture Porn*, specifically the section titled "'Perhaps I Am Getting Old, but . . .': Nostalgia and Generic Decline," 22–26.

51 Sharrett, "Problem of *Saw*," 32.

52 Ibid., 33.

53 Kim Newman, "Horror Will Eat Itself," *Sight and Sound* 19 (May 2009): 38.

54 For a discussion of films that are "about something" versus torture porn films that are supposedly empty spectacles, see Brenda Cromb, "Gorno: Violence, Shock and Comedy," *Cinephile* 4 (2008), http://cinephile.ca/archives/volume-4-post-genre/gorno-violence-shock-and-comedy/.

55 Roger Ebert wrote in his review of *Wolf Creek*, "There is a role for violence in film, but what the hell is the purpose of this sadistic celebration of pain and cruelty?" Ebert, "*Wolf Creek*," December 22, 2005, RogerEbert.com, 2005, http://www.rogerebert.com/reviews/wolf-creek-2005. Ebert says effectively the same thing about *Saw*: "Do we care enough about the characters to share what they have to endure? I didn't." Ebert, "*Saw*," October 28, 2004, RogerEbert.com, 2004, http://www.rogerebert.com/reviews/saw-2004. Interestingly, there is a "revisionist" disclaimer to Ebert's original 1969 review of *Night of the Living Dead*, intended as an "apology" perhaps: "NOTE (2004): This reaction to a screening of *Night of the Living Dead* is not, properly speaking, a review—or rather, it is a review of the audience reaction. I admire the movie itself, which I have seen twice since that 1969 afternoon, and its sequel *Dawn of the Dead* got an enthusiastic review from me. I didn't assign a star rating to *The Night of the Living Dead* because the kind of article I wrote did not seem to require one, but if I were to rate it today, I'd give it 3 1/2 stars." Ebert, "*Night of the Living Dead*" (January 5, 1969), RogerEbert.com, 2004, http://www.rogerebert.com/reviews/the-night-of-the-living-dead-1968.

56 See, for instance, Sharrett, "Problem of *Saw*," 32–37.

57 Wetmore says something similar: "Torture porn is disturbing, not only for its depiction of torture, but because it frequently justifies 'our' use of it" (*Post-9/11 Horror in American Cinema*, 115). Morris also posits, "The terror of the victim is supplanted by the delight of the torturer, which is being consciously shared by the audience: *that* is the source of horror" ("Justification of Torture-Horror," 51). Jones similarly observes that torture porn is not only about the War on Terror, but it also speaks to our culture of violence ("Lexicon of Offence," 194).

58 Susan Sontag, "Regarding the Torture of Others," *New York Times Magazine*, May 23, 2004, 26.

59 Edelstein, "Now Playing at Your Local Multiplex."

60 For a discussion of the institutionalized nature of torture, as conducted by American agents, see Jennifer Harbury's *Truth, Torture, and the American Way*. Also see Alan W. Clarke, *Rendition to Torture* (New Brunswick, NJ: Rutgers University Press, 2012). Also see Middleton, "Subject of Torture," 10. Analogously, see Robin Wood's discussion of Wes Craven's 1972 film *The Last House on the Left*, which he posits "analyzes the nature and conditions of violence and sees them as inherent in the American situation. Craven sees to it that the audience cannot escape the implications. We are spared nothing in the protracted tormenting of the two girls—our having to share the length of their ordeal is part of the point—and we cannot possibly enjoy it. They are *us*. Yet we also cannot disengage ourselves from their tormentors: *They* are us, too" (*Hollywood from Vietnam to Reagan*, 128).

61 The phrasing here derives from Susan Sontag, who wrote, "Our sympathy proclaims our innocence as well as our impotence" (*Regarding the Pain of Others*, 102).

Chapter 2 The Torture Porn Genre: Key Tropes

1 Steve Jones, "The Lexicon of Offence: The Meanings of Torture, Porn, and 'Torture Porn,'" in *Controversial Images: Media Representations on the Edge*, ed. Feona Attwood, Vincent Campbell, I. Q. Hunter, and Sharon Lockyer, 186–200 (Basingstoke, UK: Palgrave Macmillan, 2013), 187.

2 Dana R. Polan, "Eros and Syphilization: The Contemporary Horror Film," in *Planks of Reason: Essays on the Horror Film*, ed. Barry Keith Grant and Christopher Sharrett, 142–152 (Lanham, MD: Scarecrow, 2004), 143.

3 Jason Middleton, "The Subject of Torture: Regarding the Pain of Americans in *Hostel*," *Cinema Journal* 49, no. 4 (Summer 2010): 24.

4 Ibid.

5 See, for instance, Gregg Easterbrook's article "The Nation: Home Security; The Smart Way to Be Scared," *New York Times*, February 16, 2003, http://www.nytimes.com/2003/02/16/weekinreview/the-nation-home-security-the-smart-way-to-be-scared.html?pagewanted=all&src=pm.

6 Kevin J. Wetmore, *Post-9/11 Horror in American Cinema* (New York: Continuum, 2012), 86.

7 Slavoj Žižek, *Welcome to the Desert of the Real! Five Essays on September 11 and Related Dates* (New York: Verso, 2002), 27.

8 Jean Baudrillard, *The Spirit of Terrorism and Other Essays*, trans. Chris Turner (New York: Verso, 2003), 61.

9 See Catherine Soussloff, "Post-colonial Torture: Rituals of Viewing at Abu Ghraib," in *Ritual and Event*, ed. Mark Franko, 159–187 (New York: Routledge, 2007), 172.

10 Jeremy Morris, "The Justification of Torture-Horror: Retribution and Sadism in *Saw*, *Hostel*, and *The Devil's Rejects*," in *The Philosophy of Horror*, ed. Thomas Fahy, 42–56 (Lexington: University Press of Kentucky, 2010), 48. Regarding role reversals and identification with torturers, see ibid., 44–45.

11 René Girard, *Violence and the Sacred*, trans. Patrick Gregory (Baltimore: John Hopkins University Press, 1989), 4.

12 Carol J. Clover, *Men, Women, and Chain Saws: Gender in the Modern Horror Film* (Princeton, NJ: Princeton University Press, 1992), 213. Also see ibid., 23. In addition, see Isabel Cristina Pinedo, *Recreational Terror: Women and the Pleasures of Horror Film Viewing* (Albany: State University of New York Press, 1997).

13 Barbara Creed, *The Monstrous-Feminine: Film, Feminism, Psychoanalysis* (New York: Routledge, 1993), 7.

14 See Madeleine Smith's chapter "Monstrous Bodies and Gendered Abjection," in *To See the "Saw" Movies: Essays on Torture Porn and Post-9/11 Horror*, ed. James Aston and John Walliss, 157–175 (Jefferson, NC: McFarland, 2013). Smith's chapter is thoroughly enjoyable to read, and she makes some impressive observations regarding the treatment of gender in the *Saw* franchise—and many of her observations can be extrapolated and applied across the genre. However, she amplifies Barbara Creed's errors by suggesting that Julia Kristeva deems abjection as the sole province of femininity.

15 Ibid., 166.

16 Steve Jones makes similar observations regarding Srdjan Spasojevic's 2010 film *A Serbian Film*, in which the primary character, Milos, through the device of the flashback, "witnesses not just his wrongdoing, but also his own slippage between torturer and tortured positions." Steve Jones, *Torture Porn: Popular Horror after "Saw"* (New York: Palgrave, 2013), 99.

17 There is a precedent for an unaccounted gaze and most especially for the way this is deployed in the slippage of gender categories—as in classic slasher films such as *Friday the 13th*. See Clover, *Men, Women, and Chain Saws*, 56.
18 For a discussion of this scene, see Jeffrey Sconce's chapter "Spectacles of Death: Identification, Reflexivity, and Contemporary Horror," in *Film Theory Goes to the Movies*, ed. Jim Collins, Hilary Radner, and Ava Preacher Collins, 103–119 (New York: Routledge, 1993), 111–112.
19 Ibid., 114.
20 Ibid.
21 Wetmore, *Post-9/11 Horror in American Cinema*, 118. Drawing on Douglas Cowan, Wetmore adds that the nihilistic plots of contemporary horror ultimately lead toward "the narrative denial of catharsis." Douglas E. Cowan, *Sacred Terror: Religion and Horror on the Silver Screen* (Waco, TX: Baylor University Press, 2008), 261.
22 Wetmore, *Post-9/11 Horror in American Cinema*, 2–3.
23 Ibid., 74. Wetmore adds, "As in terrorists' videos, the quality [of Jigsaw's videos] is grainy, the focus is on a disguised person—while the terrorists cover their faces with scarves, sunglasses and bandanas, Jigsaw uses the doll—who issues a series of demands and threats" (ibid., 75).
24 Catherine Zimmer, "Caught on Tape? The Politics of Video in the New Torture Films," in *Horror after 9/11: World of Fear, Cinema of Terror*, ed. Aviva Briefel and Sam J. Miller, 83–106 (Austin: University of Texas Press, 2011), 84.
25 Jones, *Torture Porn*, 97.
26 Ibid.
27 Morris, "Justification of Torture-Horror," 44.
28 When the director of the FBI, Robert Mueller, in 2008 was asked if enhanced interrogation techniques had stopped another terrorist attack in the United States, he responded, "I don't believe that has been the case." Robert Mueller, quoted in Cullen Murphy, *God's Jury: The Inquisition and the Making of the Modern World* (Boston: Houghton Mifflin Harcourt, 2012), 222.
29 Clover, *Men, Women, and Chain Saws*, 31–32.
30 Elaine Scarry, *The Body in Pain: The Making and Unmaking of the World* (New York: Oxford University Press, 1985), 41.
31 Clover, *Men, Women, and Chain Saws*, 30–31. Also see Robin Wood's idea of the "Terrible House," in his *Hollywood from Vietnam to Reagan* (New York: Columbia University Press, 1986), 90.
32 Michel Foucault, "Of Other Spaces," trans. Jay Miskowiec, *Diacritics* 16, no. 1 (Spring 1986): 24.
33 On the archive as a heterotopic site, see ibid., 26.
34 Ibid.
35 Ibid.
36 Ibid., 27.
37 Clover, *Men, Women, and Chain Saws*, 30–31.
38 Evangelos Tziallas, "Torture Porn and Surveillance Culture," *Jump Cut* 52 (Summer 2010), http://www.ejumpcut.org/archive/jc52.2010/evangelosTorturePorn/.
39 Ibid.
40 Ibid.
41 Ibid.
42 Creed, *Monstrous-Feminine*, 27.

43 I want to acknowledge my student Jonathan Knapp, who pointed out this connection between clockworks and Jigsaw's devices.

44 Žižek, *Welcome to the Desert of the Real!*, 10–11.

45 Ibid., 11.

46 Jean Baudrillard also implies that the 9/11 attack, in its likeness to a movie, was pornographic. See Baudrillard, *Spirit of Terrorism and Other Essays*, 7. Simon Stow did not refer to the event itself as pornographic but does characterize the "grief industry" around it as pornographic. Simon Stow, "Portraits 9/11/01: The *New York Times* and the Pornography of Grief," in *Literature after 9/11*, ed. Jeanne Follansbee Quinn and Ann Keniston, 224–241 (New York: Routledge, 2008).

47 Adam Lowenstein, "Spectacle Horror and *Hostel*: Why 'Torture Porn' Does Not Exist," *Critical Quarterly* 53, no. 1 (2011): 52.

48 *Oxford English Dictionary*, s.v. "torture." My student Ashley Nunes initially called my attention to the Latin origins of the term "torture."

49 David Edelstein, "Now Playing at Your Local Multiplex: Torture Porn," *New York* 39, no. 4 (February 6, 2006), http://nymag.com/movies/features/15622/.

50 Anecdotally, one of my students noted that while watching *Saw III* with her partner, during the scene with rotting pigs being eviscerated, he suddenly jumped up ran to the bathroom and vomited. He was never in peril, but nonetheless affected by what he saw.

51 Linda Williams, "Film Bodies: Gender, Genre, and Excess," *Film Quarterly* 44, no. 4 (Summer 1991): 4. For more on the visceral reception of the cinematic text, see Jennifer Barker, *The Tactile Eye: Touch and the Cinema Experience* (Berkeley: University of California Press, 2009).

52 Jeffrey Bullins, "Hearing the Game: Sound Design," in Aston and Walliss, *To See the "Saw" Movies*, 185.

53 Edelstein, "Now Playing at Your Local Multiplex."

54 Scarry, *Body in Pain*, 42.

55 Ibid., 41.

56 See Wetmore, *Post-9/11 Horror in American Cinema*, 100.

57 The extraordinary rendition program is still in operation, although former CIA director Leon Panetta under the Obama administration before the Senate Intelligence Committee in 2009 assured the senators that detainees would no longer be sent to countries that torture. See the report by *60 Minutes* on the rendition program: http://www.cbsnews.com/video/watch/?id=678566n.

58 Assistant Attorney General Jay S. Bybee to Alberto R. Gonzales, Counsel to the President, August 1, 2002, Office of the Attorney General, US Department of Justice, 46. Cullen Murphy observes that the manipulation of legal rhetoric with the "Torture Memos" corresponds to "what the papal bull *Ad extirpanda* did" in 1252 when Pope Innocent IV authorized torture (*God's Jury*, 221).

59 Soussloff, "Post-colonial Torture," 172.

60 For more on flagellants, see "The Theater of the Flagellants," chapter 4 in Niklaus Largier's book *In Praise of the Whip: A Cultural History of Arousal* (New York: Zone Books, 2007).

61 For more on death as spectacle, see Sconce, "Spectacles of Death."

62 Clover, *Men, Women, and Chain Saws*, 51.

63 Linda Williams, *Hard Core: Power, Pleasure, and the "Frenzy of the Visible"* (Berkeley: University of California Press, 1989), 72–73.

64 Jones, "Lexicon of Offence," 188.

65 Bullins, "Hearing the Game," 178.

66 Bullins also discusses the use of camera flashes and specifically the audio design associated with the eruption of a flash; see ibid., 187–189.

67 Zimmer, "Caught on Tape?," 85.

68 Wetmore, *Post-9/11 Horror in American Cinema*, 84.

69 Matt Hills also compares Jigsaw to a puppeteer; see his "Cutting into Concepts of 'Reflectionist' Cinema? The *Saw* Franchise and Puzzles of Post-9/11 Horror," in Briefel and Miller, *Horror after 9/11*, 199.

70 Michael Ignatieff, "The Terrorist as Auteur," *New York Times*, November 14, 2004, http://www.nytimes.com/2004/11/14/movies/14TERROR.html. Ignatieff continues, comparing horrific scenes to pornography: "This is terrorism as pornography, and it acts like pornography: at first making audiences feel curious and aroused, despite themselves, then ashamed, possibly degraded and finally, perhaps, just indifferent. The audience for this vileness is global. A Dutchman who runs a violent and sexually explicit Web site that posts beheadings notes, in his inimitable words, that 'during times of tragic events like beheadings,' his site, which usually gets 200,000 visitors a day, gets up to 750,000 hits" (ibid.).

71 Julia Kristeva, *Powers of Horror: An Essay on Abjection*, trans. Leon S. Roudiez (New York: Columbia University Press, 1982), 4.

72 Zimmer, "Caught on Tape?," 101.

73 Clover, *Men, Women, and Chain Saws*, 151.

74 Sconce, "Spectacles of Death," 113.

75 Wood, *Hollywood from Vietnam to Reagan*, 80. At the conclusion of Wood's chapter, he suggests that the horror genre articulates "the sense of a civilization condemning itself, through its popular culture, to ultimate disintegration, and ambivalently (with the simultaneous horror/wish-fulfillment of nightmare) celebrating the fact" (ibid., 94). Torture porn might be read in these terms as well.

76 Zimmer, "Caught on Tape?," 85–86.

77 See Hills, "Cutting into Concepts of 'Reflectionist' Cinema?," 116. Žižek makes a similar observation, taking issue with the liberal commentator Alan Dershowitz, who wants to invite a debate regarding the use of torture. Žižek, *Welcome to the Desert of the Real!*, 103–104.

Chapter 3 Some Antecedents: Sadism, Exploitation, and (Neo-)Slashers

1 Steve Jones, "The Lexicon of Offence: The Meanings of Torture, Porn, and 'Torture Porn,'" in *Controversial Images: Media Representations on the Edge*, ed. Feona Attwood, Vincent Campbell, I. Q. Hunter, and Sharon Lockyer, 186–200 (Basingstoke, UK: Palgrave Macmillan, 2012), 195.

2 Julia Kristeva, *Powers of Horror: An Essay on Abjection*, trans. Leon S. Roudiez (New York: Columbia University Press, 1982), 21.

3 Jeremy Morris, "The Justification of Torture-Horror: Retribution and Sadism in *Saw*, *Hostel*, and *The Devil's Rejects*," in *The Philosophy of Horror*, ed. Thomas Fahy, 42–56 (Lexington: University Press of Kentucky, 2010), 50. Morris situates Rob Zombie's 2005 film *The Devil's Rejects* as purely sadistic (see pages 48–52).

4 See Slavoj Žižek, "Kant with (or against) Sade," in *The Žižek Reader*, ed. Elizabeth Wright and Edmond Wright, 283–301 (Oxford, UK: Blackwell, 1999), 287. Also see Žižek, "Much Ado about a Thing," chap. 6 in *For They Know Not What They Do: Enjoyment as a Political Factor* (London: Verso, 1991).

5 Morris, "Justification of Torture-Horror," 50.

6 Jane Gallop, *Intersections: A Reading of Sade with Bataille, Blanchot, and Klossowski* (Lincoln: University of Nebraska Press, 1981), 113.

7 Jean Baudrillard, *The Spirit of Terrorism and Other Essays*, trans. Chris Turner (New York: Verso, 2003), 13.

8 Brian Collins, "A Voice and Something More: Jigsaw as Acousmêtre and Existential Guru," in *To See the "Saw" Movies: Essays on Torture Porn and Post-9/11 Horror*, ed. James Aston and John Walliss, 86–104 (Jefferson, NC: McFarland, 2013), 100.

9 Kristeva, *Powers of Horror*, 4.

10 This is also known as the "Bybee Memo," named after Assistant Attorney General Jay S. Bybee, who delivered the report August 1, 2002, to Attorney General Alberto R. Gonzales.

11 From a slightly different perspective, Steve Jones also talks about torture porn and the need to view torture beyond simple binaries—good/evil, torturer/tortured. See Steve Jones, *Torture Porn: Popular Horror after "Saw"* (New York: Palgrave, 2013), 82–83. Also see Jones's discussion of Graham Green's 2008 film *The Torturer*, on pages 93–94 of *Torture Porn*, regarding character roles and the execution of duty.

12 Mikel J. Koven, "'The Film You Are About to See Is Based on Fact': Italian Nazi Sexploitation Cinema," in *Alternative Europe: Eurotrash and Exploitation Cinema since 1945*, ed. Ernest Mathijs and Xavier Mendik, 19–31 (New York: Wallflower, 2004), 20.

13 Ibid., 22–23. Also see Saul Friedlander, *Reflections of Nazism: An Essay on Kitsch and Death*, trans. Thomas Weyr (Bloomington: Indiana University Press, 1993).

14 Koven, "The Film You Are About to See Is Based on Fact," 23.

15 It is possible, however, to read *Cannibal Holocaust* as a critical cinematic text—critical of the anthropological/ethnographic traditions that subject the exotic "other" to the colonial gaze. Furthermore, the film is highly self-aware in its artificial construction belaboring its "rawness"—hand-held camera, lens flares, images out of focus, scratches, and so on. And viewed in these terms, Deodato's film might be akin to Luis Buñuel's playful treatment of the documentary mode in his 1933 *Land without Bread*. For an excellent reading of *Cannibal Holocaust*, see Julian Petley, "*Cannibal Holocaust* and the Pornography of Death," in *The Spectacle of the Real: From Hollywood to "Reality" TV and Beyond*, ed. Geoff King, 173–185 (Portland, OR: Intellect, 2005).

16 As a fan and aficionado of the exploitation genre, Quentin Tarantino also draws from the *Ilsa* films. In the faux 2007 double feature *Grindhouse* (Quentin Tarantino and Robert Rodriguez), between the two feature films, *Death Proof* (Quentin Tarantino) and *Planet Terror* (Robert Rodriguez), a series of fabricated trailers are screened, including *Werewolf Women of the S.S.*, directed by Rob Zombie, which in many respects is a composite of the most popular Naziploitation films. Tarantino, of course, produced both *Hostel* films and cast the director of these films, Eli Roth, as Sergeant Donny Donowitz, the Bear Jew, in *Inglourious Basterds* (2009). Roth also directed *Nation's Pride*, the German film screened in *Inglourious Basterds*.

17 Archival footage (without sound) from Ilse Koch's war crimes tribunal is available through archive.org: http://www.archive.org/details/1948-10-28_Ilse_Lock_war_crimes_trial.

18 Alexandra Przyrembel, "Transfixed by an Image: Ilse Koch, the 'Kommandeuse of Buchenwald,'" trans. Pamela Selwyn, *German History* 19, no. 3 (October 2001): 369.

19 In the punishment cell in Jesus Franco's 1975 film *Women behind Bars*, like the playpen, women are whipped, and electrodes are placed on the genitals.
20 See Jason Middleton, "The Subject of Torture: Regarding the Pain of Americans in *Hostel*," *Cinema Journal* 49, no. 4 (Summer 2010): 1–24.
21 Kevin Wetmore, who is interested in post-9/11 horror in general, rather than torture porn specifically, observes, "On the one hand, 9/11 transforms horror, rendering gender no longer a central issue. A collapsing building or crashing a plane does not care about one's gender, orientation or relationship with one's father: everybody dies. Random and anonymous death is not concerned with oppression or gendered identity." Viewed from a different perspective, taken from Susan Faludi's book *The Terror Dream: Fear and Fantasy in Post-9/11America* (New York: Metropolitan Books, 2007), one might posit that the September 11 attacks emasculated American masculinity (no wonder why Al-Qaeda chose such phallic representative images of American prowess). Summing up Faludi's position, Wetmore states, "In short, 9/11 was not gender biased, but our culture's understanding and reconstruction of it is." Kevin J. Wetmore, *Post-9/11 Horror in American Cinema* (New York: Continuum, 2012), 14–15.
22 Jones, "Lexicon of Offence," 188–189. Also see revised data in Jones, *Torture Porn*, 133.
23 Clover, *Men, Women, and Chain Saws*, 143.
24 Linda Williams, "Film Bodies: Gender, Genre, and Excess," *Film Quarterly* 44, no. 4 (Summer 1991): 5.
25 Rikke Schubart, *Super Bitches and Action Babes: The Female Hero in Popular Cinema, 1970–2006* (Jefferson, NC: McFarland, 2007), 81.
26 Valerie Wee, "Resurrecting and Updating the Teen Slasher: The Case of *Scream*," *Journal of Popular Film and Television* 34, no. 2 (Summer 2006): 60.
27 Janet Weeks, "*Scream* Movies Cultivate Special Audience: Girls," *USA Today*, December 12, 1997, 1A.
28 John Carpenter, interviewed by Todd McCarthy, "Trick and Treat," *Film Comment* 16 (1980): 23–24; also quoted in Clover, *Men, Women, and Chain Saws*, 48–49.
29 Clover, *Men, Women, and Chain Saws*, 29.
30 Collins, "A Voice and Something More," 99. Similarly, Jacob Huntley observes that by the end of the *Saw* franchise, "Jigsaw is no longer really a nickname that neatly applies to one person and instead it would be better to talk of the Jigsaw effect or the Jigsaw assemblage." Jacob Huntley, "The Jigsaw Assemblage," in Aston and Walliss, *To See the "Saw" Movies*, 123.
31 Wetmore notes that in the post-9/11 context, "traditional monsters must transform to equal the horror of terrorism otherwise they fade into irrelevance" (*Post-9/11 Horror in American Cinema*, 154).
32 Ibid., 197.
33 Wetmore observes that in the remake of *Friday the 13th*, sexuality is not a problem as such. "Jason slaughters them all. He does not distinguish between the sexually active and the 'pure.' While Whitney and her boyfriend do not have crazy, loud sex as their companions do, it is made clear that they, too, expect to have relations during the camping trip" (*Post-9/11 Horror in American Cinema*, 197).
34 Barbara Creed, *The Monstrous-Feminine: Film, Feminism, Psychoanalysis* (New York: Routledge, 1993), 54–55.
35 Similarly, in one of the cheeky lines of *Scream 3*, Sidney, having gamed her brother, the monster, astride him says, "I guess we think alike," as she reveals a bulletproof

vest. Her brother also wears a bulletproof vest and is thus able to enact the roll of the supernatural boogieman, apparently impervious to bullets.

36 In Wes Craven's 2011 film *Scream 4*, Sidney's cousin, Jill, turns out to be one of the killers. Among other examples of intimate relations between the final girl and the monster, Freddy's own daughter plays the role of the final girl in *Freddy's Dead: The Final Nightmare* (Rachel Talalay, 1991). Clover also discusses the affiliation between the final girl and the monster; see *Men, Women, and Chain Saws*, 38.

Chapter 4 The *Saw* Franchise: Videogames and the Sadistic Pro(an)tagonist Jigsaw

1 Later in this chapter, I argue that Jigsaw is a sadist par excellence; the insurance executive Easton, though, might also be a sadist—reducing all human life to economics, utterly devoid of compassion. Easton, nevertheless, is arrogant and greedy, revealing in the end that emotions are governing his disposition. Sadists, though, are not above preying on one another.

2 Matt Hills, drawing from Cynthia Freeland, compares Jigsaw to Pinhead in *Hellraiser*; see his, "Cutting into Concepts of 'Reflectionist' Cinema? The *Saw* Franchise and Puzzles of Post-9/11 Horror," in *Horror after 9/11: World of Fear, Cinema of Terror*, ed. Aviva Briefel and Sam J. Miller, 107–123 (Austin: University of Texas Press, 2011), 114.

3 Leigh Whannell, interview by MakingOf, "Screenwriter Leigh Whannell Talks 'Insidious,'" YouTube, August 8, 2011, http://www.youtube.com/watch?v=xjAjUCHlOjo.

4 Hills, "Cutting into Concepts of 'Reflectionist' Cinema?," 108.

5 See, for instance, Christopher Sharrett, "The Problem of *Saw*: 'Torture Porn' and the Conservatism of Contemporary Horror Films," *Cineaste* 35, no. 1 (Winter 2009): 32–37; and Kim Newman's "Horror Will Eat Itself," *Sight and Sound* 19 (May 2009): 37–38. Newman, to his credit, all but acknowledges his own criticism as curmudgeonly.

6 The film was shot in eighteen days, breakneck speed for the most accomplished and veteran filmmaker, truly herculean for first-time filmmakers.

7 Catherine Zimmer in a passing comment makes the same observation: "The *Saw* films, clearly influenced by the tremendous success of David Fincher's *Se7en* (1995), tell the story of the serial killer 'Jigsaw,' who kidnaps people and places them in scenarios that require them to make torturous choices in order to survive or save others, thus, according to Jigsaw, learning the 'real' value of life." Catherine Zimmer, "Caught on Tape? The Politics of Video in the New Torture Films," in Briefel and Miller, *Horror after 9/11*, 85.

8 Kevin Wetmore makes an interesting observation about the name "Tapp" and his partner's name, "Sing": they are "the detectives in charge of tracking down Jigsaw in the first film, [but their] . . . names suggest they are 'song and dance men,' giving a good show but not up to the task of actually doing anything." And more than this, the torture porn genre, in its (supposed) lack of narrative and reliance on spectacle, makes *Saw* little more than a Busby Berkeley musical tinged with a little bit of blood. Kevin J. Wetmore, *Post-9/11 Horror in American Cinema* (New York: Continuum, 2012), 102.

9 In an early rough cut of *Saw*, Wan had apparently placed Nine Inch Nails music into the film as a placeholder prior to Clouser joining the project.

10 Other films that serve as a model for *Saw* include Robert Fuest's 1971 film *The Abominable Dr. Phibes* and Vincenzo Natali's 1997 film *Cube*. For a comparative analysis of the former, see Fernando G. Pagnoni Berns and Amy M. Davis's chapter "From Jigsaw to Phibes: God, Free Will and Foreknowledge in Conflict," in *To See the "Saw" Movies: Essays on Torture Porn and Post-9/11 Horror*, ed. James Aston and John Walliss, 73–85 (Jefferson, NC: McFarland, 2013).

11 David Edelstein, "Now Playing at Your Local Multiplex: Torture Porn," *New York* 39, no. 4 (February 6, 2006), http://nymag.com/movies/features/15622/.

12 Carol Clover, *Men, Women, and Chain Saws: Gender in the Modern Horror Film* (Princeton, NJ: Princeton University Press, 1992), 45.

13 Ibid. Jeffrey Sconce's discussion of identification in the horror film suggests that we identify with positions, not characters as such. He posits, "Viewers identify with Freddy not so much as a character but as a facilitator, the dynamic 'source' of the phantasmagoric imagery." Jeffrey Sconce, "Spectacles of Death: Identification, Reflexivity, and Contemporary Horror," in *Film Theory Goes to the Movies*, ed. Jim Collins, Hilary Radner, and Ava Preacher Collins, 103–119 (New York: Routledge, 1993), 114.

14 Hills, "Cutting into Concepts of 'Reflectionist' Cinema?," 114. See Cynthia A. Freeland, *The Naked and the Undead: Evil and the Appeal of Horror* (Boulder, CO: Westview, 2000), 266.

15 There are clear affinities between the games in the *Saw* films and the games played on reality television programs (see Wetmore, *Post-9/11 Horror in American Cinema*, 78). Indeed, on programs such as *Hell's Kitchen*, characters plead for their "lives," hoping to survive at least until the next round; Chef Ramsay, like Jigsaw, sets up challenges, and over the course of the game, players/characters reveal themselves, in some instances, to be quite nasty. In torture porn, too, players/victims are not particularly likeable, and their "elimination" might very well be welcome.

16 For a discussion of this scene, see Sconce, "Spectacles of Death," 111–112.

17 Warren Buckland analyzes Luc Besson's 1997 film *The Fifth Element* in a similar fashion; see Buckland, "Video Pleasure and Narrative Cinema: Luc Besson's *The Fifth Element* and Video Game Logic," in *Moving Images: From Edison to the Webcam*, ed. John Fullerton and Astrid Söderbergh Widding, 159–164 (London: John Libby, 2000), 161. Also see Evangelos Tziallas's chapter "The Spectacle of Correction: Video Games, Movies and Control," in Aston and Walliss, *To See the "Saw" Movies*, 45–72. Although specifically viewed through the lens of control, Dean Lockwood's chapter "Work Is Hell: Life in the Mannequin Factory," particularly in the latter half, also discusses (video)gaming; this essay is also found in Aston and Walliss, *To See the "Saw" Movies*, 139–156.

18 For more on Jigsaw's disembodied voice, see Brian Collins, "A Voice and Something More: Jigsaw as Acousmêtre and Existential Guru," in Aston and Walliss, *To See the "Saw" Movies*, 86–104. Also see Jeffrey Bullins's chapter "Hearing the Game: Sound Design," in ibid., 189–191.

19 Wetmore, *Post-9/11 Horror in American Cinema*, 74.

20 For more on the FPS, see Will Brooker, "Camera-Eye, CG-Eye: Videogames and the 'Cinematic,'" *Cinema Journal* 48, no. 3 (Spring 2009): 128. While Brooker considers films such as *Cloverfield*, even more characteristic of the FPS aesthetic is Gus Van Sant's 2003 film *Elephant*, which tracks students relentlessly (usually from behind) as they pass through the halls of a high school.

21 I would like to acknowledge my graduate student Patrick Brame, who pointed out

the relationship between the game controller and the adoption of the disembodied camera. In addition, Andrew Clark, also one of my graduate students, identified the similarities between the cinematography in *Saw* and games such as *Prince of Persia: The Sands of Time.*

22 Alexander R. Galloway, *Gaming: Essays on Algorithmic Culture* (Minneapolis: University of Minnesota Press, 2006), 62; emphasis in original.

23 Ibid., 63; emphasis in original.

24 Whannell, a self-aware screenwriter, utilizes Hitchcock's strategies for creating suspense. Though Wetmore does not connect this device to Hitchcockian strategies as such, he observes that in the post-9/11 era, the ticking time bomb comes with added connotations: "*Saw 2* even features a 'ticking bomb' scenario in which the clock is counting down, but in reverse. The justification frequently given for 'enhanced interrogation' is that if a terrorist knows a bomb is about to go off, it is morally justifiable to torture him in order to learn where the bomb is and save lives" (*Post-9/11 Horror in American Cinema*, 103).

25 Steven Shaviro, "Regimes of Vision: Kathryn Bigelow, *Strange Days*," *Polygraph* 13 (2001): 62.

26 Rob Sachs, "Charlie Clouser's Scary Soundtrack for *Saw*," *Day to Day*, NPR, October 29, 2004, http://www.npr.org/templates/story/story.php?storyId=4132853.

27 K. J. Donnelly, "*Saw* Heard: Musical Sound Design in Contemporary Cinema," in *Film Theory and Contemporary Hollywood Movies*, ed. Warren Buckland, 105–123 (New York: Routledge, 2009), 107. For an excellent discussion of the sound design in the *Saw* franchise, see Bullins, "Hearing the Game," 176–193.

28 Donnelly, "*Saw* Heard," 107.

29 Listen, for instance, to the sound on the film's 2004 DVD menu page, which loops an industrially inspired track.

30 For a discussion of this score, see Bullins, "Hearing the Game," 187.

31 Hills, "Cutting into Concepts of 'Reflectionist' Cinema?," 117.

32 Jean Baudrillard, *The Spirit of Terrorism and Other Essays*, trans. Chris Turner (New York: Verso, 2003), 17.

33 Sachs, "Charlie Clouser's Scary Soundtrack for *Saw*." There is perhaps another Kubrick connection: "The music cue [in the score 'Hello Zepp'] itself bears some similarity to the Catholic hymn 'Dies Irae,' which is featured during the opening credits of *The Shining* (1989). Though the hymn describes events during the Day of Judgment, which is certainly in line with Jigsaw's modus operandi, it is unknown if Clouser, either consciously or subconsciously, was channeling the score from the classic Kubrick film or from Catholic liturgy" (Bullins, "Hearing the Game," 187).

34 Hills observes that the "emphasis on narrative trickery is stressed through the repeated use of Charlie Clouser's 'Hello Zepp' music cue. This piece of music, in a variety of realizations, plays over key dramatic twists in every entry in the franchise. It is as much a part of the series' format as Jigsaw and his traps, sonically reinforcing the *Saw* brand not as graphic horror per se, but rather as a series of audacious, heightened narrative games and reveals" ("Cutting into Concepts of 'Reflectionist' Cinema?," 120).

35 Brooker, "Camera-Eye, CG-Eye," 124.

36 Ibid., 123.

37 Wan, disappointed with his own rough cut of the original film, in an interview recalls lamenting that he had made a PG-13 drama and decided to reshoot close-ups to add a bit more gore. See jigsawsl8n8, "30 Even More

Scary Movie Moments 3 Saw" (Wan interview), YouTube, January 7, 2009, http://www.youtube.com/watch?v=OERSfSPL71c&feature=autoplay&list=PL22774D70EFD8D690&index=3&playnext=1.

38 Buckland, "Video Pleasure and Narrative Cinema," 160. Buckland cites Simon Gottschalk, "Videology: Video-Games as Postmodern Sites/Sights of Ideological Reproduction," *Symbolic Interaction* 18, no. 1 (1995): 13.

39 Buckland, "Video Pleasure and Narrative Cinema," 160.

40 Gottschalk, "Videology," 5. Gottschalk notes that John Fiske refers to video arcades as "the semiotic brothels of the machine age," further suggesting the ways in which the discourse of videogames eroticizes the execution of rules. See John Fiske, *Reading the Popular* (Boston: Unwin Hyman, 1989), 93.

41 Buckland, "Video Pleasure and Narrative Cinema," 160.

42 Ibid., 161. Also see Dean Lockwood, "All Stripped Down: The Spectacle of 'Torture Porn,'" *Popular Communication* vol. 7, no. 1 (2009): 46–45.

43 This conception of a more efficient judicial process—one that forgoes due process—is echoed in the disposition of gaming. Gottschalk's article "Videology" outlines eight assumptions about the discourse of videogames, the eighth assumption being that videogaming "affirms the existence of reliable, decipherable, and systematic rules, a purely objective computer 'order' which promises control and survival in the midst of electronic excess" free from the bounds of human compassion and the mores of civil discourse (14).

44 The trap that Jigsaw sets for Hoffman finds affinities with one of the episodes in *Salò*. The prize for winning the "best ass contest" is immediate execution. When a "winner" is selected, the Bishop holds his pistol against the youngster's head and pulls the trigger—we find that the pistol was never loaded. Rather, it was part of a ruse to perpetuate humiliation and anguish; the abductees can only be killed once, but they can be humiliated endlessly.

45 For a detailed discussion of rape-revenge narratives, see Clover's chapter "Getting Even," in her *Men, Women, and Chain Saws*, 114–165. Also see Alexandra Heller-Nicholas's book-length study *Rape-Revenge Films: A Critical Study* (Jefferson, NC: McFarland, 2011).

46 At fair length, Slavoj Žižek talks about "cutters"—those who self-mutilate: "cutting is a radical attempt to (re)gain a hold on reality, or (another aspect of the same phenomenon) to ground the ego firmly in the bodily reality, against the unbearable anxiety of perceiving oneself as nonexistent." The cutting allays anxiety—ameliorates the crisis. "So, although, of course, cutting is a pathological phenomenon, it is none the less a pathological attempt at regaining some kind of normality, at avoiding a total psychotic breakdown." Slavoj Žižek, *Welcome to the Desert of the Real! Five Essays on September 11 and Related Dates* (New York: Verso, 2002), 10. *Saturday Night Live* star Darrell Hammond candidly discusses his own experience as a cutter in his memoir *God, If You're Not Up There, I'm F*cked* (New York: Harper, 2011); also listen to his revealing and quite moving interview with Terry Gross on *Fresh Air* (November 7, 2011).

47 Madeleine Smith, "Monstrous Bodies and Gendered Abjection," in Aston and Walliss, *To See the "Saw" Movies*, 171.

48 Ibid., 171–172.

49 "For Sade," Pierre Klossowski observes, "the substitution of Nature in the state of perpetual motion for God signifies, not the arrival of a happier era for humanity, but only the beginning of tragedy and its conscious and deliberate acceptance."

Pierre Klossowski, *Sade My Neighbour*, trans. Alphonso Lingis (London: Quartet Books, 1991), 81.

50 In *Salò*, the abductees do not win the spectator's sympathy either, but this is because we never really learn enough about the characters, they turn against each other, and they finally only really act as foils for the libertines' fantasies and rage.

51 Mikel Koven makes the same observation in his short assessment of the first film in *101 Horror Movies You Must See before You Die*, ed. Steven Jay Schneider, 402 (London: Quintessence, 2009). Also see Wetmore, *Post-9/11 Horror in American Cinema*, 102.

52 Wetmore, *Post-9/11 Horror in American Cinema*, 102–103.

53 Ibid., 103.

54 A camera flash is also used in Marcus Grave's 2010 film *Choose*, but in this case, it is used by the perpetrator. The perpetrator uses successive camera flashes to disorientate a vain fashion model—the misogynistic violence of the perpetrator is paired with the voyeuristic/sadistic gaze associated with the camera.

55 Zimmer, "Caught on Tape?," 86–87.

56 Jones similarly observes that female nudity is rare in the *Saw* films, but reviewers extract the single instance in *Saw III*, when Danica is strung up in a freezer, "as proof that the whole franchise is misogynistic (see Kinsella, 2007). Subsequently detractors have propagated that presumption, erroneously conclude that *Saw* is fixated on 'starlet being strung up' (Orange, 2009) and 'taboo-breaking sex and violence' (Graham, 2009a)" (Jones, *Torture Porn*, 132–133), citing Warren Kinsella, "Torture Porn's Dark Waters," *National Post*, June 7, 2007; Michelle Orange, "Taking Back the Knife," *New York Times*, September 6, 2009; Jane Graham, "Caught in a Trap, and I Can't Back Out," *Guardian*, October 16, 2009.

57 This scene is actually set immediately adjacent to the Roy Thomson Hall in Toronto, Ontario, home of the Toronto Symphony. Although most probably coincidental, this location seems to correspond to the arrangement found in the closing moments of *Salò* in its relation to the opera.

58 Wetmore, *Post-9/11 Horror in American Cinema*, 104.

59 Michel Foucault, *Discipline and Punish: The Birth of the Prison*, trans. Alan Sheridan (New York: Vintage Books, 1995), 48. For more regarding Foucault and the *Saw* franchise, see Tziallas, "Spectacle of Correction," 45–72.

60 Foucault, *Discipline and Punish*, 47.

61 "The public execution did not re-establish justice," Foucault observes; "it reactivated power" (ibid., 49). See Gabrielle Murray's article on *Hostel: Part II* for a discussion of the term "pornography" and its relation to concealing from sight: Gabrielle Murray, "*Hostel II*: Representations of the Body in Pain and the Cinema Experience in Torture-Porn," *Jump Cut* 50 (Spring 2008), http://www.ejumpcut.org/archive/jc50.2008/TortureHostel2/. Jason Middleton also briefly discusses torture porn in relation to the denial of sight; see his article "The Subject of Torture: Regarding the Pain of Americans in *Hostel*," *Cinema Journal* 49, no. 4 (Summer 2010): 9.

62 Zimmer, "Caught on Tape?," 87.

63 Catherine Soussloff, "Post-colonial Torture: Rituals of Viewing at Abu Ghraib," in *Ritual and Event*, ed. Mark Franko, 159–187 (New York: Routledge, 2007), 171.

64 Jeremy Morris, "The Justification of Torture-Horror: Retribution and Sadism in *Saw*, *Hostel*, and *The Devil's Rejects*," in *The Philosophy of Horror*, ed. Thomas Fahy, 42–56 (Lexington: University Press of Kentucky, 2010), 47.

65 Zimmer, "Caught on Tape?," 85.

66 Klossowski, *Sade My Neighbour*, 51.
67 Slavoj Žižek, "Kant with (or against) Sade," in *The Žižek Reader*, ed. Elizabeth Wright and Edmond Wright, 283–301 (Oxford, UK: Blackwell, 1999), 288.

Chapter 5 The *Hostel* Films: Consuming Bodies

1 Truth be told, though these are directing/screenwriting conceits: Paxton using a scalpel (the very tool that the businessman employs) and the echoed imagery, which Paxton would have no way of knowing, all are a product of narrative construction. The conceit works, though, and further illustrates Roth's investment in narrative despite what critics might otherwise suggest.
2 Steve Jones, *Torture Porn: Popular Horror after "Saw"* (New York: Palgrave, 2013), 89.
3 Jeremy Morris, "The Justification of Torture-Horror: Retribution and Sadism in *Saw*, *Hostel*, and *The Devil's Rejects*," in *The Philosophy of Horror*, ed. Thomas Fahy, 42–56 (Lexington: University Press of Kentucky, 2010), 44–45; Jason Middleton, "The Subject of Torture: Regarding the Pain of Americans in *Hostel*," *Cinema Journal* 49, no. 4 (Summer 2010): 4.
4 See Adam Lowenstein, "Spectacle Horror and *Hostel*: Why 'Torture Porn' Does Not Exist," *Critical Quarterly* 53, no. 1 (2011): 42–60.
5 Middleton, "Subject of Torture," 4.
6 Ibid.
7 Ibid., 4–5.
8 Ibid., 5.
9 Ibid., 22.
10 Interestingly, and this plays into the ways in which the contours of the Holocaust materialize in Roth's films, the character biography for Donowitz, as stated on the Internet Movie Database (http://www.imdb.com/character/ch0101641/bio), evokes the Jewish myth of the golem: "Sgt. Donny Donowitz is a member of the Basterds. Also known as 'The Bear Jew,' Donowitz's weapon of choice is a wooden baseball bat, signed by fellow members of his Boston Jewish community with names of their loved ones in Europe. He is so feared amongst the German military that some believe he is a golem."
11 David Edelstein, "Now Playing at Your Local Multiplex: Torture Porn," *New York* 39, no. 4 (February, 6, 2006), http://nymag.com/movies/features/15622/.
12 See Barbara Creed's discussion of Countess Elizabeth Bathory in *The Monstrous-Feminine: Film, Feminism, Psychoanalysis* (New York: Routledge, 1993), 60.
13 Discussing the Bathory sequence, Roth explicitly stated at the Austin premiere of *Hostel: Part II* that the "violence is a substitute for sex": Anne Heller, "AICN Presents Eli Roth at Hostel 2 Austin Premiere," YouTube, August 13, 2007, https://www.youtube.com/watch?v=rRivo8R7XA4.
14 The lion's share of Wesley Morris's review of *Hostel: Part II*, for the *Boston Globe*, focuses on the Bathory scene. Seemingly paralyzed by this scene, and without saying as much, like Edelstein, Morris suggests that Roth's error is that he privileges spectacle over narrative, thus emphasizing "what a movie can show," versus what a movie can "say." Morris concludes that Roth and his contemporaries have no "interest in actually scaring us" and that Roth's "moviemaking is driven only by contempt; he wants to nauseate us into submission." Wesley Morris, "*Hostel* Sequel Is Pure

Torture," *Boston Globe*, June 8, 2007, http://www.boston.com/ae/movies/articles/2007/06/08/hostel_sequel_is_pure_torture/.

15 Kaleem Aftab, "*Drag Me to Hell*—Don't Lose Your Head," *Independent*, June 5, 2009, http://www.independent.co.uk/arts-entertainment/films/features/drag-me-to-hell--dont-lose-your-head-1697053.html.

16 Edelstein, "Now Playing at Your Local Multiplex."

17 Middleton makes similar observations; see "Subject of Torture," 21.

18 Kanye West on *A Concert for Hurricane Relief*, a Red Cross fundraiser that aired September 2, 2005, on the NBC network.

19 Aftab, "*Drag Me to Hell*." Peter Hutchings argues, "the only people who could actually enjoy this sort of thing are either sick or stupid." Peter Hutchings, *The Horror Film* (Harlow, UK: Pearson Longman, 2004), 83.

20 While preparing for *Hostel*, Roth notes, "I read the history of medieval tortures—witch torture and gladiators. Looking through human history I found that people have this sick need to do harm to another human being. The thing that really shocked me was New Orleans [after Hurricane Katrina]. I was in Prague, we were scoring *Hostel* at the time, and we turned on the TV and bodies were floating down the street. People were raping, and I thought, 'Oh my God, this is what people do when no one is looking. People will go right to that place of total insanity.' It's some part of human nature that everybody has. It's within everybody's capacity to behave that way, and it's horrifying to think that you yourself could almost do that to someone. That was really what I wanted to explore in the sequel." Eli Roth, interviewed by Jason Guerrasio, "The Vacation Planner," *Filmmaker* 15, no. 3 (Spring 2007), *Film and Television Literature Index*, EBSCO*host* (accessed March 15, 2013).

21 Cullen Murphy, *God's Jury: The Inquisition and the Making of the Modern World* (Boston: Houghton Mifflin Harcourt, 2012), 215.

22 See ibid., 222.

23 *Beneath the Skin*, DVD special feature for *Cabin Fever* (Eli Roth, 2002).

24 Also see (or, perhaps more accurately, listen to) another instance in *Ju-on* (19:10), as Kazumi Tokunaga mounts the stairs: when she first sees a ghostly figure, there is a cacophony of multiple piano keys slamming down all at once—though the sound is abstracted and reverberant. This is actually a technique that Akira Ifukube used in the sound design of *Gojira* (Ishiro Honda, 1954).

25 Roth, interviewed by Guerrasio, "Vacation Planner."

26 StrawberryAphrodite1, "Eli Roth on *Hostel*" (February 2006), YouTube, June 14, 2010, http://www.youtube.com/watch?v=j5ArtKwbobY.

27 See, for instance, the review of *Hostel: Part II* (June 6, 2007) on the Australian television program *At the Movies*, hosted by film critics Margaret Pomeranz and David Stratton. The review can be found on YouTube or at the *At the Movies* website: http://www.abc.net.au/atthemovies/txt/s1941379.htm.

28 The use of gas to sedate an individual in a cell also happens in *Captivity* and *Choose*.

29 Roland Barthes, *Camera Lucida*, trans. Richard Howard (New York: Hill and Wang, 1981), 27.

30 On October 7, 1944, the Sonderkommando blew up one of the crematoria at Auschwitz-Birkenau using gunpowder smuggled from a munitions factory and orchestrated an uprising.

31 With the German-speaking torturer, we are invited to make associations with Mengele. See Middleton, "Subject of Torture," 16.

32 Ka Tzetnik 135633 was the pseudonym for Yehiel De-Nur, who took his

concentration-camp numerical identification as his penname. Ka Tzetnik 135633 (aka Yehiel Dinur), *The House of Dolls*, trans. Moshe M. Kohn (London: Frederick Muller, 1965).

33 Another sign of Josh's Jewishness is that, while in the hostel spa, he compares his circumcised penis to Oli's uncircumcised penis.

34 See Elaine Scarry, *The Body in Pain: The Making and Unmaking of the World* (New York: Oxford University Press, 1985), 41.

35 Ibid., 42.

36 Ibid., 41.

37 Ibid.

38 This term is attributed to SS officer Heinz Thilo, a physician stationed at Auschwitz. See Antoni Kępiński, "Anus Mundi," *Archives of Psychiatry and Psychotherapy* 4 (2007): 85.

39 Big Sister, the brothel that the pair visit, is a real brothel in Prague, not in Slovakia, outfitted with multiple webcams that allows subscribers to the Big Sister website to watch.

40 Marquis de Sade, *The 120 Days of Sodom and Other Writing*, trans. Austryn Wainhouse and Richard Seaver (New York: Grove Weidenfeld, 1987), 237–238.

41 Roland Barthes, *Sade/Fourier/Loyola*, trans. Richard Miller (Berkeley: University of California Press, 1989), 146.

42 Maisha Wester, "Torture Porn and Uneasy Feminism: Re-thinking (Wo)men in Eli Roth's *Hostel* Films," *Quarterly Review of Film and Video* 29 (2012): 392. Also see Jones, *Torture Porn*, 145.

43 Elvis Mitchell's interview with Eli Roth on his radio program *The Treatment* is available as part of the special features on the *Hostel: Part II* DVD. *The Treatment* is produced by KCRW, in Santa Monica, California, a National Public Radio affiliate.

44 Middleton offers a similar reading; see "Subject of Torture," 20.

45 For more on the rape-revenge narrative, see Carol Clover's chapter "Getting Even," in *Men, Women, and Chain Saws: Gender in the Modern Horror Film* (Princeton, NJ: Princeton University Press, 1992), 114–165. Also see Alexandra Heller-Nicholas, *Rape-Revenge Films: A Critical Study* (Jefferson, NC: McFarland, 2011).

46 Middleton, "Subject of Torture," 21.

47 Ibid., 17.

48 Ibid.

49 The CBS news program *60 Minutes* reported that in 2007, "it is estimated that Americans now spend somewhere around $10 billion a year on adult entertainment, which is as much as they spend attending professional sporting events, buying music or going out to the movies." Rebecca Leung, "Porn in the U.S.A.," *60 Minutes*, December 5, 2007, http://www.cbsnews.com/news/porn-in-the-usa-21-11-2003/.

50 Kelly Dennis, "Leave It to Beaver: The Object of Pornography," in *Strategies for Theory: From Marx to Madonna*, ed. R. L. Rutsky and Bradley Macdonald (Albany: State University of New York Press, 2003), 187.

51 "Squirting" is the porn vernacular for female ejaculation.

52 Middleton, "Subject of Torture," 6.

53 Ibid.

54 Ibid.

55 Ibid., 7–8.

56 Linda Williams, *Hard Core: Power, Pleasure, and the "Frenzy of the Visible"* (Berkeley: University of California Press, 1999), 48.

57 Ibid.
58 John Berger, *Ways of Seeing* (New York: Viking Penguin, 1985), 47.
59 Roth's *The Green Inferno* (2013) clearly references *Cannibal Holocaust*.
60 Eadweard Muybridge, *Muybridge's Complete Human and Animal Locomotion* (New York: Dover, 1979), 1100–1101. For an animated presentation of this image series, see the University of Southern California Digital Library, http://digitallibrary.usc.edu/search/controller/view/rbm-m678.html. I would like to acknowledge my student Jonathan Knapp, who initially brought this comparison to my attention.
61 Wester, "Torture Porn and Uneasy Feminism," 395.
62 Dennis, "Leave It to Beaver," 187.
63 Wester, "Torture Porn and Uneasy Feminism," 395.
64 Williams, *Hard Core*, 40–41.
65 Clover, *Men, Women, and Chain Saws*, 29.
66 See Linda Williams, "Film Bodies: Gender, Genre, and Excess," *Film Quarterly* 44, no. 4 (Summer 1991): 2–13.
67 Jones discusses spatial issues in the genre, particularly with respect to the crossing of boundaries, citing how characters in *Hostel* "move from 'seeing' to 'feeling,'" from touched (tortured) to toucher (torturer) (*Torture Porn*, 103–104).
68 Slavoj Žižek, *Welcome to the Desert of the Real! Five Essays on September 11 and Related Dates* (New York: Verso, 2002), 10–11.
69 Ibid., 11.
70 Tomas Geyskens, "Painting as Hysteria—Deleuze on Bacon," in *Sexuality and Psychoanalysis: Philosophical Criticisms*, ed. Jens De Vleminck and Eran Dorfman, 215–229 (Leuven, Belgium: Leuven University Press, 2010), 224.
71 Gilles Deleuze, *Francis Bacon: The Logic of Sensation*, trans. Daniel W. Smith (Minneapolis: University of Minnesota Press, 2004), 19.
72 Geyskens, "Painting as Hysteria," 224.

Chapter 6 "I Think We Took a Wrong Turn . . ."

1 See Jason Middleton, "The Subject of Torture: Regarding the Pain of Americans in *Hostel*," *Cinema Journal* 49, no. 4 (Summer 2010): 8–9.
2 Speaking about John Boorman's 1972 film *Deliverance*, Carol Clover observes that the "city approaches the country [with] guilt, and by aligning our sympathies relentlessly with the city people, director Boorman invites us to participate not only in their arrogance ('Give him a couple of bucks'), but also in their palpable nervousness at having to face directly those they recognize, at some level of consciousness, as the rural victims of their own city comfort." Carol Clover, *Men, Women, and Chain Saws* (Princeton, NJ: Princeton University Press, 1992), 128–129. For further discussion on the urban/rural conflict in the horror genre, see specifically Clover's chapter "Getting Even."
3 For a succinct discussion of the Sawney Bean legend and how it informs contemporary popular culture and the tourist economy, see Sandy Hobbs and David Cornwell, "Sawney Bean, the Scottish Cannibal," *Folklore* 108 (1997): 49–54.
4 See *The Directors: The Films of Wes Craven* (Robert Emery, 1999).
5 One could also presumably even find earlier sources for this trope in literature—perhaps the oracle in *Oedipus Rex* or the soothsayer in Shakespeare's *Julius Caesar*.
6 The Splat Pack is usually given as Alexandre Aja (*High Tension*, *Piranha*), Darren Lynn Bousman (*Saw II*, *III*, and *IV*), Neil Marshall (*The Descent*, *Doomsday*), Greg

Mclean (*Wolf Creek*, *Rouge*), Eli Roth (*Cabin Fever*, *Hostel*, *Hostel: Part II*), James Wan (*Saw*, *Death Sentence*), Leigh Whannell (*Saw*, *Dead Silence*), and Rob Zombie (*House of 1000 Corpses*, *The Devil's Rejects*). For an interesting survey of the Splat Pack, see Mark Henry and Frank H. Woodward's 2011 documentary *The Splat Pack*.

7 The sequel to the 2006 film, *The Hills Have Eyes II* (Martine Weisz, 2007), is, interestingly enough, shot in Morocco and exhibits overt references to the current geopolitical circumstances.

8 For a discussion of the feminization of Jewish male characters, see, for instance, the work of Judith Doneson: "The Jew as a Female Figure in the Holocaust Film," *Shoah: A Review of Holocaust Studies and Commemorations* 1, no. 1 (1978): 11–13, 18; "The Image Lingers: the Feminization of the Jew in *Schindler's List*," in *Spielberg's Holocaust: Critical Perspectives on "Schindler's List,"* ed. Yosefa Loshitzky, 140–152 (Bloomington: Indiana University Press, 1997); *The Holocaust in American Film*, 2nd ed. (Syracuse, NY: Syracuse University Press, 2002).

9 President George W. Bush, quoted in Brian Knowlton, "Terror in America / 'We're Going to Smoke Them Out': President Airs His Anger," *New York Times*, September 19, 2001, http://www.nytimes.com/2001/09/19/news/19iht-t4_30.html.

10 Clover, *Men, Women, and Chain Saws*, 162–163.

11 Linnie Blake makes a similar observation: "like the cowboy hero and his successor, the serial killer, the hillbilly amply illustrates the limits placed on liberty by an increasingly organized and urbanized society." Linnie Blake, "'I Am the Devil and I'm Here to Do the Devil's Work': Rob Zombie, George W. Bush, and the Limits of American Freedom," in *Horror after 9/11: World of Fear, Cinema of Terror*, ed. Aviva Briefel and Sam J. Miller (Austin: University of Texas, 2011), 196. Also, for a discussion of the relationship between the western and horror genres, see the latter part of Clover's chapter "Getting Even," in *Men, Women, and Chain Saws*, 160–165.

12 George Will, quoted in Frank Rich, "No News Is Good News," *New York Times*, October 13, 2001, https://www.nytimes.com/2001/10/13/opinion/journal-no-news-is-good-news.html?src=pm.

13 Ibid.

14 Secretary of Defense Donald Rumsfeld, interviewed by Tim Russert on *Meet the Press*, December 2, 2001; transcript available at http://www.defense.gov/transcripts/transcript.aspx?transcriptid=2585.

15 U.S. National Commission on Terrorist Attacks upon the United States, *The 9/11 Commission Report* (Washington, DC: U.S. GPO, 2004), 339.

16 For more on the "prison without bars" motif, see Steve Jones, *Torture Porn: Popular Horror after "Saw"* (New York: Palgrave, 2013), 105–108.

17 There are clear affinities between the stalking sequence in *Captivity* and Michael Powell's 1960 film *Peeping Tom*. Dean Lockwood also discusses the similarities between *Captivity* and *Peeping Tom*; see "All Stripped Down: The Spectacle of 'Torture Porn,'" *Popular Communication* 7, no. 1 (2009): 43.

18 Jennifer Harbury, *Truth, Torture, and the American Way* (Boston: Beacon, 2005), 16.

19 Lockwood, "All Stripped Down," 45.

20 Jennifer Lynch, interviewed by Tyler Doupe, "Shock Interview: Jennifer Lynch and Vincent D'Onofrio on *Chained*," Fun With Horror, November 13, 2012, http://www.funwithhorror.com/?p=1874.

21 There are startling affinities between *Chained* and the real-life case of abduction

in Cleveland, Ohio, in which Ariel Castro apparently held three young women in captivity for a decade.

22 Michel Foucault, "Of Other Spaces," trans. Jay Miskowiec, *Diacritics* 16, no. 1 (Spring 1986): 27.

23 Julia Kristeva, *Powers of Horror: An Essay on Abjection*, trans. Leon S. Roudiez (New York: Columbia University Press, 1982), 4.

24 See Foucault, "Of Other Spaces," 27.

25 PremiereScene, "Chained UK Premiere—Jennifer Chambers Lynch Interviews," interview by Claire Bueno, YouTube, August 2012, http://www.youtube.com/watch?v=gON1Pg5qQGw.

26 Kevin J. Wetmore, *Post-9/11 Horror in American Cinema* (New York: Continuum, 2012), 109. Brandon Nutt's 2009 film *The Last Resort* envisions the performance, as Diana Palaversich calls it, between gringos and Mexicans. For more on the gringo/Mexican encounter, see Diana Palaversich, "La vuelta a Tijuana en seis escritores," *Aztlán: A Journal of Chicano Studies* 28, no. 1 (2003): 116, cited in Fiamma Montezemolo, René Peralta, and Heriberto Yépez, *Here Is Tijuana!* (London: Black Dog, 2006), 31.

27 Mary Louise Pratt, *Imperial Eyes: Travel and Transculturation* (New York: Routledge, 1994), 6.

28 Ibid., 6–7.

29 Ibid., 7.

30 Or as Marc Augé phrases it, "The traveler's space may thus be the archetype of *non-place*." Marc Augé, *Non-Places: Introduction to an Anthropology of Supermodernity*, trans. John Howe (New York: Verso, 1995), 86.

31 Wetmore, *Post-9/11 Horror in American Cinema*, 111.

32 Recently, this issue came to light when the collapse of a Bangladesh garment factory killed more than eleven hundred workers—paid little more than thirty-eight dollars a month. This incident initiated some soul searching regarding the true costs of cheap apparel, but a few short months later, it has all but left public consciousness.

33 Elizabeth Swanson Goldberg, "Splitting Difference: Global Identity Politics and the Representation of Torture in the Counterhistorical Dramatic Film," in *Violence and American Cinema*, ed. David Slocum, 245–270 (New York: Routledge, 2001), 260.

34 Ibid., 268.

35 Regarding American peril, see James Aston and John Walliss, "'I've Never Murdered Anyone in My Life. The Decisions Are Up to Them': Ethical Guidance and the Turn toward Cultural Pessimism," in *To See the "Saw" Movies: Essays on Torture Porn and Post-9/11 Horror*, ed. James Aston and John Walliss, 13–29 (Jefferson, NC: McFarland, 2013), 25.

36 James Clifford, *Routes: Travel and Translation in the Late Twentieth Century* (Cambridge, MA: Harvard University Press, 1997), 32.

37 Ibid., 31.

38 Ibid., 33.

39 Ibid.

40 Wetmore, *Post-9/11 Horror in American Cinema*, 134.

41 Slavoj Žižek, *Welcome to the Desert of the Real! Five Essays on September 11 and Related Dates* (New York: Verso, 2002), 27.

42 Blake, "I Am the Devil and I'm Here to Do the Devil's Work," 189.

43 Kathleen Stewart, *A Space on the Side of the Road: Cultural Poetics in an "Other" America* (Princeton, NJ: Princeton University Press, 1996), 3.
44 Regarding the repulsive and fascinating qualities of the hillbilly, see Blake, "I Am the Devil and I'm Here to Do the Devil's Work," 188.
45 Clifford, *Routes*, 34.
46 Ibid., 34–35.
47 Stewart, *Space on the Side of the Road*, 44, 46.
48 Ibid., 44. Stewart is referencing Susan Stewart's research here; see Susan Stewart, *On Longing: Narratives of the Miniature, the Gigantic, the Souvenir, the Collection* (Baltimore: John Hopkins University Press, 1984), 154.
49 Stewart, *Space on the Side of the Road*, 18.
50 Blake, "I Am the Devil and I'm Here to Do the Devil's Work," 193.
51 Ibid., 194.
52 In the DVD commentary, Zombie notes that something peculiar happens when Tiny finally reemerges in the narrative to break Wydell's neck and to save Baby and the others: "Now here's where you'd think the audience would be upset, but every time we show this, it gets a huge round of applause when the good guy dies. So I don't know what that means."
53 Regarding the tension of identification in Zombie's films, see Blake, "I Am the Devil and I'm Here to Do the Devil's Work," 195.

Chapter 7 Soft-Core, and Beyond Torture Porn

1 Alfred Hitchcock, interview in François Truffaut, *Hitchcock*, rev. ed. (New York: Simon and Schuster, 1985), 73.
2 Simon Brown and Stacey Abbott, "The Art of the Sp(1)atter: Body Horror in *Dexter*," in *Dexter: Investigating Cutting Edge Television*, ed. Douglas L. Howard, 205–220 (London: I. B. Tauris, 2010), 212–213. To my recollection, I do not think I have ever heard Dexter's power tools—dismemberment of the body takes place off-screen.
3 Linda Williams, *Hard Core: Power, Pleasure, and the "Frenzy of the Visible"* (Berkeley: University of California Press, 1989), 49.
4 Douglas Howard, "'You're Going to Tell Me Everything You Know': Torture and Morality in Fox's *24*," in *Reading 24: TV against the Clock*, ed. Steven Peacock, 133–145 (London: I. B. Tauris, 2007), 140.
5 Steve Jones makes a similar case when citing Linnie Blake's analysis of Christopher Smith's 2004 film *Creep*: "Her argument hinges on the same supposition that pervades popular journalistic responses to torture porn: that such violence requires justification." Steve Jones, *Torture Porn: Popular Horror after "Saw"* (New York: Palgrave, 2013), 137–138.
6 John Yoo, *War by Other Means: An Insider's Account of the War on Terror* (New York: Atlantic Monthly Press, 2006), 172.
7 "It is true that, for a time, the interrogators at Guantánamo, operating without guidance, often amateurs, and under extreme pressure to show results, improvised as best they could. They gleaned ideas from the Fox drama *24* . . . . But the explicit sanction of torture, and the demand that it be used, came from above." Cullen Murphy, *God's Jury: The Inquisition and the Making of the Modern World* (Boston: Houghton Mifflin Harcourt, 2012), 222. Also regarding the emulation of *24* tactics, see Tung Yin,

"Jack Bauer Syndrome: Hollywood's Depiction of National Security Law," *Southern California Interdisciplinary Law Journal* 17, no. 2 (Winter 2008): 280.

8 Peter Lattman, "Justice Scalia Hearts Jack Bauer," *Law Blog, Wall Street Journal,* June 20, 2007, http://blogs.wsj.com/law/2007/06/20/justice-scalia-hearts-jack-bauer/.

9 Dahlia Lithwick, "How Jack Bauer Shaped U.S. Torture Policy," *Newsweek,* July 25, 2008, http://www.thedailybeast.com/newsweek/2008/07/25/the-fiction-behind-torture-policy.html.

10 Lindsay Coleman, "'Damn You for Making Me Do This': Abu Ghraib, *24*, Torture, and Television Masochism," in *The War Body on Screen*, ed. Karen Randell and Sean Redmond, 199–214 (New York: Continuum, 2008), 199–200.

11 Michael J. Lewis, "Making Modern Evil: Terrorism, Torture, and the Creation of Evil in *24*," in *Vader, Voldemort and Other Villains: Essays on Evil in Popular Media*, ed. Jamey Heit, 162–174 (Jefferson, NC: McFarland, 2011), 164.

12 Coleman, "Damn You for Making Me Do This," 206–207, citing *Saw* (James Wan, 2004) and *Saw II* (Darren Lynn Bousman, 2005).

13 Jean Baudrillard, *The Spirit of Terrorism and Other Essays*, trans. Chris Turner (New York: Verso, 2003), 61.

14 Howard, "You're Going to Tell Me Everything You Know," 141.

15 Lithwick, "How Jack Bauer Shaped U.S. Torture Policy."

16 David Edelstein, "Now Playing at Your Local Multiplex: Torture Porn," *New York* 39, no. 4 (February, 6, 2006), http://nymag.com/movies/features/15622/.

17 Coleman, "Damn You for Making Me Do This," 212.

18 Mark Hosenball, "Report Reveals CIA Conducted Mock Executions," *Newsweek,* August 20, 2009, http://www.thedailybeast.com/newsweek/2009/08/20/report-reveals-cia-conducted-mock-executions.html.

19 Lewis, "Making Modern Evil," 171.

20 Ibid., 172.

21 Julia Kristeva, *Powers of Horror: An Essay on Abjection*, trans. Leon S. Roudiez (New York: Columbia University Press, 1982), 4.

22 Lewis, "Making Modern Evil," 170–171.

23 Ibid., 170.

24 Yin, "Jack Bauer Syndrome," 295. Yin also posits elsewhere an interesting question: "Why does Bauer not torture women? The answer is probably that viewers might stop viewing him as the dedicated hero who does whatever it takes to save the nation, and start seeing him as a monster" (ibid., 290).

25 Ibid., 279.

26 Coleman, "'Damn You for Making Me Do This,'" 213.

27 Stan Beeler, "From Silver Bullets to Duct Tape: Dexter versus the Traditional Vigilante Hero," in Howard, *Dexter*, 222. Also, for a brief discussion of Jigsaw as superhero, see Evangelos Tziallas's chapter "The Spectacle of Correction: Video Games, Movies and Control," in *To See the "Saw" Movies: Essays on Torture Porn and Post-9/11 Horror*, ed. James Aston and John Walliss, 45–72 (Jefferson, NC: McFarland, 2013), 49. For more on Dexter as a superhero, see Anthony Letizia, "The Origins of Dexter Morgan and Bruce Wayne," Geek Pittsburgh, January 5, 2011, http://www.geekpittsburgh.com/reflections/dexterorigins.htm.

28 Edelstein, "Now Playing at Your Local Multiplex."

29 Douglas Howard, "Harry Morgan: (Post)Modern Prometheus," in Howard, *Dexter*, 61.

30 Ibid., 62.

31 Dexter says in the opening episode of season 3, titled "Our Father," and the religious connotations of the episode title are wholly appropriate here, "There were so many lessons in the vaunted Code of Harry, twisted commandments handed down from the only God I ever worshipped. One through ten. Don't get caught—that I got covered. But killing someone without knowing if he's guilty—I'd love some help on this one, but my God is dead now."

32 Howard, "Harry Morgan," 66.

33 Mary Shelley, *Frankenstein* (New York: Bantam Books, 1981), 42.

34 Howard, "Harry Morgan," 68.

35 There might be an instance of sexual sublimation in the place of killing in "The Dark Defender," the fifth episode of the second season. Dexter confronts the man who murdered his mother, nearly kills him, but is talked down by Lila Tournay, his addiction sponsor. (Dexter enters an addiction program, first as cover, then as an effort to keep his Dark Passenger at bay.) Instead of killing the man, Dexter finds solace in Lila's arms. For more on the sublimation of the libidinal drive in *Dexter*, see Beth Johnson, "Sex, Psychoanalysis, and Sublimation in *Dexter*," in Howard, *Dexter*, 78–95.

36 When Dexter kills in passion in season 6, episode 6, "Just Let Go," it is not Harry who appears but rather the specter of Dexter's elder brother, Brian, also born of the same trauma as Dexter and also a serial killer. But whereas Dexter was given the Code, Harry's word, an incarnation of the superego, Brian is capricious; he kills for the love of killing, free of any code, and is an embodiment of the id. In the following episode, "Nebraska," Dexter goes on a road trip with his brother and does things totally out of character. At the end of this episode, however, he rejects his brother and returns, as the Prodigal Son, to the father.

37 Kristeva, *Powers of Horror*, 21.

38 Ibid., 4.

39 Michele Byers, "Neoliberal *Dexter*?," in Howard, *Dexter*, 144.

40 Ibid., 148.

41 Ibid., 156.

42 My graduate student Patrick Brame quite astutely notes the uncanny affinities between this closing and the unseemly celebrations following the news of the killing of Osama bin Laden.

43 Günter Grass, *Two States—One Nation?*, trans. Krishna Winston and A. S. Wensinger (San Diego: Harcourt Brace Jovanovich, 1990), 123.

44 Jones, *Torture Porn*, 64.

45 Jason Middleton, "The Subject of Torture: Regarding the Pain of Americans in *Hostel*," *Cinema Journal* 49, no. 4 (Summer 2010): 2.

46 Guy Debord, *Society of the Spectacle, trans. Black and Red* (Detroit: Black and Red, 1983), fragment 18.

47 Edelstein, "Now Playing at Your Local Multiplex."

Bibliography

Aftab, Kaleem. "*Drag Me to Hell*—Don't Lose Your Head." *Independent*, June 5, 2009. http://www.independent.co.uk/arts-entertainment/films/features/drag-me-to-hell--dont-lose-your-head-1697053.html.

Aston, James, and John Walliss. "'I've Never Murdered Anyone in My Life. The Decisions Are Up to Them': Ethical Guidance and the Turn toward Cultural Pessimism." In *To See the "Saw" Movies: Essays on Torture Porn and Post-9/11 Horror*, edited by James Aston and John Walliss, 13–29. Jefferson, NC: McFarland, 2013.

———, eds. *To See the "Saw" Movies: Essays on Torture Porn and Post-9/11 Horror*. Jefferson, NC: McFarland, 2013.

Attwood, Feona, Vincent Campbell, I. Q. Hunter, and Sharon Lockyer, eds. *Controversial Images: Media Representations on the Edge*. Basingstoke, UK: Palgrave Macmillan, 2013.

Augé, Marc. *Non-Places: Introduction to an Anthropology of Supermodernity*. Translated by John Howe. New York: Verso, 1995.

Badt, Karin. "Family Is Hell and So Is the World." *Bright Lights Film Journal* 50 (November 2005). http://brightlightsfilm.com/50/hanekeiv.htm.

Barker, Jennifer. *The Tactile Eye: Touch and the Cinema Experience*. Berkeley: University of California Press, 2009.

Barker, Martin, and Julian Petley, eds. *Ill Effects: The Media/Violence Debate*. New York: Routledge, 1997.

Barthes, Roland. *Camera Lucida*. Translated by Richard Howard. New York: Hill and Wang, 1981.

———. *Sade/Fourier/Loyola*. Translated by Richard Miller. Berkeley: University of California Press, 1989.

Bataille, Georges. *Erotism: Death and Sensuality*. Translated by Mary Dalwood. San Francisco: City Lights Books, 1986.

———. *The Tears of Eros*. Translated by Peter Connor. San Francisco: City Lights Books, 1989.

Baudrillard, Jean. *The Spirit of Terrorism and Other Essays*. Translated by Chris Turner. New York: Verso, 2003.

Beeler, Stan. "From Silver Bullets to Duct Tape: Dexter versus the Traditional Vigilante Hero." In *Dexter: Investigating Cutting Edge Television*, edited by Douglas L. Howard, 221–230. London: I. B. Tauris, 2010.

Berger, John. *Ways of Seeing*. New York: Viking Penguin, 1985.

Berns, Fernando G. Pagnoni, and Amy M. Davis. "From Jigsaw to Phibes: God, Free Will and Foreknowledge in Conflict." In *To See the "Saw" Movies: Essays on Torture Porn and Post-9/11 Horror*, edited by James Aston and John Walliss, 73–85. Jefferson, NC: McFarland, 2013.

Beugnet, Martine. *Cinema of Sensation: French Film and the Art of Transgression*. Carbondale: Southern Illinois University Press, 2007.

Black, Joel. *The Reality Effect: Film Culture and the Graphic Imperative*. New York: Routledge, 2002.

Blackwood, Gemma. "*Wolf Creek*: An UnAustralian Story?" *Continuum: Journal of Media and Cultural Studies* 21, no. 4 (December 2007): 489–497.

Blake, Linnie. "'I Am the Devil and I'm Here to Do the Devil's Work': Rob Zombie, George W. Bush, and the Limits of American Freedom." In *Horror after 9/11: World of Fear, Cinema of Terror*, edited by Aviva Briefel and Sam J. Miller, 186–199. Austin: University of Texas, 2011.

———. *The Wounds of Nations: Horror Cinema, Historical Trauma and National Identity*. Manchester: Manchester University Press, 2008.

Briefel, Aviva, and Sam J. Miller, eds. *Horror after 9/11: World of Fear, Cinema of Terror*. Austin: University of Texas Press, 2011.

Brooker, Will. "Camera-Eye, CG-Eye: Videogames and the 'Cinematic.'" *Cinema Journal* 48, no. 3 (Spring 2009): 122–128.

Brottman, Mikita. *Offensive Films*. Nashville, TN: Vanderbilt University Press, 2005.

Brown, Simon, and Stacey Abbott. "The Art of Sp(1)atter: Body Horror in *Dexter*." In *Dexter: Investigating Cutting Edge Television*, edited by Douglas Howard, 205–220. London: I. B. Tauris, 2010.

Brunette, Peter. *Michael Haneke*. Urbana: University of Illinois Press, 2010.

Buckland, Warren. "Video Pleasure and Narrative Cinema: Luc Besson's *The Fifth Element* and Video Game Logic." In *Moving Images: From Edison to the Webcam*, edited by John Fullerton and Astrid Söderbergh Widding, 159–164. London: John Libby, 2000.

Bullins, Jeffrey. "Hearing the Game: Sound Design." In *To See the "Saw" Movies: Essays on Torture Porn and Post-9/11 Horror*, edited by James Aston and John Walliss, 176–193. Jefferson, NC: McFarland, 2013.

Burrill, Derek A. *Die Tryin': Videogames, Masculinity, Culture*. New York: Peter Lang, 2008.

Byers, Michele. "Neoliberal *Dexter*?" In *Dexter: Investigating Cutting Edge Television*, edited by Douglas L. Howard, 143–156. London: I. B. Tauris, 2010.

Caputi, Jane. "Advertising Femicide: Lethal Violence against Women in Pornography and Gorenography." In *Femicide: The Politics of Woman Killing*, edited by Jill Radford and Diana E. H. Russell, 203–221. New York: Twayne, 1992.

Clarke, Alan W. *Rendition to Torture*. New Brunswick, NJ: Rutgers University Press, 2012.

Clifford, James. *Routes: Travel and Translation in the Late Twentieth Century*. Cambridge, MA: Harvard University Press, 1997.

Clover, Carol J. *Men, Women, and Chain Saws: Gender in the Modern Horror Film*. Princeton, NJ: Princeton University Press, 1992.

Coleman, Lindsay. "'Damn You for Making Me Do This': Abu Ghraib, *24*, Torture, and Television Masochism." In *The War Body on Screen*, edited by Karen Randell and Sean Redmond, 199–214. New York: Continuum, 2008.

Collins, Brian H. "A Voice and Something More: Jigsaw as Acousmêtre and Existential Guru." In *To See the "Saw" Movies: Essays on Torture Porn and Post-9/11 Horror*, edited by James Aston and John Walliss, 86–104. Jefferson, NC: McFarland, 2013.

Collins, Jim, Hilary Radner, and Ava Preacher Collins, eds. *Film Theory Goes to the Movies*. New York: Routledge, 1993.

Collins, Max Allan, and James L. Traylor. *One Lonely Knight: Mickey Spillane's Mike Hammer*. Bowling Green, OH: Bowling Green State University Popular Press, 1984.

Cooper, James Fenimore. "From Bates to Bush: The New Slasher Film." Master's thesis, Oklahoma State University, 2011. ProQuest (1501027).

Cowan, Douglas E. *Sacred Terror: Religion and Horror on the Silver Screen*. Waco, TX: Baylor University Press, 2008.

Creed, Barbara. *The Monstrous-Feminine: Film, Feminism, Psychoanalysis*. New York: Routledge, 1993.

Cromb, Brenda. "Gorno: Violence, Shock and Comedy." *Cinephile* 4 (2008). http://cinephile.ca/archives/volume-4-post-genre/gorno-violence-shock-and-comedy/.

Debord, Guy. *Society of the Spectacle*. Translated by Black and Red. Detroit: Black and Red, 1983.

Deleuze, Gilles. *Francis Bacon: The Logic of Sensation*. Translated by Daniel W. Smith. Minneapolis: University of Minnesota Press, 2004.

Dennis, Kelly. "Leave It to Beaver: The Object of Pornography." In *Strategies for Theory: From Marx to Madonna*, edited by R. L. Rutsky and Bradley Macdonald, 187–224. Albany: State University of New York Press, 2003.

De Vleminck, Jens, and Eran Dorfman, eds. *Sexuality and Psychoanalysis: Philosophical Criticisms*. Leuven, Belgium: Leuven University Press, 2010.

Dixon, Wheeler Winston, ed. *Film and Television after 9/11*. Carbondale: Southern Illinois University Press, 2004.

Doneson, Judith. *The Holocaust in American Film*. 2nd ed. Syracuse, NY: Syracuse University Press, 2002.

———. "The Image Lingers: the Feminization of the Jew in *Schindler's List*." In *Spielberg's Holocaust: Critical Perspectives on "Schindler's List,"* edited by Yosefa Loshitzky, 140–152. Bloomington: Indiana University Press, 1997.

———. "The Jew as a Female Figure in the Holocaust Film." *Shoah: A Review of Holocaust Studies and Commemorations* 1, no. 1 (1978): 11–13, 18.

Donnelly, K. J. "*Saw* Heard: Musical Sound Design in Contemporary Cinema." In *Film Theory and Contemporary Hollywood Movies*, edited by Warren Buckland, 105–123. New York: Routledge, 2009.

Douthat, Ross. "The Return of the Paranoid Style," *Atlantic Monthly* 301, no. 3 (April 2008): 52–59.

Easterbrook, Gregg. "The Nation: Home Security; The Smart Way to Be Scared." *New York Times*, February 16, 2003. http://www.nytimes.com/2003/02/16/weekinreview/the-nation-home-security-the-smart-way-to-be-scared.html?pagewanted=all&src=pm.

Ebert, Roger. "*Night of the Living Dead*." RogerEbert.com, January 5, 1969. http://www.rogerebert.com/reviews/the-night-of-the-living-dead-1968.

———. "*Saw*." RogerEbert.com, October 28, 2004. http://www.rogerebert.com/reviews/saw-2004.

———. "*Wolf Creek*." RogerEbert.com, December 22, 2005. http://www.rogerebert.com/reviews/wolf-creek-2005.

Edelstein, David. "Audience Is Loser in Haneke's Unfunny 'Games.'" *Fresh Air*, NPR, March 14, 2008, http://www.npr.org/templates/story/story.php?storyId=88230619.

———. "Now Playing at Your Local Multiplex: Torture Porn." *New York* 39, no. 4 (February 6, 2006): 63–64. http://nymag.com/movies/features/15622/.

———. "A Threat, Hidden in Plain Sight." *Fresh Air*, NPR, January 13, 2006. http://www.npr.org/templates/story/story.php?storyId=5156201.

Fahy, Thomas, ed. *The Philosophy of Horror*. Lexington: University Press of Kentucky, 2010.

Faludi, Susan. *The Terror Dream: Fear and Fantasy in Post-9/11America*. New York: Metropolitan Books, 2007.

Featherstone, Mark, and Beth Johnson. "'Ovo Je Srbija': The Horror of the National Thing in *A Serbian Film*." *Journal for Cultural Research* 16, no. 1 (January 2012): 63–79.

Fiske, John. *Reading the Popular*. Boston: Unwin Hyman, 1989.

Foucault, Michel. *Discipline and Punish: The Birth of the Prison*. Translated by Alan Sheridan. New York: Vintage Books, 1995.

———. "Of Other Spaces." Translated by Jay Miskowiec. *Diacritics* 16, no. 1 (Spring 1986): 22–27.

Freeland, Cynthia A. *The Naked and the Undead: Evil and the Appeal of Horror*. Boulder, CO: Westview, 2000.

French, Karl, ed. *Screen Violence*. London: Bloomsbury, 1996.

Friedlander, Saul. *Reflections of Nazism: An Essay on Kitsch and Death*. Translated by Thomas Weyr. Bloomington: Indiana University Press, 1993.

Frost, Craig. "Regendering the Final Girl: Eli Roth's *Hostel*." *Cinemascope* 12 (January–June 2009): 1–10.

Fullerton, John, and Astrid Söderbergh Widding. *Moving Images: From Edison to the Webcam*. London: John Libby, 2000.

Galloway, Alexander R. *Gaming: Essays on Algorithmic Culture*. Minneapolis: University of Minnesota Press, 2006.

Galloway, Patrick. *Asia Shock: Horror and Dark Cinema from Japan, Korea, Hong Kong, and Thailand*. Berkeley: Stone Bridge, 2006.

Geyskens, Tomas. "Painting as Hysteria—Deleuze on Bacon." In *Sexuality and Psychoanalysis: Philosophical Criticisms*, edited by Jens De Vleminck and Eran Dorfman, 215–229. Leuven, Belgium: Leuven University Press, 2010.

Girard, René. *Violence and the Sacred*. Translated by Patrick Gregory. Baltimore: John Hopkins University Press, 1989.

Goldberg, Elizabeth Swanson. "Splitting Difference: Global Identity Politics and the Representation of Torture in the Counterhistorical Dramatic Film." In *Violence and American Cinema*, edited by David Slocum, 245–270. New York: Routledge, 2001.

Gottschalk, Simon. "Videology: Video-Games as Postmodern Sites/Sights of Ideological Reproduction." *Symbolic Interaction* 18, no. 1 (1995): 1–18.

Grant, Barry Keith, and Christopher Sharrett, eds. *Planks of Reason: Essays on the Horror Film*. Lanham, MD: Scarecrow, 2004.

Grass, Günter. *Two States—One Nation?* Translated by Krishna Winston and A. S. Wensinger. San Diego: Harcourt Brace Jovanovich, 1990.

Green, Amy M. "The French Horror Film *Martyrs* and the Destruction, Defilement, and Neutering of the Female Form." *Journal of Popular Film and Television* 39, no. 1 (2011): 20–28.

Grey, Sarah Cameron Loyd. "Dead Time: Aporias and Critical Videogaming." *symploke* 17, nos. 1–2 (2009): 231–246.

Gross, Sheryl W. "Guilt and Innocence in *Marathon Man*." *Literature Film Quarterly* 8, no. 1 (1980): 52–68.

Gruno, Kristina E. "*Martyrs*." *Journal of Feminist Family Therapy* 23, no. 2 (2011): 151–158.

Guerrasio, Jason. "The Vacation Planner." *Filmmaker* 15, no. 3 (Spring 2007). *Film and Television Literature Index*, EBSCO*host* (accessed March 15, 2013).

Gunning, Tom. "The Cinema of Attraction[s]: Early Film, Its Spectator and the Avant-Garde." In *The Cinema of Attractions Reloaded*, edited by Wanda Strauven, 381–388. Amsterdam: Amsterdam University Press, 2006.

Hambling, David. "Interrogation Drugs at Gitmo Alleged." *Wired*, November 21, 2008. http://www.wired.com/dangerroom/2008/11/interrogation-d/.

Hammond, Darrell. *God, If You're Not Up There, I'm F*cked*. New York: Harper, 2011.

———. Interview with Terry Gross, *Fresh Air*, NPR, November 7, 2011.

Haneke, Michael. Interview by Nick James. "Darkness Falls." *Sight & Sound* 13, no. 10 (October 2003): 16–18.

Harbury, Jennifer. *Truth, Torture, and the American Way*. Boston: Beacon, 2005.

Hartigan, John. *Odd Tribes: Toward a Cultural Analysis of White People*. Durham, NC: Duke University Press, 2005.

Haskell, Molly. *From Revenge to Rape: The Treatment of Women in the Movies*. New York: Holt, Rinehart, and Winston, 1975.

Hawkins, Joan. *Cutting Edge: Art-Horror and the Horrific Avant-Garde*. Minneapolis: University of Minnesota Press, 2000.

Heit, Jamey, ed. *Vader, Voldemort and Other Villains: Essays on Evil in Popular Media*. Jefferson, NC: McFarland, 2011.

Heller-Nicholas, Alexandra. *Rape-Revenge Films: A Critical Study*. Jefferson, NC: McFarland, 2011.

Henry, Katherine. "Life-in-Death: The Monstrous Female and the Gothic Labyrinth in *Aliens* and 'Ligeia.'" In *Horrifying Sex*, edited by Ruth Bienstock Anolik, 27–39. Jefferson, NC: McFarland, 2007.

Hills, Matt. "Cutting into Concepts of 'Reflectionist' Cinema? The *Saw* Franchise and Puzzles of Post-9/11 Horror." In *Horror after 9/11: World of Fear, Cinema of Terror*, edited by Aviva Briefel and Sam J. Miller, 107–123. Austin: University of Texas Press, 2011.

Hobbs, Sandy, and David Cornwell. "Sawney Bean, the Scottish Cannibal." *Folklore* 108 (1997): 49–54.

Horkheimer, Max, and Theodor Adorno. *The Dialectic of Enlightenment*. Translated by John Cumming. New York: Continuum, 1996.

Hosenball, Mark. "Report Reveals CIA Conducted Mock Executions." *Newsweek*, August 20, 2009. http://www.thedailybeast.com/newsweek/2009/08/20/report-reveals-cia-conducted-mock-executions.html.

Howard, Douglas L., ed. *Dexter: Investigating Cutting Edge Television*. London: I. B. Tauris, 2010.

———. "Harry Morgan: (Post)Modern Prometheus." In *Dexter: Investigating Cutting Edge Television*, edited by Douglas L. Howard, 61–77. London: I. B. Tauris, 2010.

———. "'You're Going to Tell Me Everything You Know': Torture and Morality in Fox's *24*." In *Reading 24: TV against the Clock*, edited by Steven Peacock, 133–145. London: I. B. Tauris, 2007.

Huntley, Jacob. "The Jigsaw Assemblage." In *To See the "Saw" Movies: Essays on Torture Porn and Post-9/11 Horror*, edited by James Aston and John Walliss, 123–138. Jefferson, NC: McFarland, 2013.

Hutchings, Peter. *The Horror Film*. Harlow, UK: Pearson Longman, 2004.

Ignatieff, Michael. "The Terrorist as Auteur." *New York Times*, November 14, 2004. http://www.nytimes.com/2004/11/14/movies/14TERROR.html.

Jackson, Neil. "*Cannibal Holocaust*, Realist Horror and Reflexivity." *Post Script: Essays in Film and the Humanities* 21, no. 3 (Summer 2002): 32–45.

Johnson, Beth. "Sex, Psychoanalysis, and Sublimation in *Dexter*." In *Dexter: Investigating Cutting Edge Television*, edited by Douglas L. Howard, 78–95. London: I. B. Tauris, 2010.

Johnson-Lewis, Erika. "Torture, Terrorism, and Other Aspects of Human Nature." In *Cylons in America: Critical Studies in "Battlestar Galactica,"* Tiffany Potter and C. W. Marshall, 27–39. New York: Continuum, 2008.

Jones, Steve. "The Lexicon of Offence: The Meanings of Torture, Porn, and 'Torture Porn.'" In *Controversial Images: Media Representations on the Edge*, edited by Feona Attwood, Vincent Campbell, I. Q. Hunter, and Sharon Lockyer, 186–200. Basingstoke, UK: Palgrave Macmillan, 2013.

———. "'Time Is Wasting': Con/sequence and S/pace in the *Saw* Series." *Horror Studies* 1, no. 2 (2010): 225–239.

———. *Torture Porn: Popular Horror after "Saw."* New York: Palgrave, 2013.

———. "Twisted Pictures: Morality, Nihilism and Symbolic Suicide." In *To See the "Saw" Movies: Essays on Torture Porn and Post-9/11 Horror*, edited by James Aston and John Walliss, 105–122. Jefferson, NC: McFarland, 2013.

Ka Tzetnik 135633 (aka Yehiel Dinur). *The House of Dolls*. Translated by Moshe M. Kohn. London: Frederick Muller, 1965.

Kępiński, Antoni. "Anus Mundi." *Archives of Psychiatry and Psychotherapy* 4 (2007): 85–87.

King, Geoff, ed. *The Spectacle of the Real: From Hollywood to "Reality" TV and Beyond*. Portland, OR: Intellect, 2005.

King, Geoff, and Tanya Krzywinska, eds. *Screenplay: Cinema/Videogames/Interfaces*. New York: Wallflower, 2002.

Klossowski, Pierre. *Sade My Neighbour*. Translated by Alphonso Lingis. London: Quartet Books, 1991.

Knowlton, Brian. "Terror in America / 'We're Going to Smoke Them Out': President Airs His Anger." *New York Times*, September 19, 2001. http://www.nytimes.com/2001/09/19/news/19iht-t4_30.html.

Koven, Mikel J. "'The Film You Are About to See Is Based on Fact': Italian Nazi Sexploitation Cinema." In *Alternative Europe: Eurotrash and Exploitation Cinema since 1945*, edited by Ernest Mathijs and Xavier Mendik, 19–31. New York: Wallflower, 2004.

———. "*Saw*." In *101 Horror Movies You Must See before You Die*, edited by Steven Jay Schneider, 402. London: Quintessence, 2009.

Kristeva, Julia. *Powers of Horror: An Essay on Abjection*. Translated by Leon S. Roudiez. New York: Columbia University Press, 1982.

———. *Strangers to Ourselves*. Translated by Leon S. Roudiez. New York: Columbia University Press, 1991.

Lane, Anthony. "Happy Haneke." *New Yorker*, October 5, 2009. http://www.newyorker.com/reporting/2009/10/05/091005fa_fact_lane.

———. "Recurring Nightmare." *New Yorker*, March 17, 2008. http://www.newyorker.com/arts/critics/cinema/2008/03/17/080317crci_cinema_lane.

Largier, Niklaus. *In Praise of the Whip: A Cultural History of Arousal*. New York: Zone Books, 2007.

Lattman, Peter. "Justice Scalia Hearts Jack Bauer." *Law Blog, Wall Street Journal*, June 20, 2007. http://blogs.wsj.com/law/2007/06/20/justice-scalia-hearts-jack-bauer/.

Leaver, Tama. "'Humanity's Children': Constructing and Confronting the Cylons." In *Cylons in America: Critical Studies in "Battlestar Galactica,"* edited by Tiffany Potter and C. W. Marshall, 131–142. New York: Continuum, 2008.

Lee, Nathan. "Evil Dead: *Hostel: Part II*: Lame, Tame, and Not Worth Moralizing." *Village Voice*, June 5, 2007. http://www.villagevoice.com/2007-06-05/film/evil-dead/full/.

Letizia, Anthony. "The Origins of Dexter Morgan and Bruce Wayne." Geek Pittsburgh, January 5, 2011. http://www.geekpittsburgh.com/reflections/dexterorigins.htm.

Lewis, Michael J. "Making Modern Evil: Terrorism, Torture, and the Creation of Evil in*24*." In *Vader, Voldemort and Other Villains: Essays on Evil in Popular Media*,Jamey Heit, 162–174. Jefferson, NC: McFarland, 2011.

Lindsay, Jeffry P. *Darkly Dreaming Dexter*. New York: Doubleday, 2004.
Lithwick, Dahlia. "How Jack Bauer Shaped U.S. Torture Policy." *Newsweek*, July 25, 2008. http://www.thedailybeast.com/newsweek/2008/07/25/the-fiction-behind-torture-policy.html.
Lockwood, Dean. "All Stripped Down: The Spectacle of 'Torture Porn.'" *Popular Communication* 7, no. 1 (2009): 40–48.
———. "Work Is Hell: Life in the Mannequin Factory." In *To See the "Saw" Movies: Essays on Torture Porn and Post-9/11 Horror*, edited by James Aston and John Walliss, 139–156. Jefferson, NC: McFarland, 2013.
Lowenstein, Adam. "Spectacle Horror and *Hostel*: Why 'Torture Porn' Does Not Exist." *Critical Quarterly* 53, no. 1 (2011): 42–60.
Mayer, Jane. "Whatever It Takes: The Politics of the Man behind *24*." *New Yorker*, February 19, 2007. http://www.newyorker.com/reporting/2007/02/19/070219fa_fact_mayer.
McAllister, Ken S. *Game Work: Language, Power, and Computer Game Culture*. Tuscaloosa: University of Alabama Press, 2004.
McCann, Ben. "Body Horror." In *To See the "Saw" Movies: Essays on Torture Porn and Post-9/11 Horror*, edited by James Aston and John Walliss, 30–44. Jefferson, NC: McFarland, 2013.
McCarthy, Todd. "Trick and Treat." *Film Comment* 16 (1980): 17–24.
McRoy, Jay, ed. *Japanese Horror Cinema*. Honolulu: University of Hawai'i Press, 2005.
Middleton, Jason. "The Subject of Torture: Regarding the Pain of Americans in *Hostel*." *Cinema Journal* 49, no. 4 (Summer 2010): 1–24.
Montezemolo, Fiamma, René Peralta, and Heriberto Yépez. *Here Is Tijuana!* London: Black Dog, 2006.
Morris, Jeremy. "The Justification of Torture-Horror: Retribution and Sadism in *Saw*, *Hostel*, and *The Devil's Rejects*." In *The Philosophy of Horror*, edited by Thomas Fahy, 42–56. Lexington: University Press of Kentucky, 2010.
Morris, Wesley. "*Hostel* Sequel Is Pure Torture." *Boston Globe*, June 8, 2007. http://www.boston.com/ae/movies/articles/2007/06/08/hostel_sequel_is_pure_torture.
Murphy, Cullen. *God's Jury: The Inquisition and the Making of the Modern World*. Boston: Houghton Mifflin Harcourt, 2012.
Murray, Gabrielle. "*Hostel II*: Representations of the Body in Pain and the Cinema Experience in Torture-Porn." *Jump Cut* 50 (Spring 2008). http://www.ejumpcut.org/archive/jc50.2008/TortureHostel2/.
Muybridge, Eadweard. *Muybridge's Complete Human and Animal Locomotion*. New York: Dover, 1979.
Newman, Kim. "Horror Will Eat Itself." *Sight and Sound* 19 (May 2009): 37–38.
Palaversich, Diana. "La vuelta a Tijuana en seis escritores." *Aztlán: A Journal of Chicano Studies* 28, no. 1 (2003): 97–125.
Perron, Bernard, and Mark J. P. Wolf, eds. *The Video Game Theory Reader*. New York: Routledge, 2003.
———, eds. *The Video Game Theory Reader 2*. New York: Routledge, 2009.
Petley, Julian. "*Cannibal Holocaust* and the Pornography of Death." In *The Spectacle of the Real: From Hollywood to "Reality" TV and Beyond*, edited by Geoff King, 173–185. Portland, OR: Intellect, 2005.
Pinedo, Isabel Cristina. *Recreational Terror: Women and the Pleasures of Horror Film Viewing*. Albany: State University of New York Press, 1997.
Polan, Dana R. "Eros and Syphilization: The Contemporary Horror Film." In *Planks of Reason: Essays on the Horror Film*, edited by Barry Keith Grant and Christopher Sharrett, 142–152. Lanham, MD: Scarecrow, 2004.

Porton, Richard. "Collective Guilt and Individual Responsibility: An Interview with Michael Haneke." *Cineaste* 30, no. 1 (Winter 2005): 50–51.

Potter, Tiffany, and C. W. Marshall. *Cylons in America: Critical Studies in "Battlestar Galactica."* New York: Continuum, 2008.

Pratt, Mary Louise. *Imperial Eyes: Travel Writing and Transculturation*. New York: Routledge, 1994.

Presdee, Mike. *Cultural Criminology and the Carnival of Crime*. New York: Routledge, 2000.

Priest, Dana, and Barton Gellman. "U.S. Decries Abuse but Defends Interrogations." *Washington Post*, December 26, 2002. http://www.washingtonpost.com/wp-dyn/content/article/2006/06/09/AR2006060901356.html.

Prince, Stephen. *Firestorm: American Film in the Age of Terrorism*. New York: Columbia University Press, 2009.

Przyrembel, Alexandra. "Transfixed by an Image: Ilse Koch, the 'Kommandeuse of Buchenwald.'" Translated by Pamela Selwyn. *German History* 19, no. 3 (October 2001): 369–399.

Radford, Jill, and Diana E. H. Russell, eds. *Femicide: The Politics of Woman Killing*. New York: Twayne, 1992.

Randell, Karen, and Sean Redmond, eds. *The War Body on Screen*. New York: Continuum, 2008.

Rawle, Steven. "Real-Imagining Terror in *Battlestar Galactica*: Negotiating Real and Fantasy in *Battlestar Galactica*'s Political Metaphor." In *"Battlestar Galactica": Investigating Flesh, Spirit and Steel*, edited by Roz Kaveney and Jennifer Stoy, 129–153. London: I. B. Tauris, 2010.

Rich, Frank. "No News Is Good News." *New York Times*, October 13, 2001. https://www.nytimes.com/2001/10/13/opinion/journal-no-news-is-good-news.html?src=pm.

Rizzo, John. *Company Man: Thirty Years of Controversy and Crisis in the CIA*. New York: Scribner, 2014.

Rockoff, Adam. *Going to Pieces: The Rise and Fall of the Slasher Film, 1978–1986*. Jefferson, NC: McFarland, 2002.

Ruggill, Judd Ethan, and Ken S. McAllister. *Gaming Matters: Art, Science, Magic and the Computer Game Medium*. Tuscaloosa: University of Alabama Press, 2011.

Sachs, Rob. "Charlie Clouser's Scary Soundtrack for *Saw*." *Day to Day*, NPR, October 29, 2004. http://www.npr.org/templates/story/story.php?storyId=4132853.

Sade, Donatien Alphonse François, Marquis de. *The 120 Days of Sodom and Other Writing*. Translated by Austryn Wainhouse and Richard Seaver. New York: Grove Weidenfeld, 1987.

Scarry, Elaine. *The Body in Pain: The Making and Unmaking of the World*. New York: Oxford University Press, 1985.

Schaefer, Eric. "Exploitation Films: Teaching Sin in the Suburbs." *Cinema Journal* 47, no. 1 (Fall 2007): 94–97.

Schopp, Andrew. "Interrogating the Manipulation of Fear: *V for Vendetta, Batman Begins, Good Night and Good Luck*, and America's 'War on Terrorism.'" In *The War on Terror and American Popular Culture*, edited by Andrew Schopp and Matthew B. Hill, 259–286. Madison, NJ: Fairleigh Dickson University Press, 2009.

Schubart, Rikke. *Super Bitches and Action Babes: The Female Hero in Popular Cinema, 1970–2006*. Jefferson, NC: McFarland, 2007.

Sconce, Jeffrey. "Spectacles of Death: Identification, Reflexivity, and Contemporary Horror." In *Film Theory Goes to the Movies*, edited by Jim Collins, Hilary Radner, and Ava Preacher Collins, 103–119. New York: Routledge, 1993.

Scott, A. O. "Torture or Porn? No Need to Choose." *New York Times*, May 12, 2011. http://movies.nytimes.com/2011/05/13/movies/a-serbian-film-directed-by-srdjan-spasojevic-review.html.

Self, Will. "The American Vice." In *Screen Violence*, edited by Karl French, 71–81. London: Bloomsbury, 1996.

Sharrett, Christopher. "Genocidal Spectacles and the Ideology of Death." In *Bad: Infamy, Darkness, Evil, and Slime on Screen*, edited by Murray Pomerance, 65–78. Albany: State University of New York Press, 2004.

———. "The Idea of Apocalypse in *The Texas Chainsaw Massacre*." In *Planks of Reason: Essays on the Horror Film*, edited by Barry Keith Grant, 255–276. Lanham, MD: Scarecrow, 1984.

———. "The Problem of*Saw*: 'Torture Porn' and the Conservatism of Contemporary Horror Films." *Cineaste*35, no. 1 (Winter 2009): 32–37.

Shaviro, Steven. "Regimes of Vision: Kathryn Bigelow, *Strange Days*." *Polygraph* 13 (2001): 59–68.

Shelley, Mary. *Frankenstein*. New York: Bantam Books, 1981.

Slocum, David, ed. *Violence and American Cinema*. New York: Routledge, 2001.

Smith, Madeleine. "Monstrous Bodies and Gendered Abjection." In *To See the "Saw" Movies: Essays on Torture Porn and Post-9/11 Horror*, edited by James Aston and John Walliss, 157–175. Jefferson, NC: McFarland, 2013.

Sontag, Susan. *Regarding the Pain of Others*. New York: Farrar, Straus and Giroux, 2003.

———. "Regarding the Torture of Others." *New York Times Magazine*, May 23, 2004, 24–29, 42.

Soussloff, Catherine. "Post-colonial Torture: Rituals of Viewing at Abu Ghraib." In *Ritual and Event*, edited by Mark Franko, 159–187. New York: Routledge, 2007.

Stewart, Kathleen. *A Space on the Side of the Road: Culture Poetics in an "Other" America*. Princeton, NJ: Princeton University Press, 1996.

Stewart, Susan. *On Longing: Narratives of the Miniature, the Gigantic, the Souvenir, the Collection*. Baltimore: John Hopkins University Press, 1984.

Stow, Simon. "Portraits 9/11/01: The *New York Times* and the Pornography of Grief." In *Literature after 9/11*, edited by Jeanne Follansbee Quinn and Ann Keniston, 224–241. New York: Routledge, 2008.

Strauven, Wanda, ed. *The Cinema of Attractions Reloaded*. Amsterdam: Amsterdam University Press, 2006.

Taylor, John. *Body Horror: Photojournalism, Catastrophe and War*. New York: New York University Press, 1998.

Taylor, Paul A. Interview by Srecko Horvat. *International Journal of Žižek Studies* 1, no. 0 (2007): 1–7.

Tziallas, Evangelos. "The Spectacle of Correction: Video Games, Movies and Control." In *To See the "Saw" Movies: Essays on Torture Porn and Post-9/11 Horror*, edited by James Aston and John Walliss, 45–72. Jefferson, NC: McFarland, 2013.

———. "Torture Porn and Surveillance Culture." *Jump Cut* 52 (Summer 2010). http://www.ejumpcut.org/archive/jc52.2010/evangelosTorturePorn/.

U.S. National Commission on Terrorist Attacks upon the United States. *The 9/11 Commission Report*. Washington, DC: U.S. GPO, 2004.

Ward, Russel Braddock. *The Australian Legend*. New York: Oxford University Press, 1958.

Wark, McKenzie. *Gamer Theory*. Cambridge, MA: Harvard University Press, 2007.

Wee, Valerie. "Resurrecting and Updating the Teen Slasher: The Case of *Scream*." *Journal of Popular Film and Television* 34, no. 2 (Summer 2006): 50–61.

Weeks, Janet. "*Scream* Movies Cultivate Special Audience: Girls." *USA Today*, December 12, 1997, 1A.

Welch, Michael. *Scapegoats of September 11th*. New Brunswick, NJ: Rutgers University Press, 2006.

Wester, Maisha. "Torture Porn and Uneasy Feminism: Re-thinking (Wo)men in Eli Roth's *Hostel* Films." *Quarterly Review of Film and Video* 29 (2012): 387–400.

Wetmore, Kevin J. *Post-9/11 Horror in American Cinema*. New York: Continuum, 2012.

Williams, Linda. "Discipline and Fun: *Psycho* and Postmodern Cinema." In *Reinventing Film Studies*, edited by Christine Gledhill and Linda Williams, 351–378. London: Arnold, 2000.

———. "Film Bodies: Gender, Genre, and Excess." *Film Quarterly* 44, no. 4 (Summer 1991): 2–13.

———. *Hard Core: Power, Pleasure, and "The Frenzy of the Visible."* Berkeley: University of California Press, 1989.

Williams, Patrick, Sean Q. Hendricks, and W. Keith Winkler, eds. *Gaming as Culture: Essays on Reality, Identity and Experience in Fantasy Games*. Jefferson, NC: McFarland, 2006.

Wolf, Mark J. P., ed. *The Medium of the Videogame*. Austin: University of Texas Press, 2001.

———. *Virtual Morality: Morals, Ethics, and New Media*. New York: Peter Lang, 2003.

Wood, Robin. *Hollywood from Vietnam to Reagan*. New York: Columbia University Press, 1986.

Yeffeth, Glenn, and Jennifer Thomason, eds. *Halo Effect: An Unauthorized Look at the Most Successful Video Game of All Time*. Dallas: Benbella Books, 2006.

Yin, Tung. "Jack Bauer Syndrome: Hollywood's Depiction of National Security Law." *Southern California Interdisciplinary Law Journal* 17, no. 2 (Winter 2008): 279–299.

Yoo, John. *War by Other Means: An Insider's Account of the War on Terror*. New York: Atlantic Monthly Press, 2006.

Zimmer, Catherine. "Caught on Tape? The Politics of Video in the New Torture Films." In *Horror after 9/11: World of Fear, Cinema of Terror*, edited by Aviva Briefel and Sam J. Miller, 83–106. Austin: University of Texas Press, 2011.

Žižek, Slavoj. *For They Know Not What They Do: Enjoyment as a Political Factor*. London: Verso, 1991.

———. "Kant with (or against) Sade." In *The Žižek Reader*, edited by Elizabeth Wright and Edmond Wright, 283–301. Oxford, UK: Blackwell, 1999.

———. *Welcome to the Desert of the Real! Five Essays on September 11 and Related Dates*. New York: Verso, 2002.

Filmography

Abominable Dr. Phibes, The, Robert Fuest, 1971, 94 min.
Alien, Ridley Scott, 1979, 117 min.
American Grindhouse, Elijah Drenner, 2010, 80 min.
American Horror Story: Asylum, FX Network, 2012.
American Mary, Jen Soska and Sylvia Soska, 2012, 103 min.
Anniversary at Shallow Creek, The, Jon D. Wagner, 2001, 90 min.
Audition [*Odishon*], Takashi Miike, 1999, 115 min.
Battle Royale [*Batoru Rowaiaru*], Kinji Fukasaku, 2000, 114 min.
Battlestar Galactica, Sky One; Sci-Fi Channel, 2004–2009.
Benny's Video, Michael Haneke, 1992, 105 min.
Beyond Rangoon, John Boorman, 1995, 100 min.
Birds, The, Alfred Hitchcock, 1963, 119 min.
Blacklist, The, NBC, 2013–.
Blair Witch Project, The, Daniel Myrick and Eduardo Sánchez, 1999, 81 min.
Blob, The, Irvin S. Yeaworth and Russell S. Doughten, 1958, 86 min.
Blood Feast, Herschell Gordon Lewis, 1963, 67 min.
Book of Revelation, The, Ana Kokkinos, 2006, 118 min.
Boxing Helena, Jennifer Chambers Lynch, 1993, 107 min.
Buried, Rodrigo Cortés, 2010, 95 min.
Cabin Fever, Eli Roth, 2002, 93 min.
Cabin in the Woods, The, Drew Goddard, 2011, 95 min.
Caché [*Hidden*], Michael Haneke, 2005, 117 min.
Cannibal Holocaust, Ruggero Deodato, 1980, 95 min.
Captivity, Roland Joffé, 2007, 96 min.
Carrie, Brian De Palma, 1976, 98 min.
Chained, Jennifer Chambers Lynch, 2012, 94 min.
Choose, Marcus Graves, 2010, 83 min.
Clinic, The, James Rabbitts, 2010, 94 min.
Clockwork Orange, A, Stanley Kubrick, 1971, 136 min.
Cloverfield, Matt Reeves, 2008, 85 min.
Cold Fish [*Tsumetai nettaigyo*], Shion Sono, 2010, 144 min.
Collection, The, Marcus Dunstan, 2012, 82 min.

Collector, The, Marcus Dunstan, 2009, 90 min.
Conformist, The, Bernardo Bertolucci, 1970, 111 min.
Constant Gardner, The, Fernando Meirelles, 2005, 129 min.
Cube, Vincenzo Natali, 1997, 90 min.
Cut, Chan-wook Park, 2004, 48 min.
Damned, The, Luchino Visconti, 1969, 156 min.
Deliverance, John Boorman, 1972, 110 min.
Descent, The, Neil Marshall, 2005, 99 min.
Devil's Rejects, The, Rob Zombie, 2005, 107 min.
Dexter, Showtime, 2006–2013.
Dictator, The, Larry Charles, 2012, 83 min.
Director: The Films of Wes Craven, Robert Emery, 1999, 60 min.
Elephant, Gus Van Sant, 2003, 81 min.
Evil Dead, The, Sam Raimi, 1981, 85 min.
Excision, Richard Bates, Jr., 2012, 81 min.
Experiment, The, Paul Scheuring, 2010, 96 min.
Final, The, Joey Stewart, 2010, 93 min.
Following, The, Fox Network, 2013–.
Freddy's Dead: The Final Nightmare, Rachel Talalay, 1991, 89 min.
Friday the 13th, Sean Cunningham, 1980, 95 min.
Friday the 13th, Marcus Nispel, 2009, 97 min.
Friday the 13th Part Two, Steve Miner, 1981, 87 min.
Frontière(s) [*Frontier(s)*], Xavier Gens, 2007, 108 min.
Funny Games, Michael Haneke, 1997, 108 min.
Funny Games, Michael Haneke, 2007, 111 min.
Game of Thrones, HBO, 2011–.
Gentlemen Prefer Blondes, Howard Hawks, 1953, 91 min.
Gestapo's Last Orgy, The, Cesare Canevari, 1976, 92 min.
Girls against Boys, Austin Chick, 2012, 94 min.
Godfather, The, Francis Ford Coppola, 1972, 175 min.
Gojira [*Godzilla*], Ishiro Honda, 1954, 96 min.
Green Inferno, Eli Roth, 2013, 100 min.
Grey Zone, The, Tim Blake Nelson, 2001, 108 min.
Grindhouse, Robert Rodriguez and Quentin Tarantino, 2007, 191 min.
Halloween, John Carpenter, 1978, 91 min.
Halloween, Rob Zombie, 2007, 109 min.
Halloween II, Rick Rosenthal, 1981, 92 min.
Halloween II, Rob Zombie, 2009, 105 min.
Halloween 4: The Return of Michael Myers, Dwight H. Little, 1988, 88 min.
Hannibal, NBC Network, 2013–.
Hellraiser, Clive Barker, 1987, 94 min.
Henry: Portrait of a Serial Killer, John McNaughton, 1986, 83 min.
High Tension [*Haute Tension*], Alexandre Aja, 2003, 91 min.
Hills Have Eyes, The, Wes Craven, 1977, 89 min.
Hills Have Eyes, The, Alexandre Aja, 2006, 107 min.
Hills Have Eyes II, The, Martin Weisz, 2007, 89 min.
Homeland, Showtime, 2011–.
Hostel, Eli Roth, 2005, 94 min.
Hostel: Part II, Eli Roth, 2007, 93 min.

Hostel: Part III, Scott Spiegel, 2011, 88 min.
House of 1000 Corpses, Rob Zombie, 2003, 89 min.
Human Centipede (First Sequence), The, Tom Six, 2009, 92 min.
Human Centipede II (Full Sequence), The, Tom Six, 2011, 88 min.
Hunger Games, The, Gary Ross, 2012, 142 min.
Ichi the Killer [*Koroshiya*], Takashi Miike, 2001, 129 min.
Ilsa: Harem Keeper of the Oil Sheiks, Don Edmonds, 1976, 85 min.
Ilsa: She-Wolf of the SS, Don Edmonds, 1975, 96 min.
Ilsa: The Tigress of Siberia, Jean LaFleur, 1977, 85 min.
Ilsa: The Wicked Warden, Jesus Franco, 1977, 90 min.
In Chambers [*Bak Lukkede Dører*], Aleksander Nordaas, 2008, 9 min.
Inglourious Basterds, Quentin Tarantino, 2009, 159 min.
Inside, Alexandre Bustillo and Julien Maury, 2007, 82 min.
Invasion of the Body Snatchers, Don Siegel, 1956, 80 min.
Irreversible [*Irréversible*], Gaspar Noe, 2002, 97 min.
I Spit on Your Grave, Meir Zarchi, 1978, 101 min.
I Spit on Your Grave, Steven R. Monroe, 2010, 108 min.
Jaws, Steven Spielberg, 1975, 124 min.
Ju-on: The Grudge [*Ju-on*], Takashi Shimizu, 2002, 92 min.
Kinatay, Brillante Mendoza, 2009, 105 min.
King Kong, Merian Cooper and Ernest Schoedsack, 1933, 100 min.
King Kong, John Guillermin, 1976, 134 min.
Lady Vengeance [*Chinjeolhan geumjassi*], Chan-wook Park, 2005, 112 min.
Land without Bread, Luis Buñel, 1933, 30 min.
Last House on the Left, The, Wes Craven, 1972, 84 min.
Last Resort, The, Brandon Nutt, 2009, 75 min.
Lions for Lambs, Robert Redford, 2007, 92 min.
Love Camp 7, Lee Frost, 1969, 96 min.
Mad Max, George Miller, 1979, 88 min.
Make Them Die Slowly, Umberto Lenzi, 1981, 93 min.
Marathon Man, John Schlesinger, 1976, 125 min.
Martyrs, Pascal Laugier, 2008, 99 min.
Memory of the Camps, creative producer Sidney Bernstein, 1985, 56 min.
Night and Fog, Alain Resnais, 1955, 32 min.
Nightmare on Elm Street, A, Wes Craven, 1984, 91 min.
Night of the Living Dead, George A. Romero, 1968, 96 min.
Night Porter, The, Liliana Cavani, 1974, 118 min.
99 Pieces, Anthony Falcon, 2007, 94 min.
Oldboy [*Oldeuboi*], Chan-wook Park, 2003, 120 min.
Panic Room, David Fincher, 2002, 112 min.
Paranormal Activity, Oren Peli, 2007, 86 min.
Pawnbroker, The, Sidney Lumet, 1964, 116 min.
Peeping Tom, Michael Powell, 1960, 101 min.
Penance, Jake Kennedy, 2009, 85 min.
Pieces, Juan Piquer Simón, 1982, 89 min.
Poltergeist, Tobe Hooper, 1982, 114 min.
Psycho, Alfred Hitchcock, 1960, 109 min.
Razor's Ring, Morgan Hampton, 2008, 95 min.
Rear Window, Alfred Hitchcock, 1954, 112 min.

REC, Jaume Balagueró and Paco Plaza, 2007, 78 min.
Rendition, Gavin Hood, 2007, 122 min.
Reservoir Dogs, Quentin Tarantino, 1992, 99 min.
Rest Stop, John Shiban, 2006, 80 min.
Rest Stop: Don't Look Back, Shawn Papazian, 2008, 89 min.
Revenge, ABC, 2011–.
Ringu, Hideo Nakata, 1998, 96 min.
Road to Guantánamo, The, Mat Whitecross and Michael Winterbottom, 2006, 95 min.
Rome, Open City [*Roma, città aperta*], Roberto Rossellini, 1945, 100 min.
Rosemary's Baby, Roman Polanski, 1968, 136 min.
Ruins, The, Carter Smith, 2008, 90 min.
Salò, or the 120 Days of Sodom [*Salò o le 120 giornate di Sodoma*], Pier Paolo Pasolini, 1975, 116 min.
Salon Kitty, Tinto Brass, 1976, 129 min.
Salvador, Oliver Stone, 1986, 122 min.
Saw, James Wan, 2003, 9 min.
Saw, James Wan, 2004, 103 min.
Saw II, Darren Lynn Bousman, 2005, 93 min.
Saw III, Darren Lynn Bousman, 2006, 108 min.
Saw IV, Darren Lynn Bousman, 2007, 93 min.
Saw V, David Hackl, 2008, 92 min.
Saw VI, Kevin Greutert, 2009, 90 min.
Saw 3D: The Final Chapter, Kevin Greutert, 2010, 90 min.
Saw: A Hardcore Parody, Dick Chibbles, 2010, 100 min.
Scandal, ABC Network, 2012–
Scream, Wes Craven, 1996, 111 min.
Scream 2, Wes Craven, 1997, 120 min.
Scream 3, Wes Craven, 2000, 116 min.
Scream 4, Wes Craven, 2011, 111 min.
Searchers, The, John Ford, 1956, 119 min.
Serbian Film, A, Srdjan Spasojevic, 2010, 104 min.
Se7en, David Fincher, 1995, 127 min.
Seven Beauties [*Pasqualino Settebellezze*], Lina Wertmüller, 1975, 115 min.
Severance, Christopher Smith, 2006, 96 min.
Silence of the Lambs, The, Jonathan Demme, 1991, 118 min.
Splat Pack, The, Mark Henry and Frank H. Woodward, 2011, 43 min.
Standard Operating Procedure, Errol Morris, 2008, 116 min.
Steel Trap, Luis Cámara, 2007, 89 min.
Strangers, The, Bryan Bertino, 2008, 86 min.
Surveillance, Jennifer Chambers Lynch, 2008, 97 min.
Sympathy for Mr. Vengeance [*Boksuneun naui geot*], Chan-wook Park, 2002, 129 min.
Syriana, Stephen Gaghan, 2005, 128 min.
Taken, Pierre Morel, 2008, 93 min.
Tea Break, Scott Walker, 2004, 7 min.
Texas Chain Saw Massacre, The, Tobe Hooper, 1974, 83 min.
Thousand Cuts, A, Charles Evered, 2012, 87 min.
Torso, Sergio Martino, 1973, 92 min.
Tortured, Nolan Lebovitz, 2008, 107 min.
Tortured, The, Robert Lieberman, 2010, 79 min.

Train, Gideon Raff, 2008, 94 min.
Trouble Every Day, Claire Denis, 2001, 101 min.
Turistas, John Stockwell, 2006, 93 min.
24, Fox Network, 2001–2014.
Unthinkable, Gregor Jordan, 2010, 97 min.
Untraceable, Gregory Hoblit, 2008, 101 min.
Vacancy, Nimród Antal, 2007, 85 min.
V for Vendetta, James McTeigue, 2005, 132 min.
WΔZ (aka *The Killing Gene*), Tom Shankland, 2007, 104 min.
White Ribbon, The, Michael Haneke, 2009, 144 min.
Wolf Creek, Greg Mclean, 2005, 99 min.
Woman, The, Lucky McKee, 2011, 101 min.
Women in Cages, Gerardo de Leon, 1971, 81 min.
Women in Cell Block 7, Rino Di Silvestro, 1973, 100 min.
Woolite commercial, Rob Zombie, 2013, 33 sec.
Would You Rather, David Guy Levy, 2012, 93 min.
Wrong Turn, Rob Schmidt, 2003, 84 min.
Wrong Turn 2: Dead End, Joe Lynch, 2007, 96 min.
Wrong Turn 3: Left for Dead, Declan O'Brien, 2009, 92 min.
Wrong Turn 4: Bloody Beginnings, Declan O'Brien, 2011, 93 min.
Wrong Turn 5: Bloodlines, Declan O'Brien, 2012, 87 min.
Zero Dark Thirty, Kathryn Bigelow, 2012, 157 min.

Index

About the Author

AARON KERNER teaches in the Cinema Department at San Francisco State University. A good deal of his research surveys the ways in which historical violence materializes in visual culture, an interest that the present volume is most certainly indicative of. In fact, the catalyst for the present volume is found in his Holocaust research. In 2011, he published *Film and the Holocaust: New Perspectives on Dramas, Documentaries, and Experimental Films*, an extensive survey of films that represent the Holocaust; the book covers areas that have been largely neglected (e.g., experimental films, exploitation, and pornography), and unlike other scholarship in this area, authenticity is viewed in it as something of a red herring. While many people are concerned with a film's supposed fidelity to that catastrophic event, Kerner instead insists that the event and its representation need to be treated on their own terms. A representation is always already a translation of an event into narrative/visual form—and this is true across the board, from dramatic narratives to documentaries. The so-called War on Terror is effectively treated in the same manner here—and the author proposes that torture porn negotiates our uneasy relationship with American violence. In a similar vein, his "Gojira no hone" (Godzilla's Bones), featured in *Traumatic Affect*, illustrates how the Japanese monster functions as an "affective vessel." Kerner is currently working on a range of subjects in and around the concept of ugliness and disgust.